D0152840

International Transactions in Services

The Atwater Institute:
The World Information Economy Centre

The Atwater Institute is an independent, international, nonprofit organization devoted to public policy issues in the field of information and communication. The institute sponsors conferences and shirt-sleeve sessions designed to build a consensus on international "rules of the road" in the information area; commissions and disseminates papers on public policy; and develops educational materials on the information economy. Currently, its principal project is to act as a catalyst in the creation of an international policy framework leading to a General Agreement on Information Transfer/Trade (GAIT).

The Atwater Institute
3940 Côte des Neiges, Suite D-3
Montreal, Québec, Canada H3H 1W2
tel. (514) 931-2319

About the Book and Author

Over the past decade, the importance of international trade and foreign direct investment in services, and especially data services (transborder data flows), has increased significantly. This book begins with an examination of the rise of data services (data processing, software, data bases, and telecommunication services) and the impact of these services on international economic transactions. The author then looks at trade and foreign direct investment in services in general and reviews the policy position of the United States, the principal proponent of the international services discussion. Against this background, Dr. Sauvant analyzes the interests of various countries vis-à-vis trade and foreign direct investment in data services, looking at protection of privacy issues as well as competing values and approaches relating to the acquisition of data resources. On the basis of this analysis, Dr. Sauvant reviews the international policy discussion as it is carried out in bilateral and multilateral negotiations through the Organisation for Economic Co-operation and Development, the International Bureau for Informatics, the General Agreement on Tariffs and Trade, and the United Nations. Basic statistical data accompany the text, and key policy documents are included in the annexes.

Karl P. Sauvant is affiliated with the United Nations Centre on Transnational Corporations. He is author of *Trade and Foreign Direct Investment in Data Services* (Westview, 1986) and is coeditor (with Hajo Hasenpflug) of *The New International Economic Order: Confrontation or Cooperation Between North and South?* (Westview, 1978) and (with Farid Lavipour) of *Controlling Multinational Enterprises: Problems, Strategies, Counterstrategies* (Westview, 1976).

International Transactions in Services

The Politics of Transborder Data Flows

Karl P. Sauvant

The Atwater Series
on the World Information Economy, No. 1

Westview Press / Boulder and London

This Westview softcover edition was manufactured on our own premises using equipment and methods that allow us to keep even specialized books in stock. It is printed on acid-free paper and bound in softcovers that carry the highest rating of the National Association of State Textbook Administrators, in consultation with the Association of American Publishers and the Book Manufacturers' Institute.

Copyright © 1986 by Karl P. Sauvant

Published in 1986 in the United States of America by Westview Press, Inc.; Frederick A. Praeger, Publisher; 5500 Central Avenue, Boulder, Colorado 80301

Library of Congress Cataloging-in-Publication Data
Sauvant, Karl P.
  International transactions in services.
  (The Atwater series on the world information
economy)
  1. Information services and state. 2. Telecommuni-
cation policy. I. Title. II. Title: Transborder data
flows. III. Series.
HD9696.A2S28 1986   384'.068   85-31522
ISBN 0-8133-0310-9

Composition for this book was created by conversion of the author's word-processor disks.
This book was produced without formal editing by the publisher.

Printed and bound in the United States of America

∞ The paper used in this publication meets the requirements of the American National Standard for Permanence of Paper for Printed Library Materials Z39.48-1984.

6   5   4   3   2   1

To SdS, SCP

Contents

Annexes

Tables and Figures

Figures

Foreword

It gives us great pleasure to introduce The Atwater Series on the World Information Economy. The series is the first major publishing venture of The Atwater Institute: The World Information Economy Centre. The institute was founded on the premise that reaping the benefits of the "information age" depends above all on deepening our understanding of the increasingly central role of information in economic life. It proposes to serve as a world forum for open discussion and as an independent research and resource centre on all aspects of the information economy. The institute has begun by concentrating on critical policy issues concerning international information flows, especially as they affect international trade.

The aim of the Atwater series is to stimulate serious and informed discussion on the economic, commercial, legal, and social implications of the information revolution. We believe such discussion to be essential for the adoption of enlightened policies and strategies at all levels, and the items in our series will combine intellectual substance and practical relevance in such a way as to make a useful contribution to it. The series will be overseen by a distinguished, independent, and international editorial board.

In view of our current focus, we are especially delighted that the series is beginning with Karl P. Sauvant's *International Transactions in Services: The Politics of Transborder Data Flows*. Dr. Sauvant's book is the first comprehensive review of the international policy discussion on trade and foreign direct investment in services. More important, however, he deals in detail with the impact of data services upon international trade in services and their central significance in the services debate. Quite apart from its obvious intellectual merits, Dr. Sauvant's book is also distinguished by its timeliness: It appears in conjunction with the initiation of the new GATT round in Punta del Este, Uruguay, in September 1986, which is expected to address the very concerns taken up in this volume. In fact, this volume—strongly supported by data and original documents—is indispensable reading for anyone who wants to understand the services aspect of the new GATT round.

Dr. Sauvant's book will also make an important contribution to the discussion of an international public policy framework for trade in and transfer of information and information-intensive services that is being launched by the institute with the

Atwater 1986 Conference on "The World Information Economy: Risks and Opportunities" (Montréal, 4–7 November 1986).

We should like to make it clear that since the aim of the Atwater series is to stimulate discussion, the volumes in it will naturally espouse a variety of stances on the matters discussed and none of them should be read as statements of Atwater Institute policy.

Frank B. Common, Jr., Q.C.
Chair and Founder, Atwater Institute

Knut O.H.A. Hammarskjöld
Director General, Atwater Institute

Vishwas P. Govitrikar
Director of Operations and Research,
Atwater Institute
Series Editor

Preface

Perhaps no other development has a stronger impact on today's economy and way of life than the advent of microelectronics or data technology—technology that is based on the use of digital data signals. This data technology, in turn, has given rise to data industries: data goods (computers, computer equipment, peripherals) and data services (data processing, software, information storage and retrieval, and telecommunication data services). Data goods and data services, together with the research and development required to develop them and the capacities and skills needed for their production and application, are data resources—core resources for economic and social development for at least the remainder of this century.

Apart from becoming important industries in their own right, data industries increasingly contribute to the transformation of the modus operandi of most other industries. Microelectronic devices and the software required to operate them are more and more incorporated in products and processes, giving them a new character. For many, these changes have the quality of a new industrial revolution revolving around the use of data resources.

A central aspect of the advent of microelectronics has been the merger of computer and telecommunication technologies. As a consequence, computers—and electronic devices in general—can communicate with one another; in particular, data goods and data services can be utilized without regard to their actual location and without loss of time. The results are data flows. They may occur in any of the four forms of data services mentioned earlier, and they serve to carry out certain tasks or, to put it differently, to perform certain services. If such flows cross national frontiers—normally via transnational computer-communication systems—they become transborder data flows: data services rendered (exported/imported) across national borders.

To the extent to which the use of computers and microelectronic devices becomes more frequent, and to the extent to which information is increasingly represented and sent in digital form, the volume of data flows grows. This is facilitated by a rapid expansion of data networks capable of carrying data flows nationally and internationally. They are being linked in a world-wide grid of computer-communication systems which constitutes the infrastructure of a world economy increasingly based on the use of data technology and data flows.

In this world economy, data flows provide the informational infrastructure for trade in goods and services and increase the tradeability of certain services. Perhaps even more importantly, transnational computer-communication systems are increasingly becoming the nervous systems of the world-wide affiliate network of transnational corporations, and the data flows transmitted over these systems are becoming the lifeblood of the operations of these corporations. Data flows are not only used by transnational corporations to speed up the sending of messages, but also to improve the management of corporate systems and to change the very manner in which corporations actually engage in production.

Given the importance of data flows, the question arises, of course, as to what public-policy responses are most appropriate to them. This question arises especially sharply in an international context both because the underlying technology is non-national in nature and because there is no international authority which can deal with the legal, economic and, in the final analysis, political consequences of this new phenomenon.

In the light of all this, the first major purpose of this volume is to document the emergence of the data industries (and especially the emergence of data-service industries) and to analyze particularly the economic impact of transborder data flows.

Since the beginning of the 1980s, the discussion of transborder data flows has acquired an additional dimension: it has become part of the widening debate on an appropriate framework for international transactions in services. The services debate has its origin in the relatively recent discovery—slowly making its way into the awareness of experts and policy-makers—of the importance of services in the international economy: services account for over half of the gross national product of the developed market economies and are the single largest sector in most developing economies; the recorded value of trade in services amounts to one-quarter of that of trade in goods; and the service sector has become the single largest sector in which foreign direct investment is made. Services are, in other words, the single most important economic activity. And data flows carrying out certain tasks are, as noted earlier, a service themselves; whenever they are rendered across national frontiers, trade in data services takes place.

But data flows are more than a simple service—they are a core service. The reason is that they increase the transportability of other services. Since most services are intangible and non-storable, their production and consumption normally have to occur at the same time in the same place. This, of course, is a serious obstacle to trade in services. Real-time interactive communication via transnational computer-communication systems changes this situation. By collapsing time and space, transactions can take place *at the same time* but *at different places*. As a result, the tradeability of such services as banking, insurance, accounting, design and engineering, legal services, advertising, research and development, consulting and, of course, data services themselves, increases considerably. And other services that are information-intensive (e.g., travel, shipping, tourism) acquire a new informational infrastructure. Transborder data flows change, therefore, the parameters which determine how certain services can be delivered to foreign markets. They thereby open large new opportunities for trade in services. This potential underlines the importance of an international public-policy framework for transborder data flows.

Since data flows represent a service, and since the nature of data services as a core service is becoming recognized, the discussions of such a framework are undertaken as part of the broader negotiations on trade in services in general. In other words, any international framework created for trade in services will also deal with transborder data flows. In fact, it is likely that any international negotiations on services will give priority attention to data services.

Given this, the second major purpose of this volume is to review briefly the importance of the service sector and, particularly, to document international transactions—trade and foreign direct investment—in services. In addition, the forces that shape the international services debate, and a number of the issues that have arisen in its context, are also reviewed since they are of immediate relevance to the discussion of a public-policy framework for transborder data flows.

The third major purpose of this volume, then, is to deal with the question of an international public-policy framework for transborder data flows. The interests that shape this discussion are analyzed and the status of various efforts at the bilateral, regional and international levels is reviewed. As these discussions are inextricably interwoven with those on a framework for trade and foreign direct investment in services, this review deals with data services as part of services in general. An effort has been made to take developments up to the end of 1985 into account.

It is almost certain that data technologies will be at the center of national economic development in years to come. It is very likely that the international dimension of the application of these technologies, especially in the form of transborder data flows, will be regarded with increasing attention in international economic discussions. And it is equally likely that the broader context in which these discussions take place—the services debate—will be one of the central issues on the international agenda in the decade ahead. If this volume contributes to a clearer understanding of these issues, it will have fulfilled its purpose.

Finally, I wish to acknowledge with gratitude the assistance obtained from Craig Johnson and Jörg Weber and the generous advice I have received from many of my colleagues on particular parts of this study. Most of them are members of the TDF "mafia"—a small, but rapidly growing group of persons in business, government and academia dedicated to furthering the understanding of transborder data flows and the issues associated with them. They include Ray Austin, Carol Balassa, Hugh Donaghue, T. L. Early, Murray Gibbs, Vishwas Govitrikar, Kathryn Hauser, Ricardo Maciel, G. Russell Pipe, Cynthia Rich, Peter Robinson, Miguel Rodriquez, Istvan Sebestyen, François Vuilleumier, and Zbigniew Zimny. To all of them: thank you very much! My debt to Silvana da Silva is other and greater. To her this book is dedicated.

Naturally, the responsibility for any mistakes, misrepresentations or omissions in this volume is entirely my own, and the views expressed in it do not necessarily represent those of the United Nations.

Karl P. Sauvant
March 1986

Introduction and Summary

Social scientists have characterized the transition from a predominantly agricultural to a predominantly manufacturing economy during the last century as the industrial revolution. And manufacturing has continued to dominate economic thinking until today. For instance, many of the standard leading economic indicators either ignore services altogether or are biased toward manufacturing (the closely-watched measure of the wholesale price index in the US, for example, excludes services), and a broad discussion is underway about the "re-industrialization" of the United States.

Yet, a quiet and almost unnoticed revolution has taken place during the past two decades in all developed market economies and most developing countries: services have become the single largest economic sector. As documented in chapter I, trade, transport and communication, finance, public administration and defense, and other services together accounted, in 1979, for 59% of the GDP of the developed market economies as a group and 43% of the GDP of the developing countries as a group. (Even if public administration and defense are excluded, the service sector remains the single most important sector in most countries.) In the United States, the most advanced large services economy, services accounted for over two-thirds of the country's GDP at the beginning of the 1980s—compared with one-fifth for manufacturing—and 7 out of 10 jobs were in service industries. In fact, 8 out of 10 jobs created in the US during the period 1972-1982 were in service industries. Similarly, three-fifths of the European Community's GDP came from services at the beginning of the 1980s, as opposed to one-fifth from manufacturing. The decrease of employment in the Community's manufacturing sector of 4 million jobs between 1973 and 1981 was more than offset by an increase in the same period of 6 million jobs in services. In other words, many countries have actually experienced a "de-industrialization." They have become services economies.

It is astonishing that public discussion, government policy and economic theory have paid little attention to this structural change. The following quote (referring to the US) describes the gap between reality and awareness:

> In every major economic area—growth rates, standard of living, employment, balance of trade—our service sector has overtaken the goods sector in significance. Yet in spite of this dramatic change in our economy, most of our businessmen, economists and policy-makers continue to think about our economy with models and images derived from the goods-producing sector. When we think about "structural unemployment", the image is Youngstown and rusting steel mills, not filing clerks displaced by computers. When we discuss inflation, the debate revolves around oil and food, not medical care and communications services.

1

When we ponder the negative effects of the trade deficit, it is Japanese autos which drive the debate, not Korean construction firms out-bidding American ones for foreign contracts. This implicit "goods bias" in our thinking makes it difficult both to perceive the real nature of our economy and to anticipate future changes in it which will affect the welfare of our citizens. Like generals who blindly prepare for the last war, our economic policy-makers spend too much of their time thinking about the last economy.[1]

Perhaps the lack of awareness that the goods sector is no longer the center of economic development is one of the reasons why a number of economic policies are found to be less effective today than they were in the past. After all, many of these policies are being directed at a share of the economy that has been declining in importance and it is not obvious that the policy mix that is effective in an industrial economy is also effective in a service economy. For example, such tax policies as the US investment tax credit and the accelerated cost recovery system, which were meant to stimulate investment, are much more effective for capital-intensive manufacturing industries than for labor-intensive service industries. On the other hand, increases in payroll taxes have primarily a dampening effect on the services sector. The ingrained intellectual bias in favor of the goods sector must be corrected if we want to understand the realities of today's domestic and international economic developments.

In the international sphere, one result of the neglect of services has been that service transactions remain without a comprehensive international regime of rights and responsibilities and do not benefit from the discipline and predictability associated with it. As regards trade, this is so because the international trade regime, as embodied in the General Agreement on Tariffs and Trade (GATT), does not apply to trade in services but only to trade in goods. As regards foreign direct investment (FDI), this is so because no multilaterally agreed set of rules exists for this type of international transaction. Hence, governments are free, within the limits of their international obligations, to intervene in international transactions in services as and when they see fit.

Most services are intangible and non-storable. As a rule, therefore, their production and consumption have to occur at the same time in the same place. While this is a serious constraint on the tradeability of services, international transactions in services have nevertheless reached considerable proportions. This is documented in chapter I. Thus, service exports of market economies were conservatively calculated at $360 billion in 1980, about one-quarter of the exports of goods. As regards FDI, annual FDI outflows of four major capital-exporting countries (US, UK, Federal Republic of Germany, Japan) which went into services were estimated at about $15 billion during the early 1980s—over half of the total FDI outflows of these countries (see table 1). And the world's accumulated FDI stock in services of $220 billion had reached a third of the world's total FDI stock of about $580 billion. In other words, service transactions have clearly become an important component of international transactions.

If the importance of trade in services as a vehicle to deliver services to foreign markets is compared to that of FDI in services as effected through transnational corporations (TNCs), available data show that, for the leading economies, FDI is considerably more important than trade. Thus, the service exports of the principal capital-exporting countries mentioned above and Canada amounted

Table 1. Estimated world trade and foreign direct investment in services
(Billions of dollars)

Country	Exports of services a/ 1980	Foreign direct investment					Sales of foreign service affiliates 1981 b/
		Stock		Outflows, 1981-1983 (Yearly averages)			
		Total 1981	Services 1981	Total	Services		
United States	35	228	88	9c/	5c/		185
United Kingdom	34	92	31	6	3d/		65
Federal Republic of Germany	32	45	19	5	2		40
Japan	19	45	18	8	5		38
Canada	7	26	6	...	...		12
TOTAL above	127	436	162	28c/	15c/		340
Other developed market economies	165	128	47e/	9	5		99
Developing countries	66	18	7e/	...	...		15
WORLD TOTAL	358	582	216	37	20		454

Sources: UNCTAD, "Production and Trade in Services, Policies and Their Underlying Factors Bearing upon International Services Transactions", TD/B/941/Rev. 1; U.S., Department of Commerce, International Direct Investment: Global Trends and the U.S. Role (Washington: Superintendent of Documents, 1984); UNCTC, Trends and Issues in Foreign Direct Investment and Related Flows (New York: United Nations, 1985), Sales No. E.85.II.A.15; and various national sources.

a/ Private non-factor services.
b/ Estimated by applying to the services FDI stock of all countries the following ratios based on 1982 data: sales of US foreign service affiliates plus sales of foreign service affiliates in the US divided by US outward plus inward stock in services.
c/ Excluding US flows in finance. Finance was excluded because of the abnormal flows related to transactions between parent corporations in the US and their financial subsidiaries in the Netherlands Antilles. (In 1982 and 1983, large borrowings by US TNCs from their affiliates in the Netherlands Antilles took place.)
d/ Calculated by applying the 1981 share of services in the total FDI stock.
e/ Estimated by applying the average percentage share of services for the countries for which relevant data are available to those for which no separate data on services are available.

to $130 billion in 1980. On the other hand, the sales of the foreign service affiliates of TNCs from the same countries were estimated to be about twice as high—$340 billion in 1981. For the US, the data are even more impressive. While 1981 US service imports were $32 billion, the sales of US affiliates of non-US service TNCs reached $103 billion. Similarly, 1981 US service exports amounted to $34 billion, while sales of affiliates of US service TNCs established abroad amounted to $185 billion. For the UK, Japan and Canada, the volume of sales of foreign affiliates of their TNCs is about twice as high as the volume of their service exports, while for the FRG the two values are about the same.

The pattern does not, however, apply in the same manner to developing and socialist countries. The reason is that the foreign direct investments of the two groups of countries are of minor importance. For them, therefore, exports in services are more important than the services sales generated by their foreign direct investments. On the import side, on the other hand, it is quite likely that the volume of services sales by foreign affiliates located in the developing countries is higher than the volume of services imported by these countries.

In the foregoing text, trade and FDI in services were treated separately for analytical reasons. However, in reality both are very much interrelated, primarily because the provision of certain services through trade requires FDI (e.g., the export of a complex software package may require the establishment of a local affiliate to permit the adaptations necessary for its installation), and because more and more FDI requires trade in services for its operation (e.g., continued access to a central data base). In addition, regulations often provide that the sale of certain services (e.g., insurance) require a local establishment. This, in turn, has led to conceptual innovations (examined in chapter I) that reflect the special circumstances and interests associated with international service transactions. Most important here are the concepts of "right of presence" and "establishment trade". "Right of presence" grows out of the importance of access to the local distribution systems for trade in services. In the context of data services, this means that a party in one country should be allowed to link up with a party in another country for the purpose of sending data via transnational computer-communication systems. "Establishment trade" involves a broadening of the traditional definition of trade— which requires transactions between residents and non-residents, either in the form of "cross-border trade" or "within-border trade" (e.g., a tourist from country A buying services from a resident in country B)—to include those transactions emanating from locally established foreign affiliates.

These conceptual innovations require close analysis because they may have a number of public policy implications, not least regarding the boundaries between trade and FDI. If they are accepted, "right of establishment"—traditionally a key FDI concept—and "right of presence", for instance, become trade issues. This logic finds its precise expression in the US "Trade and Tariff Act of 1984" which not only elevates trade in services to a position equal to that of trade in goods, but virtually subsumes FDI under the trade regime and, therefore, defines barriers to trade explicitly as including restrictions on establishment and operation in foreign markets. At the same time, the notion of "establishment trade" implies that foreign affiliates are non-residents which, in turn, undermines a central tenet of the FDI policy of all developed market economies, namely that foreign affiliates should be granted national treatment, i.e., the same treatment that is accorded to domestic firms in like circumstances.

Emphasizing the linkages between trade and FDI is not meant to obscure the distinctions between the two kinds of transactions. One involves international trade issues, the other ownership issues in a domestic context. Accordingly, the policy and regulatory regimes applicable to these transactions differ, as do the underlying principles on which they are based. Thus, while the governing principle of the international FDI regime is that each country has the sovereign right to admit or not to admit FDI, that of the international trade regime, as enshrined in GATT, is that trade is to be admitted freely (subject to certain clearly defined conditions). These different principles have to be taken into account when discussing international policies applicable to services. The extent to which trade and FDI are being considered separately and, therefore, the extent to which these different principles are applied to each type of transaction, may well influence the character of any international public-policy framework that will eventually emerge.

This volume does not focus on services in general, although it provides some basic figures about the growth of the service sector and the dimensions of its internationalization, and outlines the international policy discussion on the subject. It concentrates rather on just one service industry only—data services— and especially the policy discussions relating to the international dimensions of these services. Since data services are a service, the broader services discussion provides the context for the focus on the narrower issues related to data services. Before dealing with these, the concept "data services" and related concepts need defining.

In the past decade, technological innovation has centered on microelectronics and has given birth to data technologies, i.e., technologies that function on the basis of digital signals. Data technologies offer vastly improved capabilities for the processing, storage, retrieval, manipulation, and transmission of data for a wide variety of purposes at (generally) declining costs. They are a core technology and as such form the nexus around which domestic economic and social activities will be restructured in the years to come. Data resources—data goods (computers, computer equipment, peripherals), data services (data processing, software, information storage and retrieval (data bases), telecommunication data services), the research required for their development (R & D), and the capacities and skills needed for their production and application—acquire, therefore, strategic importance for economic development. Within data resources, furthermore, the balance of importance is shifting from data goods to data services: an increasing share of data goods consists, in effect, of data services. For instance, software now accounts for more than three-quarters of the total life-cycle costs to the users of large computer systems. Increasingly, in other words, what a purchaser of data goods obtains are data services to which some hardware is attached. Chapter II documents the rise of the data-service industries.

Data services, like goods and other services, can be delivered to foreign markets through FDI or trade. As regards FDI, the mechanisms through which this occurs are the same as in the case of foreign direct investment in the goods sector: foreign affiliates are established which produce and sell services. Accordingly, the whole range of issues relating to FDI in general are relevant here as well, including the standards on the basis of which such affiliates ought to operate and ought to be treated.

As regards trade, matters are more complicated. Trade in data services is the result of the merger of telecommunication and informatics and its extension

Figure 1.   Telecommunications, informatics, telematics, and TDF

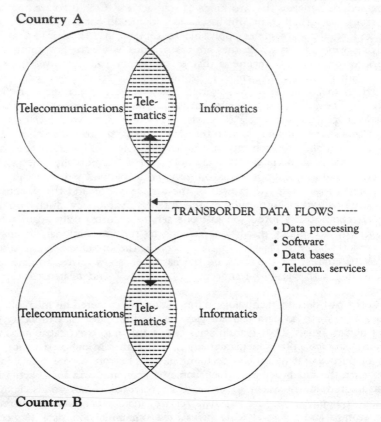

Country A

Country B

into the international realm (see fig. 1). Formally, trade in data services—or transborder data flows (TDF)—is defined as point-to-point movements of machine-readable data across national boundaries. The data involved are normally of a proprietary nature, and the movements are usually based on contractual relationships between parties. (Media products which involve mass diffusion—especially broadcasting and television—are, therefore, excluded.) Such movements can be effected by non-electronic means, e.g., magnetic tapes, discs, punched cards, or other media. Increasingly, however, electronic means are used, which presuppose the availability of a telecommunication infrastructure. In these cases, transnational computer-communication systems are established, i.e., arrangements whereby one or several computers in one or several countries are linked to affiliated computers in other countries and through them (or directly) to remote terminals. The trend in TDF is toward the greater usage of transnational computer-communication systems. Apart from the factors discussed earlier, the rapidly increasing use of micro-computers and the trend toward the automated office are likely to give a special boost to the growth of TDF. The same effect can be expected from the rapid spread of home computers. The last development, in fact, gives the TDF discussion a new dimension because it leads to growing involvement of private households in TDF.

Trade in data services can either involve arm's-length commercial transactions between independent firms (e.g., when a firm located in one country accesses a commercial data base located in another country) or intra-company transactions between entities of the same corporate system (e.g., when an affiliate located in one country accesses a data base in the parent corporation located in another country). Although this may appear to be a rather broad conceptualization of trade in data services, it is no broader than that applying to trade in goods, which also includes commercial and intra-firm transactions. However, while only an estimated 30% of the total goods trade of market economies consists of non-commercial transactions, perhaps 80–90% of trade in data services consists of non-commercial or intra-firm transactions. For this reason, attention has traditionally focused on these intra-firm (or corporate) transactions, under the name of transborder data flows (TDF). But even the TDF discussion usually combines commercial and corporate data flows, although the latter normally overshadows—because of its greater importance—the former. The point that must be emphasized is that in each case data services are rendered, regardless of whether they are transactions in their own right, or constitute the infrastructure for trade in goods, trade in services or the operations of TNCs, and regardless of whether they are specifically identified and recorded as data services, paid for or not. Transborder data flows are, therefore, for the most part nothing other than traded data services. For this reason, the concept "transborder data flows" is being used here interchangeably with the concept "trade in data services".

This is not to say that TDF involve only trade issues and that the subject does not have broader implications for, e.g., privacy, dependency, vulnerability, corporate structures, industrialization or economic development in general. In fact, it is because of their implications for, above all, economic development that TDF are important. The approach taken in this volume is to review first briefly these implications in order to establish the importance of TDF, and then to narrow the discussion to the trade aspect of the problematique.

Given the importance of data resources in general and data services in particular, I suggest that data services are a core service: more and more, they change the parameters for the operations of most other services and, indeed, most economic activities. An analogy is perhaps the invention of electricity. That invention not only led to the creation of new industries (e.g., power generators, electrical appliances), but also changed the manner in which other national and international economic activities were undertaken; in fact, it played a crucial role in bringing about the way of life we know.

A number of reasons support this assertion. One is that data services are rapidly becoming important industries in their own right. Second, data services are changing the modus operandi of existing industries and play a pivotal role in the new industrial revolution that is taking place. Third, they change international economic transactions by giving rise to trade and foreign direct investment in data services; by becoming the infrastructure for trade in goods and especially for trade in services; by redefining the modalities for the operations of TNCs; and by increasing the tradeability of certain services (see fig. 2). These points are documented briefly in chapter II, whose purpose is to outline the importance of data services as strategic economic resources. The third of these changes, the impact of data

Figure 2. The nature of data services as a core service

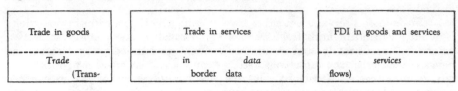

Trade in goods	Trade in services	FDI in goods and services
Trade (Trans-	*in data* border data	*services* flows)

Figure 3. The role of TNCs in trade and foreign direct investment in data services

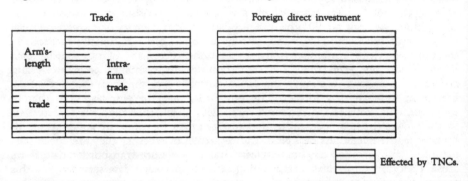

services on international economic transactions, is of particular interest for this volume in view of its focus on policy discussions concerning the international dimensions of data services.

In the context of the services discussion, it is particularly important that the advent of transnational computer-communication systems increases the tradeability of certain services. It has already been pointed out that, because of the nature of services, their production and consumption have normally to occur *at the same time in the same place* and that this represents a serious obstacle to trade. Real-time, interactive communication via transnational computer-communication systems changes this situation. By collapsing time and space (at decreasing costs), transactions can take place *at the same time but in different places.* As a result, the tradeability of certain services increases considerably, affecting especially such key business services as banking, insurance, accounting, design and engineering, legal services, management consulting, and, of course, data services themselves. This impact may have profound implications for international service transactions in general. For one, where tradeability increases, this creates a considerable potential for an actual expansion of trade in services. Second, since increased tradeability broadens the options of both sellers and buyers as regards the manner in which services can be delivered or obtained, the need for FDI in services may decrease.

In sum, data services are becoming an important component of international economic transactions. They are rapidly becoming the infrastructure for trade in goods, trade in services and the operations of TNCs. In addition, they increase the tradeability of a whole range of services. This central role makes data services a core service. It is a core service, furthermore, whose international transactions are overwhelmingly effected by TNCs (see fig. 3): in FDI by definition; in trade because most of it consists of intra-firm (and hence TNC-internal) trade and much of the remainder involves TNCs as suppliers, buyers or providers of the infrastructure.

It is against the background of the importance of service transactions and the importance of data resources that the issues relating to trade and FDI in data services have to be seen. Originally, policy attention focused on transborder flows of personal data and the privacy considerations associated with them. Two international instruments (briefly discussed in chapter III) were adopted in this respect: the OECD "Guidelines Governing the Protection of Privacy and Transborder Flows of Personal Data" and the Council of Europe "Convention for the Protection of Individuals with Regard to Automatic Processing of Personal Data."

Since the beginning of the 1980s, however, the emphasis has clearly shifted toward the transborder flow of economic data and especially the trade aspect of this phenomenon. In the process, the discussions of trade and FDI in data services have become part and parcel of the discussions of trade and FDI in services generally. The reason is simple: the principal proponent of these discussions, the US, seeks to establish a multilateral framework for trade in services in general. It is explicitly meant to be an umbrella framework under which ideally all service industries would be moving in the same direction, namely liberalization. It would, thus, be a framework applicable to data services as well. In fact, given the core nature of data services, the international discussion of services and the design of a framework for them may well proceed in a manner that gives special attention to data services. Throughout this volume, therefore, the discussion of the politics of trade and FDI in data services is intertwined with the discussion of the politics of trade and FDI in services generally.

Before these politics can be examined, the interest situations of countries and regions vis-à-vis TDF and the competing values they bring to bear on the formulation of policies in this area must be examined.

Given the importance of data resources for economic development, it is not surprising that countries increasingly seek, first and foremost, to strengthen domestic data resources; second, to ensure access to those data services that cannot reasonably be developed locally; and third, to improve their physical and intellectual data infrastructure (informatics, telecommunications and skills) to place the country in the best position to use data resources. In this context, one feature of transnational computer-communication systems becomes of central importance: they permit it that data resources can be accessed internationally. While this obviously and greatly facilitates the achievement of the second of the objectives just mentioned, it may hamper the achievement of the first objective. The principal reason is that the availability of data resources through TDF may decrease the need to develop such resources locally, or may make such local development difficult because of the strength of international competition.

Given a full recognition of the importance of data resources, the key issue—and the main subject of chapter III—is what approach governments adopt to acquire data resources. Two main variables, it appears, determine the selection of an appropriate approach. One is the extent to which countries consider that they already have sufficient data resources. The other is the extent to which countries consider it necessary and feasible to pursue data-resource acquisition strategies that aim either at building up domestic data resources or at obtaining access to them abroad.

For countries that do not think that they have sufficient data resources and so consider it necessary and feasible to build up their domestic resources in this area, the *principal objective* is to obtain competitive capabilities in as many data resources as possible. This, in turn, would permit them to (1) have a maximum of economic resources central to future development located on their national territory; (2) capture the direct and indirect benefits (including skills) associated with the development of such resources; (3) stimulate the development of other industries because of the close linkages of data resources with the rest of the economy; and (4) establish a basis for savings of foreign exchange through import substitution, generation of foreign exchange through exports, and participation in the world market for data resources. The *rationale* for such a national approach lies in the belief that—in spite of the immediate costs of an infant-industry policy—the realization of hitherto underdeveloped domestic capabilities adds, in the longer run, to national and international welfare. This consideration is particularly attractive because of the strategic importance of data resources for development and because distance-insensitive transportation costs and the homogeneity of certain data services may offer specialization advantages that facilitate the growth of competitive industries. The main *policy instruments* of this approach include subsidies, performance requirements, procurement policies, the favoring of national champions (i.e., chosen domestic corporations to advance national objectives through which the growth of domestic data resources can be stimulated), and the wide range of traditional protectionist measures through which fledgeling domestic industries can be sheltered against overwhelming international competition. Also crucial in this context are various forms of control of TDF. As mentioned earlier, the principal reason for such control is that transborder data flows permit international access to data resources which, therefore, need not be developed locally. In addition, wherever there is a potential for local development, TDF, for competitive reasons, may inhibit it. In other words, since transborder data flows can have an influence on the location of data resources, any comprehensive national policy aimed at strengthening domestic data resources has to pay attention to these flows. Moreover, it is also often thought important that the data resources to be built up are not merely located on national territory but also domestically controlled (i.e., not controlled by TNCs headquartered elsewhere). Under these circumstances, a country may discriminate (e.g., in procurement policy) against foreign affiliates. Developed (e.g., Canada, the European Community, France) and developing countries (e.g., Brazil, India, Mexico) alike pursue policies that contain some of these elements.

Countries that do not see themselves as having sufficient data resources but are in a weak position to build up domestic capacities (especially for data services) have to rely on transborder data flows. In other words, data resources are not physically but only functionally acquired. While the actual resources remain located abroad, access to them is gained via transnational computer-communication systems. For instance, instead of building up local data bases or having copies of data bases located in the country, it is considered sufficient to have access to data bases located abroad. Under such an access-oriented acquisition approach, the *principal objective* is to have the widest possible access to the use of data resources located elsewhere. This, in turn, requires an environment in which undisrupted access to international data resources is guaranteed (this is, in fact, the precondition for this approach) and barriers to trade in data services and other measures that could disrupt TDF are reduced or eliminated. (Barriers to FDI in data services would, however, be of little interest because, presumably, no important domestic data-resource firms exist.) Beyond this, and to the extent to which data resources are needed for international transactions (e.g., banking), the objectives are in many respects similar to those of countries that possess well-developed data resources (see below), especially concerning the desire to benefit fully from the application of data services in international transactions. The *rationale* for such a functional acquisition approach is the desire to avoid the opportunity costs entailed in the development of domestic capacities and to benefit from international specialization by utilizing imported data resources for other economic activities in which the country is thought to have a comparative advantage. The principal costs of this approach are dependence on critical resources located elsewhere and the learning benefits and spin-off effects forgone in the development of domestic data resources. The main *policy instrument* is to ensure by international agreement that access to data resources abroad is guaranteed. In other words, countries with data resources need to be obliged to permit transborder access to them. In fact, such a right of access is a sine qua non for all those countries that are willing to forgo the development of domestic data resources and/or to rely on TDF for obtaining access to such resources. In a sense, therefore, therefore "right of access" is a necessary complement to "right of presence" (and especially to one of its components, the "right of non-establishment"): unless access is guaranteed, a right of presence—which implies that critical data resources may be located elsewhere and are merely available via telecommunication lines—may become a risky undertaking for countries.

Countries that possess well-developed data resources are, of course, in a different interest situation. Their approach in this area flows from their desire to benefit as much as possible from their technological and commercial lead in data industries. Accordingly, their *principal objective* is to promote an international environment in which (1) barriers to trade and FDI in data services and other measures that could disrupt TDF are reduced or eliminated; (2) data-services transactions and applications can take place as freely, non-discriminatorily and securely as possible so that data industries can grow internationally through exports and FDI; (3) other international transactions can benefit fully from the application of data services; (4) corporations can develop new services based on data technology; (5) the functioning of corporate transnational computer-communication systems (i.e., the operation of TNCs) is not hampered; and (6) the worldwide technical infrastructure for TDF is as efficient as possible to permit transactions in data services. Most of these goals are also shared by the major users of TDF, especially TNCs. The *rationale* for this approach lies in the belief that—analogous to trade in goods—the world as a whole gains from growing trade and FDI in data services because they contribute to a more efficient international allocation of resources and increase the efficiency of doing transnational business, and that trade in services, like trade in goods, is an engine of growth. The aims of this approach cannot be realized nationally (as those of countries lacking data resources may be), but require rather an international approach: other countries have to be convinced not to establish barriers to international transactions in data services. Accordingly, the main *policy instrument* is the adoption of an enforceable liberal international regime that specifies the responsibilities of countries as regards trade and FDI in data services, or, short of that, the conclusion of appropriate bilateral and regional agreements. The latter, in any event, may bring about immediate improvements of the situation and, in addition, may encourage multilateral negotiations.

The strategies described so far are, in their pure form, ideal types seldom to be found in the real world. Even the country that comes closest to the first option, Brazil, pursues a mixture of strengthening domestic data resources and seeking access to international data resources. Mixed strategies allow a country to strengthen its domestic capacities for certain segments of an industry (e.g., microcomputers), but to rely on access to international data resources for other segments (e.g., main-frame computers). Another mix of interests arises if a country desires to strengthen its domestic data resources, but another of the country's industries (e.g., banking) needs state-of-the-art data services and, independently of that, needs an open international system for TDF to remain (or become) competitive internationally. Many countries are likely to be in mixed-interest situations of this sort. This is all the more likely to be the case when countries already have other industries that are dependent on data services, especially countries that have information-intensive, internationally oriented service industries and countries that are the headquarters of TNCs. Most developed market economies fall in this category, but also a number of developing countries. The dilemma for the developing countries is, however, less pronounced because few of them are the headquarters of TNCs with transnational computer-communication systems, or have information-intensive service industries that are active internationally. The developing countries can, therefore, more easily pursue national acquisition policies for data resources.

In the context of this volume, the approach which aims at establishing an enforceable liberal international regime for data-service transactions is, of course, of particular interest, because it fuels the international policy discussion in this area. The principal proponents of this approach are the international business community (most notably in the US) and, most importantly, the US government. A number of factors—some of them already mentioned, others to be elaborated in the main body of the volume—explain why the US administration is the principal proponent of this approach and has initiated the international discussion on services:

1. The US is the most advanced service economy of international importance. Its service sector accounts for two-thirds of GDP, it is the major source of new employment, and it is looked upon as a new engine of growth and a principal source of structural adjustment. The US was the first country to recognize the importance of the service sector, both in its domestic and in its international contexts.

2. As pointed out earlier, international transactions in services have reached considerable proportions, in FDI more so than in trade. However, considering that the share of services involved in international transactions is considerably lower than that of industry or agriculture or, for that matter, the share of services in GDP, the potential for a substantial increase in international service transactions is high. The US would be among the principal beneficiaries if this potential were realized.

3. The US is by far the most important exporter of services foreign direct investment. Services FDI has been the most dynamic component of the country's outward FDI, accounting for almost 40% of total stock (more than manufacturing investment) and a similar share of total flows. As a result, US-based TNCs are occupying leading positions in most international service industries.

4. The US is also, with approximately $35 billion in 1980, the world's largest exporter of services, although the service exports of the United Kingdom, France, and the Federal Republic of Germany are of the same magnitude, and the ratio of service to merchandise exports of the United Kingdom and France is almost twice that of the US.

5. Prospects for an expansion of trade in services are particularly promising for those services whose tradeability has increased because of the advent of transnational computer-communication systems and the rising importance of transborder data flows.

6. Since the US is leading in data services, it is best-placed to lead in these new forms of international trade as well, and to benefit from the increased tradeability of certain services.

7. For the same reason, the US has also been the first to recognize trade in data services as an important activity in its own right and to recognize the impact it has on the infrastructure for trade and FDI in general.

8. The importance of international transactions in services, and especially the importance of transborder data flows, have been fully recognized by the US business community, which has been pressing the US government to take action regarding services in general and data services in particular.

9. For all these reasons, the US is strongly interested in an open international environment for service transactions in general and data-service transactions in particular. The US is, therefore, vigorously pursuing the establishment of an enforceable liberal international regime to govern trade and FDI in services and especially data services.

10. The establishment of such a framework is in harmony with the country's commitment in principle to a liberal trade and FDI regime and its conviction that, ultimately, such a regime is the most beneficial for all countries. However, the establishment of such a framework is resisted by a number of countries, especially developing ones. They fear that a liberal regime would effectively hinder the growth of indigenous service industries, because international competition could be overwhelming in many instances.

11. Most developed countries are in a more mixed-interest situation. While most of them lag behind the US in the development of most data services, they can benefit immediately from the application of these services for their own purposes, be it to improve the operations of their TNCs, to strengthen the competitiveness of their service industries, or to exploit the new tradeability of certain services. The US can, therefore, build on a certain commonality of interests with these countries (which includes a desire of all of them to have access to the markets of developing countries) when advancing its quest for a liberal framework for international service transactions.

The combination of these factors has led to a full recognition of the importance of international service transactions in the country's legislation and policies and to vigorous efforts to pursue the matter on the international level.

Because of the leading role of the US in this matter, the policy objectives of that country as regards international service transactions are likely to influence strongly the contents of international discussions in this field. Particularly relevant here is the "Trade and Tariff Act of 1984" which is examined in detail in chapter III because it provides the mandate, the objectives, the instruments and the resources for the government's service policy. The Act gives services a status equal to that of goods under US trade law and, to a large extent, covers FDI as well, thus bringing this activity also under the purview of US trade law to a certain extent. Furthermore, services are specifically understood to include data services, since the definition of services includes specifically transfers of information. This gives data services, so to speak, legal status. The principal objective identified by the Act for international negotiations is to reduce or eliminate barriers and other distortions to trade and FDI in services. To achieve this objective, the Act provides the Administration with negotiating authority for bilateral and multilateral agreements, and gives it a range of powers to entice or pressure other governments to be more amenable to US objectives. Most important among these powers is the strengthening of Section 301 of the 1974 Trade Act and the clarification that it applies to services as well—and, for that matter, to FDI with implications for trade in goods and services. (Section 301 invests the Administration with broad discretionary powers to negotiate for the reduction or elimination of barriers to US service exports and FDI flows, and to take punitive action against countries that do not reduce or remove such barriers.) In addition, the Act grants powers to the Administration regarding *new* export performance requirements imposed by other countries; provides that customs duties can be modified in the area of high technology products and services (mostly the area of data industries); and, to a certain extent, makes the granting of beneficiary status under the Generalized System of Preferences a negotiating tool with which developing countries can be enticed or pressured to accept US objectives regarding trade in services and FDI flows. This prepares the US well for negotiations on international transactions in services.

This preparation covers, and is immediately relevant to, trade in data services as well. Beyond that, a host of committees—mostly in the US, but also in the framework of the International Chamber of Commerce—have examined the questions pertaining to TDF in great detail and have elaborated the objectives and key elements for an international agreement on that subject (see chapter III). Based on this preparatory work, the US administration has formulated its policy stance which it pursues vigorously on the regional and international levels. The objective is to ensure an open international system for trade and FDI in data services. The principles advocated to advance this objective are unrestricted flow of information and market-place competition. At the operational level, this means, first and foremost, to reduce or eliminate any obstacles to international transactions in data services and to prevent the imposition of new ones. "Obstacles" are defined broadly and include the introduction of taxes or tariffs on the value of data-service flows, certain conditions placed on the operation of leased lines, certain data-protection provisions, local content requirements, lack of software protection, market access barriers, certain equipment policies, and telecommunication monopolies. These matters are further discussed in chapter III.

The manner in which these interest situations shape the discussions of trade and FDI in data services at the bilateral, regional and international levels is the subject of chapters IV and V. Particular attention is given to three questions:

1. How do the interest situations of countries influence the choice of forum for discussion or negotiation?
2. How are these discussions or negotiations shaped by the principal competing values regarding international transactions in services in general and data services in particular?
3. What has been achieved so far?

With a few exceptions, the discussions and negotiations on data services have so far been conducted mostly in the framework of the general services discussion, a discussion in which the US is the driving force. At the bilateral level, the US administration is paying more attention than in the past to services when concluding bilateral investment protection and promotion treaties; it has concluded an agreement with Israel about the establishment of a free trade area between the two countries which includes comprehensive (but as yet non-binding) provisions on services; and it is pursuing negotiations with Canada about a sectoral free trade agreement for computer services. The agreement with Israel, in particular, may well acquire the character of a model.

More important, however, are the initiatives in the OECD. The basic philosophy of that organization is to favor an open international economic system, and it deals both with FDI and trade issues. On the FDI side, the Code of Liberalisation of Capital Movements and the Declaration and Decisions on International Investment and Multinational Enterprises constitute a framework which also covers FDI in services. It was strengthened, in 1984, with the extension of the Capital Movements Code to cover certain important aspects of the right of establishment. On the trade side, the Code of Liberalisation of Current Invisible Operations offers a basic framework, but one with a number of limitations, one of them being that it does not cover data services. Efforts to strengthen this Code have been initiated.

Recognizing the central importance of data services, the US initiated in 1982—within the framework of the OECD's general services discussion—work on a "Declaration on Transborder Data Flows." After three years of negotiations, the text of the Declaration was adopted in April 1985 by the OECD's Council of Ministers. Its central thrust is to promote access to data and information and related services and to avoid the creation of unjustified barriers to the international exchange of data and information. At the same time, the Declaration acknowledges that the ability of member countries to reap the benefits associated with TDF may vary, that national policies which affect TDF reflect many different social and economic goals, and it observes that governments may adopt varied means to achieve their policy goals. The Declaration is the first multilateral instrument dealing specifically with the transborder flow of economic data, and its adoption is a breakthrough for all those who seek an international commitment to maintaining an open environment for TDF. Because of the core nature of data services, it is an agreement with far-reaching implications for trade in other services and for the operations of TNCs. As the first agreement reached in the context of the trade-in-services discussion in general, the Declaration is a sign post for the desired direction in these discussions. Furthermore, it establishes a minimum platform for the developed market economies for the most important part of the services discussions—data services—shortly before negotiations actually begin.

This is most likely to occur in GATT. Given the importance of the impending services negotiations in GATT, most of chapter V deals with the considerations that the contracting parties bring to these negotiations, their objectives, and the progress made so far. On the initiative of the US, GATT agreed in November 1984 to initiate a work program on services. For the proponents of the international services discussion, this represented a breakthrough, precisely because the free-trade persuasion underlying the institution's Articles of Agreement suits their interests perfectly. In fact, it is almost certain that the next GATT round of multilateral trade negotiations will have services on its agenda, and it is very likely that the outcome will include a framework for trade in services, including data services. When actual negotiations commence, it can be expected that, as in the OECD, special attention will be given to data services. The US, at least, has indicated its priority in this regard and has informed GATT's contracting parties accordingly.

The developing countries as a group strongly oppose the inclusion of services in GATT's work program. The overwhelming majority of developing countries have a relatively weak indigenous service sector, which is reflected in their balance-of-payments deficit in this area. These countries fear, therefore, that a liberal service-trade regime could effectively hinder the growth of indigenous service industries, because international competition could be overwhelming in many instances. This fear is exacerbated by the expectation that (given the nature of services) negotiation in this area must unavoidably include certain FDI issues—a matter developing countries certainly do *not* wish to bring into the GATT framework. In addition, the developing countries fear that the inclusion of a "new issue" like services would shift attention away from negotiations on trade in goods, which are much more important for developing countries, and for which an agreed-upon work program exists, as adopted in 1982 by the GATT Ministerial Meeting. Thus, developing countries have pointed out that the GATT framework is not applicable to services because GATT was specifically devised for trade in goods, not trade in services, a position which the US held at one point as well. Although the developing countries could not prevent the inclusion of services in the GATT work program, a number of them can be expected to continue to oppose or slow down actual negotiations on services, although it may be very difficult to resist the determination of the US—and the support of the US by most other developed market economies—to establish an international framework for trade in services. The developing countries prefer UNCTAD as the forum for services discussions because they see their interests better represented in that organization, and because UNCTAD already has considerable experience in dealing with a number of service industries. In fact, UNCTAD decided in March 1985 to initiate a work program on services, and it can be expected to pay special attention to TDF as a core service.

The OECD, GATT and UNCTAD are not the only fora in which international transactions in data services are discussed. As reviewed in chapters IV and V, the Latin American Economic System (SELA), the International Telecommunication Union (ITU), UNESCO, the United Nations Commission and Centre on Trans-national Corporations, and the Intergovernmental Bureau for Informatics (IBI) also pay attention to this subject. SELA is doing this with a view to adopting a regional policy in this area and influencing the position of the Group of 77 as a whole. The ITU focuses entirely on the technical infrastructure of TDF and has not dealt with the economic implications of data services—nor does it seem to have any intention of doing so. UNESCO's interest in this subject follows from its interest in the New International Information Order and from its work on informatics and new information and communication technologies. The Commission and Centre on Transnational Corporations approach the subject primarily from the point of view of research on the role of TNCs in TDF and services and the fact that service FDI falls under the United Nations Code of Conduct on Transnational Corporations. The IBI, on the other hand, focuses specifically on TDF. For that purpose, it established a high-level International Consultative Commission on Transborder Data Flow Development at the end of 1984 and endowed it with a broad mandate. The IBI is thus in a position to assume a leadership role in the international TDF discussion, which would be to the advantage of IBI's main constituency, the developing countries. Endowed with considerable resources and supported by its own secretariat, the Commission could direct IBI's policy discussion and research program and influence the TDF policies of developing countries through IBI's technical assistance work. In any event, the work of IBI will certainly play an important role in raising the awareness of the developing countries in TDF matters and focusing it on the issues considered important by IBI, as well as in assisting developing countries directly in dealing with the issues raised by this phenomenon.

The focus of the discussion in international fora has so far been on trade in services and data services, although, as pointed out earlier, FDI is considerably more important than trade in delivering services to foreign markets. In addition, barriers to FDI in services are probably more important than barriers to trade in services, and the FDI aspect in the trade-in-services negotiations is likely to slow them down. One would assume, therefore, that FDI in services ought to receive more attention than trade in services from the proponents of a liberal regime for international transactions in services. But this is strangely not the case. The issues related to this matter are taken up in the concluding chapter of this volume. Perhaps the most important reasons for the neglect of the FDI dimension are the trade-related importance of TDF—especially their role as a core service, as the informational infrastructure for trade in goods and for the operations of TNCs, and their role in increasing the tradeability of certain services—and ignorance of the relative importance of FDI in services compared to that of trade in services. This neglect is all the more astonishing since an international agreement on FDI— the United Nations Code of Conduct on Transnational Corporations—is within reach. When concluded, the Code will define the rights and responsibilities of transnational corporations and states in the area of FDI (including FDI in services) and thereby establish a stable, predictable and transparent framework for the most important dimension of international transactions in services. Whatever the reasons for this neglect, the economic reality—perhaps helped by political necessity—of the greater importance of FDI in services is bound to assert itself sooner or later in the discussion of an appropriate framework for international transactions in services.

Notes

[1] US, Congress, House of Representatives, Committee on Banking, Finance and Urban Affairs, Subcommittee on Economic Stabilization, "Service Industries: The Changing Shape of the American Economy" (Washington: Government Printing Office, 1984), mimeo., p. 1.

I

Services

A. The domestic service sector

1. Classification and measurement

The study of services has long been—and still is—a much neglected subject, "the stepchild of economic research".[1] To a large extent, this has been the result of the nature and heterogeneity of services: they are normally intangible and cannot be stored, and they have little in common except their intangibility and non-storability.[2] Because of the nature of services, their production and consumption normally have to occur at the same time in the same place (e.g., transportation, tourism), or otherwise these services are very cumbersome or impractical to provide across distances (e.g., banking, trade). As a result, it is very difficult to define, measure and aggregate services. These characteristics of the service sector invite separate industrial rather than aggregate sectoral analysis and partly explain the conceptual neglect that the sector as a whole has suffered in economic analysis.

Conceptual neglect has its origin also in the classical view, reaching back to Adam Smith, that services (as opposed to goods) are of a non-productive nature since the result of the labor and capital required to produce them cannot be stored—services "perish in the very instance of their performance"[3]—and hence are of little value to society. Karl Marx embraced a similar view, as a result of which the national accounting systems of the socialist countries only include those services that are considered to be "material services" (e.g., transport, communications and trading). Other economists (e.g., Friedrich List[4]) recognized, however, the importance of services for development. But it was only in the mid-1930s and 1940s that the work of Allan G. B. Fisher and Colin Clark began to lead to a more systematic body of knowledge about the role and importance of services.[5] In particular, Fisher and Clark conceived of economic development as a process involving sectoral shifts from the primary via the secondary to the tertiary sectors. The work since then, however, has failed to provide a broadly-shared definition and classification of services, so that today "no authoritative consensus on either the boundaries or the classification of the service industries" exists.[6]

Apart from the conceptual undervaluation of the importance of services, this is also a result of the problems inherent in defining, classifying and measuring a broad range of intangible activities. As has been observed, "the measurement of price and volume changes for most services remains primitive and rudimentary. There is little understanding about the nature of the physical units in which most

18

services should be quantified, and consequently their prices are also vague and ill-defined."[7]

To begin with, the principal national accounts systems—the United Nations system (used by most countries), the material product system (used by the socialist countries) and the Courcier system (used by France and most French-speaking developing countries)—take different approaches to the classification of industrial and service activities.[8] Besides, the classification systems are much cruder for services than for goods: the Standard Industrial Classification (SIC) system used by the US Census Bureau, for instance, has twice as many SIC codes for goods than for services, although two-thirds of the US economy consists of the service sector. In addition, individual countries often make their own adaptations and many of them do not have time-series data. As a consequence, comparisons between countries and over periods are fraught with difficulties and insufficiencies. Moreover, particularly in developing countries, the informal sector is quite important, i.e., a substantial number of service activities go unrecorded.[9] Under-recording also occurs because services are produced outside the institutional framework of the service sector. Since a great variety of services is produced in-house in the context of the production of goods, these activities are counted as part of the value added in the goods sector. For instance, if a steel company prepares its accounts in-house, this activity is an integral part of steel production; if the task is contracted out to an accounting firm, it is classified as a service. Hence, one source of the growth of the service sector is merely a change in industrial organization and the division of labor in that, as a result of differentiation, standardization of knowledge, and the emergence of economies of scale, service activities leave the intra-firm context and enter the market-place.[10]

Difficulties also arise in the valuation of services. While output in the goods sector can be valued on the basis of physical units of measurement, this is considerably more difficult in the case of services and thus leads to a wide range of methods of valuation. Furthermore, where services are strongly regulated (e.g., railway services), their prices may be subsidized in the interest of social objectives and hence not reflect their market value, with the result that output is underestimated; conversely, in some cases of public monopolies (e.g., telecommunication services), services may be overpriced, with the result that the service output is overvalued.

Even where data are available, they are normally aggregated in very broad categories; in particular, the rapidly growing category of "other services" contains a wide range of services which should properly be reported separately to permit a more meaningful analysis. The reported data, moreover, do not as a rule distinguish between the production of indigenous enterprises and that of foreign affiliates. This makes analysis very difficult, especially as regards the role of foreign capital in individual service industries.

In sum, statistics on services are inadequate and under-report service production by an unknown (but probably high) percentage. This reflects partly the fact that national accounts systems were established when services were regarded as unimportant, and partly the existence of inherent difficulties in measuring service output. The lack of comprehensive and detailed time-series data is a serious obstacle to analysis of the service sector both nationally and internationally.

In line with the intellectual tradition of the services discussion, a broad definition of services would include all economic activities outside the agricultural, mining and manufacturing sectors. Under the United Nations system of national accounts, these are construction, utilities, trade, transport, finance, community services (mostly public administration and defense), and others. (A further breakdown of these categories, using the International Standard Industrial Classification of All Economic Activities (ISIC), is contained in table I-1.) Under this definition, the service sector accounted, at the end of 1979, for 64% of the GDP of market economies—67% of that of the developed market economies and 51% of that of the developing countries (see table I-2). These services together amounted to $5,200 billion in 1979, of which $4,500 billion were produced in developed market economies and $760 billion in developing countries; the corresponding figures for 1970 were $1,500 billion, $1,400 billion and $170 billion, respectively (see tables I-3 to I-5).

Such a broad definition is, however, not generally accepted. If one considers the output of services as non-storable and intangible, construction clearly provides a tangible output and, therefore, should be excluded from the definition. The construction sector contributed, in 1979, $530 billion to the GDP of the market economies, $430 billion in the case of the developed and $100 billion in the case of the developing countries. Similarly, public administration and defense could be regarded as comprising a separate set of activities, among other reasons because a good part of it falls outside the market economy. On the other hand, a number of services that are provided by the government in some countries are provided by the private sector in others. The exclusion of government services—which contributed $630 billion to the GDP in the developed and $110 billion to the GDP of the developing market economies in 1979—from the services discussion thus introduces some distortion into international comparisons. Finally, utilities are frequently not included in services, principally on the grounds that they involve heavy capital equipment and produce mostly visible (e.g., water) or storable (e.g., gas) outputs.[11] Utilities contributed about $170 billion to the GDP of the developed and $20 billion to the GDP of developing countries in 1979.

The exclusion of construction, public administration and defense, and utilities leaves a narrow definition of services, comprising trade and finance, transport and communication, and other services. In most of the literature, these activities are regarded as the core of the services sector, and the following discussion, unless indicated otherwise, focuses on them. Depending on the service industry and the country, a good part of these activities is carried out by private agents, for which reason they are often referred to as "private sector services." Furthermore, in a number of service industries—accounting, advertising, information storage and retrieval, tourism, insurance, re-insurance, banking, and shipping—a limited number of TNCs play an important and at times dominant role, especially in the industries' international dimensions.[12]

This set of activities accounted, in 1979, for 47% of the GDP of market economies (representing $3,800 billion of production), 49% ($3,300 billion) in the case of the developed market economies and 37% ($500 billion) in the case of the developing countries. Even narrowly defined, the service sector is, therefore, the single largest sector of the world economy (see table I-6). In the US, Australia, Denmark, and Belgium the service sector (including public administration and defense) has reached two-thirds of GDP; private business services alone range typically between 40% and 50% (see table I-7).

Figure I-1   Employment growth in the US, by sector, 1962–1982 (millions of jobs)

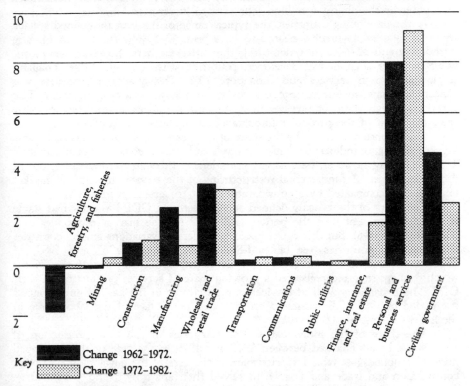

Key   ▇ Change 1962–1972.
      ▨ Change 1972–1982.

Source: New York Stock Exchange, U.S. International Competitiveness: Perception and Reality (New York: New York Stock Exchange, 1984), p. 33.

The importance of the service sector is even higher if measured by employment figures. The broadly defined service sector is by far the largest employer in both developed and developing market economies.[13] In the former, private sector services and administration and defense accounted for between 53% and 75% of total employment at the beginning of the 1980s, compared to 24–28% in industry and 6–8% in agriculture (see table I-7). In the US, this share was above 70% of employment in 1980. In fact, 82% of the US employment growth between 1962 and 1972 was accounted for by personal and business services, civilian government, and wholesale and retail trade; during 1972 and 1982, the combined share of these activities was 77% (see fig. I-1). This compares, respectively, with 12% and 4% for manufacturing. The service sector will remain the principal source of new job growth in the period to 1995, while the employment contribution of the manufacturing sector will continue to decline.[14] The job category in the US with by far the highest growth rate (88%) between 1982 and 1995 is forecast to be computer programers and systems analysts (up from 520,000 to 980,000)—an occupation centered on data resources.[15] Similarly, the over 4 million jobs that were lost in manufacturing in the European Community between 1973 and 1981 were more than offset by the almost 6 million jobs created in services.[16]

In the developing countries, the typical range of the broadly defined service sector in total employment appeared to have been 40–53% (compared to 14–30% in industry and 32–44% in agriculture); the variations here, however, were considerably larger than in the developed countries, with a country like Thailand employing 21% in services and Singapore 70%. The quality of statistics and conceptual discrepancies may account for this variation to a certain extent. The surprisingly high share of services in developing countries is probably in many cases the result of the particular importance of public sector services.

One important reason why the share of services in employment is considerably higher than that of industry are different levels and rates of growth of productivity.[17] This factor may, however, be changed considerably through the increasing use of data technologies. A fundamental restructuring of the service employment market may occur, accompanied by a considerable boost to service productivity.

The share of the broadly defined service sector in GDP has remained stable at about 64 per cent over the period 1970–1979 for the market economies as a whole (see table I-6). But this figure masks considerable variations among countries and groups of countries (see tables I-8 and I-9). Between 1965 and 1983, 54 countries—including a number of least developed countries—out of the 76 for which data are reported registered a growing share of services production in their GDP. The dynamic growth of services is even clearer in the case of employment: the period of 1965–1981 witnessed an increased percentage of the labor force in services in 97 out of 103 countries.[18]

The share of the individual service categories in the total production of services has barely changed between 1970 and 1979 in the case of the developed market economies (see table I-4). However, in the case of the developing countries, construction and trade and finance increased their share by 3 and 4 percentage points respectively, while that of "other services" decreased by 7 percentage points (see table I-5). In the case of trade and finance, this change was mostly due to increased activities in this category in the non-oil-exporting countries, while in the case of construction the increase was largely due to oil-revenue-induced activities in the oil-exporting countries. As to "other services", both oil-exporting and non-oil-exporting countries experienced a decline, the latter more so than the former.[19]

These figures do not, of course, capture relative changes within service categories. The category "other services", in particular, contains data services, key services of the future; such important business services as consultancy services, accounting, engineering, franchising, legal services, and leasing; and such consumer growth services as tourism, entertainment, car rental and health services. Systematic data on these components are not available, but indications are that the share of a number of these services has been increasing rapidly during the past decade, at least in developed market economies.

The developing countries' share in the total production of services of all market economies ranged, in 1979, from 10% to 20%, with "other services" as the lower end of the range and construction at the upper end (see table I-10). All service categories, except "other services", increased their share in total production during the decade of the 1970s, led by construction (by seven percentage points) and followed by trade and finance (by five points) and public administration and defense as well as transport and communication (by 4 points each). "Other services" is the only category that decreased, a development which is not unimportant since this category contains many key business services. Overall, the developing countries share in the total production of services in market economies has increased steadily during the 1970s, from 11% in 1970 to 13% in 1975 and 15% in 1979.

2. Role in development

The figures presented in the preceding section indicate the importance of the service sector in its own right. Equally important, the service sector has vital linkages with other sectors of the economy and influences their competitiveness. This is not the place for a full discussion of the role of services in development.[20] Suffice it to say that the service sector is a key part of the infrastructure for economic, social, cultural and political development. For instance, an efficient transport, communication and trading system is indispensable for the production and distribution of goods and other services and thus for balanced economic growth and the avoidance of bottlenecks. Similarly, the development of a banking system plays a crucial role in mobilizing and channeling domestic savings and foreign financial resources for national development. And no modern economy can do without such business services as accounting, consulting, and engineering. Finally, the growing data-service industry plays a key role in the evolution toward what has been called the information economy.[21]

To quantify these linkages is difficult. Perhaps the best approach is to note that a good percentage of domestically consumed services is not directed toward final consumers, but rather represents—within an evolving division of labor— intermediate inputs to other production processes. Using input-output data for Australia, Canada, the United Kingdom, and the United States, it has been calculated that, during the 1970s, about one-third of the broadly-defined service sector's output consisted of intermediate services.[22] This percentage varied, of course, across service categories, increasing to about one-half for transport and communication and falling to one-seventh for construction. More specifically, data for the US suggest that 10% of the agriculture sector's contribution to GNP consists of such services as soil preparation and forest services; the figure for minerals and mining is 20%.[23] In manufacturing, the share of production workers decreased from 82% of the work force in 1950 to 70% in 1980. In fact, "about 25 percent of U.S. GNP originates in services used as inputs by goods-producing industries—more than the value added to GNP by the manufacturing sector."[24]

Increasing demand for intermediate services may well be one of the principal sources of growth of the service sector, together with growing demand for services from final consumers whose income increases (income elasticity of demand for services). A further factor (touched upon earlier) that may influence the growth of service production is the lower rate of increase in labor productivity in the service sector (compared to the goods sector). The relative role of each of these factors in the growth of the service sector is subject to increasing research.[25]

In sum, the service sector is important in and by itself, and also because of its interlinkages with the rest of the economy. What this amounts to is that services "have overtaken industry in its role as the engine of growth."[26] (It is, therefore, not surprising that the Commission of the European Community considers it "no exaggeration to see the establishment of a common market in services as one of the main preconditions for a return to economic prosperity."[27]) A competitive services sector plays, therefore, a key role in economic development. In this light, special attention has to be given to the service sector in developing countries and special efforts have to be made to ensure that services critical to the development process are adequately provided. This, in turn, requires a considerably better understanding of the role of services in the development process—an objective which could be furthered by the development of better statistics and in-depth studies at the national level.[28]

B. Trade and foreign direct investment in services

Like industry and agriculture, the service sector has undergone a process of internationalization through trade and FDI. As will be seen in the following, FDI has played a more important role in this respect than trade, although the low tradeability of services—partly a result of their nature—may change with the increased use of data technologies.

1. Conceptual issues and statistical limitations

As defined by the International Monetary Fund (IMF), trade involves transactions between residents of a given country and non-residents.[29] International service transactions can actually cross borders ("cross-border trade"—e.g., passenger services, shipping, data processing, information storage and retrieval, advertising, motion pictures), or they can be undertaken within a country between residents and non-residents ("within-border trade"—e.g., hotel services, port and airport services). The characteristic common to both types of trade is that services produced by residents of one country are bought by residents of another country. For balance-of-payments reporting purposes, the traded services that are distinguished are shipment, other transport, travel, and "other private services" (see table I-11). The following discussion is based on this definition of trade in services.[30]

Those services that are not storable and do not lend themselves to transport and hence to cross-border trade can be provided abroad through FDI, i.e., they are produced directly in a foreign market. Following the IMF definition, FDI is "investment that is made to acquire a lasting interest in an enterprise operating in an economy other than that of the investor, the investor's purpose being to have an effective voice in the management of the enterprise".[31] Normally, such investments are undertaken by corporations—which, in this manner, become transnational corporations—through the establishment of foreign affiliates. This is particularly the case in such service activities as banking, insurance and hotel services, but it also applies to air transport, newspaper agencies, and engineering and software consultancy which, while tradeable, often require facilities abroad in order to provide maintenance and similar support services.

The measurement (credit and debits) of trade in services faces, of course, many of the same difficulties encountered in the domestic context in the quantification of services.[32] Trade in goods involves the movement of physical units which are normally recorded, for customs purposes, at the border. Trade in services, on the other hand, normally involves intangible and non-storable products (consisting, in the case of data services, often merely of information) which, in most cases, are not subject to tariffs. While the former set of characteristics makes it difficult to trace or monitor and hence measure service movements, the latter fact explains why no comprehensive recording mechanism exists. Many service-trade transactions go, therefore, unrecorded and have to be estimated;[33] particularly well-known examples are open registry fleets[34] and a whole range of trade transactions between tourists and residents. Many traded services are furthermore combined with goods transactions and reported as such. This is, for instance, the case where manufacturers export services (e.g., engineering services) to independent customers in connection with FDI or trade in goods. Similarly, many services are embodied in goods and their value is not reported separately. For instance, a complete computer system includes both hardware and software, the latter being a service; as a rule, however, the service component is not reported separately. Perhaps even more importantly, a whole range of services crosses international boundaries within transnational corporate systems, typically provided by the parent corporation (e.g., advertising, accounting, data processing, software, legal services). Data on such intra-firm trade are largely unavailable and, in any event, often lumped together, in the case of goods TNCs, with the trade in goods of the corporations concerned. The data that are available often have no historic depth (especially in the case of developing countries) and—as the categories listed above indicate—are highly aggregated. The US, for example, maintains trade statistics for about 10,000 classes of physical goods, grouped in approximately 3,000 categories. Trade in services, on the other hand, is lumped together under just six categories, viz., travel, passenger fares, other transportation, fees and royalties from foreigners, US government miscellaneous services, and other private services. Most notably, the category "other private services" contains a number of diverse and important services, including non-merchandise insurance, communications, advertising, brokerage, management, certain operational leasing, processing and repair, merchanting, and other professional and technical services. Since many of these services are growing dynamically, their aggregation within such a broad category is increasingly a considerable obstacle to meaningful analysis. Finally, in distinction to trade in goods, the IMF does not provide data on the direction of service trade.

The situation is even more serious as regards FDI statistics. The IMF collects only aggregate data on FDI flows. It does not distinguish between direct investments in the goods and service sectors, nor does it furnish information on the direction of FDI flows. The secretariat of the Organisation for Economic Co-operation and Development (OECD) reports investment flows for the members of the Development Assistance Committee,[35] but only to developing countries and without distinguishing between goods and services. One must, therefore, have recourse to national data, but these again are most inadequate and subject to the limitations pointed out earlier.

A general problem is the meaning of the value of FDI outlays in services. The recorded investment value of a foreign branch or representative office of a bank, for instance, normally bears no relationship to the actual importance of these establishments in terms of the business they create. In other words, a services FDI dollar may generate a higher ratio of sales or assets than an industrial FDI dollar. Data for the US seem to indicate that this is, in fact, the case (see table I-12). In 1982, $77 billion of US outward stock in services generated $433 billion in sales, $892 billion in assets and 1.8 million jobs. The corresponding figures for manufacturing were $84 billion for stock, $359 billion in sales, $266 billion in assets and 4.4 million jobs. This results in a ratio of 1:6 for services FDI to associated sales, 1:12 for associated assets and (per invested $100,000) 1:2 for employment. The corresponding ratios for manufacturing are 1:4 for sales, 1:3 for assets and (per invested $100,000) 1:5 for employment. (Data on inward stock yield a similar picture.)

This suggests that FDI in services creates a higher value of economic activities than FDI in manufacturing. In other words, services FDI creates more assets and sales with fewer people than manufacturing FDI. This, in turn, implies a higher productivity of FDI in services. These differences suggest that the conventional measurement of FDI through capital underrepresents the economic importance of services as compared to that of other sectors. If world FDI could be recalculated on the basis of either sales or assets, the share of the service sector in total FDI might well be considerably higher than conventional measurement through stocks or flows suggests—but the data for such a recalculation are lacking. This situation is complicated further by the growth of non-equity forms (franchising, leasing, licensing agreements, subcontracting, and the like), a phenomenon particularly prevalent in a number of service industries (e.g., hotels). While some of them may turn foreign firms into quasi-foreign affiliates, the values involved are reported nowhere.

In sum, the state of statistics on trade and FDI in services is dismal. Transactions are under-reported or not reported at all, by an unknown but most probably significant factor. Therefore, the available data reported here indicate orders of magnitude only. This paucity of data imposes serious limitations on any analysis of trade and FDI in services.

2. Trade in services

Given the characteristics of services, the production of services in general has remained mostly domestically oriented. That part of the services production of market economies which is traded internationally increased from 7% in 1970 to 11% in 1980, which compares to an increase from 32% to 45% for agricultural and 30% to 55% for industrial production (see table I-13). Thus, the internationalization of services through trade has increased, but at a slower pace and at a considerably lower level than that of other economic activities. While the proportion that is traded varies from country to country, the overall pattern is consistent: the proportion of service trade is considerably lower than that of goods. For instance, only 4% of Japan's services were exported in 1980, compared to 35% for goods. The US exported 3% and 19%, respectively, in the same year. The UK exported 11% of its services and over 60% of its goods in 1980, while Canada exported 8% and 28% respectively in 1977.[36] However, this general picture of the low trade internationalization of services does not necessarily apply to individual service industries. For example, maritime and air transport are largely international by nature, and the part of their production that is being traded is substantial.

In 1980, service exports of market economies (as measured by credits) were $360 billion, compared to merchandise exports of $1,760 billion; developed market economies exported $290 billion, developing countries $70 billion (see table I-14). In 1985, service exports surpassed $500 billion—but, given the under-reporting discussed earlier, they are likely to be considerably higher. Service exports of market economies grew at an average annual rate of 18% between 1970 and 1980, compared to 21% for merchandise exports, 22% for foreign-direct-investment income and 14% for GDP.[37] As a result—and in spite of the increasing trade internationalization of services observed in the preceding paragraph—the share of services in merchandise trade decreased from 25% in 1970 to 20% in 1980. The 'most important traded service category remained, throughout the decade, "other private services" (with a volume of $130 billion in 1980), followed closely by travel. The share of "other private services" in total trade remained stable throughout the decade—an indication of the dynamic nature of individual components of that category.

Paralleling the developed market economies' share in the production of services, their share in the service exports of market economies as a group was 82% in 1980, down from 87% in 1970. Of their (in 1980) $292 billion in exports and $284 billion in imports, the principal export and import category of these countries was, throughout the period, "other private services", followed by travel (see table I-14). It was also a category which (together with "other transportation") grew fastest and in which these countries registered a surplus—$3 billion in 1970, $14 billion in 1980. The developed market economies' service account as a whole moved from a $1 billion surplus in 1970 to an $8 billion surplus in 1980. (During the same period, these countries' merchandise balance changed from a surplus of $6 billion to a deficit of $79 billion.)

The share of the developing countries in service exports of market economies grew to almost one-fifth in 1980, compared to over one-quarter for imports. Out of $66 billion of exports in 1980, travel constituted, in 1970 as in 1980, the principal export category, although "other private services" reached almost equal importance in 1980 and grew at the highest rate (see table I-14). Of the $103 billion in imports in 1980, shipping constituted, with $38 billion, the largest single category, followed by travel and "other private services" (each about $25 billion). Thus, the developing countries' service account as a whole registered a deficit of $37 billion in 1980, compared to a deficit of $4 billion in 1970. The principal contribution to the 1980 deficit came from shipping ($31 billion) Almost all of the deficit ($32 billion) was accounted for by oil-exporting developing countries, which registered sizable deficits in shipping ($16 billion), travel ($9 billion) and other private services ($7 billion). In the case of the non-oil-exporting developing countries, the deficit in shipping ($15 billion) was somewhat balanced by surplusses in travel ($6 billion) and other private services ($4 billion), with other transport being in balance.[38]

Of the 20 largest exporters of services in 1980, 16 were industrialized countries; the 10 largest exporters were all industrialized countries (see table I-15). The US led the list ($35 billion), followed closely by the UK ($34 billion), France ($33 billion), and the Federal Republic of Germany ($32 billion). The three most important developing countries were Mexico ($7 billion), Singapore ($6 billion), and Yugoslavia ($5 billion). On the import side, the main importing developing countries were Saudi Arabia, Iran and Mexico (see table I-16). The list was led by the Federal Republic of Germany ($50 billion), followed by Japan, the US, and France. Country data exhibit wide differences as far as the composition of service exports is concerned. Countries that are touristically attractive—e.g., Mexico, Austria, Spain, Switzerland, Italy, Greece, and Yugoslavia—derived between 72% and 33% of their export earnings from travel. In absolute terms, other countries have important foreign income from travel as well. However, this does not translate into highest shares in their service accounts because of relatively high exports in other categories, particularly in "other private services". This is the largest item for the FRG, France, the UK, the US, Belgium, Sweden, Denmark, and the Republic of Korea. Among "other private services", financial services can be quite important. In the case of the UK, for instance, the net earnings of the City of London's financial institutions in 1983 were over £5 billion (see table I-17), three times higher than in 1977 and accounting for over 70% of the UK's net surplus in invisibles in 1983.[39] Shipping weighs heavily in the receipts of Norway and even in those of Japan. "Other transportation" is of greatest importance for The Netherlands and Singapore. Generally speaking, developed countries have a much more diversified structure of service exports than the developing ones, with Singapore being the most notable exception among the latter. For a number of countries, the relative importance of service trade is rather high. More specifically, in the cases of Spain, Austria, Yugoslavia and Greece, the ratio of service to merchandise exports was 50% or higher in 1980, mostly because of tourism credits.

3. Foreign direct investment in services

As the figures in the preceeding section indicate, only a small share of the services produced are traded. The principal reason for this low ratio is precisely that most services are of an intangible nature and can, therefore, neither be stored nor transported, but rather must be produced when and where they are consumed. This means that, traditionally, FDI has been the principal vehicle for the major developed countries through which services have been delivered to foreign markets.

The comparative importance of trade and FDI in delivering services to foreign markets has already been indicated at the beginning of this volume: sales by foreign service affiliates in 1981 amounted to an estimated $450 billion, compared to service exports of $360 billion in 1980; for the leading economies, however, foreign affiliate sales appear to be about twice as important as exports (see table 1). Better data exist for the US (see table I-18). US affiliates of non-US service TNCs sold services in the value of $22 billion in 1974, compared to US service imports of $15 billion during that year. By 1982, services sold through foreign affiliates in the US had increased to $125 billion, compared to $33 billion imported the same year. As to sales by service-industry affiliates of US TNCs abroad, data exist only for three years. Affiliates of US service TNCs operating abroad sold services in the value of $37 billion in 1974, compared to $13 billion of US service exports that year. By 1977, services sold by foreign affiliates had tripled to $114 billion, compared to $18 billion exported that year. And by 1982, sales associated with services FDI had increased to $178 billion. If wholesale trade affiliates are added, the sales of foreign service affiliates in the US increased to $355 billion, and those of US foreign service affiliates abroad to $415 billion in 1982. However, wholesale trade affiliates should be considered separately because their sales figures consist mostly of goods; their inclusion would, therefore, distort the patterns of service sales.

These data permit a number of important observations. First, FDI is in fact more important than trade for the major developed countries in delivering services to foreign markets. Overall, it appears that—for major developed countries—sales of foreign service affiliates are approximately twice as important as service exports. This average masks, however, wide variations. In the case of the US, the ratio for service exports to sales by US service affiliates abroad was almost 1:3 in 1974 and increased to 1:6 in 1977 and then decreased to 1:5 in 1982. In other words, at the beginning of the 1980s, US outward FDI was over five times more important than the country's exports in delivering services to international markets. FDI in services also appears to be considerably more important than service trade for other developed countries, especially as regards the US market. The ratio for service imports to sales by foreign services affiliates in the US was 1:1.5 in 1974, remained the same in 1977 and then rose each year to reach almost 1:4 in 1982. In this case, in other words, sales from services FDI in the US were almost four times more important than US service imports at the beginning of the 1980s. It should be noted that this pattern—at least as the export side is concerned—does not apply to developing and socialist countries, because these countries participate only minimally in FDI. (On the import side, on the other hand, sales by foreign affiliates in developing countries may well be more important than imports.) Second, the higher reliance of major economies on FDI as opposed to trade as the principal vehicle to deliver services to foreign markets also becomes apparent if the trade and foreign-affiliate sales pattern in the service sector is compared with that in the manufacturing sector (see table I-19). While on the export side that pattern (for the US) was, as just mentioned, more than 1:5 for services in 1982, it was less than 1:3 for manufacturing. Similarly, on the import side the ratio of service imports to sales by foreign service affiliates in the US was almost 1:4 in 1982, compared to a ratio of 1:1 for manufacturing imports to sales by foreign manufacturing affiliates in the US. The situation is similar in mining. In the case of agriculture, in fact, exports and imports were considerably higher than the respective sales of foreign affiliates. Only in petroleum is the ratio of exports to affiliate sales higher than in services (see table I-19). Third, sales by foreign service affiliates have, on the whole, been considerably more dynamic than trade. In the case of the US, service exports increased at an average annual growth rate of 11% between 1974 and 1977 and sales of foreign affiliates at 46%; between 1977 and 1982, however, exports grew, with 13%, faster than the 9% for sales of foreign affiliates. On the import side, service imports grew by 10% and sales of foreign service affiliates by 11% between 1974 and 1977, but they rose, respectively, by 11% and 33% between 1977 and 1982. Fourth, the sharply declining growth pattern of foreign sales by US affiliates during 1977–1982 suggests that US services FDI abroad may have reached a plateau (although it is also possible that a good part of this decline is the result of disinvestments from the Netherland Antilles). At the same time, the sharply increasing growth pattern of sales of foreign affiliates in the US during the period 1977–1982 probably reflects a catching-up effort on the part of non-US TNCs, a matter to be discussed later. In fact, the growth pattern of non-US TNCs during 1977–1982 (33%) is rather similar to that of US TNCs during 1974–1977 (46%). This can also be seen from the fact that the ratio of sales by US service affiliates abroad to that of foreign services affiliates in the US declined considerably, from 4:1 in 1977 to 1.5:1 in 1982.

The importance of the service sector is also reflected in the composition of the stock and especially the flow of FDI. The changes that have taken place there over the last decade and a half are almost dramatic: the service-sector share in the world stock of FDI is now over one-third and that in total FDI flows is perhaps over one-half. For a number of countries, the stock and flow of services FDI has become the single largest component in total FDI. Exact figures on the sectoral distribution of world stock and flows of FDI are not available, but some estimates exist for the majority of the leading capital exporters, which are also the most important recipients of FDI. These estimates differ according to source but, by and large, show similar trends regarding the position of services in direct investment.

The data that are available indicate that, at least during the 1970s, services FDI has, in fact, grown rapidly and, almost without exception, at a higher rate than other FDI. This is reflected in the share of services FDI in the total outward FDI stock of seven home countries for which data are available. Between 1971 and 1978, the aggregate services FDI stock of these countries—which account for about 80% of world FDI—more than doubled from $43 billion to $87 billion. Since the growth rate of services FDI was above that of FDI as a whole (11% compared to 8%), the share of services FDI in total FDI rose from 24% to 29% (see table I-20). The US alone accounted for 62% of the FDI services stock in 1978 (compared to 57% of total FDI), followed by Japan (13%) and the UK (10%). (It should be noted, however, that no data are available on a number of other important service exporters, most notably France and Switzerland.) Japan, Italy and the US have each more than 30% of their FDI stock in services; in fact, for the first two countries services FDI represents the largest FDI sector. Although in the case of Canada and Italy the services share in total FDI decreased between 1971 and 1978, it rose in the cases of the Federal Republic of Germany, Japan, the Netherlands, the UK and the US between 3 and 7 percentage points. Over the same time period, the stock of services FDI in the developing countries nearly tripled from $10 billion to $28 billion; as a result, the share of the developing countries in the total services FDI of this group of capital-exporting countries rose from 24% to 32% (see table I-20) and lies, therefore, somewhat above the share of developing countries in total FDI. The US accounted for 70% of services FDI stock in developing countries, followed by Japan (15%). Most dynamic were the US and Japan, each of which registered an increase of 10 percentage points in the services FDI in developing countries over the period. In other words, the developing countries have been particularly attractive for services FDI, reflecting, perhaps, weak indigenous capacities in this sector.

More detailed data, covering longer periods or more recent years, are available for selected countries only (see table I-21). They, too, indicate a major expansion of FDI in services during the 1970s. Furthermore, they suggest that the economic crisis of the early 1980s led not only to decreased growth of FDI in general, but also to slower growth of services FDI. In the case of the Federal Republic of Germany, the share of services stock in total FDI increased from 40% in 1976 to over 45% in 1984. In the case of Japan, this share nearly doubled from 20% in 1960 to 39% in 1969, then remained at that level until 1980, to rise to nearly 50% in 1984. In the case of the US, finally, services were already quite important as early as 1950, involving one-third of the outward stock of FDI. In the 1970s, a substantial shift toward services in the sectoral composition of investment abroad took place, raising the share of services to over 40% in 1977, especially at the cost of extractive industry. Between 1977 and 1983, the stock of FDI in services continued to grow in value from $59 to over $80 billion. But due to the faster increase of stock in the extraction and processing of petroleum and gas (which more than doubled) and especially because of heavy divestments from the Netherland Antilles, the services' share in the total stock declined to 36% in 1983. The early leading role of the US as an exporter of service capital is also supported by the fact that, in the early 1970s, sales by US service affiliates abroad were already increasing at an average annual rate of 46%, while those of foreign affiliates in the United States—i.e., services FDI of non-US TNCs—only accelerated during the period 1977 to 1982, and then, with 33% average annual growth, considerably so (see table I-18). (However, it is also possible that this acceleration is not so much the result of an increase of the export of services FDI by non-US TNCs, but rather the consequence of a redirection of services FDI flows toward the US.)

Data on the flow of FDI reflect more accurately shifts in the composition of FDI because they are not influenced by the historical weight of FDI stock in industry, although they, like stock data, suffer from the shortcomings discussed above, namely that the measurement of FDI through equity capital underrepresents the economic importance of services as compared to that of other sectors. Data for France indicate the important and growing role of services in French FDI during the 1970s. Services accounted for almost 40% of the cumulative outflow of investment capital in the years 1972–1975, increasing to about 50% in the period of 1976–1980, and declining thereafter (see table I-22). A similar picture characterizes outflows from the UK: from a share of 41% in 1970–1971, the services component increased to 49% in 1978–1980. In the case of the FRG, the services' share in the flow of FDI increased from 45% during 1977–1980 to one-half during 1981–1984. The most dramatic change, however, was taking place in the FDI flows of Japan: the service share rose from 20% in 1975 to 67% in 1984. For Japan, which traditionally placed heavy emphasis on raw materials, this indicates a substantial restructuring of its outward FDI stock. Thus, flow data, especially for recent years, indicate more clearly than stock data that services have become the most important and dynamic component of FDI.

The picture that emerges from outward FDI flows is supported by the composition of FDI stock in selected host countries (see table I-23). For all developed market economies for which data are available, the share of services FDI in total FDI increased between 1971 and 1978, except for Italy, in which the share remained stable. The highest increase was registered by services FDI in the US, where the services share increased from 29% to 41%, and the Federal Republic of Germany, where the services share increased from 18% to 28%. The US has by far the highest share of services FDI in total FDI. The same pattern characterizes the developing countries on which data are available. The services FDI share rose during 1971 and 1978 in almost all developing countries on which data are available, but the extent of this increase and the actual share of services FDI in total FDI vary considerably. While in the case of the developed host countries the increases ranged between 0 and 12 percentage points, the range in the developing host countries was between −23 and +16 percentage points. Similarly, while in the developed host countries the typical share of services FDI in total FDI ranged between 20% and 30%, in the case of the developing countries for which data are available it ranged from 6% in Indonesia on the one hand to 52% in Morocco on the other.

The scant data available on the composition of services FDI are difficult to interpret because coverage and specificity differ from country to country. However, it appears that the most important position in services FDI is occupied by investment in wholesale and retail trading (see table I-24). This activity accounted for between one-third and one-half of the outward and inward stock of the US, the FRG, Japan, and (outward only) The Netherlands. The second single largest item appears to be banking, usually combined with insurance. It involved as much as 42% of

the UK's outward stock, over one quarter of the FRG's outward stock, over half
of the US inward stock, one third of the US outward stock, and 47% of French
outward service flows during 1972-1980.[40] In the case of the US, outward stock
in finance, insurance and banking has grown faster than any other industry
category.[41]

Not surprisingly, most of the world's largest service TNCs are headquartered
in the principal capital-exporting countries (see table I-25). Japan and the US alone
accounted for 44 out of the 75 largest service TNCs. Overall, trading and banking
(61 companies) dominate the group. With one exception, the ten largest service
TNCs consisted in 1983 of trading companies, led by five Japanese trading houses
(sogo shoshas) and including three US retailers. The largest transnational bank
occupied only the eleventh position. If, however, assets were taken as a criterion
instead of revenues, banks would be in the lead. If data for US FDI abroad and
data for FDI in the US can be generalized, foreign service affiliates account for
over 50% of all foreign affiliates.[42]

The leading role of the US in the international service sector is reflected
in the fact that corporations from that country occupy commanding positions in
such service industries as data services, advertising, market research, accounting,
hotel chains, fast food chains, and air lines (see table I-26); that they play a leading
role in many host countries; and that their degree of internationalization (as
measured by such variables as the geographic spread and share of foreign activities
in total activities) is usually higher than that of TNCs from other countries. A
number of service industries have, furthermore, a relatively high degree of concentration, particularly as far as international transactions are concerned.[43]

A number of factors explain the internationalization of services through
FDI.[44] They include the rapid expansion of trade in goods and services (which
stimulates accompanying FDI in services),[45] rapid advances in communications,
competitive advantages over firms in host countries, a regulatory environment
restricting service trade, deregulations increasing competitive pressure, the emergence
of Eurocurrency markets, the rise of international lending, migrations of labor,
and the growth of tourism. Apart from the non-tradeability of certain services,
however, the most basic factor that fueled the growth of services FDI in spite of
all obstacles was the expansion of industrial TNCs. To a certain extent, this factor
either incorporates or is based on a number of the ones just mentioned. The
growing network of foreign industrial affiliates pulled service companies along,
especially in trading, banking, insurance, accounting, advertising and legal services,
to continue to serve their clients abroad. Eventually, this motivation was complemented by a desire to exploit new business opportunities and the competitive
edge of experience gained domestically and internationally. In any case, the patterns
of growth of industrial and service FDI seem to support this basic explanation:
the rapid expansion of industrial FDI in the 1960s and early 1970s was followed
by an accelerated expansion of services FDI since the middle of the 1970s. In the
case of the US, this process had started earlier, partly because the main outward
thrust of US FDI had begun earlier than that of other developed countries and
partly because services had played a greater role at an earlier time in the US
economy than in other economies. This is suggested by the data on trade and
sales of foreign service affiliates discussed earlier (see table I-18), and it is supported
by FDI flow and stock data covering the period 1960-1983.

It should be noted that FDI in services increased, especially in developing countries, in spite of a number of obstacles. FDI in such industries as shipping, airlines, banking and insurance is often not permitted or permitted only within clearly defined parameters and, in most cases, subject to strict regulatory control.[46] Furthermore, service foreign affiliates experienced a wave of nationalizations, especially during the first half of the 1970s (see table I-27). Thus, for instance, the number of foreign insurance affiliates decreased in the developing countries from 1,636 in 1968 to 599 in 1982 (see table I-28). Needless to say, the incidence of nationalization affected negatively the share of services in FDI stock, but it was obviously more than offset by new services FDI, except, perhaps, in the case of the UK's outward FDI.

C. Implications

1. Interrelationships and the blurring of boundaries

In spite of the basic domestic orientation of the service sector, services have undergone a dynamic process of internationalization through trade and FDI. However, the patterns in which this has occurred differ. Shipping, other transport and to a certain extent travel are predominantly trade-oriented; they constitute the bulk of trade in services. On the other hand, trading, banking and other financial services, which belong to the rather heterogeneous group of "other private services", dominate FDI in services. Between the two modes of delivering services to foreign markets, FDI has clearly been the more important and dynamic one.

One factor which explains these different patterns is the extent to which services are currently tradeable. Services such as ocean shipping, tourism and air transport are almost by definition international in nature (which, however, does not exclude FDI). Trade in other services, especially in the category "other private services", is very cumbersome or impractical. In these cases, FDI becomes more attractive.

A second factor involves national regulations. In some service industries—like air transport, shipping (especially cabotage), telecommunication, banking—foreign ownership is excluded or subject to more or less substantial restrictions on entry and/or operations. This encourages internationalization through trade. However, when FDI restrictions are eased, internationalization through FDI may advance. An example is the liberalization in banking in many developed countries during the 1970s and the subsequent increase of FDI in banking (see table I-29). Conversely, when trade in some service industries is restricted—as, for instance, in advertising, some data services, insurance—corporations may have recourse to FDI as the vehicle for delivering services to foreign markets. However, when service trade restrictions are liberalized, internationalization through trade may advance. In other words, national regulations may bias the delivery of service to foreign markets in the direction of trade or in that of FDI.

At the same time, trade in services and FDI in services are intimately linked with each other. For one, trade and FDI in certain services (e.g., data processing) can be substituted for each other, i.e., can be provided either locally through foreign affiliates or across borders. Second, many service industries rely increasingly on data services (e.g., information storage and retrieval), which are often provided from abroad or locally by foreign affiliates. Third, trade in services can lead to supporting services FDI. And fourth, services FDI can lead to service trade.[47]

The interrelationship between trade and FDI in services is perhaps nowhere clearer than in the relationship between travel and air transport on the one hand, and hotel and lodging services on the other (see table I-30). Large airlines, in particular, have expanded most notably into tourism. Many of them have interests in hotels and tour operations, and a number of them are expanding into activities like computer services, insurance and catering. Air France, for instance, owns the Meridien Hotel chain; Finnair owns the Finlandia Travel Agency; Lufthansa owns part of Avis; and Pan American World Airways, through Pan Am World Services Inc., provides a wide range of technical and management-contract services in engineering and design, general aviation, aerospace and base support. These activities can provide a considerable portion of the airlines' total revenues, e.g., 36% for Aer Lingus and 29% for Union de Transports Aériens-UTA in 1983.

These examples draw attention to another important development: the blurring of the boundaries between different service corporations and, indeed, between service and industrial corporations.[48] The discussion in the preceding paragraph shows this for one set of industries. It can easily be expanded to other industries, especially in the banking/insurance/financial services field. Aided strongly by deregulation, the boundaries between these industries are rapidly disappearing in a number of important countries. Allianz Worldwide, for instance, one of the world's largest international insurance corporations headquartered in the Federal Republic of Germany, decided in December 1984 to reorganize itself in a manner that would permit it to provide services other than insurance, especially in the area of financial services.[49] In fact, certain financial services are now also provided by retail chains. For instance, Sears, Roebuck and Co., the world's largest retailing chain, provides life insurance. The blurring of the boundaries between service and industrial corporations is particularly obvious in the data industries. There, the largest producers of data goods are also the most important producers of data services. Beyond that, it has been observed that "non-bank, non-financial enterprises that are leaders in computers and telecommunication systems *could* play a growing and increasingly direct role in the provision of financial services and finance-related services. For example, it is quite conceivable that corporations like IBM and AT&T might evolve over ten or twenty years from the provision of equipment and communication grids to provision of information, management and even financial services".[50] Since this was written in 1983, IBM has entered into an agreement (in February 1984) with Sears, Roebuck and Co. and CBS to develop a nation-wide videotex service for households in the US with personal and home computers, and it entered into a joint venture with Merrill Lynch to develop a computerized information and order-execution system for brokers. It is developments like these that have led to the prediction that "the walls between banking, insurance and brokerage will completely crumble. And competition will be international. The large players will be Citibank, Sears, American Express, maybe American Can or Security Pacific, BankAmerica, AT&T and I.B.M., large German and French banks and Japanese trading houses".[51]

The common denominator for many of these developments is that the services provided are information-intensive and that the corporations concerned can capitalize on their own transnational computer-communication systems and the data services developed and provided by them. Thus, one of the considerations behind the expected diversification of Allianz into financial services is the fact that the company's more than 1,000 branches are already linked through a computer network which can not only be used for insurance transactions but also for banking transactions. Similarly, Eastman Kodak, the world's largest photographic products group, announced in November 1984 that it planned to set up a new communication division. The division will market enhanced-value telecommunication services to business and commercial customers, using as its basis its existing internal network, which in 1984 handled about seven million long-distance calls and moved nearly one million data files between 225 locations worldwide.[52]

To the extent that service corporations—and, for that matter, industrial corporations—come to depend for both FDI and trade on transnational computer-communication systems (a matter to be discussed in the next chapter), oligopolistic tendencies in some service industries may increase. The reason is that the establishment of such systems is highly capital intensive. American Express, for instance, is spending $500 million every year on its computer-communication system; Air France is reported to be planning to invest as much in its communication system as in aircraft in the decade ahead; and BankAmerica spent approximately $1.2 billion in the computer and communication area in 1985, in which 9,000 employees were involved, most of them professionals.[53] Hence, these systems may only be affordable by large corporations, unless public data networks are available and/or shared use of private systems (a sensitive public-policy issue) is permitted. However, while this situation may create new barriers to entry for potential competitors, it also *invites* new entrants as the examples above demonstrate, namely those corporations that have already created their own transnational computer-communication systems.

2. Conceptual innovations

None of these developments changes the basic relationship between trade and FDI in services. But a middle ground between FDI on the one hand and trade on the other is created by the importance of access to a country's delivery system for providing newly tradeable services.

Consider, for example, highly complex software packages which can be exported as a data service. Normally these packages require extensive adaptation, which means that they can only be exported if the exporter is permitted to engage in a long-term working relationship with the importer in the importing country, i.e., establishes a foreign-data service affiliate. Conversely, even after a software package is fully installed, it may require continuing access to a central data base to ensure effective operation and ongoing maintenance, i.e., data trade is required. In this particular example, however, the service can only be provided if market presence is granted, i.e., access to the local (telecommunication) infrastructure. Or consider a travel agency abroad, providing certain travel services to clients in the host country and relying heavily on the corporation's transnational computer-communication system. Is the office a foreign-direct-investment establishment, or merely an operating agency which markets and distributes services produced by the parent corporation in the home country? It could be regarded as an FDI establishment because, after all, it involves assets in a host country which are controlled from abroad, and these would appear as such in the host and home countries' balance of payments. On the other hand, these assets are minimal and only incidental to the service provided. The production of that service depends primarily on the corporation's central data base and its transnational computer-communication system through which the service is imported, for delivery to the customer in the host country. Or consider an insurance agent traveling abroad who carries a portable computer in her brief-case which she plugs into the telecommunication network whenever need arises. Although, strictly speaking, this computer could be regarded as an FDI asset—and as a substitute, in fact, for a foreign affiliate—it would be very difficult to record it as a foreign direct investment and to classify such an activity as anything other than trade.

These examples suggest that the boundaries between FDI and trade are blurring in certain services, a development likely to accelerate given the growing complexity and rising data-technology content of modern products and production and the services and servicing requirements associated with them. Despite clear conceptual differences among them, FDI (which involves the acquisition of a lasting interest in a corporation), market presence (which involves the need to have access to parts of another country's distribution system) and pure trade (which involves merely access to another country's market) lie on a continuum. The specific forms that can be used along this continuum (from FDI to pure trade) to deliver services to foreign markets include franchising, management contracts, licensing, subcontracting, joint ventures, representative offices, agencies and branches, and majority-owned subsidiaries.

From the point of view of the corporations which deliver services to foreign markets it is merely a question of business strategy whether to choose trade, FDI or any form in between to serve a foreign market. It is thus important for corporations that they have, in fact, the freedom to choose among the various forms of conducting business and that they are not constrained by government regulations, especially regulations that would put them in a less advantageous position than domestic corporations. For service firms, these options have an even greater importance, especially in the grey area of market presence and toward the FDI end of the continuum.

"Market presence" is a new concept, begotten by the services debate. Its importance lies in the fact that, without access to the national distribution system, certain services cannot be provided through trade. The advent of data services and their impact on the tradeability of certain services makes this concept even more important. The US would like access to the national service distribution system to be treated like access to the national goods distribution system as foreseen by GATT: once foreign goods have overcome the legitimate barriers at the border, they enjoy the same rights as domestic goods as regards access to the domestic distribution system (national treatment). For the US, this means that, for instance, data-processing companies can sign contracts or leasing agreements with local companies to provide data-processing services, thus acquiring access to, or the right of presence in, a foreign market. In this approach, the *ownership* of the domestic distribution system remains a separate (FDI) question, although it is recognized that the right to invest in the distribution system would often improve trade possibilities considerably. In other words, optimal liberalization of trade in services would also require the liberalization of FDI in services.

All this has led some to postulate a "right of presence." This grants a party in one country the right to have access to the local distribution system in another country or, more broadly, to have a commercial presence in that country. In the case of data services, this means that a party in one country can link up with a party in another country for the purpose of sending data via transnational computer-communication systems. The "right of presence" thus encompasses such component rights as the "right to deliver" or the "right to sell" a service, which means either that the service provider is permitted to have access to the market from abroad and can compete in it on an equal footing with domestic firms, or it means (in addition?) that the service provider has a "right of establishment" (to be discussed below); the "right to connect", for instance with foreign affiliates, customers or brokers; the "right to receive" services from suppliers abroad; the "right to plug in" necessary equipment to the national telecommunication network; perhaps even the right to establish local marketing, sales and distribution systems needed to sell services and to use foreign employees to maintain these systems; and, in a sense, the "right of non-establishment", namely the right *not* to be forced to locate certain activities, for example data bases or data-processing facilities, in a host country. Since the right of presence does not necessarily involve ownership, it is being considered by the US as a trade rather than an FDI issue and, therefore, regarded as being in the purview of GATT. However, this may at times be debatable because a number of contractual relationships may well have the effect of granting foreigners "an effective voice in the management of the enterprise"—the litmus test of the IMF's definition of FDI quoted earlier in this chapter. The importance of non-equity forms as one aspect of FDI is a well-established (and apparently growing) phenomenon.[54] In brief, the distinction between FDI and trade issues is not always easy to make and may at times be made arbitrarily. However, such arbitrariness can have profound political implications because the international regime governing FDI is different from that governing trade.

The private sector in the US has strongly urged the US administration to ensure that the right of presence be recognized in a new international system of trade-in-services rules. A statement prepared in April 1985 for the US Trade Representative by the Services Policy Advisory Committee (the US private sector's principal official channel to make its views on services known to the US administration) recommended with the overwhelming support of its members that:

> The overriding goal of U.S. negotiators should be the achievement of equal access to foreign markets so that the U.S. and other trading nations can take full commercial advantage of the opportunities afforded in host-country markets. Market access should be ensured through strong provisions for non-discrimination, national treatment (e.g., the principle that imported goods and services be accorded the same treatment as domestic goods and services) and the right of establishment.[55]

The statement continued to specify that the aim would be a package which would consist of, among other things, "government guaranteed access to distribution systems."[56] This would give a foreign supplier of services "the right to engage in or contract with local businesses or government authorities (e.g. telecommunication networks), either from within the country or from remote markets, for the distribution of services"; furthermore, "a local presence could also be accomplished through the establishment of a subsidiary, affiliate, a shared joint venture, minority interests with management control or some type of licensing agreement."[57] More generally, and most importantly, the statement suggested that "in any situation where the domestic regulatory system required a local presence as a condition for doing business, the right of establishment would become a negotiable trade issue rather than an investment issue."[58]

The new concept of market presence has found its way already into one international instrument, the "Declaration on Trade in Services", annexed to the Agreement on the Establishment of a Free Trade Area between the Government of the United States of America and the Government of Israel.[59] Among the principles enumerated in it, the third one specified that "Each party will endeavor to provide that a supplier of a service produced within the other nation is able to *market or distribute* that service under the same conditions as a like service produced within the first nation, including situations where a *commercial presence* within the nation is necessary to facilitate the export of a service from the other nation or is required by that Party" (emphasis added). An explanatory footnote further states that "in the area of commercial banking, the concept of a commercial presence refers to the activities of representative offices, but not to agencies, branches or subsidiaries of commercial banks." In other words, representative offices of commercial banks are *not* to be regarded as foreign direct investment— as they are, under certain circumstances, in US FDI statistics[60]—but rather as an activity that falls under the heading of trade or, more precisely, under the heading of market presence. Presumably, this was done because representative offices are not seen as producing anything locally but as merely facilitating trade. Obviously, it is very difficult to draw a line through the point where trade in services ends and local production through FDI begins. If one seeks to apply the concept of market presence, this point has to be defined for each service separately. The function of this concept is clearly to expand the realm of issues traditionally covered by the trade regime.

The peculiar nature of most services has led to another conceptual innovation as well. It involves a broadening of the standard definition of trade by taking into account the fact that most services, unlike goods, normally have to be produced when and where they are consumed. In other words, the intangible nature of a given service (e.g., hospital services) makes a local establishment (or some other more permanent local arrangement) intrinsically necessary to provide the service.[61] Similarly, foreign service providers may in some cases be competitive only if they can establish a foreign affiliate; this may, for instance, be the case for complex software packages because of the need to adapt these packages and undertake a certain amount of on-the-spot follow-up servicing. Or a government may require that a service company (e.g., an insurance firm) has to establish a local office if it wishes to undertake business in the country. Wherever these conditions apply, a service firm has to establish an affiliate in a foreign market to deliver its product to that market. The innovation is to add to the traditional categories of "cross-border trade" and "within-border trade" the new category of "establishment trade", namely those transactions emanating from locally established affiliates of foreign-owned TNCs. For instance, when the OECD Committee on Financial Markets initiated in 1982 a study on obstacles to trade in banking services, it

> agreed to adopt a broad definition of "trade in services", encompassing (i) "establishment trade in services", which involves the establishment of the foreign-controlled bank supplying banking services in the country of the

consumer of those services; (ii) "across-the-border trade in services", which relates to those banking services which are provided by a bank in the exporting country to a consumer of those services in another country; and (iii) trade-in-service operations arising from a combination of these two approaches (e.g. the establishment of foreign-controlled banks in a financial centre to participate in the provision of banking services to customers in third countries).[62]

Thus, if the aim is to reduce obstacles to trade in services, then among the restrictions to be dismantled are restrictions on the right of establishment (or on the right of presence). The right of establishment (traditionally a core FDI concept), as well as the right of presence thus become trade issues. As will be discussed in chapter III, this logic finds its precise expression in the 1984 US Trade and Tariff Act, which not only elevates trade in services to a position equal to that of trade in goods but virtually subsumes FDI under the trade regime and, therefore, explicitly defines barriers to trade as including restrictions on establishment and operations in foreign markets.

To define establishment trade as part of international trade may be advantageous from the point of view of the exporters of services and services FDI because it maximizes their right to gain access to foreign markets. This is especially the case since the right of establishment has as yet no international recognition. However, such a definition has far-reaching implications. The reason that the IMF does not consider establishment trade a form of trade is that foreign affiliates are regarded as residents. Consequently, the transactions between them and other residents of their host countries are domestic transactions, not trade, and, therefore, should not normally feature in the trade-in-services discussion. Implicit in the notion that establishment trade is international trade is, therefore, the view that foreign affiliates are non-residents of host countries. This in turn undermines the central tenet of the FDI policy of all OECD countries, namely that foreign affiliates should (with certain qualifications) be granted national treatment. For FDI-importing countries, on the other hand, the acceptance of the notion of establishment trade (and the considerations accompanying it) could signal the loss of the right to admit or not to admit FDI and would thus require a rather unlikely reversal of current policies. Given all these implications, no more may be attainable than a clearer and narrower definition of rights and responsibilities along the lines of "right of presence" or "market access", helped by the increasing tradeability of certain services.

This emphasis on the links between FDI and trade is meant to alert the reader to the fact that measures taken in one area affect the other and that policy measures dealing with these matters have to be fine-tuned to a greater extent than in the past. It is *not* meant to obscure the fact that the two types of transaction are distinct. One involves international trade issues; the other raises much more sensitive issues such as ownership, the question of control over the domestic economy and, ultimately, considerations of national sovereignty. While for corporations it may merely be a question of economic factors or business strategy whether (regulations permitting) to choose trade or FDI to serve a market, the considerations involved for governments are different, depending on which of the two types of transaction is involved. Accordingly, the policy and regulatory regimes applicable to these transactions differ, as do the underlying principles informing them. While the international FDI regime is governed by the principle that each country has the sovereign right to admit or not to admit FDI, the international trade regime, as enshrined in GATT, is governed by the principle that trade is to be admitted freely (subject to certain clearly defined conditions). These differences have to be taken into account when discussing international policies applicable to services. The choice of the governing principle and the choice of the type of transaction one considers more important may well influence the character of any international public-policy framework that may eventually emerge.

In any event, it is clear that the current discussion has generated important new concepts whose implications call for careful consideration. A crucial issue here is how narrowly or broadly these concepts are defined. This applies in particular to the "right of presence." It is one thing to define this concept narrowly, restricting it essentially to transport aspects only. It is another thing to define it so broadly that it is virtually indistinguishable from the "right of establishment". In the latter case, the introduction of the concept of right of presence may simply be regarded as a tactical ploy to bring an issue into the trade discussion and into GATT under a new name which otherwise could not be introduced in this discussion and the purview of this organization under its old name.

D. Policy challenges

The vital role of the service sector raises the familiar policy question of how these services should be provided: domestically, through the establishment of indigenous capacities, or from abroad, through trade or FDI. These options are not new, nor are the arguments that have been advanced in their support. Many of them turn on the most efficient use of scarce economic resources in the short and in the long run and often center on infant-industry and performance-requirement considerations. It is not necessary to review these arguments here. Clearly, priorities have to be set and choices have to be made about the extent to which domestic and foreign resources should be utilized in the development of the service sector.

These choices are complicated by a number of factors. For example, the determination of comparative advantage for the production of services may be even more difficult than for the production of goods, because many services, especially business services, are knowledge-intensive and, therefore, do not lend themselves easily to traditional factor-proportion analysis.[63] This is not to say that comparative-advantage theory is not applicable, but that it has to be adapted—perhaps considerably—to the pecularities of the service sector. In particular, the relative abundance of land, raw materials and capital equipment as principal factors of production may be considerably less important for the production of services (except for special cases like tourism) than the relative abundance of human capital (know-how) and labor. Since human capital and labor, furthermore, are relatively mobile, a country's factor endowment for the production of services may be subject to much greater change than that for the production of goods. For instance, any country that has a small number of skilled persons and access to the world telecommunication system can set up, at least in principle, an international data base. At the same time, however, the comparative advantage developing countries may have in labor-intensive services may be offset by restrictions on migration and the lack of the technology needed to deliver modern services. Furthermore, many services operate increasingly at a global level, and the economies of scale and geographic scope necessary to be competitive at that level are not always easy to achieve. This is especially so because many service industries are highly concentrated and often dominated by TNCs. Finally, the increasing resistance of particularly the US to performance requirements makes it more difficult to use this device to promote national service industries. In other words, barriers to entry can be formidable. The continuing dominance of London as a banking and insurance center bears this out. On the other hand, the emergence of such regional centers as Hong Kong or Bahrain shows that these barriers are not insurmountable. In sum, the continuing relevance of the theory of comparative advantage depends on the proper identification of the principal factors of production, of the factors that determine their relative abundance for a particular location, and of the conditions under which they can be exploited.

The choices concerning the development of service industries are still further complicated by the emergence of data services, which have increased the tradeability of services and which may change the international economics of the service sector. In the developed market economies, data services are one of the most dynamic among services, with far-reaching consequences for future economic growth: they belong to the nexus around which economic activities are being restructured. In the developing countries, on the other hand, data services are weak or non-existent and most countries are linked only peripherally to the international data-telecommunication and informatics infrastructure. To the extent that this situation persists, it could mean that the developing countries will benefit only to a limited extent from the new tradeability of certain services, particularly as far as exports are concerned. In fact, the situation may have detrimental implications for the international competitiveness of some of their own service and goods exports.[64] Imports of data services are likely to grow at the same time. The principal reason is that TNCs are increasingly building their own corporate (i.e., private) transnational computer-communication systems. As will be discussed in the next chapter, these systems link their world-wide affiliate networks and permit them to provide a growing range of services. If these developments occur, they could further aggravate the growing services deficit of the developing countries as a group, a trend which emerged strongly during the 1970s.

Policy discussions of the service sector must start from the fact that the provision and use of services have traditionally received close policy attention, more so than the production and consumption of goods. Two main reasons explain this attention. The first is that the invisible nature of many services requires greater specificity in prescribing how services are to be rendered, since they cannot be physically inspected like goods. The second is the economic, social, cultural and political importance and implications of a number of services: banking, for instance, involves monetary policy; mass media involve cultural identity; and air and maritime transport involves defense issues. The results have been (a) public ownership (often public monopoly) has become a feature of important services in many countries; (b) foreign ownership is often excluded; (c) where private ownership (domestic or foreign) is permitted, many services are highly regulated and subject to strict requirements and supervisory control; and (d) trade is frequently closely controlled. There are, however, certain indications of change. In some important countries, services such as air transport, telecommunications and banking have recently been partially deregulated, a development which can affect international competition in services, if only by suggesting to other countries that they follow a similar path. This process receives further impetus from the blurring of the boundaries between service industries in major countries since it diffuses the application of service regulations. The latter development, however, may require special public-policy attention, because it could make traditional regulatory frameworks obsolete in certain circumstances and frustrate regulatory intentions. The same effect may be created by the increased use of data services. To illustrate, many countries have strict regulations for the establishment and operations of foreign banks. It may be important to examine to what extent national regulations geared to FDI in banking can be circumvented through the increased tradeability of banking services which, therefore, need to be suitably adapted. Similarly, teleservices may substitute, up to a point, for the mobility of highly skilled labor. For example, instead of software specialists or architects moving from one country to another, they can provide their services via transnational computer-communication systems. This, in turn, has implications for immigration policies and, possibly, trade policies.

International transactions in this area have also received much policy attention. The OECD, for instance, has long undertaken work on services in the framework of specialized committees on such subjects as insurance, banking, tourism, and shipping. Similarly, since its establishment in 1964, UNCTAD has been concerned with such services as shipping and insurance. And even the developing countries of the non-aligned movement have identified such services as transport, telecommunication, insurance and tourism as fields of activities deserving special attention in the movement's action program for economic co-operation. A number of these activities have found their expression in specific agreements or organizations, such as UNCTAD's Code of Conduct for Liner Conferences, the OECD's Code of Liberalisation of Current Invisible Transactions, the International Maritime Organization (IMO), the International Civil Aviation Organization (ICAO), the International Air Transport Association (IATA), the World Tourism Organization (WTO), INTERSPUTNIK, INTELSAT, the International Telecommunication Union (ITU) and the World Intellectual Property Organization (WIPO). All of these agreements or organizations reflect a *sectoral* approach. They do not look at services from an integrated, *global* perspective. It is this new perspective that the current international discussion brings to service transactions: it deals with all services and their relationship to FDI. This perspective is further encouraged by the fact that a number of important services such as data services, banking and related financial services, insurance, tourism, and other services whose tradeability has increased because of the advent of TDF are not covered by an international regime. The absence of a regime governing trade in services in general, combined with a strong desire to prevent the establishment of new barriers (standstill) and to decrease existing barriers (roll-back) to service transactions are central to the current debate on a liberal international framework for trade in services.

This is not to say that the only outcome of this debate can be a comprehensive framework for international transactions in all services. In fact, many countries continue to think primarily in terms of services of special importance to them and do not focus on the service sector as a whole. Also, it is recognized that the peculiarities of individual service industries require sectoral treatment. Furthermore, it is unclear to what extent such a framework is also supposed to deal with FDI issues. As discussed earlier, the link is provided by the fact that, given the nature of services, FDI is often required to sell services internationally. Therefore, certain trade-related FDI issues could fall within such a framework. Some of these considerations have found expression in the new emphasis on trade-related FDI issues, the importance accorded to right of establishment, the attempts to reduce barriers to FDI in general, and the emergence of the concept of right of presence. On the other hand, GATT (the principal forum in which service matters are currently being discussed) has no competence in FDI issues proper, and governments usually treat trade and investment issues separately and through different international agreements and organizations.

In spite of these open questions, most of the proponents of the trade-in-services debate feel that a number of issues are common to most service industries. As will be seen below, the most important issues in this context are right of presence, right of establishment, non-discrimination, national treatment, and stand-still and roll-back of restrictions, especially as regards transborder data flows. What the proponents of the services debate desire, therefore, is a global, inter-sectoral and enforceable framework for the service sector as a whole which resolves these issues in a liberal fashion. Such a broad framework, in turn, would give the necessary political impetus to sectoral approaches. In other words, a broad framework for service trade and sectoral agreements on individual services are seen as complementary and mutually supporting, with the broad framework giving the direction for sectoral agreements. It is this approach and perspective which is new and which, if implemented, is likely to establish a new framework for sectoral activities in such organizations as the OECD, UNCTAD and the non-aligned movement.

The discussions have begun. Although traditional services will continue in the foreseeable future to make up the bulk of service exports and imports, the emerging forms of service trade are the most dynamic and future-oriented ones. In fact, it is in part the potential of these new forms that has focused attention on the range of policy issues that are raised by the importance of the service sector and its internationalization through trade and foreign direct investment. These matters will be taken up in the next chapter.

Notes

[1] Victor R. Fuchs, *The Service Economy* (New York: National Bureau of Economic Research, 1968), p. XXIII. Similarly, D. F. Channon observed in 1978 that services are "still the Cinderella industries of academics and politicians alike", see *The Services Industries* (London: Macmillan, 1978), p. XV.

[2] Too much, however, should not be made of the heterogeneity of services: after all, a space shuttle and a pencil have not much more in common than their tangibility and storability. Jagdish N. Bhagwati, "Splintering and Disembodiment of Services and Developing Nations", *The World Economy*, 7 (June 1984), pp. 133–144, citing Irving B. Kravis ("Services in the Domestic Economy and in World Transactions", Working Paper No. 1124 (Cambridge: National Bureau of Economic Research, 1983), mimeo.), suggests that a working definition of services should be based on their non-storability.

[3] Adam Smith, *An Inquiry into the Nature and Causes of the Wealth of Nations* (London: Encyclopaedia Britannica, 1955), Book Two, p. 143. Or elsewhere (p. 142): "There is one sort of labour which adds to the value of the subject upon which it is bestowed: there is another which has no such effect. The former, as it produces a value, may be called productive; the latter, unproductive labour. Thus the labour of a manufacturer adds, generally, to the value of the materials which he works upon, that of his own maintenance, and of his master's profit. The labour of a menial servant, on the contrary, adds to the value of nothing."

⁴ See the discussion in Henryk Kirzkowski, "Services in the Development Process and Theory of International Trade" (Geneva: Graduate Institute of International Studies, 1984), mimeo.

⁵ See Allan G. B. Fisher, *The Clash of Progress and Security* (London: Macmillan, 1935) and "Production: Primary, Secondary and Tertiary", *The Economic Record*, 15 (June 1939), pp. 24-38; and Colin Clark, *The Conditions of Economic Progress* (London: Macmillan, 1940).

⁶ George J. Stigler, *Trends in Employment in the Service Industries* (Princeton: Princeton University Press, 1956), cited approvingly 12 years later by Fuchs, *op. cit.*, p. 14.

⁷ T.P. Hill, "On Goods and Services", *The Review of Income and Wealth*, 23 (December 1977), p. 15. For a very useful discussion of conceptual and definitional questions related to services, as well as data on services, see UNCTAD, "Production and Trade in Services, Policies and Their Underlying Factors Bearing upon International Services Transactions", TD/B/941 (and Corr. 1) of 1 March 1983, UNCTAD, "Services and the Development Process", TD/B/1008 of 2 August 1984, and Jacques Nusbaumer, *Les services: Nouvelle donne de l'économie* (Paris: Ed. Economica, 1984).

⁸ See United Nations, *Comparisons of the System of National Accounts and the System of Balances of the National Economy* (New York: United Nations, 1981), part II.

⁹ See in this context J. Charmes, "Comment mesurer la contribution du secteur non structuré à la production nationale dans les pays du Tiers-Monde?" *The Review of Income and Wealth*, 29 (December 1983), pp. 429-444.

¹⁰ Bhagwati (*op. cit.*) describes this as a process whereby services splinter from goods, with the consequence that the resulting services will tend to be technically advanced (because they are the result of further economic development) and that they are independent of demand influences as such (because they merely involve a shift from intra to inter-firm transactions).

¹¹ This is, of course, also a consideration that applies to transport and communications, although these sectors are generally considered as services. For a contrary view see Fuchs, *op. cit.*

¹² See, for instance, Frederick F. Clairmonte and John H. Cavanagh, "Transnational Corporations and Services: The Final Frontier", *Trade and Development: An UNCTAD Review*, 5 (1984), pp. 215-274. See also the reports prepared by the United Nations Centre on Transnational Corporations (UNCTC) on service industries, especially *Transnational Corporations in Advertising* (New York: United Nations, 1979), Sales No. E.79.II.A.2, *Transnational Reinsurance Operations* (New York: United Nations, 1980), Sales No. E.80.II.A.10, *Transnational Banks: Operations, Strategies and Their Effects in Developing Countries* (New York: United Nations, 1981), Sales No. E.81.II.A.7, *Transnational Corporations and Transborder Data Flows* (New York: United Nations, 1982), Sales No. E.82.II.A.4, *Transnational Corporations in International Tourism* (New York: United Nations, 1982), Sales No. E.82.II.A.9, and *Transborder Data Flows: Access to the International On-line Data Base Market* (New York: United Nations, 1983), Sales No. E.83.II.A.1.

¹³ For the following statistics, which are based on a sample of countries, see UNCTAD, "Production and Trade in Services", *op. cit.*, pp. 32-35, unless specified differently.

¹⁴ US, Congress, House of Representatives, Committee on Banking, Finance and Urban Affairs, Subcommittee on Economic Stabilization, "Service Industries: The Changing Shape of the American Economy" (Washington: Government Printing Office, 1984), mimeo., p. 20.

¹⁵ See New York Stock Exchange, *U.S. International Competitiveness: Perception and Reality* (New York: New York Stock Exchange, 1984), p. 48.

[16] European Community, "European Communities' Study on International Trade in Services" (Geneva: GATT, 1984), mimeo., p. 6.

[17] See, for instance, Jonathan Gershuny and Ian Miles, *The New Service Economy: The Transformation of Employment in Industrial Societies* (London: Frances Pinter, 1983).

[18] Data on the socialist countries are difficult to obtain. As indicated earlier, the national accounts system of these countries are based on the net material product (NMP), which comprises only the "material" services transport, trade and communication; all other services are considered as non-productive. Data on the input of total services into domestic production are, therefore, systematically lower than those based on the system of national accounts used by other countries. Estimates made for Poland for 1977 on a system-of-national-accounts basis indicate that the country's total services share in GDP was 33–35%, compared to 22% on the basis of NMP. See UNCTAD, "Services and the Development Process", *op. cit.*, annex I, p. 5.

[19] See UNCTAD, "Production and Trade in Services", *op. cit.*, p. 27.

[20] See UNCTAD, "Services and the Development Process", *op. cit.*

[21] See, e. g., Marc Uri Porat, *The Information Economy: Definition and Measurement* (Washington, D.C.: US Government Printing Office, 1977).

[22] See Australia, Bureau of Industry Economics, *Features of the Australian Service Sector* (Canberra: Australian Government Publishing Service, 1980).

[23] US, Office of the U.S. Trade Representative (USTR), *Annual Report of the President of the United States on the Trade Agreements Program, 1983* (Washington: USTR, 1984), p. 25.

[24] *Ibid.*

[25] For a brief review, see Gershuny and Miles, *op. cit.* It should be noted that the growth of the service sector in and by itself does not necessarily represent sound economic development. It may, for instance, be the result of unemployment which could lead to a growth of the public service sector or to the establishment of many small service undertakings (e.g., repair shops).

[26] Nusbaumer, *op. cit.*, p. 3.

[27] Commission of the European Communities (COC), *Completing the Internal Market: White Paper from the Commission to the European Council* (Brussels: COC, 1985), p. 26.

[28] Such studies are undertaken by contracting parties of the GATT and members of the United Nations Conference on Trade and Development (UNCTAD). The United Nations Centre on Transnational Corporations (UNCTC) has sponsored national studies as well, but they focus on one sector only, data services.

[29] See IMF, *Balance of Payments Manual* (Washington: IMF, 1977), fourth edition, p. 11. It should be noted that foreign affiliates in a country are regarded as residents.

[30] There is little controversy that shipment, other transport, and travel should be included in any discussion of trade in services. No consensus exists, however, to what extent direct and portfolio investment income, unrequitted transfers (especially private migrant transfers and workers remittances) and "other goods, services and income" should be included. As regards the first two of these categories (also called "factor services"), the argument has been made that the flow of factor income is linked to FDI, not trade, and, therefore, does not belong into a trade-in-services discussion. Besides, the inclusion of factor income distorts any analysis by inflating the size of the service account dramatically. For example, if factor income is included, roughly two-thirds of all US service exports in 1980 would have consisted of the return of profits on US FDI abroad, three-fifths of which is in industry and agriculture. On the other hand, the point has been made that the provision and management of capital and labor constitutes a service and that, therefore, it is appropriate to include investment

income under services. In addition, profits of TNCs may include charges levied by headquarters on their foreign affiliates for services rendered by it for the corporate system as a whole (e.g., advertising). As far as the third category—"other goods, services and income"—is concerned, it lumps together "official transactions" (e.g., expenditures for embassies, consulates and military personnel abroad) and the private transactions of labor and property income (i.e., wages of foreigners, fees, royalties) as well as "other goods and services". Official transactions are a category sui generis, and many of the arguments made about factor services also apply to labor and property income. That leaves "other goods and services"—or "other private services"—which, as will be discussed below, contain a wide range of mostly business services. (The sum of factor and non-factor services is also referred to as "invisibles".) Since statistics on service trade often do not indicate on what definition they are based, discrepancies can often arise. Often, for instance, official transactions are included (for instance by UNCTAD), as is certain property income (for instance by certain US statistics).

³¹ IMF, Balance of Payments Manual, op. cit., para. 408.

³² For a review, see UNCTAD, "Production and Trade in Services", op. cit., and "Services and the Development Process", op. cit. For an in-depth analysis of the methodological difficulties in measuring international transactions in services, see Evelyn P. Lederer, Walther Lederer and Robert L. Sammons, "International Services Transactions of the United States: Proposals for Improvement in Data Collection" (Washington: Department of State, 1982), mimeo.

³³ The US, Office of the US Trade Representative (USTR), "U.S. National Study on Trade in Services" (Washington: USTR, 1983), mimeo., noted, for instance, that "undervaluation of trade transactions [in services] is likely to be widespread" (p. 13) and "there is substantial cause to believe that current methods of data collection on service industries trade may regularly underestimate total transaction value" (p. 108).

³⁴ Since open registry fleets do not belong to any country, their receipts and expenditures are not recorded in balance-of-payments statistics. As a result, the balance of world shipping services in 1979 was calculated to be $30 billion, instead of the expected zero; this figure alone accounts for nearly one-half of that year's discrepancy in the service account; see UNCTAD, "Production and Trade in Services", op. cit., p. 18.

³⁵ See OECD, Development Co-operation (Paris: OECD, annually). For a detailed discussion of the status of FDI statistics, see "Data on Foreign Direct Investment, Including Capital Inflows and Outflows, and on Other Aspects of the Activities of Transnational Corporations, and Suggestions for Further Action", E/C.10/1986/3 of 30 January 1986.

³⁶ See GATT, "Japan's National Study on Trade in Services" (Tokyo, 1984), mimeo., p. 7, GATT "Canada's National Study on Trade in Services" (Ottawa, 1984), p. 19, and Survey of Current Business, 63 (July 1983).

³⁷ See "U.S. National Study", op. cit., p. 110.

³⁸ See UNCTAD, "Production and Trade in Services", op. cit., pp. 52–53.

³⁹ See British Invisible Exports Council, Annual Report 1983/84, p. 23.

⁴⁰ See H. Kraegenau, Internationale Direktinvestitionen: Ergaenzungsband 1982 (Hamburg: HWWA, 1983).

⁴¹ See US, Department of Commerce, International Direct Investment: Global Trends and the U.S. Role (Washington: Superintendent of Documents, 1984), p. 12.

⁴² See US, Department of Commerce, Foreign Direct Investment in the United States (Washington: Superintendent of Documents, 1983), United States Direct Investment Abroad, 1977 (Washington: Superintendent of Documents, 1981), and U.S. Direct Investment Abroad: 1982 Benchmark Survey Data (Washington: Superintendent of Documents, 1985). In 1977,

53% of US affiliates abroad were in services; in 1982, this ratio was 55% (10,090 out of 18,339). In 1981, 73% of foreign affiliates in the US were service foreign affiliates.
   [43] For a detailed discussion of the role of TNCs, see Clairmonte and Cavanagh, *op. cit.*, Karl P. Sauvant and Zbigniew Zimny, "FDI and TNCs in Services", *The CTC Reporter*, 20 (Autumn 1985), pp. 24–28, and UNCTC, *Trends and Issues in Foreign Direct Investment and Related Flows* (New York: UN, 1985), Sales No. E.85.II.A.15.
   [44] For an elaboration, see UNCTC, *Trends and Issues, op. cit.*
   [45] For instance, the US insurance industry has tended to establish affiliates in countries in which it already had significant insurance exports. See, US, International Trade Commission (ITC), "The Relationship of Exports in Selected U.S. Service Industries to U.S. Merchandise Exports" (Washington: ITC, 1982), mimeo.
   [46] See, e.g., UNCTC, *Transnational Banks, op. cit.*, and R. M. Pecchioli, *The Internationalization of Banking: The Policy Issues* (Paris: OECD, 1983).
   [47] Trade and FDI in services are, of course, also linked to trade and FDI in goods. This is not a new situation. Trade in automobiles, for instance, has always depended, to a certain degree, on the establishment of a servicing network. But it appears that with the growing complexity and especially the increasing software content of certain traded products, supporting FDI—especially for maintenance purposes—becomes more important. Similarly, as discussed earlier, many foreign service affiliates were set up to service transnational industrial corporations.
   [48] The emergence of service conglomerates is one of the major points made by Clairmonte and Cavanagh, *op. cit.*
   [49] See *Der Spiegel*, 39 (7 January 1985), p. 60.
   [50] Harold Malmgren, "Negotiating International Rules for Services" (Washington: Malmgren Inc., 1983), mimeo., p. 8.
   [51] Jeffrey B. Lane, vice chairperson and chief executive officer of Shearson, a part of American Express, quoted in Ken Auletta, "The Fall of Lehman Brothers: The Men, the Money, the Merger", *The New York Times Magazine*, 24 February 1985, p. 38.
   [52] See *Financial Times*, 21 November 1984.
   [53] See, respectively, Peggy Turbett, "Banks Keep the Barrier Watch to Maintain Global Data Flow", *American Banker*, 4 February 1985, Geza Feketekuty and Jonathan David Aronson, "Meeting the Challenges of the World Information Economy", *The World Economy*, 7 (March 1984), p. 63, and private communication. Expenditures on telecommunications in the magnitude of 5% of operating expenses other than those related to payroll are not uncommon among service-sector firms; see Ray Austin, "Business Needs for Innovation in the Service Sector" (London: Unilever, 1985), mimeo., p. 3.
   [54] See Charles Oman, *New Forms of International Investment in Developing Countries* (Paris: OECD, 1984).
   [55] "Chairman's Report on a New Round of Multilateral Trade Negotiations. Submitted to the United States Trade Representative, May 15, 1985" (Washington: USTR, 1985), mimeo., contribution by the Services Policy Advisory Committee, p. 5.
   [56] *Ibid.*
   [57] *Ibid.*
   [58] *Ibid.*
   [59] US, Office of the Trade Representative, April 1985, mimeo., discussed in chapter IV, and reprinted in annex VIII to this volume.
   [60] In US FDI statistics, representative offices of commercial banks are generally not considered FDI. However, if representative offices produce revenues from services provided to unaffiliated persons (e.g., loans, receiving funds, or operating with a set of books), they

are counted as FDI. See the "Instruction Booklet" in *1982 Benchmark Survey Data, op. cit.*, pp. 5-6.

[61] This discussion is entirely in terms of *corporate* providers of services. The provision of services through *individuals* raises a whole set of different problems which are not being considered here.

[62] OECD, *International Trade in Services: Banking. Identification and Analysis of Obstacles* (Paris: OECD, 1984), p. 7.

[63] For a discussion of the factors determining comparative advantage in services, see André Sapir and E. Lutz, "Trade in Services: Economic Determinants and Development-Related Issues", World Bank Staff Working Paper No. 480, August 1981, and André Sapir, "Trade in Services: Policy Issues for the Eighties", *Columbia Journal of World Business*, 17 (Fall 1982), pp. 77-83.

[64] For instance, banks from developing—and, for that matter, other countries—may face increasing difficulties in participating in international financial transactions if they do not utilize computer-communication networks, be it in the context of SWIFT or such systems as automated teller machine networks.

Table I-1. Service activities according to the United Nations
system of national accounts

Sector	ISIC classification	Activity
Construction	5	Includes general and special trade contractors primarily engaged in contract construction. Maintenance or repair work done by maintenance staff in the full-time employ of enterprises are excluded.
Utilities	4, 92	Includes electricity, gas and steam, gas manufacture and distribution, steam heat and power, water supply, and sanitary services.
Trade	6 (excl. 63)	Includes wholesale and retail trade.
Transport, storage and communication	7	Includes land, water, and air transport and services allied to transport (e.g., storage and warehousing and communication).
Financing, insurance, real estate	8 (excl. 832, 833)	Includes banks and other financial institutions, insurance and real estate.
Public administration and defense	91	Excludes governmental activities other than administrative in such fields as transport, communication, education, health, production marketing, and the operation of financial institutions, each of which is classified in the appropriate ISIC industry group.
Other services	63,832, 833 93 - 96	Includes restaurants and hotels; business services (e.g., legal services, accounting, data processing, engineering, advertising) machinery and equipment rental and leasing; social and related community services (educational services, research and scientific nstitutes, health services, welfare institutions, business, professional and labor associations, other community services), recreational and cultural services (motion pictures and other entertainment, libraries, museums, other recreational services), personal and household services (repair, laundries, domestic services, other) and international bodies.

Source: United Nations, Indexes to the International Standard Industrial Classification of all Economic Activities (New York: United Nations, 1971).

Table I-2. The domestic service sector as a share of GDP
in market economies, 1979
(Per cent)

Definition of service	Market economies	Developed market economies	Developing countries
Broad definition (Construction, public administration and defense, utilities, trade, finance, transport and communication, other services)	64	67	51
Restrictive definition (Excluding construction)	58	61	45
More restrictive definition (Excluding construction and public administration and defense)	49	51	39
Narrow definition (Excluding construction, public administration and defense and utilities)	47	49	37

Source: UNCTAD, "Production and Trade in Services, Policies and Their Underlying Factors Bearing upon International Services Transactions", TD/B/941 (and Corr. 1) of 1 March 1983.

Table I-3. The production of services in market economies,
by service category, 1970, 1975, 1979

(Billions of dollars and per cent of all domestic services activities)

Service category	1970		1975		1979	
	Value	Per cent	Value	Per cent	Value	Per cent
Construction	147	10	303	10	530	10
Utilities	56	4	111	4	190	4
Public administration and defense	227	15	480	16	739	14
Trade and finance	593	39	1 016	35	2 046	39
Transport and communication	156	10	297	10	525	10
Other services	351	23	734	25	1 209	23
TOTAL	1 530	100	2 941	100	5 239	100

Source: Same as table I-2.

Table I-4. The production of services in developed market economies,
by service category, 1970, 1975, 1979

(Billions of dollars and per cent of all domestic service activities)

Service category	1970		1975		1979	
	Value	Per cent	Value	Per cent	Value	Per cent
Construction	130	10	258	10	428	10
Utilities	51	4	101	4	170	4
Public administration and defense	206	15	425	16	634	14
Trade and finance	529	39	1 016	38	1 722	38
Transport and communication	136	10	254	9	437	10
Other services	313	23	651	24	1 086	24
TOTAL	1 365	100	2 705	100	4 477	100

Source: Same as table I-2.

Table I-5. The production of services in developing countries,
by service category, 1970, 1975, 1979

(Billions of dollars and per cent of all domestic service activities)

Service category	1970		1975		1979	
	Value	Per cent	Value	Per cent	Value	Per cent
Construction	17	10	46	12	103	13
Utilities	5	3	10	3	21	3
Public administration and defense	22	13	55	14	105	14
Trade and finance	64	39	154	39	324	43
Transport and communication	20	12	43	11	87	11
Other services	38	23	83	21	123	16
TOTAL	166	100	391	100	763	100

Source: Same as table I-2.

Table I-6. The sectoral composition of the GDP
of market economies, 1970, 1979
(Per cent)

Sector	Market economies 1970	Market economies 1979	Developed market economies 1970	Developed market economies 1979	Developing countries 1970	Developing countries 1979
Agriculture	7	7	4	4	25	17
Industry	29	30	30	29	25	32
Services Broad definition a/	64	64	64	67	50	51
Narrow definition a/	..	47	..	49	..	37

Source: Same as table I-2.
a/ For the definition, see table I-2.

Table I-7. The role of services in developed market economies a/
(Per cent)

Country	Year	Share in GNP/GDP Private sector services	Share in GNP/GDP Public sector services	Share in GNP/GDP Total	Share in employment Private sector services	Share in employment Public sector services	Share in employment Total
US	1980	...	...	66	...	...	72
Australia	1982/83	...	...	66	...	...	75 b/
Denmark	1982	42	24	66	35	32	67
Belgium	1983	50	16	66	30	27	57
Canada	1981	...	...	63	...	...	64
France	1984	...	...	63	...	...	61
Sweden	1982	37	25	62	33	32	65
European Community	1981	43	15	58	38	20	58
Netherlands	1983	45	12	57	53	15	68
Japan	1981	53	3	56	55	1	56
UK	1982	40	16	56	42	20	62
FRG	1982	...	...	55	...	...	53
Italy	1982	...	...	53	...	...	58
Finland	1983	35	17	52	...	...	53
Norway	1983	36	14	50	40	23	63

Source: Based on the national studies submitted to GATT.
a/ Since not all countries use the same definitions, the data are not strictly comparable.
b/ 1984/85.

Table I-8. The share of services in the GDP
and employment of individual countries

Country and region	GDP			Employment		
	Share of services in GDP (Per cent)		Changes 1965-1983 (Percentage points)	Share of services in total employment (Per cent)		Changes 1965-1981 (Percentage points)
	1965	1983		1965	1981	
Developed countries						
Australia	50	...	...	52	61	9
Austria	45	58	13	36	54	18
Belgium	53	63	10	48	56	8
Canada	61	68	7	56	66	10
Denmark	60	72	12	49	58	9
Finland	52	60	8	39	54	15
France	...	...	...	42	53	11
Germany, Fed. Rep. of	...	52	...	42	50	8
Greece	49	53	4	27	35	8
Ireland	...	...	...	41	45	4
Italy	48	54	6	34	44	10
Japan	48	55	7	42	49	7
Netherlands	...	63	...	48	49	1
New Zealand	...	59	...	51	55	4
Norway	59	55	-4	48	56	8
Portugal	...	51	...	30	37	7
South Africa	48	...	...	38	41	3
Spain	49	...	...	31	46	15
Sweden	53	66	13	46	61	15
Switzerland	...	...	...	40	49	9
United Kingdom	56	66	10	51	56	5
United States	59	66	7	59	66	7

(Table I-8 cont'd)

Country and region	GDP			Employment		
	Share of services in GDP (Per cent)		Changes 1965–1983 (Percentage points)	Share of services in total employment (Per cent)		Changes 1965–1981 (Percentage points)
	1965	1983		1965	1981	
Developing countries						
Africa						
Algeria	51	40	-11	27	50	23
Benin	38	47	9	38	38	0
Burkina-Faso	32	40	8	4	5	1
Burundi	...	26	...	7	11	4
Cameroon	50	45	-5	8	10	2
Central African Rep.	38	42	4	4	8	4
Chad	41	...	...	4	8	4
Congo	62	38	-24	34	40	6
Egypt	45	47	2	29	20	-9
Ethiopia	28	36	8	8	13	5
Ghana	41	40	-1	23	27	4
Guinea	...	39	...	6	7	1
Ivory Coast	47	50	3	10	17	7
Kenya	47	46	-1	10	12	2
Lesotho	30	55	25	5	25	20
Liberia	34	38	4	11	16	5
Libya	33	34	1	38	53	15
Madagascar	38	48	10	5	9	4
Malawi	37	...	...	5	9	4
Mali	38	43	5	3	15	12
Mauritania	32	45	13	6	23	17
Morocco	49	51	2	25	27	2
Nigeria	29	40	11	21	27	6
Rwanda	18	...	...	5	7	2
Senegal	56	54	-2	12	13	1
Sierra Leone	38	48	10	11	16	5
Somalia	24	39	15	8	10	2
Sudan	37	51	14	9	12	3
Tanzania	40	33	-7	8	11	3
Togo	34	50	16	9	18	9

(Table I-8 cont'd)

	GDP			Employment		
	Share of services in GDP (Per cent)		Changes 1965–1983 (Percentage	Share of services in total employment (Per cent)		Changes 1965–1981 (Percentage
Country and region	1965	1983	points)	1965	1981	points)
Tunisia	54	50	-4	27	33	6
Uganda	35	...	...	7	11	4
Zaire	51	44	-7	9	12	3
Zambia	32	48	16	16	22	6
Zimbabwe	48	57	9	21	25	4
West Asia						
Iran	38	...	...	24	27	3
Iraq	36	...	...	30	32	2
Israel	55	67	12	53	57	4
Jordan	...	61	...	43	60	17
Kuwait	27	38	11	65	64	-1
Lebanon	67	...	...	47	62	15
Oman	16	...	...	...	...	...
Saudi Arabia	31	32	1	20	25	5
Syria	49	55	6	27	36	9
Turkey	41	48	7	15	33	18
United Arab Emirates	...	34	...	...	...	...
Yemen, Arab Rep.	...	62	...	11	14	3
Yemen, PDR	...	...	...	16	40	24
Yugoslavia	35	...	...	22	36	14
Other Asia						
Afghanistan	...	...	...	9	13	4
Bangladesh	36	40	4	10	15	5
Burma	52	39	-13	...	23	...
China	22	18	-4	...	13	...
Hong Kong	58	69	11	40	40	0
India	31	38	7	15	16	1
Indonesia	29	35	6	20	30	10
Korea	37	47	10	29	37	8
Malaysia	45	44	-1	27	34	7
Nepal	23	27	4	3	5	2
Papua New Guinea	41	...	...	7	10	3
Philippines	46	42	-4	27	37	10
Singapore	73	62	-11	68	59	-9
Sri Lanka	51	47	-4	30	32	2
Thailand	42	50	8	13	15	2

(Table I-8 cont'd)

Country and region	GDP			Employment		
	Share of services in GDP (Per cent)		Changes 1965–1983 (Percentage points)	Share of services in total employment (Per cent)		Changes 1965–1981 (Percentage points)
	1965	1983		1965	1981	
Latin America						
Argentina	42	49	7	48	59	11
Bolivia	49	52	3	22	26	4
Brazil	48	53	5	34	46	12
Chile	52	55	3	53	62	9
Colombia	46	51	5	35	53	18
Costa Rica	53	50	−3	33	48	15
Dominican Rep.	53	55	2	23	33	10
Ecuador	50	46	−4	25	31	6
El Salvador	49	59	10	23	28	5
Guatemala	...	...	...	20	24	4
Haiti	...	...	...	16	19	3
Honduras	41	47	6	20	17	−3
Jamaica	53	60	7	41	47	6
Mexico	54	52	−2	29	38	9
Nicaragua	51	47	−4	27	47	20
Panama	63	...	...	39	49	10
Paraguay	45	48	3	26	32	6
Peru	55	51	−4	31	41	10
Trinidad & Tobago	57	...	...	42	51	9
Uruguay	53	60	7	52	57	5
Venezuela	71	53	−18	46	55	9

Source: The World Bank, World Development Report 1985 (New York: Oxford University Press, 1985), pp. 178–179, 214–215.

Table I-9. Changes in the share of services in GDP and employment,
by country group
(Number of countries)

Area	Number of countries with share:			Total number of countries in the sample
	Growing	Constant	Decreasing	
Share in GDP between 1965 and 1983				
Developed market economies	11	–	1	12
Developing countries	43	–	21	64
TOTAL	54	–	22	76
Share in employment between 1965 and 1981				
Developed market economies	22	–	0	22
Developing countries	75	2	4	81
TOTAL	97	2	4	103

Source: Based on table I-8.

Table I-10. The share of developing countries in the total production
of services in market economies, 1970, 1975, 1979
(Per cent)

Service category	1970	1975	1979
Construction	12	15	19
Utilities	9	9	11
Public administration and defense	10	11	14
Trade and finance	11	15	16
Transport and communication	13	14	17
Other services	11	11	10
TOTAL	11	13	15

Source: Based on tables I-3 to I-5.

Table I-11. Service categories in the IMF balance-of-payments
reporting system

Category	Description
Shipment	Freight, associated insurance and other distributive services.
Other transport	Passenger services (i.e., the transport of persons by vessel or airline), port services, charters of carriers, miscellaneous transport.
Travel	Goods and services acquired from an economy by travelers during their stay in that economy to use themselves or to give away. (Travelers include tourists, business travelers and students and trainees.)
Other private services not included elsewhere	Covers all goods and services not specifically allocated to other items in the current account. The main components include non-merchandise insurance, communications, advertising, brokerage, management, operational leasing, subscriptions to periodicals, processing and repair, merchanting and professional and technical services.

Source: IMF, Balance of Payments Manual (Washington: IMF, 1977), fourth edition.

Table I-12. US outward and inward direct investment, selected data for affiliates, by industry of affiliate

Industry	Direct investment position a/ Billion dollars	Per cent	Total assets b/ Billion dollars	Per cent	Total sales Billion dollars	Per cent	Employment Thousands	Per cent	Number of affiliates	Assets/sales per invested dollar Assets	Sales	Jobs per invested hundred thousand dollars
	1		2		3		4		5	2:1	3:1	4:1
A. Outward investment (1982)												
All industries c/	207	100	1 349	100	1 027	100	6 816	100	18 339	6.5	5.0	3.3
Mining	5	3	17	1	8	1	141	2	180	3.2	1.5	2.7
Petroleum	40	19	136	10	187	18	266	4	712	3.5	4.7	0.7
Manufacturing	84	40	266	20	359	35	4 433	65	7 005	3.2	4.3	5.3
Services	77	37	892	66	433	42	11 765	26	10 090	11.6	5.6	2.3
of which:												
Trade	25	12	69	5	151	15	944	14	4 034	2.8	6.1	3.8
Banking	10	5	554	41	87 d/	9	139	2	882	53.8	8.5	1.5
Finance	10	5	137	10	14	1	46	1	1 685	13.8	1.5	0.5
Insurance	7	4	44	3	17	2	82	1	627	6.1	2.3	1.1
Petroleum services	18	9	59	4	142	14	145	2	1 089	3.3	7.9	0.8
Other services	7	3	29	2	22	2	390	6	1 773	4.2	3.2	5.7
B. Inward investment (1980)												
All industries c/	80	100	522	100	436	100	2 112	100	7 676	6.5	5.4	2.6
Mining	1	2	7	1	3	1	25	1	69	5.2	2.6	1.9
Petroleum	10	13	35	7	64	15	79	4	138	3.4	6.2	0.8
Manufacturing	31	39	82	16	98	23	1 102	52	1 232	2.6	3.2	3.6
Services	36	45	394	76	293	67	854	40	5 595	10.9	8.1	2.3
of which:												
Trade	14	18	60	11	221	51	521	25	1 553	4.2	15.4	3.6
Banking	5	6	230	44	24 d/	5	78	4	366	51.1	5.2	1.7
Finance	1	2	32	6	5	1	25	1	233	26.9	3.9	2.1
Insurance	6	8	36	7	15	3	62	3	125	5.9	2.4	1.0
Petroleum services	2	2	9	2	20	5	22	1	97	4.8	10.2	1.2
Other services	8	10	27	5	10	2	146	7	3 221	3.4	1.2	1.8

Sources: US, Department of Commerce, U.S. Direct Investment Abroad: 1982 Benchmark Survey Data (Washington, D.C.: Superintendent of Documents, 1985); and Foreign Direct Investment in the U.S. 1980 (Washington, D.C.: Superintendent of Documents, 1983).

a/ Equal to parents' equity in and net outstanding loans to their foreign affiliates.
b/ Equal to the sum of total owners' equity in affiliates held by parents and all other persons and total liabilities owed by affiliates to both parents and all other persons.
c/ Including "other industries".
d/ Total income.

Table I-13. The internationalization of economic sectors
of market economies, 1970, 1980
(Billion of dollars and per cent)

Sector	GDP		Exports		Exports as percentage of GDP	
	1970	1980	1970	1980	1970	1980
Agriculture	182	603	58	273	32	45
Mining and manufacturing	727	2 770	218	1 522	30	55
Services[a]	1 458	5 644	100	610	7	11
TOTAL	2 367	9 017	376	2 405	16	27

Source: Frederick F. Clairmonte and John H. Cavanagh, "Transnational Corporations and Services: The Final Frontier", Trade and Development: An UNCTAD Review, 5 (1984), p. 224.
  [a] The figures include factor services.

Table I-14. Service trade of market economies, by country group, 1970, 1980
(Billions of dollars)

Service category	1970			1980			Credit growth 1970-80 (Per cent)
	Credit	Debit	Net a/	Credit	Debit	Net a/	
Developed market economies	2.2	11.6	0.6	50.0	48.4	1.6	15
Developing countries	0.8	4.5	-3.7	6.8	38.0	-31.2	24
Total	13.0	16.1	-3.1	56.8	86.4	-30.6	16
Other transportation							
Developed market economies	10.8	13.3	-2.5	59.2	64.0	-4.8	19
Developing countries	1.7	1.6	0.1	14.9	14.9	0	24
Total	12.5	14.9	-2.4	74.1	78.9	-4.8	19
Travel							
Developed market economies	15.5	15.2	0.3	77.1	80.3	-3.2	17
Developing countries	4.0	3.0	1.0	22.9	25.5	-2.6	19
Total	19.5	18.2	1.3	100.0	105.8	-5.8	18
Other private services							
Developed market economies	18.4	15.7	2.7	105.6	91.4	14.2	19
Developing countries	2.2	3.3	-1.1	21.4	24.8	-3.4	26
Total	20.6	19.0	1.6	127.0	116.2	10.8	20
TOTAL							
Developed market economies	56.9	55.8	1.1	291.9	284.1	7.8	18
Developing countries	8.7	12.4	-3.7	66.0	103.2	-37.2	22
GRAND TOTAL	65.6	68.2	-2.6	357.9	387.3	-29.4	18
Memorandum							
Merchandise trade							
Developed market economies	223	217	6	1 254	1 333	-79	19
Developing countries	49	44	5	503	391	112	26
Total	272	261	11	1 757	1 724	33	21

Source: Same as table I-2.
   a/ In theory, the sum of credits and debits for each component should equal
zero. The net figure is, therefore, due to incomplete country coverage (especially
as regards the socialist countries), under-reporting by individual countries, the lag
in the recording of transactions, and statistical discrepancies.

Table I-15. The 20 largest exporters of services, by category, 1970, 1980
(Billions of dollars and per cent)

Country	Value 1970	Value 1980	Composition 1980 Shipment	Composition 1980 Other transpor- tation	Composition 1980 Travel	Composition 1980 Other private services	Per cent of merchandise export 1980
US	10	34.7	3.7	10.3	10.1	10.6	16
UK	8	34.4	5.8	8.3	6.9	13.4	31
France	5	33.0	4.0	6.8	8.2	14.0	31
FRG	5	32.3	5.6	4.6	6.7	15.4	17
Italy	2	22.6	3.2	2.4	9.0	8.0	30
Japan	3	18.9	7.4	5.6	0.6	5.3	15
Netherlands	3	17.5	3.6	6.2	1.7	6.0	26
Belgium	2	11.7	2.4	1.9	1.8	8.6	26
Spain	2	11.6	1.1	1.9	6.9	1.7	57
Austria	1	10.2	...	.1	6.5	3.6	63
Norway	2	8.7	5.0	1.5	.8	1.4	39
Switzerland	2[a]	8.5	.4	...	4.1	4.0	29
Sweden	1	7.7	1.7	1.3	1.0	3.7	24
Mexico	2[a]	7.4	...	.4	5.2	1.8	46
Canada	2	7.0	.8	.7	2.9	2.6	10
Denmark	1	6.0	1.8	...	1.6	2.6	39[a]
Singapore	.5	5.5	.5	2.0	1.3	1.7	33
Yugoslavia	.7[a]	4.5	.4	1.0	1.6	1.5	50
Rep. of Korea	.2	4.4	.9	.6	.4	2.5	26
Greece	.5[a]	3.1	.1	.1	1.7	1.2	97
Total market economies	73.0	358	57	74	100	127	22[a]

Sources: UNCTAD, "Production and Trade in Services," op. cit., and "U.S. National Study," op. cit.
  a/ Including official services.

Table I-16. The 15 largest importers of services, by category, 1970, 1980
(Billions of dollars and per cent)

Country	Value 1970	Value 1980	Composition 1980 Shipment	Other transportation	Travel	Other private services
FRG	8.5	49.6	5.4	5.6	20.8	17.8
Japan	4.8	32.3	4.2	13.1	4.6	10.4
US	9.0	28.9	6.1	8.4	10.4	4.0
France	4.3	27.5	4.8	6.3	6.0	10.3
UK	6.2	24.3	3.9	8.9	6.4	5.1
Netherlands	2.9	17.4	4.7	2.6	4.7	5.4
Italy	3.7	16.2	5.1	1.9	1.9	7.2
Belgium	2.0	14.0	2.0	1.9	3.3	6.8
Saudi Arabia	0.2	11.7	5.1	1.0	3.5	...
Iran	0.5	9.8	3.7	...	2.9	1.9
Canada	2.9	9.3	1.1	0.4	3.9	3.9
Sweden	1.1	7.2a/	...	2.3	2.2	...
Mexico	1.2	7.2a/	0.9	0.9	4.2	1.1
Norway	0.9	7.0a/	...	3.6	1.5	...
Switzerland	0.9	6.5a/	...	...	2.9	2.8
Total market economies	68.2	487.0	86.0	79.0	106.0	116.0

Sources: UNCTAD, "Production and Trade in Services," op. cit.
a/ Including small amounts of official services.

Table I-17. Net trade earnings of UK financial institutions,
1977-1983
(Million pounds)

Financial service	1977	1978	1979	1980	1981	1983
Banking	330	701	207	447	1 329	1 842
Insurance	913	1 039	1 009	855	974	1 595
Pension funds	17	24	46	87	107	396
Commodities	110	163	140	180	160	350
Merchanting a/	120	132	145	160	200	275
Baltic Exchange	155	153	200	181	285	246
Investment trusts	51	52	58	82	91	162
Other brokerage	37	54	88	123	137	157
Unit trusts	12	15	22	33	39	104
Solicitors	36	44	52	61	67	79
Stock exchange	20	21	25	43	35	71
Lloyd's Register of Shipping	21	20	18	23	28	37
TOTAL	1 822	2 418	2 010	2 275	3 452	5 314

Sources: Committee on Invisible Exports, Annual Report 1982/83, p. 29, and
British Invisible Exports Council, Annual Report 1983/84, p. 23.
a/ Profits of non-commodity third-country trade.

Table I-18. Trade and sales of foreign affiliates in services: the US case, 1974-1982

(Billion of dollars and per cent)

Transaction	1974	1977	1978	1979	1980	1981	1982	Average annual growth rate 1974-1977	1977-1982
Exports	13	18	21	25	29	34	33	11	13
Foreign sales by US affiliates	...	276	...	...	...	...	415	...	9
Excluding affiliates in wholesale trade	37	114	...	...	...	...	178	46	9
Ratio of affiliates' sales to exports	2.8	6.3	...	...	...	...	5.4		
Imports	15	20	23	26	29	32	33	10	11
Sales by foreign affiliates in US	100	127	165	227	298	345	355	8	23
Excluding affiliates in wholesale trade	22	30	41	63	82	103	125	11	33
Ratio of affiliates' sales to imports	1.5	1.5	1.8	2.4	2.8	3.2	3.8		

Sources: US, Department of Commerce, "United States Service Industries in World Markets" (Washington: Department of Commerce, 1976), mimeo., pp. 18-20, United States, Department of Commerce, Bureau of Economic Analysis, Staff Paper 41, U.S. International Trade and Investment in Services: Data Needs and Availability (Washington: Superintendent of Documents, 1984), Survey of Current Business, December 1985, and data obtained from the United States Department of Commerce.

Table I-19. Trade and sales of foreign affiliates in various sectors: the US case, 1982[a]
(Billion of dollars)

Transaction	Mining	Petroleum	Manufacturing	Agriculture	Services[b]
Sales of US affiliates abroad (1)	8	187	359	1.5	178
US exports (2)	3	13	135	39.1	33
Ratio (1:2)	2.7	14.4	2.7	0.04	5.4
Sales of foreign affiliates in the US (1)	6	40	141	1	125
US imports (2)	3	61	136	22	33
Ratio (1:2)	2.0	0.7	1.0	0.05	3.8

Sources: Same on table I-18, Survey of Current Business, December 1984, and UNCTAD, Handbook of Trade and Development Statistics, 1983 and 1985.
[a] Trade with market economies, FOB basis.
[b] Sales exclude wholesale trade affiliates, but include construction affiliates.

Table I-20. Share of services in outward FDI stock, selected home countries, 1971, 1978

(Billions of dollars and per cent)

Country	Total FDI (Billion dollars)		Total services				Share of developing countries			
			Billion dollars		Share in total stock a/		Billion dollars		Percentage a/	
	1971	1978	1971	1978	1971	1978	1971	1978	1971	1978
US	101	168	26	54	26	32	6.7	19.5	26	36
Japan	10	27	4	11	36	42	1.0	4.2	27	37
UK	24	31	6	8	2?	27	1.5	1.7	27	20
FRG	7	32	1	7	16	22	0.3	2.5	27	34
Netherlands	15	20	2	3	13	17	...	1.0	...	29
Canada	7	11	2	3	33	29	...	...	...	...
Italy	3	3	2	1	48	38	0.3	0.1	19	9
TOTAL	167	292	43	87	24	29	9.8b/	28.0b/	24b/	32b/

Source: United Nations, Salient Features and Trends in Foreign Direct Investment (New York: United Nations, 1983).

a/ Calculated on the basis of non-rounded figures.
b/ Excluding Canada and The Netherlands.

Table I-21. Stock of FDI in services, selected home
countries, various years
(Value and per cent)

Country and currency	Year	Value		Share of services in total FDI (Percentage)
		Total FDI	FDI in services	
United States[a]	1950	12	4	33
(Billion dollars)	1957	25	8	31
	1966	52	16	31
	1977	146	59	41
	1980	215	84	39
	1981	228	88	39
	1982	221	83	37
	1983	226	81	36
Growth rates	1966 - 1977	9.8	12.6	
	1977 - 1983	7.6	5.4	
Federal Republic of Germany[b]	1976	49	20	40
	1977	53	22	42
(Billion DM)	1978	61	23	38
	1979	70	23	33
	1980	85	36	42
	1981	102	42	42
	1982	109	45	41
	1983	124	53	43
	1984	145	60	45
Growth rates	1976 - 1978	10.9	9.0	
	1978 - 1984	15.7	19.0	
Japan				
(Billion dollars)	1960	.3	.06	20
	1965	1	.3	29
	1969	4	1	39
	1975	16	6	38
	1977	21	8	37
	1980	36	14	39
	1981	45	18	40
	1982	53	23	43
	1983	61	28	45
	1984	71	34	48
Growth rates	1965 - 1977	28.9	31.5	
	1977 - 1984	19.0	23.0	

Sources: Based on US, Department of Commerce, International Direct
Investment: Global Trends and the U.S. Role (Washington: Superintendent of
Documents, 1984); Japan, Export-Import Bank, Bulletin of the Research Institute
for Overseas Investment, various issues; Deutsche Bundesbank, "Statistische
Beihefte zu den Monatsberichten der Deutschen Bundesbank", Reihe 3, April 1984
and February 1986; and data supplied by the US Department of Commerce.
    a/ Including construction and petroleum-industry related services.
    b/ By industry of foreign affiliate, primary and secondary investment.

Table I-22. Average flows of FDI in services, selected
home countries, various years
(Value and per cent)

Country and currency	Year (Averages)	Value Total FDI	FDI in services	Share of services in total FDI
France)	1972-1975	5	2	39
(Billion FF)	1976-1980	6	3	50
	1979-1980	7	3	42
	1981-1983	20	7	35
United Kingdom a/	1970-1971	1.4	0.6	41
(Billion dollars)	1975-1977	3.3	1.2	37
	1978-1980	6.9	3.4	49
Japan	1973	3.5	1.2	39
(Billion dollars)	1975	3.3	1.4	20
	1982	7.7	4.7b/	44
	1983	8.1	4.9b/	60
	1984	10.2	6.8b/	67
Federal Republic	1977-1980	8.9	4.0	45
of Germany	1981-1984	15.2	7.6	50
(Billion DM)				

Sources: Calculated from Kraegenau, op. cit., United Kingdom, Business
Statistics Office, Business Monitor: Overseas Transactions, various issues;
and Japan, Export-Import Bank, Bulletin of the Research Institute for Overseas
Investment, various issues, Deutsche Bundesbank, Statistische Beihefte, op.
cit., and "La balance des paiements de la France : Rapports annuels, annexes",
various years.
    a/   Excluding oil.
    b/   Excluding construction.

Table I-23. Share of services in stock of inward FDI, selected host countries, 1971, 1978
(Million of dollars and per cent)

Country	Value of total stock 1971	Value of total stock 1978	Value of services stock 1971	Value of services stock 1978	Share of services in total 1971	Share of services in total 1978	Change in share (percentage points)
Developed countries							
United States	13 914	40 931	4 053	16 657	29	41	+12
Netherlands	7 506	11 884	2 018	3 581	27	30	+ 3
Italy	6 155	5 764	1 863	1 741	30	30	0
Germany, Federal Republic of	9 155	29 172	1 687	8 158	18	28	+10
Canada	27 857	42 903	6 212	10 759	22	25	+ 3
United Kingdom	13 827	22 277	1 625	4 426	12	20	+ 8
Japan	851	1 920	95	381	11	20	+ 9
Developing countries							
Philippines	116 a/	976	61 a/	294	53 a/	30	−23
Morocco	20 f/	239 c/	8 f/	125 c/	42 f/	52 c/	+10
Venezuela	1 237 e/	1 479 c/	499 e/	552 c/	40 e/	37	− 3
Panama	207 a/	270 c/	64 a/	94 c/	31 a/	35 c/	+ 4
Nigeria	2 010	3 700 b/	327	1 202 b/	16	32 b/	+16
India	2 185	2 405 d/	507	697 d/	23	29 d/	+ 6
Ecuador	438	723 b/	63	199 b/	14	28 b/	+14
Colombia	503 a/	843	134 a/	228	27 a/	27	0
Korea, Republic of	115 f/	1 004 e/	25 f/	250	22 f/	25	+ 3
Thailand	70 g.	244 c/	2 g/	46 c/	3 g/	19 c/	+16
Mexico	3 174 a/	5 050	514 a/	944 b/	16 a/	19 b/	+ 3
Peru	851 d/	998	128 d/	162	15 d/	16	+ 1
Brazil	3 404 a/	13 740	320 a/	2 281	9 a/	17	+ 8
Indonesia	3 225 a/	6 555 c/	48 a/	420 c/	2 a/	6 c/	+ 4

Source: Same as table I-20.
a/1972. b/1976. c/1977. d/1974. e/1975. f/1973. g/1969.

Table I-24. Composition of outward and inward stock of FDI
in services, by category, selected developed countries,
various years
(Value and per cent)

Country and industry	Outward stock		Inward stock	
United States	1983 Billion dollars	1983 Per- centage	1984 Billion dollars	1984 Per- centage
Trade	28.5	35	30.5	39
Banking	11.5	14	10.2	13
Finance, insurance, real estate	17.2	21	29.9	38
(Insurance)	(7.9)	(10)	(8.8)	(11)
Transportation	2.0	3	1.3	2
Communication	0.7	1	0.3 a/	0.4
Other services	6.6	8	2.3	3
(Hotels)	(1.1)	(1)	(0.5)	(0.6)
(Advertising)	(0.5)	(0.6)	(...)	(...)
(Accounting)	(0.5)	(0.6)	(...)	(...)
Services related to petroleum industry	14.6	18	3.3	4.2
TOTAL services	81.1	100	77.8	100

Federal Republic of Germany b/

	1984 Billion DM	1984 Per- centage	1984 Billion DM	1984 Per- centage
Trade	29.5	45	20.3	41
Transport and communication	1.5	2	1.4	3
Banking, insurance and other finance	19.4	29	9.2	19
(Banking)	(8.0)	(12)	(6.9)	(14)
(Insurance)	(6.7)	(10)	(0.3)	(1)
(Other finance)	(4.6	(7)	(1.9)	(4)
Other services c/	15.6	24	18.4	37
(Holding companies and other property administration)	(7.2)	(11)	(14.2)	(29)
(Real estate)	(6.1)	(9)	(1.9)	(4)
(Others)	(2.1)	(3)	(2.2)	(5)
TOTAL services	66.0	100	49.3	100

Japan	1984 Billion dollars	1984 Per- centage	1984 Billion dollars	1984 Per- centage
Trade	11.1	33	0.7	48.3
Banking, insurance	7.0	21	...	...
Transport and communication	4.7	14	0.014	1
Real estate	1.3	4	0.034	2.3 f/
Other services c/ d/	9.6	28	0.7	48.3
TOTAL services	33.7	100	1.5	100

(Table I-24 cont'd)

Country and industry	Outward stock		Inward stock
United Kingdom	1981	1981	
	Billion £	Percentage	
Trade	3.8	25	
Banking	3.5	23	
Insurance	3.0	19	
Transport and communication	1.0	6	
Property owning and managing	2.0	13	...
Other services c/	2.2	14	
TOTAL services	15.5	100	
Netherlands	1976	1976	
	Billion guilders	Percentage	
Trade	3.9	45	
Banking, insurance	1.9	22	...
Others	2.8	33	
TOTAL services	8.6	100	

Sources: US, Department of Commerce, Survey of Current Business, various issues, OECD, Recent International Direct Investment Trends (Paris: OECD, 1981), Deutsche Bundesbank, Statistische Beihefte, op. cit., Bank of England Quarterly Bulletin, June 1984, Business Monitor, Overseas Transactions, Supplement 1981, Japan, Import-Export Bank, Research Institute Report on Overseas Investment, and data supplied by the United States Department of Commerce.

   a/ 1983.

   b/ Primary and secondary FDI by branch of economic activity of the foreign affiliate abroad (outward FDI) and by branch of economic activity of the foreign affiliate in the FRG (inward FDI).

   c/ Excluding construction.

   d/ Professional services, hotels, etc., including public utilities.

   e/ Including construction.

Note: Discrepancies between tables concerning absolute and relative figures for services are the results of differences in coverage of services. Unclear industries include construction, public utilities, real estate and services related to petroleum sector (United States). It is not possible to avoid these discrepancies, since some sources do not indicate detailed coverage of services. Besides, some countries provide two statistical series on FDI which are not strictly comparable.

Table I-25. The world's 75 largest transnational service corporations, 1983

Rank	Name	Country	Industry	Revenues	Assets	Profit or net income	Employees (Thousands)	Foreign content (percentage of total) Revenue	Assets	Profit	Number of foreign affiliates
				(Total in million dollars)							
1	Mitsui & Co. Ltd.	Japan	Wholesaler	63 149	21 017	27	12.9	...	...	...	267 a/
2	Mitsubishi Corp.	Japan	Wholesaler	62 831	21 340	102	14.3	...	...	...	228 a/
3	C. Itoh & Co. Ltd.	Japan	Wholesaler	48 436	15 612	1	10.0	...	...	...	213 a/
4	Marubeni Corp.	Japan	Wholesaler	46 816	16 543	2	10.6	...	...	...	252 a/
5	Sumitomo Corp.	Japan	Wholesaler	45 806	10 914	92	11.5	...	...	...	148 a/
6	Sears, Roebuck	USA	Retailer	35 883	46 176	1 301	450.0	9.0	4.5	NA	
7	Nissho Iwai Corp.	Japan	Wholesaler	34 039	9 835	20	7.7	...	...	...	104 a/
8	Phibro-Salomon	USA	Diversified services	29 757	42 017	470	6.7	67.5	11.9	50.0	...
9	K Mart	USA	Retailer	19 479	8 359	...	250.0	8.7	7.5	5.7	...
10	Safeway Stores	USA	Retailer	18 585	4 174	183	162.1	24.4	26.3	45.9	...
11	Citicorp	USA	Banking	17 037	127 923	860	63.7	56.6	59.1	54.4	236 b/
12	Toyo Menka Kaisha Ltd.	Japan	Wholesaler	16 865	5 364	2	5.5	...	...	...	80 b/
13	Kanematsu-Gosako Ltd.	Japan	Wholesaler	15 105	4 894	5	4.5	...	...	...	90 a/
14	Nichimen Corp.	Japan	Wholesaler	14 770	5 450	2	3.5	...	...	...	... b/
15	Bank America	USA	Banking	13 299	123 045	390	91.1	44.7	40.1	47.4	259 b/
16	Nippon Life Insurance Co.	Japan	Insurance and other financial services	12 604	34 039	1 880	15.1	...	...	...	...
17	CIGNA	USA	Insurance and other financial services	12 563	35 116	...	...	...	...	...	
18	Travelers Corp.	USA	Insurance and other financial services	12 002	32 875	438	123.0	...	...	...	400
19	Barclays Bank Group	UK	Banking	11 937	94 150	187	60.6	...	...	...	...
20	Barque Nationale de Paris Group	France	Banking	11 335	101 019	...	...	...	...	...	194 b/
21	Credit Lyonnais Group	France	Banking	11 272	88 123	119	45.9	...	...	...	99 b/
22	National Westminster Bank PLC	UK	Banking	9 953	87 061	602	91.7	...	...	...	65 b/
23	American Express	USA	Financial services	9 770	43 981	685	70.5	25.2	35.5	55.3	30 b/
24	Midland Bank Group	UK	Banking	9 245	76 320	173	82.6	...	...	...	68 b/
25	Tengelmann Group	FRG	Retailer	9 200	...	...	78.0	...	...	...	...
26	Société Générale Group	France	Banking	9 030	86 346	117	48.1	...	...	...	64 b/
27	Bank Leumi Le Israel BM	Israel	Banking	8 527	21 428	69	15.3	...	...	...	20 b/
28	Chase Manhattan	USA	Banking	8 523	81 920	430	37.2	58.0	56.6	42.1	188 b/
29	Banco do Brasil	Brazil	Banking	7 947	53 057	869	117.0	...	...	...	47
30	Royal Bank of Canada	Canada	Banking	7 758	68 707	390	38.7	...	...	...	75 b/

(Table I-25 cont'd)

Rank	Name	Country	Industry	Revenues	Assets	Profit or net income	Employees (Thousands)	Foreign content (percentage of total) Revenue	Assets	Profit	Number of foreign affiliates
				(Total in million dollars)							
31	Deutsche Bank Group	FRG	Banking	7 680	77 160	249	47.3	...	...	...	66 b/
32	Dai-Ichiykangyo Bank	Japan	Banking	7 613	110 036	150	23	...	...	...	29 b/
33	Fuji Bank Ltd.	Japan	Banking	7 401	102 979	234	17.2	...	...	...	36 b/
34	Bank of Tokyo Ltd.	Japan	Banking	7 271	78 934	118	14.4	...	...	...	95 b/
35	Bell Canada Enterprises	Canada	Communications	7 201	12 006	655	96.3	...	...	...	
36	Sumitomo Bank Ltd.	Japan	Banking	6 944	96 933	237	15.5	...	...	...	31 b/
37	Lloyds Bank Group	UK	Banking	6 925	55 749	419	69.3	...	...	...	80 b/
38	S&W Berisford PLC	UK	Commodity broker	6 756	2 032	29	9.0	...	...	...	
39	Mitsubishi Bank Ltd.	Japan	Banking	6 678	97 384	163	18.3	...	...	...	32 b/
40	Manufacturers Hanover	USA	Banking	6 996	64 332	337	28.2	44.7	65.2	48.7	56 b/
41	George Weston Ltd.	Canada	Retailer	6 329	1 742	62	60.0	...	...	...	
42	Sanwa Bank Ltd.	Japan	Banking	6 320	93 094	147	16.6	...	...	...	35 b/
43	Sunkyong Group	S.Korea	Wholesaler	6 213	2 376	41	83.7	...	...	...	
44	Canadian Imperial Bank of Commerce	Canada	Banking	6 088	55 263	256	35.5	...	...	...	56 b/
45	Bank of Montreal	Canada	Banking	6 038	51 273	230	29.1	...	...	...	36 b/
46	Allianz Worldwide	FRG	Insurance	6 000	6 665	100	25.1	20.3	...	...	3 c/
47	City Investing	USA	Diversified services	5 948	8 361	53.6	...	14.5	10.8	6.1	
48	JP Morgan	USA	Banking	5 764	58 023	460	...	59.8	52.8	54.3	50 b/
49	Industrial Bank of Japan Ltd.	Japan	Banking	5 710	76 356	171	5.2	...	...	...	45 b/
50	Dresdner Bank	FRG	Banking	5 629	59 048	145	31.9	...	...	...	66 b/
51	Halliburton	USA	Diversified services	5 522	5 834	501	73.2	30.4	33.7	42.3	...
52	Continental Group	USA	Diversified services	5 522	5 463	345	...	18.7	10.3	17.3	...
53	Woolworth (FW)	USA	Retailer	5 456	2 364	308	114.6	42.0	47.3	40.3	
54	Fluor	USA	Diversified services	5 301	4 085	274	34.1	34.9	22.1	62.4	...
55	Daiei Inc.	Japan	Retailer	5 270	3 893	-16	4.9	...	...	...	
56	Chemical New York	USA	Banking	4 903	51 165	306	19.5	38.4	37.4	42.2	57 b/
57	Standard Chartered Bank Group	UK	Banking	4 837	41 948	136	55.1	...	...	...	124 b/
58	Mitsui Bank Ltd.	Japan	Banking	4 830	68 760	100	12.0	...	...	...	32 b/
59	Kawasho Corp.	Japan	Wholesaler	4 787	1 627	2	2.0	...	...	...	
60	Karstadt Group	FRG	Retailer	4 811	4 398	142	22.8	...	...	...	
61	Bank of Nova Scotia	Canada	Banking	4 718	44 469	283	25.5	...	...	...	85 b/
62	Migros-Genossenschafts	Switzerland	Retailer	4 626	2 947	66	54.0	...	...	...	
63	Ito-Yokado Co. Ltd.	Japan	Retailer	4 578	2 048	98	22.8	...	...	...	
64	Nationale-Nederlanden	Netherlands	Insurance	4 555	18 593	166	17.7	...	...	...	5 c/
65	Tokai Bank Ltd.	Japan	Banking	4 554	65 784	99	14.7	...	...	...	21 b/

(Table I-25 cont'd)

Rank	Name	Country	Industry	Revenues	Assets	Profit or net income	Employees (Thousands)	Foreign content (percentage of total)			Number of foreign affiliates
				(Total in million dollars)				Revenue	Assets	Profit	
66	Continental Illinois Long Term Credit	USA	Banking	4 381	42 097	101	12.2	34.8	38.5	7.9	74 b/
67	First Interstate	USA	Banking	4 341	44 423	247	...	16.5	19.5	6.1	...
68	Carrefour	France	Retailer	4 278	1 370	60	27.0	...	...	...	...
69	Toyoda Tsusho Kaisha Ltd.	Japan	Wholesaler	4 277	1 105	19	1.6	...	...	...	...
70	Marks & Spencer PLC	UK	Retailer	4 261	2 545	248	39.0	...	...	...	...
71	Swiss Re Group	Switzerland	Insurance	4 150	10 386	50	13.7	95.0	...	...	...
72	Vendex Intr. BV	Netherlands	Retailer	4 072	14 441	66	31.0	...	...	...	...
73	Suez Group	France	Banking	4 010	27 096	136	10.9	...	...	...	36 b/
74	Société Générale de Banque SA	Belgium	Banking	4 004	32 217	60	15.7	...	...	...	27 b/
75	American International Group	USA	Financial services	3 997	10 556	473	...	46.1	40.9	64.1	...

Sources: Forbes, 2 July 1984; Fortune, 11 June 1984; "Japanese Multinational Facts and Figures", Oriental Economist, 1983 and 1984; UNCTC, Transnational Banks: Operations, Strategies and Their Effects in Developing Countries (New York: UN, 1981), Sales No. E.81.II.A.7.

a/ As of 31 March 1982.
b/ 1978.
c/ Data only for affiliates in the United States.

Note: Only those companies were included whose basic activity is in services.

Table I-26. The world's largest service TNCs, by industry

	Trading (Revenue, Rank $bn) 1984	Banking (Revenue $bn) 1984	Reinsurance (Total net premium income, $bn) 1982	Accounting (Revenue $bn) 1983	Advertising (Gross income $bn) 1982	Market research (Sales $bn) 1982	Airlines a/ (Passenger RPKs, b/ $bn) 1983	Airlines (Cargo FTKs, c/ millions) 1983	Hotels d/ (Thousand rooms) 1983	Fast food e/ restaurant chains (No. of units worldwide) 1983	Data processing industry, W. Europe (Revenue $bn) 1983	Data processing industry, world (Revenue $bn) 1984
1	Mitsui & Co Ltd. Japan 68.6	Citicorp USA 20.5	Munich Re FRG 3.5	Arthur Andersen USA 1.2	Dentsu Japan 0.40	Nielsen USA 0.433	Pan Am USA 46.4	Flying Tigers USA 2.9	Holiday Inns USA 310.3	McDonalds Corp. USA 7589	IBM USA 10.8	IBM USA 44.3
2	Mitsubishi Corp. Japan 66.9	Bank America USA 14.4	Swiss Re Switzerl. 2.9	Peat Marwick, USA 1.2	Young & Rubicam USA 0.3	IMS USA 0.125	TWA USA 44.3	JAL Japan 2.3	Sheraton Corp. USA 124.0	KFC Corp. USA 6969	Bull, France 1.4	Digital Equipment Corp., USA 6.2
3	C Itoh & Co. Ltd. Japan 56.9	Bank Leumi Israel BM Israel 12.9	General Re USA 1.3	Coopers & Lybrand USA 1.1	Ted Bates USA 0.36	SAMI USA 0.085	British Airways UK 34.4	Air France France 1.9	Ramada Intl. USA 95.6	Intl. Dairy Queen USA 4763	Siemens FRG 1.4	Burroughs Corp. USA 4.5
4	Marubeni Corp. Japan 50.9	Barclays Group UK 12.3	Gerling FRG 0.7	Price Waterhouse USA 1.0	J.Walter Thompson USA 0.35	Arbitron USA 0.080	JAL Japan 32.2	Lufthansa FRG 1.9	Hilton Hotels Corp. USA 88.9	Pizza Hut USA 4300	Olivetti Italy 1.3	Control Data Corp. USA 3.8
5	Sumitomo Corp. Japan 49.8	Banque Nationale de Paris France 11.4	Employers Re USA 0.6	Arthur Young USA 1.0	Ogilvy & Mather USA 0.31	AGB Research UK 0.074	Air France France 27.6	KLM Netherland 1.9	Quality Intl. USA 73.5	Burger King USA 3499	Digital, USA 1.1	NCR Corp. USA 3.7

	Trading (Revenue Rank $bn) 1984	Banking (Revenue $bn) 1984	Reinsurance (Total net premium income, $bn) 1982	Accounting (Revenue $bn) 1983	Advertising (Gross income $bn) 1982	Market research (Sales $bn) 1982	Airlines a/ (Passenger RPKs, b/ $bn) 1983	Airlines (Cargo FTKs, c/ millions) 1983	Hotels d/ (Thousand rooms) 1983	Fast food e/ restaurant chains (No. of units worldwide) 1983	Data processing industry, W. Europe (Revenue $bn) 1983	Data processing industry, world (Revenue $bn) 1984
6	Sears, Roebuck USA 38.8	National Westminster Bank Plc,UK 11.1	Mercantile General Re,UK 0.6	Ernst & Whinney USA 0.9	McCann-Erickson USA 0.28	Burke MS USA 0.052	Lufthansa FRG 22.7	Pan Am USA 1.0	Trust-house, Forte UK 72.0	Baskin-Robbins Ice Cream USA 2770	ICL UK 1.0	Fujitsu Ltd. Japan 3.5
7	Nissho Iwai Corp. Japan 35.1	Crédit Lyonnais, France 10.9	Cologne Re FRG 0.5	Deloitte Haskins & Sells USA 0.9	BBDO Intl. USA 0.24	Research Intl. UK 0.048	Air Canada Canada 19.6	British Airways UK 0.9	Imperial Group UK 61.3	Wendy's Intl. USA 2671	Burroughs Corp. USA 1.0	Sperry Corp. USA 3.5
8	Kmart USA 22.1	Midland Bank Group UK 10.3	Prudential Re USA 0.4	KMG Main Hurdman, UK,Jap, FRG, 0.9	Leo Burnett Co USA 0.22	Infratest FRG 0.032	KLM Netherlands 15.9	United USA 0.9	Accor France 56.8	Hardee's USA 2180	Nixdorf FRG 0.9	Hewlett-Packard USA 3.4
9	Safeway Stores USA 19.6	Chase Manhattan USA 9.9	SCOR, France 0.4	Touche Ross USA 0.8	Saatchi & Saatchi Compton USA/UK 0.19	Market Facts USA 0.025	Iberia Spain 15.6	American USA 0.8	Marriott Corp. USA 53.8	Kozo Sushi Center Japan 2060	Philips Netherlands 0.8	NEC Corp. Japan 2.8
10	Toyo Menka Kaisha Ltd. Jap 18.6	Société Générale France 9.8	Frankona Re FRG 0.4	...	Foote, Cone & Belding USA 0.18	GFK Nuernberg FRG 0.024	Saudia Saudi Arabia 14.6	Alitalia Italy 0.6	Club Médi-terranée France 47.7	Chef & Brewer UK 1500	Hewlett Packard USA 0.8	Siemens AG FRG 2.8

Sources: Based on Forbes, 29 July 1985; International Insurance Monitor, April/May 1984; Advertising Age, 18 April 1983, 18 July 1983; Air Transport World, No.10, 1984; Hotels & Restaurants International, March 1984, August 1984; Datamation, June 1984, June 1985; and Datamation DP Industry Survey 1984; and various UNCTC publications.

a/ IATA airlines. Three US airlines (United, American, Eastern) have not been included, because their operations are mainly domestic.
b/ Revenue passenger kilometers. Scheduled services.
c/ Freight tonne kilometers.
d/ All hotel chains (TNCs and domestic).
e/ Some of the listed companies are mainly domestically oriented.

Table I-27. The sectoral distribution of acts of takeovers, by sector,
1960-1979
(Per cent)

Sector	1960-64	1965-69	1970-75	1976-79
Agriculture	10.9	7.4	8.9	8.0
Mining	7.3	14.8	11.9	14.3
Petroleum	14.5	17.2	19.6	19.5
Manufacturing	25.5	25.9	28.6	23.8
Finance	12.7	12.3	11.9	11.5
Other[a]	29.1	22.4	19.1	22.9
TOTAL	100.0	100.0	100.0	100.0

Source: Stephen J. Kobrin, "Expropriation as an Attempt to Control Foreign
Firms in LDCs: Trends from 1960 to 1979", International Studies Quarterly, 28
(1984), p. 336.
   a/ Mostly other services and utilities.

Table I-28. Foreign insurance affiliates in developing
countries, by region, 1968, 1982
(Number of affiliates)

Region	1968	1982	Percentage change
Africa	674	114	-83
Asia	705	384	-46
Latin America	257	101	-61
TOTAL	1 636	599	-63

Source: Sigma, July 1983, p. 5.

Table I-29. The importance of foreign banks in selected developed
countries: foreign banks' assets as percentages of
total assets of all banks, 1960-1981

Host country	Year				
	1960	1970	1973	1979	1981
Luxembourg a/	8.0	57.8	77.6	86.0	85.5
United Kingdom	...	...	...	59.0	60.2
Belgium	8.2 b/	22.5	28.6	35.5	46.8
Netherlands	...	...	...	13.0	18.0
France	7.2	12.3	14.1	14.3	17.4
United States	...	...	3.4	9.7	13.4
Switzerland	...	11.0	11.4	10.8	11.6
Spain	...	0.6	0.6	3.1	8.2
Federal Republic of Germany	0.5	1.4	...	3.2	3.6
Japan c/	...	...	1.6	2.6	2.5
Italy	...	...	...	1.5	2.3
Denmark	-	-	0.1	0.9	1.0
Austria c/	...	1.1	1.0	1.2	0.9

Source: R. M. Pecchioli, The Internationalization of Banking: The Policy
Issues (Paris: OECD, 1983).
    a/ Belgian-owned banks are not considered foreign banks.
    b/ 1958.
    c/ Foreign branches only.

Table I-30. Selected airlines: patterns of related activities, fiscal year 1983

Airlines	Operating revenues (Million dollars)	Tour operations	Hotel interests	Car rentals	Association with other airlines a/	Other related interests b/	Incidental revenues as percentage of total 1983 revenue
Developed countries							
Aer Lingus	270	X	X		X	X	35.6
Air Canada	1 739	X			X	X	2.2
Air France	2 813	X	X		X	X	3.7
Alitalia	1 601		X		X	X	16.3
American Airlines	4 532		X		...	X	7.5
British Airways	...	X	X		X	X	...
British Caledonian Airways	574	X	X		X	X	4.7
CP Air	702	X		X	...	X	3.8
Eastern Airlines	3 942				X	X	7.3
Finnair	359	X	X		...	X	
Iberia	1 505	X	X		...	X	13.2
Japan Air Lines	3 094		X		X	X	3.0
KLM	1 628	X	X		X	X	15.3
Lufthansa	...	X	X	X	X	X	...
Pan Am	3 529	X	X	X	X	X	4.9
Qantas	...	X	X		...	X	...
Sabena	740	X	X		X	X	22.6
SAS	1 665	X	X		X	X	17.6
Swissair	1 435	X	X		X	X	5.8
Trans World Airlines	3 332	X	X		...	X	8.3
United Airlines	5 286	X	X		...	X	5.2
Union de Transports Aeriens-UTA	751	X	X		X	X	28.7
Developing countries							
Air India	755	X	X		X	X	4.6
Avianca	...	X			...	X	...
Korean Airlines	1 201	X			...	X	10.9
Pakistan International	5 861	X	X	X	X	X	...
Philippine Airlines	...	X			...	X	...
Singapore Airlines	1 291	X	X		X	X	2.2
VARIG	807		X		X	X	0.2

Sources: Annual reports; ICAO, Financial Digest, 1983; World Air Transport Statistics, 1984; and Moody's International Manual, 1984.

a/ Refers to ownership and other links among airlines.
b/ Including such miscellaneous activities as catering airport ground services, world-wide aviation insurance and re-insurance international merchant banking, etc.

Note: X signifies activities in this area.

II

Data Services and Their Impact

A. The rise of data-service industries

Transborder data flows and the data technologies that make them possible are an outgrowth of microelectronics-based developments in informatics and telecommunications.[1] In informatics, technological developments have dramatically decreased the physical size of electronic data-processing devices and the price of computing power, and increased their robustness, computing speed, memory capacity, reliability, accessibility, and user-friendliness. As a result, electronic data-processing devices have become versatile instruments which are being used in a rapidly increasing range of applications, both in service and manufacturing industries. The versatility and accessibility of computer systems have increased as developments in telecommunications have come to permit the remote input and output of data, first through the traditional telephone network, then increasingly through special networks for digital data. Public national data networks are in existence or nearing completion in virtually all developed and a few developing countries. They are complemented by expanding public or quasi-public regional and international networks, both of a terrestrial and a satellite variety. Falling data-transmission costs,[2] coupled with improvements in the reliability, quality and speed of transmissions, have led to a considerable rise in the use of data telecommunication facilities. The telecommunication infrastructure is particularly important for trade in data services because without it, access cannot be gained to data resources located elsewhere.

The rapid advances in both data-processing and telecommunication technologies over the past decade have led to their convergence into a new activity, telematics, and the rise of computer communication. It is estimated that this kind of communication—which is considered one of the perhaps four most fundamental changes in the history of communication technology[3]—increased at a rate of about 28% per annum in the US during the 1970s (and may continue to rise at this rate for decades to come) and "has now become the seminal medium in the changing world of communications."[4] A key aspect of data communication is that, apart from just delivering messages, it can also create and transform messages through the artificial intelligence provided by the various data services and, in this manner, reduce information overload.[5]

The merger of informatics and telecommunications can be exemplified by the corporate strategies of the principal corporations within these two industries: IBM and ATT (see table II-1 and fig. II-1). Both used to be corporations that did

Figure II-1.   IBM and ATT in the telematics market, 1985

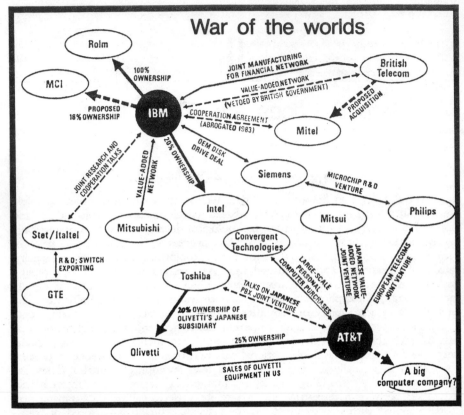

Source: *The Economist*, 29 June 1985, p. 63.

not favor joint ventures with other firms. This has changed drastically under the
impact of technological developments and competitive pressures. In fact, both
companies have embarked on a global struggle, involving far-flung alliances, to
secure their share of the world information-technology market. In the process,
the character of both companies is changing. Traditionally, IBM built computers
and ATT carried messages. Today, both computers and telephones operate on the
basis of data technologies. Thus, while ATT sells computers to be used on its
communication networks, IBM markets communication networks to accompany
its computers. The moves of both corporations during 1984 and 1985 bear this
out.

IBM, the premier corporation in the international computer market, was a
partner (together with Aetna Life Insurance) in Satellite Business Systems (SBS),
a satellite-based communication system designed primarily for the transmission of
data. It sold its share to MCI Communications (the second largest long-distance
telephone company in the US) in June 1985 and took a stake (which may reach
up to 30%) in MCI. With this acquisition, IBM entered the telecommunication

market and put itself in direct competition with ATT. This is as yet the most dramatic example of the convergence of the telecommunication and computer fields. Further, IBM had announced, in May 1984, its intention to enter the local-area-network market and acquired, in the autumn of that year, Rolm Corporation, an important producer of private branch exchanges (which play an increasing role in intra-office and local-area communication). IBM entered during the same year in a joint venture with Merrill Lynch, the largest US brokerage house, to develop a new computerized information-and-order-execution system for brokers, for which Merrill Lynch alone has committed $90 million over the next several years. In February 1984, IBM announced that it would develop, together with CBS and Sears, Roebuck and Co., a nationwide commercial videotex service for home shopping, banking and information services.

ATT, the world's largest telecommunication corporation until the end of 1983, agreed to a reorganization which became effective on 1 January 1984. As part of the agreement, it divested itself of about $120 billion in assets to form seven independent regional telephone companies in order to obtain permission to enter, among other things, the data-processing market. Within four months, ATT had entered the computer market-place with a range of six computers and had arranged a co-operation agreement with Olivetti to enter the office-equipment market and, in particular, to establish itself in the desk-top computer market. In June 1985, ATT announced that it had formed a joint venture with Chemical Bank, Time Inc. and BankAmerica. The purpose of the venture—to be initially based on Chemical Bank's Pronto home-banking service which had, at that time, 20,000 customers in 16,000 households—would be to provide such videotex services as home banking, home shopping, brokerage services, news, and ticket reservations. This venture would challenge Trintex, a similar joint venture between CBS, Sears, Roebuck & Company and IBM. Later that month, ATT and Quotron (an electronic information group) announced plans to develop and sell a sophisticated computer-based financial information system through which, for example, stock transactions can be executed. The first customer of the system will be Shearson Lehman Brothers (a subsidiary of American Express) which, eventually, will link it to its 5,500 brokerage branches in the US. With this venture, ATT will compete directly with the IBM-Merrill Lynch venture mentioned earlier. This is another strategic move through which ATT is expanding into the highly competitive, though fast-growing, market for electronically delivered market and financial information.[6] It would not be surprising if ATT's next move were to acquire a major computer company.

This blurring of the boundaries is not limited to the leaders of their respective fields. Technological developments are changing the shape of the data industry as a whole. While in the past the manufacturers of various data goods and services were normally separate companies, the distinction between market segments is increasingly disappearing (see table II-1). As a result, manufacturers of data goods and services are competing in a market with few boundaries.

In what follows, attention is given chiefly to the principal data services associated with telematics: data processing, software, information storage and retrieval (data bases), and telecommunication services, because they are at the heart of trade and FDI in data services. Each of these industries has experienced substantial growth since the mid-1970s.

The most important component of the data-services industry is *data processing* (including time-sharing), an activity which involves the tabulation, analysis and other transformation of data inputs in a computer. In 1980, the data-processing market in the OECD countries amounted to $21 billion; by the end of 1984, this market was estimated to have reached a volume of over $40 billion (see table II-2). Over half of the market is located in the US, where revenues nearly doubled between 1980 and 1984—from $12 billion to $22 billion. The corresponding figures for Western Europe were $7 billion and $14 billion. No figures are available for the socialist and developing countries, but it can be assumed that the volume of data processing in at least the latter is small.[7]

As hardware prices fall and make it less necessary to utilize external processing capabilities, the relative importance of data processing in total computer services has declined and that of *software* increased. Software consists of the machine-readable programs, procedures and rules, the application of which makes possible the performance of certain tasks by the electronic devices comprising a computer system. In 1980, the software market in the OECD countries amounted to $4 billion; by the end of 1984, this market had reached $13 billion (see table II-2). Again, over half of the market is located in the US, where software sales increased from $2 billion in 1980 to $7 billion in 1984. In Western Europe, the market quadrupled during the same period from $1 billion to $4 billion. These figures do not include the value of firmware and in-house software production of, for instance, banks; for 1981, the value of these services was estimated at $43 billion, more than half of it in the US.[8] As in the case of data processing, no figures exist for the socialist and developing countries, and again the share of at least the latter is likely to be small.[9]

The *information storage and retrieval industry* consists of off-line and on-line data bases. The market for international on-line data-bases alone has been estimated at roughly $1.5–2 billion in revenue terms in 1979.[10] While perhaps as much as 90% of these revenues accrued to corporations in the US at the beginning of the 1980s, revenues of Western European corporations operating in this market are growing faster (though on a smaller base) than those of their US counterparts (see table II-3). If projected growth rates should have proven to be correct, the three most important market segments in the US in 1985 should have been credit information ($700 million), marketing ($510 million), and economics and finance ($450 million). In Western Europe, the leading areas were expected to be economics and finance ($320 million), industry ($224 million) and econometrics ($201 million). The rapid expansion of the market is fuelled particularly by the growing conversion of public data bases from an off-line to an on-line mode. Worldwide, the total number of on-line data bases rose from about 400 in 1979 to 2,800 in 1985, an average annual growth rate of about 40% a year; over the same time period, the number of data-base producers rose from 200 to 1,300 (see table II-4).[11] Figures on the completion of public data networks and the growth of network termination points—i.e., points at which user equipment (normally a computer terminal) is connected with a data-transmission network—suggest that this growth rate will continue in the near future. In addition, the rapid spread of personal computers, word processors and dedicated terminals, combined with new technological developments in data conversion, storage, manipulation, retrieval, and transmission will further fuel the growth of this industry, as will increasing awareness and understanding of the importance of information technology. An important impetus could also come from the standardization of data-base access and software which would increase compatibility among different systems, facilitating communication and reducing learning costs users incur in utilizing new systems. While all these processes also affect the socialist and developing countries, their participation in the international on-line data-base market is, for the time being, negligible.[12]

Telecommunication services are evolving rapidly with the increasing application of microelectronics and the development of new transmission infrastructures based on satellites and fiber optic cables. The importance of these services can be gleaned from data for the US, where domestic revenues amounted to $84 billion in 1981.[13] More relevant to data traffic (although just a proxy variable) are network-termination points (NTPs). The number of NTPs in Western Europe was expected nearly to triple from 600,000 in 1981 to 1.7 million in 1987 (see table II-5); the actual number of terminals using telecommunication services will almost quadruple over the same period—from 1.1 million to 4.2 million.[14] In 1981, the UK was, in Western Europe, the leading country as far as the number of installed NTPs was concerned, although in terms of NTPs per 1,000 members of the working population, Sweden (12) and Luxembourg (10) were ahead of the UK (7). By 1987, the Federal Republic of Germany (FRG) is expected to have nearly caught up with the UK, with a number of other countries, however, having a higher ratio as far as NTPs per 1,000 members of the working population are concerned (see table II-5). The Western European average of 5 in 1981 contrasts with a value of 24 for the US in 1979—an indication of the potential development of telecommunications in Western Europe.[15] In 1981, banking and insurance was the industry with the highest number of NTPs (30% of the total), followed, in some distance, by discrete manufacturing and data-processing services (11%) (see fig. II-2). Both areas were expected to maintain their leading positions in 1987.

Since *telecommunication equipment* is used mainly to provide telecommunication services, data on the growth of this industry can also be used to give an indication of the importance of the services associated with it. Market-economy sales of telecommunication equipment were valued at $41 billion in 1980 and were projected to increase to $58 billion by 1985 (see table II-6). Switching and transmission equipment together account for nearly two thirds of the total. The developed market economies accounted for almost 90% of the total production, the US alone for almost half. This corresponds roughly to the distribution of telephones, of which only 20% are located in developing countries. Approximately four-fifths of the equipment sales of market economies are accounted for by 12 firms, all but one of which are TNCs.[16]

The information provided so far concerns data services, because these services can be rendered (domestically and internationally) via computer-communication systems and, therefore, indicate the potential for TDF. However, the potential for these flows can also be estimated by looking at the growth of *data goods* industries. The reason is that an increasing share of data goods consists, in fact, of data services, especially software (including firmware, i.e., software that is an integral part of hardware). For instance, it has been estimated that software now accounts for more than three-quarters of the total life-cycle cost to the users of large computer systems, the balance being accounted for by hardware.[17] In other words, the data-service contents of some data goods are increasing to such an extent that these goods may, at one point, have to be reclassified as services, to which some

Figure II-2. The distribution of network-termination points in Western Europe, by industry, 1981, 1987[a]

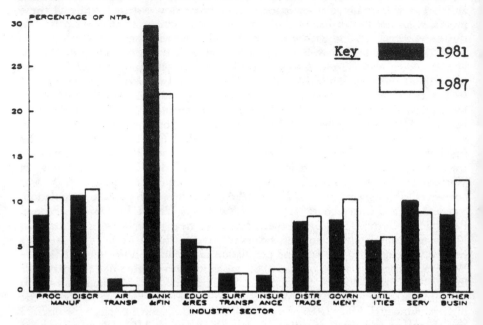

Source: Same as table II-5, p. 13.

 [a] Forecast.

hardware is attached. To the extent that data goods contain data services, the growth of the former implies a growth of the latter.

The market for data-processing equipment in market economies was estimated to amount to $78 billion in 1982, of which 45% represented computers, 38% peripherals and 17% terminals (see table II-7). In each of these market segments, the US accounted for over half of the world market, followed by Western Europe with an average of 30% and Japan with an average of 12%; other market economies, which include the developing countries, accounted on the average for 6% (see table II-8). Computers alone represent less than half of the total value of data-processing equipment. Their share is likely to decline further in the future, since peripherals are expected to grow at somewhat higher rates. In 1980, 87% of general-purpose computers (in terms of value) were installed in developed market economies, compared to 4% in developing countries.[18] The 50 largest data-processing companies (see table II-9) probably account for over four-fifths of the industry's market. In 1984, the 5 largest such companies were headquartered in the US. IBM, which accounted for $44 billion of the $120 billion in data-processing revenues of the largest 50 data-processing companies in 1984, is by far the largest corporation of the industry, followed by Digital Equipment with $6 billion. IBM's profits, in fact, are higher than Digital Equipment's revenues.

All these figures clearly indicate that the data industries have become important industries, that they are growing rapidly and that, for the time being, they are largely concentrated in the developed market economies, especially in the US. In fact, the figures provided here underestimate, for three reasons, the importance of data services. First, as already indicated, data goods contain an increasing share of data services; but this share is difficult to estimate. Secondly, systematic information is only available for services provided in the market; barely any information exists on in-house data services. That both of these factors are important is indicated by the fact that the value of firmware and in-house software production was an estimated $43 billion in 1981, compared to software-market revenues of $4 billion in 1980. And thirdly and finally, data technologies increasingly find their way into other products and hence widen the potential for data services and TDF—a topic to be considered in the next section.

B. Changes in the modus operandi
of existing industries

Data technologies are also spreading to other industries and are changing their modus operandi. The principal manner in which this occurs is that data technologies are finding a widening range of applications in traditional products and processes (see table II-10). In each case, applications depend on data services, especially software, around which these applications are structured and through which they operate. What one observes, therefore, is that as traditional products increasingly incorporate data technologies, they become data goods—which in turn consist increasingly of data services.[19] In fact, some see in this process the beginning of a "second industrial divide" which will give rise to a new paradigm of industrial organization.[20] Although an analysis of these changes goes far beyond the scope of this volume, the following points deserve mention since they help to put the importance of data resources (and especially data services) in a broader and longer-term perspective.[21]

First, and perhaps most important, the ability to use data technology, and especially the ability to adapt and develop it further, acquire a critical role in industrialization in general. With industrial and service production being increasingly based on data technology, a lack of data resources is likely to impose serious constraints on economic development and international competitiveness. Data resources, in fact, may give a special boost to productivity in services in general.

Second, the increased use of electronics in traditional industrial and service production tends to reduce the share of the cost of labor in the value-added of this production and, independently of that, may change significantly the manner in which work is undertaken. As to the first factor, for instance, the costs of components and materials represented approximately 21% of electromechanical calculators in 1964; this percentage increased to 65–70% for electrical calculators in the 1970s. At the same time, the share of labor decreased from 23 to 5–10%.[22] This, of course, has significant implications for all industries in which labor is an important factor of production and for all countries, especially developing ones, in which the price of this factor has traditionally been an important source of international competitiveness. As to the second factor, the use of computer-communication systems may increasingly allow jobs which have traditionally been performed in the office to be performed at home, thus creating "telecommuters."

In the US, perhaps as many as 300 companies (including Apple Computers, J.C. Penney, IBM, Control Data, American Express) had, in 1984, formal or informal telecommuter arrangements, involving perhaps as many as 5% of the US workforce.[23] In other words, to the extent that information-based jobs become more frequent, the potential for the number of jobs that could be done at home increases— which could lead to a revolution in work and life patterns.

Third, islands of computer-assisted activities (consisting of a network of robots and numerically controlled machine tools) are beginning to develop within the principal functional areas in which corporations are traditionally organized. These islands are increasingly linked *within* these functional areas as well as *across* them, thus permitting a new organizational approach to production.[24] (To achieve such integration, protocols have to be established to permit communication among electronic devices. One such protocol—MAP—is discussed briefly below.) In the factory of the future, machine tools will be a piece of peripheral equipment for computers: numerically controlled machine tools and robots will play an increasing role at the product-design stage through computer-aided design (CAD), at the preparatory stage of production through computer-aided manufacturing (CAM), and in the manufacturing process itself through flexible manufacturing systems (FMS), the ultimate goal being full factory automation (FA) (see fig. II-3). Accordingly, the use of electronic capital-goods systems is increasing rapidly, with Japan strongly leading in robots (see table II-11) and the US strongly leading in CAD systems (see table II-12).[25] A well-known and already widespread example is provided by electronic cash registers in supermarkets, which have become data-entry terminals linked to a central computer for maintaining inventory control and to banks for effecting financial transactions. Naturally, the various elements of such a system do not all have to be located in one country, for if they are established at different locations, they can be linked through data flows. An important implication of this development is that traditional (non-communicating) capital goods will increasingly— and perhaps rapidly—become obsolete.

Fourth, the new computer-assisted production technologies increase the flexibility of manufacturing as reprograming can be done relatively easily and quickly to accomplish different tasks. (Some of the principal characteristics of the new manufacturing environment are listed in table II-13.) As a result, the variety of parts and products that can be produced with a given electronic capital-goods system increases, while shorter production cycles can be accommodated. This, in turn, can shorten the obsolescence cycle of products, change plant economies of scale, and permit small-batch production. At the same time, the passage of materials through production systems is speeded up and results in an important efficiency gain. The Japanese automobile company Mazda, for instance, can assemble three different types of cars in one factory and hence reach the required economies of scale through one rather than three factories. This development may have profound implications for industrial organization because it may break the current imperative of long-run mass production and permit the re-emergence of smaller-scale, flexible adaptive companies which offer custom-tailored batches of output as the predominant mode of industrial production.[26]

Finally, as a result of the general tendency for the data-technology contents of goods and services to grow, it becomes increasingly difficult to distinguish between data goods and services and other goods and services. This means that a widening range of goods and services can be classified as data-related and that

Figure II-3. The concept of factory automation

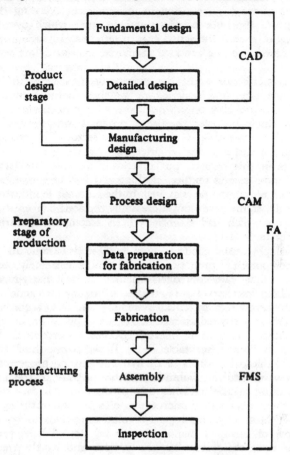

Source: "Japan's CAD Market: The Growth Phase Begins," *Quarterly Survey* (Industrial Bank of Japan), 60 (October-December 1984), p. 1.

the national and international demand for data services is likely to increase substantially. A striking illustration in this regard is telephone-switching equipment. Traditionally, such equipment consisted of electromechanical devices. With the advent of microelectronics, electronic switching equipment based on digital techniques was developed, equipment which is now becoming commonplace. As the transition to fully electronic switching progresses, a rapidly increasing part of the cost of developing a telephone switching system is accounted for by software-development cost, which is generally thought to account for at least 60% of the cost of designing new systems. What the buyer of such a system in fact obtains today is a sophisticated combination of operating systems, application programs and programing aids, plus a special-purpose computer and associated peripheral equipment. The dominance of software costs is even more marked from the customer's point of view, since software maintenance (updating the application programs) comprises the bulk of post-purchase cost—which over the product's lifetime can equal or exceed the actual cost of purchase. In such instances it could reasonably be argued that the product should be seen as falling within the data-service category.

In the *consumer* goods sector, the growing use of data technologies has been apparent for some time (e.g., calculators, watches, home computers, domestic appliances) and it is probably only a question of time until the automated home is a reality. Increasingly, however, the use of products and processes based on data technologies is also observable in the *industrial* sector. The automobile, paper/printing, mechanical and electrical engineering, and machine-tool industries have been the leaders in this respect, but practically all other industries—including such traditional industries as textiles, clothing and leather—have begun to incorporate microelectronic components as well. In the automobile industry, for example, electronic control systems have now successfully replaced conventional mechanical controls, a process which had essentially been accomplished during the period 1979 to 1981 (see table II-14).

These developments have led a recent OECD study to conclude that "Whereas ten years ago, computerized numerical control was an extremely costly technique, seldom found in numerically-controlled machine tools, it has almost become the norm now. Similarly, microprocessors are quickly coming into general use for robot control, and minicomputers in CAD systems."[27] In fact, according to a study undertaken in 1984, a weighted average of 51% of all plants in the FRG employing more than 20 people were using microelectronics, a percentage that was 47 in the UK and 38 in France (see table II-15). Between one-third and one-half of these plants used microelectronics in their manufacturing processes. Applications in products, however, still lag behind, probably because of the time needed to move products using microelectronics into production. All data suggest that the growth rate of the application of microelectronics in manufacturing is accelerating sharply and that "a quiet technological revolution appears to be gathering pace at the grassroots of Europe's manufacturing industry."[28] It is probably safe to assume that the same observation applies to Japan and North America.

The blurring of the boundaries between data resources and other goods and services is also reflected in the changing character of corporations. IBM, for instance, entered the market of sophisticated capital goods in 1984 by offering a range of robotics and manufacturing systems which offer a building-block approach to factory automation based on standard IBM computer technology. Apparently, IBM's goal is to become the world's leading supplier of computer-integrated manufacturing systems.[29] Most dramatic, however, has been a recent wave of acquisitions of data-resource capabilities by major automobile producers. In 1984, *General Motors* acquired Electronic Data Systems for $2.5 billion, at that time the world's largest independent data-processing company. In 1985, GM bought Hughes Aircraft for $5 billion, which is an important electronics supplier and satellite producer and has considerable experience with flexible manufacturing systems. Apparently, GM aims at linking all of its computer and telecommunication system "to give GM an integrated information system that would link the factory floor with the chairman's office".[30] This system would include the design and production of models, the provision of supplies by any of GM's 30,000 US suppliers and the ordering of products by customers from any of GM's 16,000 domestic dealers. Similarly, *Ford* Motor Company announced in May 1985 that it was buying an interest (for $20 million) in the American Robot Corporation, following a joint project Ford had initiated with the General Electric Company to produce electric motors in a highly automated, computerized factory. Ford's objective was to acquire the technology needed to coordinate production on the factory floor by computer so as to cut overhead and production costs; in this case, the principal earnings were expected to come from reducing white-collar staff.[31] *Chrysler* moved in the same direction when, in 1985, it bought Gulfstream Aerospace for $640 million. In Europe, *Daimler-Benz* undertook similar moves when, in 1985, it acquired Dornier, an aerospace company, and AEG, a company that is also active in such fields as telecommunications, satellite technology, microelectronics, and automated office systems. This strategy of increased reliance on data technology has repercussions beyond the companies directly involved. In the UK, for instance, Ford is reported to have informed its suppliers that, by the end of the 1980s, contracts may be conditioned on suppliers having CAD equipment. Austin Rover is already further along the automation path. It informed its suppliers that it would have its automated equipment in place before the end of 1985 and expected its suppliers to follow suit.[32]

One reason for this rapid acquisition of electronics, aerospace and other high-technology firms by automobile corporations is certainly the desire to diversify into new, high-technology fields with strong growth prospects. But another reason is certainly the need to acquire the technology and experience required to automate the production process and to increase the electronic contents of cars. In the process, traditional automobile firms acquire more and more the character of data-resource corporations; GM, in fact, is now thirty-fifth on the list of the world's largest data-processing companies (see table II-9).

Another indication of the blurring of the boundaries between data-resource companies and traditional industrial firms is the involvement of the latter in a core area of data technology, namely the development of standards for communication among programmable devices. This can be illustrated by the leadership role GM has played in this regard.[33] In 1984, GM was using 40,000 programmable devices on its plant floors, a number that is expected to increase to 200,000 by 1990. Only 15% of these devices communicate with others, principally because the devices are bought from different manufacturers and are hence often incompatible. This is inefficient, as it prevents progress toward a computer-integrated automated plant and creates considerable costs in establishing communication among devices. In fact, approximately 30–50% of the costs for new automation involve communication costs. It is therefore in the interest of the user to develop standards for factory networking, i.e., protocols that permit communication among electronic devices so that the islands of automation can be interconnected without a need to develop special software for each computer-to-computer link. Accordingly, GM set up a task force in 1980 which, on the basis of the "open systems interconnection" (OSI) standard, developed a "manufacturing automation protocol" (MAP), i.e., a standard set of communication specifications to interconnect its automated facilities on the factory floor.

Naturally, the usefulness of MAP is increased if other firms, especially GM suppliers, also adopt it. In addition, GM has an interest in convincing unrelated firms to adopt this standard as well. The reason is simple: if a large number of firms demand products with certain specifications, the suppliers of automated equipment have to produce them. This, in turn, leads to low-cost standardized products. Thus, GM sponsored, in cooperation with the McDonnell Douglas Corporation, a one-day workshop in March 1984 (attended by 39 companies), to present an overview of the MAP specifications. A follow-up workshop two months later was attended by 56 companies and another one in September 1984 by over 200 companies. On that occasion, a "MAP User Group" was formally established. Its objectives are to adopt a standard set of communication specifications using MAP as a baseline; to generate user pressure to accelerate the acceptance of such standards; and to encourage computer and device manufacturers to produce products that embody these standards. GM estimated that, by the end of December 1984, 50 firms had endorsed the protocol, including IBM, Digital Equipment Corporation, Ford, Boeing, Westinghouse, General Electric, Intel, and Motorola.[34] Then, in March 1985, a meeting took place in London at which a number of potential European users and suppliers of MAP-based products participated. In October of the same year, the European MAP User Group was formally established under the leadership of UNILEVER. Given the importance of the corporations that participate in this endeavor and the fact that MAP incorporates communication standards that are already available, it is likely that GM will succeed in bringing about an international standard for factory-floor automation. It is immaterial, incidentally, whether or not the individual devices that are being connected are located at one location or at several, at home or abroad. MAP permits, if need arises, transborder data communication at the factory floor, an issue that will be discussed further in the context of the importance of transborder data flows for transnational corporations.

In the light of this growing application of data technologies—of which this section has only given a glimpse—it is not surprising that the location of, and access to, data-resources are increasingly regarded as being of strategic importance for economic development.

C. Changes in international economic transactions

The extension of the merger of informatics and telecommunication into the international realm has given rise to transborder data flows. They were defined earlier as point-to-point movements of machine-readable data across national boundaries, increasingly via transnational computer-communication systems.[35] Data have, of course, moved across national boundaries before the advent of telematics. But it is the speed, accessibility and interactive capability made possible by the fusion of advanced electronic processing with modern telecommunication facilities that give transborder data flows their special importance.

Systematic data on the number of transnational computer-communication systems exist only for Austria, Brazil and Japan.[36] In Austria, 146 transnational computer-communication links existed in 1985 (see table II-16). In Brazil, the number of these links increased from 3 in 1979 to 29 at the beginning of 1982 (see the configuration in fig. II-4) and then doubled to 57 at the end of 1983 (see table II-16). In Japan, the number of systems tripled from 40 in 1974 to 121 in 1979, and then more than tripled again to 372 in 1983 (see table II-17). Particularly noteworthy is the extraordinary rise of systems in the manufacturing sector during the past four years, although trade and banking corporations also continued to add capacities. As the data for all three countries indicate, most transnational computer-communication links can be found in service industries, although a substantial number also exist in the manufacturing sector.

These transnational computer-communication systems are the conduits for data traffic and the reason why international economic exchanges are undergoing considerable changes. These changes manifest themselves in a number of ways: trade and FDI in data industries have become international economic activities in their own right; TDF are becoming the infrastructure for trade in goods and especially services; the modalities of the operations of TNCs are being redefined; and the tradeability of certain services is increasing.

However, the measurement of these changes is difficult. Only a relatively small share of trade in data services (perhaps not more than 10–20%) occurs on a commercial basis, i.e., at arm's-length prices in the markets for data processing, software, information storage and retrieval, and telecommunication services. But even for these services, no balance-of-payments data are collected which would permit a systematic comparative analysis. The same is true of FDI in data services and data-service sales by foreign affiliates. Data services are, of course, also rendered within transnational corporate systems, i.e., in the form of intra-firm trade. In other words, instead of buying for instance data-processing services from an unrelated computer service bureau, a TNC may establish its own corporate computer center through which data-service requirements for the corporate system as a whole are fulfilled. No figures on the value of these corporate transborder data flows exist, and it is very likely that the procedures used to determine internal transfer prices for data services and to allocate the costs of these services among the various units of a transnational corporate system vary considerably among corporations and do not necessarily always reflect market values. Similarly, no figures exist for the value of infrastructure TDF, be it in the context of trade in goods and services or FDI. Under these circumstances, a good part of the assessment of the international importance of data services has to rely on proxy measures, e.g., trade and FDI in data goods. In addition, recourse has to be had to a qualitative rather than quantitative analysis of the phenomenon, e.g., as regards the importance of TDF for trade in goods and services and the operations of TNCs.

1. Trade and foreign direct investment in data services

Data services, like data goods, can be brought to foreign markets either through trade or through foreign direct investment. No systematic data exist on the magnitude of foreign direct investment in data services. However, if data on the activities of corporations in *data-goods* industries are taken as a proxy variable— and a good part of their activities consists of data services—they indicate that a substantial share of their revenues is derived from abroad (see table II-9). For a number of the largest corporations (e.g., IBM, Burroughs, NCR, Hewlett Packard) foreign revenues are about 40% of total revenues and a good part of foreign revenues is generated by foreign affiliates. In Western Europe, for instance, 6 of the largest 10 suppliers of computer services are US-owned firms, and 3 of these are major hardware producers.[37] Clearer data are available for France. French computer-service firms received 15% of their services from foreign affiliates in 1983

Figure II-4. International communication links of Brazil, March 1982

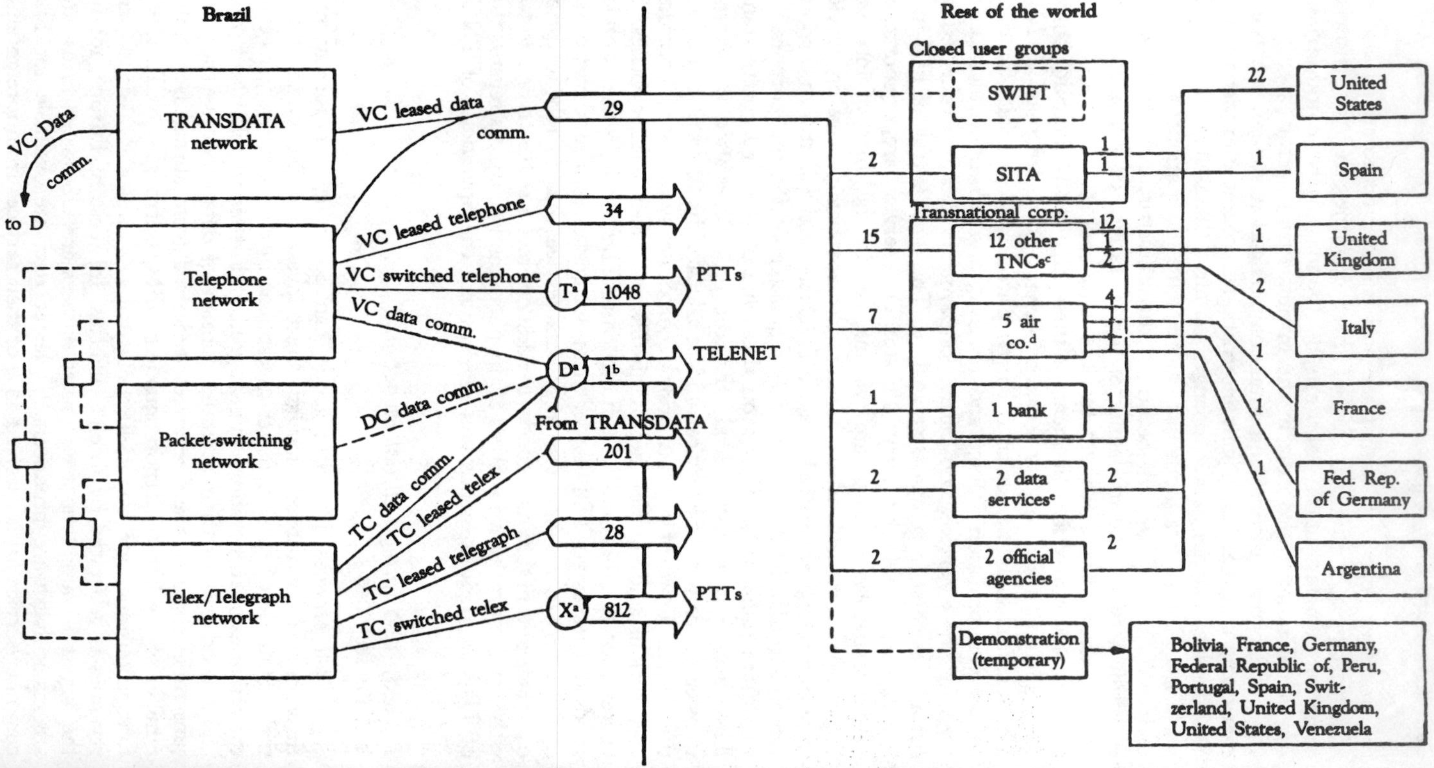

Key   Interconnection interface:
VC Voice channels
TC Telegraph channels
DC Data communication channels
‥‥‥ Link being installed
—— Existing link

Source: Transborder Data Flows and Brazil, op. cit.

[a] Gateways in Rio de Janeiro: T = Telephone; X = Telex; D = Data (TELENET node being tested).
[b] Single voice channel being tested.
[c] Including 3 Brazilian transnational corporations.
[d] Including 1 Brazilian airline corporation.
[e] All Brazilian corporations.

(see table II-18), nearly half of which were from affiliates located in other Western European countries.[38]

In trade, United States exports of *software* and *data processing* amounted to $3 billion in 1981, up from $2.4 billion in 1980 (see table II-19). Exports of software products accounted for 22% of total software revenues in 1981, while exports in processing, professional services and integrated systems accounted for an average of 8% to 10% of total revenues.[39] But even for these figures the extent to which they include service sales by US computer hardware manufacturers is far from clear. Clearer data are again available for France. They show that 6% of total French computer-service revenues were earned through exports in 1983, up 7% from 1982 (see table II-18). The developing countries' share in software trade is minimal, although the shares of a few show considerable increases. Indian exports, for instance, increased from $0.7 million in 1975/76 to $24 million in 1982/83.[40]

A separate and unique form of commercial TDF consists of *remote-sensing data*—data generated by the examination, study, exploration and monitoring of the earth and its resources from satellites. The uniqueness lies in the fact that remote sensing not only permits the transmission of data between countries, but also involves the creation of new data about particular countries and their dissemination to other countries.[41] Until 1986, the US operated the only remote-sensing system—Landsat—which provides commercially available data. (In 1986 the French system SPOT became operational.) In the US (and, as far as we know, in other countries as well), the most important users of remote-sensing data are corporations and the government. Average sales to corporations in the US between fiscal years 1979/1980 and 1981/1982 accounted for 41% of the photographic frames and 53% of the computer-compatible tapes sold. Large TNCs in oil, natural gas and minerals have been the most important users of remote-sensing data and a number of them employ these data routinely as one input into their decision-making process. Several major oil companies maintain extensive in-house Landsat libraries and are expanding their photo-interpretation and digital-analysis capabilities. Some of those corporations employ 10 to 20 professionals to work with remote-sensing data, invest annually up to $200,000 for the acquisition of data alone and usually have their own processing capabilities. The number of remote-sensing satellite systems will certainly increase in the near future, with perhaps six or more systems operational by the end of this decade. This reflects the growing importance of remote-sensing data as one important data source for the management of oil and of mineral and agricultural resources.

Little information exists on the value of trade in *information storage and retrieval*. Since on-line data bases are routinely accessed from abroad—especially within Western Europe and between Western Europe and the United States—the volume of trade may be considerable and expanding rapidly with the increasing number of data bases becoming available on-line. At the moment, however, the international share of the industry appears to be rather small, an indication perhaps of the internationalization potential of the industry. For instance, in 1982, merely 19% of the $14 billion revenues of the US information service industry (data-base development, on-line information services, document-supply services and customized search and abstracting services) came from abroad, be it from exports or foreign affiliates (see table II-20). Growth rates suggest that the domestic market continues to be more dynamic for US firms over the immediate future, although a number of firms seem to believe that the domestic market for some data-base services has matured and that foreign markets may acquire greater importance.[42]

Some systematic data exist, however, for Sweden.[43] Total on-line use of data bases in Sweden increased from 10,000 hours in 1979 to 16,000 hours in 1981 to 26,000 hours in 1983 to 35,000 hours in 1984. In 1983, 45% of this use involved Swedish data bases, 26% US data bases, 25% Western European data bases, and 4% Canadian data bases. Foreign use of Swedish data bases amounted to 5,000 hours in 1983.

In *telecommunications*, 60% of world traffic over telephone-grade circuits was routed over the transatlantic axis and about 20% over the transpacific axis in 1979.[44] The value of international telephone revenues related to the US alone rose from $600 million in 1970 to $3 billion in 1980, for an annual growth rate of 18% over the period (see table II-21).[45] An important role in the growth of international telecommunication traffic is played by international value-added networks. Apart from merely transporting data, these networks have such value-added features as packet switching, automatic rerouting, intermediate storage, various compatibility services, maintenance-related support services and electronic mail services. The operators of value-added networks normally lease lines from basic carriers (e.g., ATT in the US, the PTTs in Western Europe) and combine them with computer equipment of their own, thus creating an enhanced communication network dedicated solely to data transmission. International packet-switched networks of this kind can be created by the linking-up of national networks, a process that is virtually completed among developed market economies and also involves a growing number of developing countries (see fig. II-5). In addition, a number of networks have been created (principally through operating agreements with PTTs) with the specific purpose of providing regional or international services to the public. Most notable among them are such networks as TELENET, TYMNET and UNINET (see table II-22). They link virtually all developed market economies but leave out, at least for the moment, most developing countries.[46] TYMNET and TELENET are also linked, via Vienna (Radio Austria), with the socialist countries. These countries have a network of their own which is star-shaped and centered on Moscow (see fig. II-6).

Information available for Western Europe suggests that the number of transactions between data-communication users per average working day will increase from approximately 136 million transactions in 1979 to almost 800 million in 1987; of these, the share of international transactions is expected to rise from 10 to 15%.[47] The countries with the highest volume of TDF are the UK, Sweden, Belgium, the Federal Republic of Germany, and Italy which together accounted for three-fourths of Western Europe's total TDF in 1979. The UK's very high share of nearly one-quarter in this total is founded on its traditional role as a communication and service center (partly stemming from the colonial era), the attractiveness of London as a location for regional headquarters of TNCs, and the country's function as the principal gateway of data flows from Western Europe to the US. (More than 3 million daily transactions in 1979, or 25% of all Western European international data transactions, were destined for the US.) Sweden's high share reflects the fact that a number of time-sharing bureaux and TNCs with international networks are headquartered in Sweden. Belgium's share, on the other hand, may be attributed to its being the traditional site for regional headquarters of TNCs and also for some data networks (e.g., SWIFT).

96

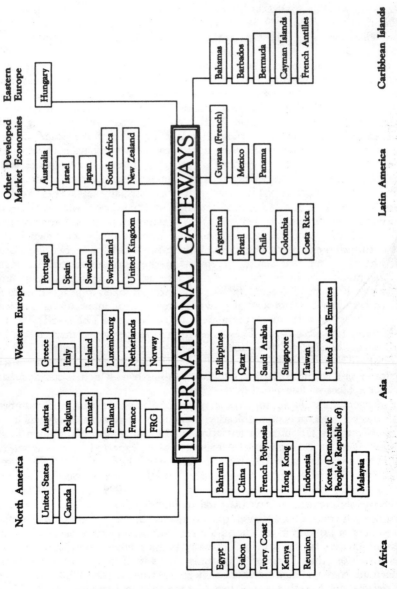

Figure II-5. The international public packet-switched data-transmission network, 1985

Sources: FRG, Federal Ministry of Posts and Telecommunications, *The Deutsche Bundespost: Your Partner for Data Transmission* (Bonn: DBP, 1985) and ITU, *Operational Bulletin,* various issues.

Figure II-6.   The dedicated leased-lines network in socialist countries

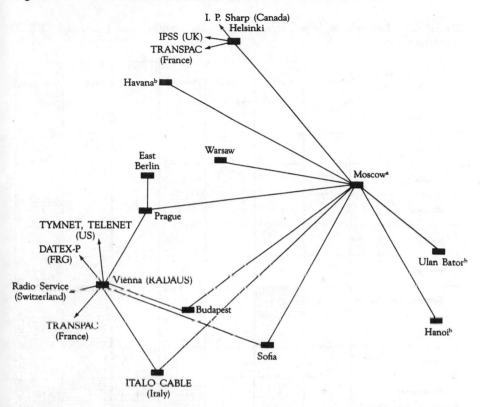

Source: "Adatátviteli Kapcsolat Budapest és Moszkva Koezoett," *Számítástechnika*, 16 (May 1985), pp. 1, 9, and information supplied by Istvan Sebestyen.

[a] All Union Research Institute for Automated Information Systems (VNIIPAS), the switching centre in the USSR for incoming and outgoing information searches. It provides on-line access to, among other things, VINITI, the largest USSR host (containing 28 bibliographical data bases), NTMIK (the data base of the International Centre of Scientific-Technical Information of the CMEA countries), and INION (a data-base host containing social-sciences data bases).
[b] Satellite connections.

The growth of data traffic is also indicated by the development of international leased lines.[48] In the OECD area, the number of these lines rose from nearly 9,000 in 1976 to almost 15,000 in 1981, and the number of those carrying data from about 3,000 in 1976 to nearly 6,000 in 1981. Annual growth rates for individual countries ranged typically from 5% to 20% for international lines generally and from 10% to 30% for data-carrying circuits. The two principal regional clusters of data traffic are North America and Western Europe (see fig. II-7). The two clusters are linked with each other mainly via the UK which, as observed earlier, occupies the position of an intercontinental and intra-Western-European data-traffic hub. This position is strengthened by the UK's low international telecom-

Figure II-7. Network of leased international data circuits among selected OECD countries (Number)

To \ From	Australia	Austria	Canada	Denmark	Finland	France	Germany, Fed. Rep. of
Australia							
Austria				2			33
Canada	1			2			
Denmark		1			7		27
Finland				9			7
France	1	2		2			106
Germany, Fed. Rep. of		33		17	4	53	
Italy		2		2		24	20
Japan							
Netherlands		9		12	1	27	132
Norway				34			7
Spain				2		15	13
Sweden				81	28	3	13
Switzerland		11		2		39	53
United Kingdom	3	6	15	10	1	116	159
United States	31	2	488	3		24	93

Source: Hans Bergendorff, "International Data Communication in the OECD area 1976 and 1981," in Henry Ergas and Jun Okayama, eds., Changing Market Structures in Telecommunications (Amsterdam: North-Holland, 1984), pp. 71–88.

Italy	Japan	Netherlands	Norway	Spain	Sweden	Switzerland	United Kingdom	United States
2								18
2		10				9		
							21	1357
2		10	31	1	98	2	21	
					37			
40	1	30		22	2	44	186	18
16	1	84	6	10	10	44	145	35
		14		9	2	15	41	35
						2	10	140
16			6	6	12	15	145	18
		3			61		21	
5		3				5	21	18
3		10	41	1		2	21	
22	1	20		4			72	35
39	6	132	12		17	34		140
12	22	24		23	2		321	

Key: Less than 10 data circuits ░ 101 – 300 data circuits ▓
10 – 50 data circuits ▤ More than 300 data circuits ■
51 – 100 data circuits ▒

munication tariff which has persuaded about one-third of the US TNCs operating in Europe to hub their computer-communication systems in the UK.[49] The principal international data-traffic hub, however, is the US: in 1981, nearly one-third of the UK's data lines, 97% of the Canadian ones, 86% of the Australian and 71% of the Japanese terminated in the US.

Figures for the trade of equipment also give an indication of the importance of the telecommunication market. Exports of OECD countries in 1980 amounted to about $16 billion, of which approximately 45% were absorbed by developing countries.[50]

Firmer data also exist for trade in *data goods*. The value of the market economies' exports of data-processing equipment doubled between 1978 and 1982, from $7 billion to $14 billion (see table II-23). Ninety-seven percent of these exports were generated by the developed market economies; these countries also absorbed 88% of imports. What percentage of this trade actually consists of data services is not known.

An increasingly important source for transactions in data services is the spread of data technology to existing industries. As pointed out earlier in this chapter, traditional products, processes and services are becoming data-based products, processes and services, and more and more of them are being integrated into larger systems that function through data flows. This, in turn, increases the demand for data-service transactions—be it because of continued linkages through TDF (e.g., data-processing, access to data bases), or through the establishment of on-site servicing facilities (e.g., for maintenance purposes). No data exist on the extent to which this is actually occurring. It is, however, safe to assume that the importance of such transactions will increase as the data technology spreads, the associated activities are organized in systems, the complexity of products, processes and services grows, and the telecommunication infrastructure improves and becomes cheaper.

This phenomenon can be illustrated by the growing trade in numerically controlled machine tools (see table II-24). In the case of Japan, for instance, the share of numerically controlled machine tools in total machine-tool exports increased from 24% in 1976 to 71% in 1981; in the case of the United Kingdom, that share went up from 9% in 1977 to 23% in 1982. Since software is an important part of this equipment, it can be expected that certain numerically controlled machine tools will eventually become integral parts of transnational computer-communication systems and hence the source of TDF. Thus, as industrial production based on data technologies is becoming more common, data-service transactions derived from them will increase as well.

Fragmentary as the data are, they do indicate that trade and FDI in data industries have increased rapidly between the mid-1970s and the mid-1980s. These figures alone do not, however, capture the actual importance of the role of data services in international transactions. The following sections have to be taken into account as well.

2. TDF as infrastructure for trade in goods and services

Increasingly, data flows via transnational computer-communication systems are being used to facilitate, monitor and direct trade in goods and services. By allowing real-time large-scale processing, storage, retrieval and manipulation of information, TDF are becoming the informational infrastructure of international trade. This trend is most apparent in such information-intensive industries as international air transport, the credit card industry, trading, insurance, and banking. Corporations in these industries are increasingly becoming data-processing firms.

In the *air transport industry*, extensive information flows are necessary to coordinate the airplanes, crews, passengers and cargo which make up an international air-transport network. Airlines have been able to improve greatly the efficiency of their international operations through the use of data flows. The principal mechanism is the Société internationale de télécommunications aéronautiques (SITA) which was formed in 1947. Based originally on telex, SITA is now made up of a world-wide network of leased lines which carried over 8 billion messages among 273 airlines in over 100 countries in 1984.[51] The most important service offered by SITA is flight and reservation information. More advanced services such as meteorological information and credit-card authorization are also available. SITA plans to add further services such as cargo and baggage handling, air-to-ground communications and flight planning. In addition, many large airlines maintain private data networks which provide capabilities beyond those of SITA. For instance, private networks allow airlines to improve the efficiency of many internal operations such as crew scheduling and maintenance, or, by providing access to more extensive data bases, to offer hotel and rental reservations and tourist information. The cost of a private network is normally justified by increased efficiency and the enhanced competitiveness derived from the ability to offer a broad range of travel services beyond basic transport. The importance of computer-communication systems for the air-transport industry transcends even the East-West divide. Thus, the Bulgarian, Hungarian and Polish national airlines book even local flights through a reservation system running on a computer located in Atlanta, Georgia.[52]

In the *credit and charge card industry*, new and complex challenges have arisen from the greater national mobility of card holders who increasingly wish to use a card domiciled in one country to make transactions in another. Compounding this challenge is the growing number of persons who utilize credit and charge cards and the widening range of establishments which accept them. Competition in the provision of credit and charge services involves increasing the number of both customers and receptive establishments, encouraging (through higher credit or charge ceilings) greater use of the cards, and on reducing the delay between the use of a card and payment. It would be virtually impossible to implement these strategies at an international level without centralized card verification and authorization procedures which minimize the risk of fraud and provide for efficient and high-speed procedures for transmitting transaction information. These functions depend heavily on TDF.

The *trading industry* is an industry which, almost by definition, is heavily dependent on information. Japan's general trading companies, the sogo shosha, epitomize this industry. The major Japanese trading companies maintain more than 100 offices in business centers around the world, all linked through modern telecommunication systems (see fig. II-8). Each of the nine largest sogo shosha devote substantial resources to communication purposes, typically between 3–5% of total sales expenditures (see table II-25). It is a ratio comparable to that of research and development (R&D) to sales in the manufacturing sector: the R&D-to-sales ratio in such a technology-intensive industry as electronics, for instance,

Figure II-8. The communication system of a major sogo shosha

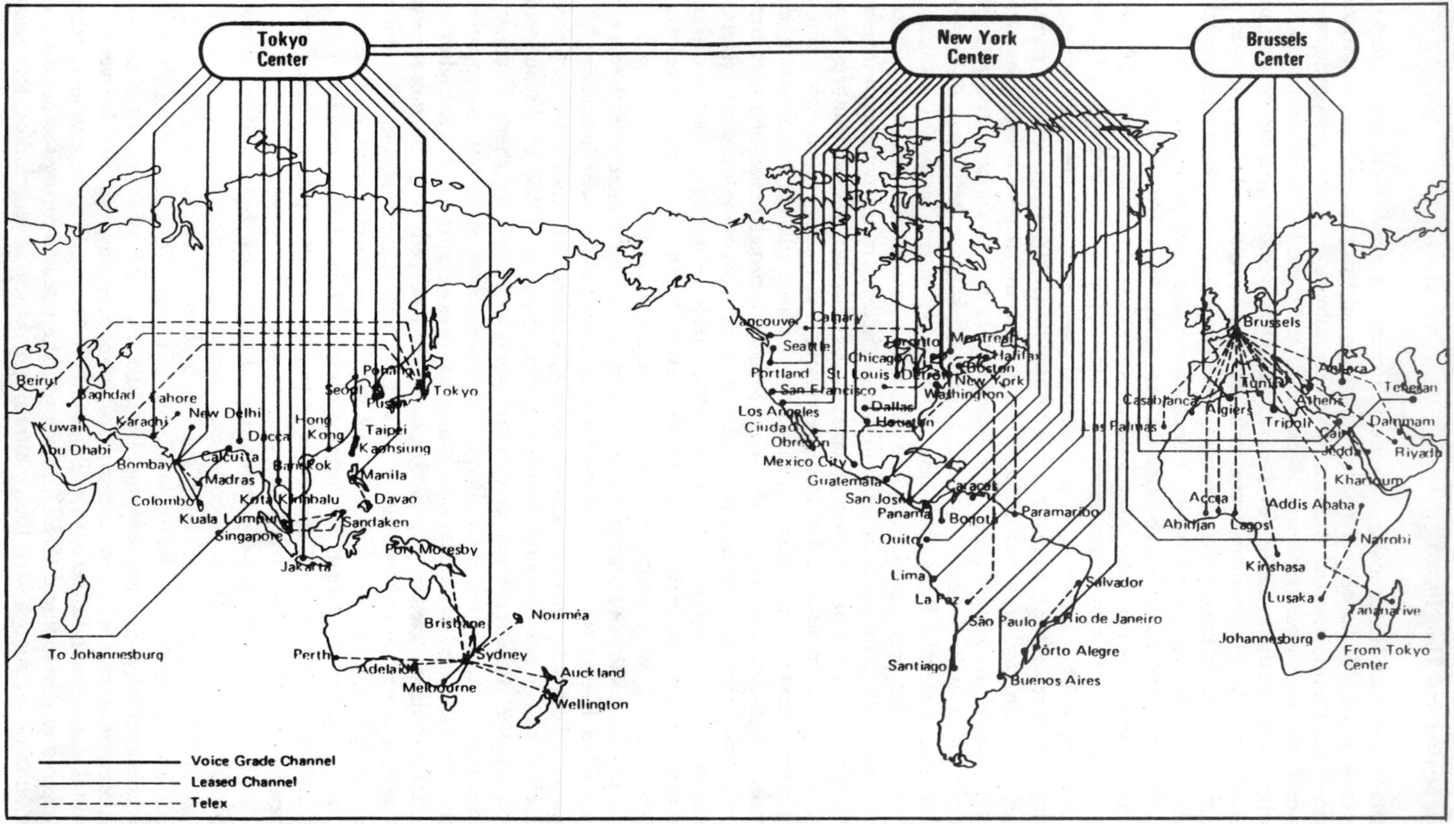

Source: JETRO, The Role of Trading Companies in International Commerce (Tokyo: JETRO, 1983), pp. 12–13.

is 4%.[53] For trading companies, communication expenditures are an investment, just as R&D expenditures are an investment for industrial corporations. The most extensive and sophisticated information-gathering system has been established by Mitsui.[54] Its communication expenditures of $60 million in 1978 amounted to 10% of total sales expenditures, equivalent to one-third of the company's total payroll (see table II-25). As in other sogo shosha, Mitsui's telex-cum-computer-communication system is centered on the home office in Japan, and a specially trained communication corps is responsible for the information-gathering function. In 1978, the daily volume of messages amounted to an estimated 80,000 dispatches and receipts.

Transborder data flows are also affecting the range of services provided internationally by *insurance firms*, particularly in the property insurance area. The continued internationalization of firms has led to a strong demand in TNCs for international insurance coverage, i.e., for insurance on a range of facilities worldwide. International insurance firms increasingly use TDF to monitor their exposure to risks held by a single transnational corporate client in several countries, and to inform their clients of the evolution of their insurance positions.

In *banking*, finally, transborder data flows have made it possible to handle more efficiently the rapidly increasing volume of financial transactions arising from the growth of world trade, FDI and tourism, and from the internationalization of capital markets. At the same time, international banks have come to provide new TDF-based services which respond to the changing needs of transnational corporate clients.[55] In particular, banks are making available to corporate customers the international cash management services they originally developed for their internal foreign-exchange management needs. These services, which facilitate the handling of exchange-rate risk in TNCs, also allow international banks to make further use of their large and increasingly sophisticated internal communication networks.[56] Over the long term, they seem likely to lead international banks increasingly into the area of providing electronic information services on a global basis. To deal with their own international transactions, banks, like airlines, have established an interbank data network for international transactions: SWIFT. SWIFT became operational in 1977 with 518 member banks in 15 countries (see table II-26). By the end of 1985, SWIFT encompassed 1,275 banks in 46 countries. Between 1978 and 1985, the number of messages carried annually increased from 21 million to 157 million. After a change in its by-laws, SWIFT can now also offer certain data-processing products and services.

Both SITA and SWIFT have become the backbone of international transactions of their respective industries. Both industries are no longer thinkable without these data networks. At the same time, it is impossible to gauge this importance in quantitative terms. Both are examples of how TDF have become an indispensable part of the international operations of certain industries.[57]

3. The importance of TDF for TNCs

Transborder data flows are also increasingly becoming the infrastructure for the operations of TNCs. TNCs control almost all of the world's FDI stock which, in 1983, amounted to over $600 billion. Over 95% of this stock originated in developed countries, led by the US (38% of the total), the UK (12%), the Federal Republic of Germany (9%), Japan (8%), Switzerland (7%), The Netherlands (6%),

Canada (5%), and France (5%).[58] The total stock of FDI—about a quarter of which is located in developing countries—represents about 20,000 TNCs with at least 100,000 foreign affiliates, not counting firms tied to TNCs through non-equity forms. The largest 50 TNCs alone control almost half of the world's FDI stock[59] and, therefore, probably a similar proportion of foreign affiliates. Through the corporate systems of TNCs flows a considerable share—perhaps one-third—of world trade (intra-firm trade) and in some countries, like the US, they account for over 90% of imports and exports. TNCs are also the principal channels for the transfer of technology as measured by licensing fees; thus, for instance, over 80% of the fees and royalties received annually by the US came from affiliate companies abroad, and this percentage has been increasing.[60] Finally—and not counting FDI flows, which averaged $44 billion per annum during 1981-1983[61]— TNCs in the form of transnational banks are also the principal conduits for international financial flows. For these reasons, they have become the most important private actors in the international economic system as well as in many national economies. In fact, to a certain extent they have internalized a good share of the most important international transactions of this system.

The overwhelming majority of the transnational computer-communication systems currently in operation are established by TNCs from developed market economies. As a number of recent studies found,[62] the importance of TDF for TNCs is high and is expected to increase even further in the near future. This is perhaps best summarized in the following quote from a survey undertaken by Business International:

> The ability to transmit, exchange and access machine-readable information around the world has clearly become an important tool for the multinational corporation. It is a tool that MNCs are coming to rely on to bring greater cohesion to the management of their geographically far-flung and functionally disparate operations. It is a tool they are counting on in ever greater numbers to gain a competitive edge, or merely to maintain their ability to compete. For many, . . . it is opening up new business opportunities. And, as important as TBDF is today, the survey confirms that it will be even more so in the near future.[63]

More specifically, the Business International study found that 88% of the companies participating in the study considered TDF important or very important for at least one corporate function, a percentage which increased to over 90 when managers were asked to predict importance for 1988. Financial management is the corporate function in which TDF are most used (see table II-27). To draw again on the Business International study, 60% of all TNCs surveyed considered TDF important or very important in this area in 1983 and 73% so considered them for 1988. That evaluation did not differ substantially between US and Western European firms, except that more than 80% of the latter were convinced of the future importance of TDF in this area. Financial management was followed relatively closely by marketing and distribution, ordering, inventory control and invoicing as far as the perceived importance of TDF to users was concerned, although the volume of flows involved was smaller. TDF were also considered quite important for production (especially in extractive industries), management (including strategic planning) and research and development (especially in some manufacturing and extractive industries) but less so for personnel and payroll management. Noteworthy are the relatively high ratings for manufacturing, strategic planning and computer-assisted design/management/engineering (CAD/CAM/CAE). The last function, in fact, had the highest growth rate in the Business International study: almost twice as many companies as in 1983 expected TDF to be important in this corporate activity within five years. However, TDF were also expected to grow in importance in virtually all other activities in most industries. Little wonder, then, that a recent study prepared by the National Telecommunications and Information Administration of the US government should observe: "International data communications have become crucial to the operation of U.S. multinational companies".[64] This is echoed in the Business International study which concluded that TNCs "are dependent on computerized flows of information to conduct their business today—and will be more so tomorrow".[65]

The extent to which TDF have become the lifeblood or the nervous system of TNCs can best be illustrated with reference to American Express and the Dresser case. As to American Express, the following quote from one of the senior vice-presidents of the corporation best describes the importance that TDF have assumed for the corporation:

> By the end of the mid 1960s, American Express had one international telecommunications link with a capacity of just 100 words per minute. By 1980 we had grown to some 28 international telecommunications links with a total capacity of 70,000 bits per second. Today, we have 75 international links with a total capacity of more than 450,000 bits per second.
>
> Amex expenditures on telecommunications and data processing have increased more than 100 fold in the past 20 years. For American Express the cost of developing, operating and maintaining these information processing systems and communications networks ranges more than a *half billion dollars* annually.
>
> Today American Express could not function without the capacity to move information across national borders with speed, accuracy, reliability and security. We rely on our international systems to allow us to provide a wide range of services: authorization of credit card transactions, replacement of lost or stolen travelers' cheques, travel reservations and other travel services, banking transactions by our international bank, and trading in securities, bonds and a host of other financial instruments.
>
> International communications also have made it possible for American Express to develop new services for our cardholders and for the establishments that accept the American Express card.
>
> Our international "point-of-sale" network links establishments accepting the American Express card with our central data processing facilities enabling them to "swipe" the card through a terminal to authorize card transactions with minimal delay. This provides a measure of protection and convenience not otherwise possible for both the cardholder and the retail establishment, making our card an even more attractive product.
>
> Another new product that is the direct result of information-age technology is the automatic teller machine, which enables our traveling cardholders to withdraw cash or travelers' cheques in a rapidly growing number of outlets around the world.[66]

The Dresser case arose when Dresser, a major US supplier of oilfield and pipeline equipment and related technology, was required to comply with the orders of the US export-control authorities in regard to the export of goods produced by its foreign affiliate in France with US-originated technology. According to *Business Week*, compliance with the sanction was easy:

> All Dresser had to do to comply with Reagan's embargo was to change the entry key to a computer in Pittsburgh on Aug. 26, the day the sanctions took effect. That effectively barred Dresser's French subsidiary from access to the technology it needs to complete orders it has on the books and to compete for new ones. And the Paris-based company faced the consequences almost immediately. Within a few weeks of its first, controversial delivery on Aug. 25, Dresser-France lost to Dresser's Clark Division based in Olean, N.Y., a $3.5 million order to supply three compressors to Australia's Santos, a gas producer.
>
> Without access to Dresser's computerized data bank, Dresser-France's engineers lack vital information to build the made-to-order compressors that account for about three-quarters of the company's business. "Without that computer, the only thing we can do is duplicate compressors we've already made", says Jean Luc Nevet, a Dresser-France systems engineer.[67]

These quotes indicate a number of the reasons for which TNCs establish transnational computer-communication systems. Foremost among them is the desire to raise the operational efficiency of their corporate networks. This is particularly important for corporations which provide a multitude of services in a wide range of markets with different economic, fiscal, legal, and political regimes. Proper management under such conditions requires a vast quantity of data, some of which (as in the case of reservation systems, credit authorization, currency management, and inventory control) must remain accessible virtually on an on-line basis, while others (like financial transactions) must be validated immediately. Furthermore, the very availability of the technology and the opportunities it offers (especially under pressures on earnings) to strengthen coordination, reduce inefficiency and cut unit costs invites corporations to improve their corporate communication systems by upgrading them to a computer-to-computer mode. Once the new systems are in place, they can, of course, be used for purposes other than communication as well.

Put into a broader context, TDF are a major element in the process by which TNCs take advantage of new technological possibilities, adjust to the changing economic environment and increase the efficiency of their operations. More specifically, the use of TDF has had three major efficiency implications: first, it has encouraged greater integration within TNCs (with headquarters increasingly becoming data-processing centers), permitting specialization gains ensuing from closer international interdependence; secondly, it has expanded the international supply of new services such as access to computerized data bases and on-line software maintenance, accelerating the diffusion of technological advances; and thirdly, it has improved the financial management in TNCs.

On the sectoral level,[68] the major factor driving the increasing use of TDF by manufacturing companies has been the growing turbulence of the economic environment in which TNCs must operate. Slower and more erratic growth consequent upon the post-1974 developments in the price of oil, together with profound structural changes in the world economy, has led to intensified international competition, paralleled by greater instability in the international monetary and financial systems. This changed environment has had three major implications for the strategies of TNCs. First, given slower growth in demand and output and greater competition on product markets, it has become increasingly important to achieve economies of scale in manufacturing and distribution through the international rationalization and integration of facilities. Secondly, the reduction of fixed costs has become more important, and is reflected in attempts to curtail duplication in research and development, to contain the growth of clerical costs and administration overhead, and to reduce working capital requirements through better inventory management. Thirdly, faced with much more unstable foreign-exchange and financial markets, the management of international financial risk has become an increasingly important function.

TDF play a growing role in TNCs' attempts to meet these strategic challenges. To begin with, transnational computer-communication systems have emerged as the crucial infrastructure for the international integration of production facilities. Integrating production facilities in several countries—each of which produces a specialized part of a final product—involves considerable coordination through data flows, if large scheduling of materials and substantial inventory control costs are to be avoided. TDF networks provide the speed and accuracy needed to perform these functions, especially the coordination of manufacturing and distribution schedules. Secondly, TDF are increasingly used within TNCs to contain the growth of fixed costs, thus lowering the firms' break-even points. One aspect of this is the growing automation of clerical tasks, particularly of the order, control and billing process. In addition to reducing administrative overheads, tighter management of accounts receivable allows firms to improve their cash flow. Equally important for reducing fixed costs is the control of inventory requirements, which increasingly involves the use of computerized international-inventory-management systems. These systems interface with the computerized systems used for production management on the one hand, and billing on the other; in addition to reducing costs, this improves the quality of the information available to management for financial control and corporate planning. Finally, given greater turbulence in world financial markets, the control of foreign-exchange exposure and of day-to-day financial strategy has increasingly been transferred in TNCs from foreign affiliates to regional or world headquarters. This transfer can only be successful if large volumes of financial information can be transmitted, frequently on a daily basis, from affiliates to headquarters and from headquarters to foreign exchange markets. TDF links between affiliates and headquarters, and between headquarters and financial institutions, are thus a necessity.

In sum, TNCs rely more and more heavily on transnational computer-communication systems. They do this not only to speed up the sending of messages (e.g., for ordering, marketing, distribution, and invoicing) but also to improve the management of corporate systems (an effect which cuts across all areas but is of particular importance in such corporate functions as financial control, strategic planning and inventory control) and to change the very manner in which corporations actually engage in production (e.g., in manufacturing, R & D, design and engineering, CAD/CAM/CAE). The last two developments in particular underline the role of TDF in transforming the international modus operandi of economic activities and in creating a new international system of production.

4. The increased tradeability
of certain services

Perhaps one of the most intriguing aspects of the emergence of TDF concerns the extent to which the advent of transnational computer-communication systems increases the tradeability of certain services. It will be recalled that most services are intangible and non-storable and that, therefore, the production and consumption of these services normally have to occur at the *same time* in the *same place*. This, in turn, is a serious obstacle to trade in services. For instance, banking traditionally required that customers go to the premises of their bank and transact their business then and there. While certain banking transactions can be undertaken by mail, telephone, telex or travel, this is often cumbersome, time-consuming, impractical and expensive—especially if interactive transactions are required. To give another example, engineering services traditionally require the presence of the service provider on the premises of the customer; if the customer is located abroad, the establishment of a foreign affiliate by the engineering firm could be required.

Real-time, interactive communication via transnational computer-communication systems changes this situation and thereby reduces the importance of this basic obstacle to trade in certain services. By collapsing time and space (at decreasing costs), transactions can take place at the *same time* but in *different places*. As a result, the tradeability—or transportability[69]—of certain services increases considerably. In other words, the growth of a sophisticated international telecommunication grid, capable of high-speed interactive data transmission at essentially distance-insensitive costs, is bound to increase the provision of a number of services via transnational computer-communication systems.

The potential for new forms of trade can best be seen from the use which TNCs make of TDF. As described in the previous section, corporate transnational computer-communication systems are increasingly being used to undertake a wide range of corporate functions, including financial management, accounting, invoicing, portfolio management, research and development, ordering, marketing, foreign-exchange management, inventory control, sourcing, and engineering. This is done on a regular basis, and considerable efforts have been made to create appropriate software, adopt efficient procedures and routinize the work involved as far as possible.

There is no reason why some of the services currently being provided via transnational computer-communication systems *within* TNCs cannot be made available *outside* these systems. It may only be a question of time until the processes of differentiation, specialization and standardization of knowledge lead to the emergence of economies of scale which make it economically feasible to take these services out of their corporate framework and into the international market-place. In the fields of airline reservation, hotel booking and certain banking transactions, this has already occurred with the establishment of the (commercial) closed user-group networks SITA and SWIFT. Similar networks are emerging in other service industries as well.

Thus, it is quite conceivable that data technologies will make a whole range of intangible and non-storable services tradeable and, in this manner, create trade options for industries which, in the past, had to serve foreign markets primarily through foreign affiliates. Prime candidates include banking, insurance, other financial services, data services, accounting, research and development, design and engineering, advertising, legal services, education, and management consulting. Table II-28 indicates, for a range of service industries, how and how far they are affected by this development. With the increase of tradeability, the market also expands, making new and global economies of scale possible. This, in turn, is bound to have profound implications for the pattern of supply of services and the industrial structure of the service industries. Corporations which first take advantage of the potential offered by TDF may be the first to reach global economies of scale and, hence, may acquire a substantial advantage vis-à-vis local and other rivals.

Banking, in fact, is an industry in which the application of data technology has already begun to permit a measure of international business in an intangible service without, as in the past, requiring a direct presence and face-to-face contact in the local market for the generation of international transactions. Thus, for instance, electronic banking is becoming widespread and includes banking from free-standing automated teller machines (ATMs) abroad. Their number worldwide was estimated at 103,000 in 1984.[70] In principle, various local and national ATM systems can be linked relatively easily through cooperative agreements of various banks, thus permitting international electronic funds transfer (EFT) on a routine basis. The banking services that can be provided via ATMs—be it locally, nationally or via transnational computer-communication networks—now amount to a full branch service. They include bill payments, cash and cheque deposits, travellers-cheque dispensing, money transfers, cheque book or statement ordering, "fast cash" dispensing, immediate statements, and branch inquiries. Increasingly, furthermore, such services as lending to firms, consumer finance, mortgage lending, securities underwriting, currency bond trading, foreign-exchange services, brokering, custody services, cash letters, and fund collection and disbursal services are becoming available electronically.

The number of ATMs in the US alone increased from 4,000 in 1975 to 43,800 in 1983, handling about 3 billion transactions worth approximately $260 billion in 1983;[71] the number of transactions had increased to 4 billion in 1984. The ATMs in the US are organized in 8 national and over 200 regional systems. The number of ATMs installed by the national systems increased from 23,000 in December 1984 to 34,000 in August 1985—an increase of 45% over an eight-month period (see table II-29). It is estimated that the US commercial banking industry alone spent between $8–$10 billion in 1984 on computer processing. Automation-related expenditures account for 11–15% of total non-interest costs—a higher proportion than any other industry with the exception of the data-processing industry.

In other developed countries, ATM networks have reached an equal level of penetration (see table II-30). In one of the latest developments in this field, banks from 17 countries in Western Europe decided in January 1985 to link their payment systems by 1 January 1986 in order to permit customers to use a single credit card to obtain cash from bank machines virtually anywhere in Western Europe.[72] Two months later, post office banks from six Western European countries and from Japan agreed to link their cash machines. The network will accept "smart cards", a new generation of plastic cards containing a small microchip which enables more complex transactions than possible with magnetic-stripe cards. Both networks may also become the basis for an international cashless shopping system; it would allow shoppers to pay with their credit cards at points of sale (POS) (e.g., in supermarkets), with the amount being instantaneously debited to the home account. Such systems are in the stage of testing in several countries, with France (because of strong government support) taking a lead in implementing them. The spread of personal computers further strengthens this trend. Although home banking has progressed slower than originally predicted, it already plays an important role in France, Hong Kong, and Sweden (see table II-30). In the US, Chemical Bank is estimated to have spent $10 to $20 million to develop its Pronto home banking system, and in France about 10 million homes are expected to have banking facilities before the end of the 1980s.[73]

These developments require, of course, major adaptive changes from banks. Perhaps the most advanced in this respect is Citicorp, which has developed the world's largest transnational computer-communication system. It is estimated that Citibank's expenditures on in-house hardware and software development, systems, support personnel, and facilities related to global electronic delivery systems and operations amounted to more than $3.3 billion from 1979–1984.[74] These expenditures have created a network which has been described as follows:

> Virtually all of Citicorp's wholesale banking systems are now connected via "the intelligent worldwide telecommunications back-bone". Citicorp now has direct telecommunications capabilities 24 hours per day, seven days a week, in 140 cities spanning 85 countries, an increase from the direct links in 70 cities in 55 countries it had during 1983 and the 5 cities in 5 countries in 1980. In the United States, six installed and four planned earth stations connect to the company's communications satellite (whose $38-million cost has been depreciated over a three-year period). Citicorp's proprietary message and data network, with annual operation costs of approximately $25 million, also operates by means of leased international lines. Five major nodes operate under an X.25 link to establish a New York/London/Singapore axis. Moreover, Citicorp is the only U.S.-based banking institution with two direct lines into China. Regionalized access is then provided through circuit switches that have been replaced with packet switches with increased customer activity. This global communications network enables Citicorp to connect to almost any standard, allows for control over U.S. telecommunications costs by compressing the maximum amount of data over leased circuits, and provides the company with the ability to count each piece of data moving over the network and to associate each piece with the originator.[75]

Many banks will have difficulties in matching such an infrastructure and, therefore, in remaining competitive in the world financial market.

Cash management is another area in which the impact of technology can be observed. Cash-management systems typically center on the corporate treasurer's work-station. On a personal computer, they offer such services as payments made, balance reporting, forecasting and modelling, multi-currency netting systems, account information, and funds transfer. In an age of high interest rates, fluctuating exchange rates and narrow profit margins, cash management has become a crucial corporate function, and many corporations have strengthened their capacities in this respect. This can be done in several ways.

One is to establish an internal cash-management network. To illustrate, a transnational oil corporation has several hundred gasoline stations in several countries. All gasoline stations are requested to report to corporate headquarters the balance of their daily transactions by a certain time via the corporate computer-communication system. The head office aggregates all flows and provides the treasurer of the corporation with the exact cash-flow position of the enterprise. This, in turn, permits a precise assessment of such matters as which funds should be held in which currency, which funds have to be borrowed, and which can be placed into overnight money markets to earn interest. The logical extension of such an approach would be for the company involved to establish its own in-house bank, initially to handle all of the company's finances, and perhaps later to sell banking services to other companies as well. This seems to be exactly what happened when British Petroleum (BP) launched an in-house bank in January 1985. (Volvo announced in April of the same year a similar plan.) BP has financial assets of over $10 billion, an annual cash flow of $40 billion, liquid assets of about $3 billion, and huge exposures to foreign currencies. If, as planned, the bank's balance comes to consist of virtually the entire financial assets of BP, it would rank among the world's largest 100 banks and thus become a potentially important competitor for other banks. According to BP's managing director for finance and planning, this move only became possible when computer-communication technology permitted the appropriate organization of the group's finances.[76]

Instead of establishing its own data network, the oil corporation in this example could also entrust the task of cash management to a transnational bank. Thus, all gasoline stations could be asked to deposit their daily balances by a certain time into the local branches of the bank in question (or its corresponding banks). The bank would then aggregate the cash position and report the results to the headquarters of the oil corporation where the corporate treasurer is linked through a desk computer to the bank. For this service, the bank would sell the necessary software to the corporation and, of course, would charge a fee.

Both approaches to cash management are being used. In the first, in which industrial corporations bypass banks, corporations begin to perform certain functions traditionally confined to banks. In the second, an internal corporate function has been externalized and has become subject to demand-and-supply competition, i.e., it has entered the market-place.

Banks have a certain comparative advantage here because the management of financial resources is one of their principal functions and because many of them had begun early to create their own computer-communication networks and to produce the software needed for cash management. They can, therefore, offer for a fee their networks and software at a marginal cost to service other corporations in the manner described above—in fact, banks may find that an increasing share of their income will be derived in the future from fees for this type of service. In effect, banks sell packages of financial management services and thus relieve corporations of one major responsibility. This may be particularly attractive to smaller corporations which do not wish to invest the necessary resources to build their own data networks. US banks have been leading in the provision of cash-management services. After developing them for the domestic market, they began, in the late 1970s, to export them to Western Europe. Naturally, European banks were forced to develop their own cash-management services. However, while the major US banks typically use their own transnational computer-communication systems and their own networks, European banks typically rely on commercial transnational value-added networks and timesharing bureaux (e.g., GEISCO, ADP, UNINET). Since such reliance is normally less flexible and more expensive than in-house services, US banks have a certain competitive edge. At the same time, given the costs involved in establishing transnational computer-communication networks, local banks are likely to have difficulties in remaining competitive, especially as far as their transnational clients are concerned. Perhaps state-of-the-art public networks could change this situation.

More generally speaking, once a transnational computer-communication system is in place, it can be used, at least in principle, for a variety of purposes. Banks may have originally established their data networks to improve their internal cash management. From there it is only a small step to open the system to customers for automated teller transactions or to offer it, for instance, to corporate clients for cash management. In fact, since high-speed sophisticated networks are typically underused (especially where back-up systems exist) and are often operated at less than one-third of their capacity, an expansion into these and other services is a natural next step. This may well be one of the reasons why Chemical Bank established a joint venture with ATT, Time Inc., and BankAmerica to provide certain videotext services (it permits a further utilization of its Pronto home banking service which it had already established) and why Citicorp offered in 1986 to buy for $680 million Quotron Systems Inc., a worldwide provider of stock quotations and other financial data (which contributes to making the supply of information one of the five major businesses of Citicorp).[77] The logic of this situation suggests that any corporation that has its own transnational computer-communication system can either expand the range of corporate and/or commercial services it offers via these networks, or it can make a part of the network available to third-party users (see the Eastman Kodak move).

It should be noted that the strategies discussed in the preceding paragraphs are the result of technological forces and economic considerations. The extent to which they can actually be implemented depends, of course, on the regulatory framework and, in particular, the permissibility of third-party use, i.e., the degree to which a private owner of a transnational computer-communication system can sell part of the system's capacity to unrelated parties. Third-party use clashes directly with the interests of most PTTs which do not wish to see the rapidly growing, profitable data traffic siphoned off by private networks paying a flat rate for leased lines. Friction between private owners of data systems and PTTs may, therefore, increase in the future, especially if the latter do not provide state-of-the-art equipment and services.

Apart from technological and economic factors, a restrictive third-party-use policy may further increase the pressure on corporations to diversify. For if they are not permitted to sell unused capacities to customers in other fields, they may decide to enter these fields themselves, either alone or in joint ventures with others (see the examples given earlier). This, in turn, would further stimulate the blurring of boundaries between industries, discussed earlier in this chapter. The underlying technology-driven reality is that the owners of private and public transnational computer-communication systems are learning that "the total global communication network becomes a pipeline of enormous capacity. Once a world information grid is built, the incremental cost of processing or transmitting additional information in that grid is very small. Thus, the incremental cost of adding services which are information-based is very low."[78] The trend in the US and elsewhere appears to be in the direction of increased multi-purpose use of computer-communication systems.

To sum up, technological and regulatory changes facilitate—and even invite—the externalization of certain corporate functions (i.e., the transformation of certain intra-firm transactions into commercially-provided services) for those corporations that do not have their own computer-communication networks or do not wish to build certain specialized capacities. For those corporations that have their own networks, product segmentation may break down as they seek to optimize the use of their networks by offering a variety of services whose only common denominator is that they are data-based. Independently of that, the availability of a transnational computer-communication grid (be it public or accessible through third-party use) provides the infrastructure—and the opportunity—for corporations not having their own networks to offer certain services (e.g., architectural designs) via telecommunication lines. The result of these developments is not only the increased tradeability of a number of services, but also a blurring of the boundaries between service and non-service corporations.

It has to be emphasized that basic to all of these developments is the state of the telecommunication system. As the price of informatics equipment declines (while its power increases), the crucial variable for the international use and expansion of data services and of activities employing them is the quality of the telecommunication system. To put it differently, those who do not have access to a sophisticated telecommunication system will not be able to participate in the emergence of new forms of trade in services.

In any event, any international discussion of services has to recognize that the rapidly changing data technologies are giving birth to a multitude of new opportunities whose applications are difficult to predict and whose utilization blurs established demarcation lines between corporations, industries and services. This, of course, makes it difficult to predict how international trade in services will evolve. But it seems certain that a whole range of new forms of service trade will be added to traditional transactions in this area, and that the role of data services as a core service will be enhanced even further.

D. Some macro effects

1. The international division of labor

The increased use of data technologies and the data services associated with them are bringing about fundamental changes in the way in which economic (and social) activities are being carried out. Data resources have acquired strategic economic importance and are becoming central to economic development. Perhaps nowhere is this captured better than in the following quote from a well-known OECD study: ". . . *the electronics revolution will change the face of advanced industrial societies*. Production, transmission and processing of the most varied information will be at the heart of economic activity and social life . . ."; in fact, "through its links with data processing and telecommunications, . . . *the electronics complex during the next quarter of a century will be the main pole around which the productive structures of the advanced industrial societies will be reorganized*".[79] In other words, we are at the beginning of a fundamental restructuring of economic activities, a restructuring that some regard as a new industrial revolution and one which has important international implications.

In this situation, control over data resources—or at least access to them—and the ability to utilize these resources become crucially important for developed, developing and socialist countries alike. The following observation by Alain Madec, the chairperson of an influential Inter-ministerial Commission on Transborder Data Flows established by the former French President Giscard d'Estaing, captures the point: "One can, therefore, expect struggles among states for data, as one has known them for raw materials and energy. . . . *Serious consequences could result from them for middle-level industrial powers, which, through the free flow of data, could slowly be reduced to consumers only*".[80] Or to quote the Coordinator for International Communication and Information Policy in the US Department of State: "We know that the manipulation and control of information is among the greatest weapons of conquest in the modern world. We know, above all, that information is power, more valuable than oil and more precious than gold."[81]

The vision that informs Madec's prediction is a vision of an international division of labor (and, ultimately, power) based on an uneven distribution of data resources (or of access to data resources) and of the ability to utilize them—in other words, a world in which the "information rich" confront the "information poor".[82] In fact, the global distribution of data resources is at the moment highly uneven. The manufacturing of the computer equipment supporting TDF, the production of the accompanying software and the development of the underlying technology are limited to the industrialized countries, with TNCs based in the US playing a leading role. The distribution of computing facilities across geographic regions is also uneven, reflecting varying levels of development and of availability of skilled human resources. Developing countries account for only a fraction of the total market. Similarly, most capacities for telecommunications—telephones, telephone networks, submarine cables, satellites—are located in the northern hemisphere. The distribution of the equipment required for TDF is thus largely limited to developed countries.

The establishment of transnational computer-communication systems and their commercial use are also concentrated in the developed market economies. Publicly-available communication networks specifically created for the transmission of data now exist in virtually all of these countries. They are linked internationally, but do not have many extensions into developing and socialist countries. Data processing undertaken by service bureaux over the existing networks is also mostly confined to the developed market economies, as is the de facto access to the expanding network of computerized data bases. Thus, the production, processing, transport and distribution of machine-readable data for commercial use are almost exclusively a phenomenon of the developed market economies. In addition, most corporate computer-communication systems are structured in such a manner that the main processing facilities are located at the seat of the parent corporation (or elsewhere in the home country), while foreign affiliates, especially those in developing countries, are often linked to the system only through terminals. Also, the majority of principal switching centres of closed user-group networks is located in developed market economies.

Thus, the international data market and the application of TDF for corporate purposes are largely limited to the developed market economies. Almost all aspects of the market are a domain of TNCs. Developing countries participate primarily as data suppliers, buyers of the finished product (information), and purchasers of the capital goods needed for their own, so far mostly rudimentary, telematics

Figure II-9. Patterns of transborder data flows

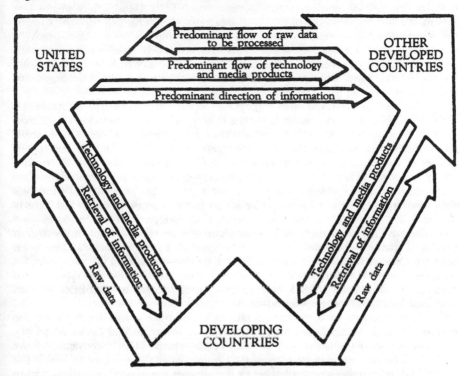

Source: Rein Turn, ed., *Transborder Data Flows: Concerns in Privacy Protection and Free Flow of Information*, vol. I, *Report of the AFIPS Panel on Transborder Data Flows* (Washington: American Federation of Information Processing Societies, 1979), p. 5.

sectors (see fig. II-9). While this pattern may change in the future, the imbalance may also grow stronger, at least in certain areas. For instance, 1981 per capita telecommunication plant gross investment amounted to $804 in the US, $76 in the FRG, $5 in Egypt and $2 in Brazil; 1982 per capita telecommunication construction expenditures were $106 for the US, $70 for the FRG, $16 for Brazil and $7 for Egypt (see table II-31). Moreover, most developed countries are rapidly expanding advanced and diversified data networks, while most of the developing countries do not even have rudimentary data networks.

What is feared in this situation is that TDF hinder the establishment of domestic data resources. To the extent that some data resources are available elsewhere (e.g., in corporate headquarters or regional centers) and can be accessed easily, market pressure to develop domestic data resources is reduced. If internationally available data resources are more competitive, local users will prefer international to nascent domestic resources, thus making it difficult for domestic infant industries to grow and to develop forward and backward linkages.

The role of TNCs in these processes deserves particular attention because they are the principal actors in international economic relations, are almost entirely headquartered in developed market economies, and account for the overwhelming share of commercial, corporate and infrastructure TDF. Hence, they play a key role in the international distribution of data resources. The present structure of the international data market, combined with the importance of TDF, leads to the concern that the developing countries may become blocked in the evolution of the international division of labor at those future activities which are comparatively less sophisticated and have fewer spin-off effects (such as research and development) associated with them.

The role of TNCs is also important because the intra-firm international division of labor of these organizations is a microcosm of the international division of labor. It may be that, within transnational computer-communication systems, less sophisticated data activities (e.g., the mere inputting of data) are located in one set of countries, while the more sophisticated ones are undertaken in another set of countries. That this fear is not entirely groundless is suggested by data pertaining to Canada which show that a vast majority of Canadian TDF involves data flows from foreign affiliates in Canada to parent corporations abroad, mostly in the US.[83] Similarly, it has been found that foreign affiliates in developing countries typically send their data to headquarters or regional centers located in developed market economies, which may suggest that the imbalance is here even stronger than in the case of Canada.[84] The increased use of TDF especially for corporate production functions may therefore have an effect on the international division of labor, even if data flows permit better access to sophisticated data resources located in developed countries.

Closely related to these considerations is the question of what impact the new information technologies have on corporate structure and decision-making. The two principal variables are the degree to which TDF encourage a more centralized or decentralized *location* of data resources and the degree to which the use of TDF encourages a centralization or decentralization of *decision-making* within TNCs. Since the technology itself permits both centralization and decentralization, key considerations in this respect are the cost of computing power, human resources, telecommunication services and corporate strategies. In recent years, the cost of computing power has declined considerably, thus encouraging decentralization. On the other hand, the costs of telecommunication have not decreased as dramatically and the costs of sophisticated data skills have risen considerably, thus encouraging centralization. Since the balance of these developments is not clear and may vary depending on the special configuration of needs of particular companies, corporate strategy—i.e., management's vision of how a corporation should be structured— plays an important role. Corporations that view their foreign affiliates more or less as independent entities would tend to prefer a decentralized location of data resources and decentralized decision-making. Corporations that prefer operational integration among the different parts of their transnational corporate systems— for example, on the level of component specialization or the link between ordering and production—have a greater need for coordination and thus for more centralized decision-making structures. While this may reduce the autonomy of each affiliate of a TNC, it is a natural and inevitable counterpart of the efficiency gains arising from greater operational integration of corporate activities. Naturally, mixed strategies are also possible. For instance, decentralized data-processing networks can be established, although centralized facilities remain in use where large processing or storage facilities are required or access to unique and complex software is involved.

Furthermore, the impact of TDF on headquarters-affiliate relationships may differ according to geographical region. It has been found in this context that inter-affiliate communications appeared to be more common in Western Europe, while affiliates in the developing countries normally send their data to regional centers or to headquarters located in developed countries.[85] This disparity, which may well reflect weaknesses in the infrastructure necessary for TDF in developing countries, could lead to a substantial difference between developed and developing countries in the impact of TDF.

In any event, the available data suggest that a broad variety of decision-making structures can coexist with different physical data-processing network structures, as long as access to any part of the network is possible. It is for this reason that one study concluded that, while it "found a definite trend toward distributed computer power and processing for certain activities, it found no definite trend toward either centralization or decentralization of management control."[86] Furthermore, decision-making can be decentralized while ex-post control can be centralized. This is reflected in the response of one of the companies that participated in this study. It believed "that the tendency is toward decentralization of decision-making, 'because you have more control'".[87] This suggests that, while TDF permit a decentralization of equipment and decision-making, they simultaneously increase the ability of headquarters to monitor corporate systems worldwide and to intervene when developments make it necessary.

The intention is not to fault TNCs for taking advantage of the possibilities offered by the new information technologies. It is rational corporate behavior to improve corporate efficiency, which, as demonstrated earlier, TDF are generally credited with doing. Often, in fact, TNCs may have little choice in their location of data resources, since local skills and the local telematics infrastructure may be too weak to permit the competitive location of certain activities in developing countries. However, a vicious cycle which reproduces itself as an outcome of basic market processes may only be avoidable if local data resources are strengthened—in many cases, to be sure, on a selective basis. This objective normally requires the adoption of appropriate government policies at the national and international levels, an issue to be discussed in the next chapter. If this does not occur, many countries, and especially developing ones, may not be in a position to benefit fully from TDF (particularly if they do not have an adequate infrastructure) and they may be more prone than not to regard these flows with suspicion and as a threat to their economic development. This suspicion may be further nourished when TDF contribute to greater centralization in TNC decision-making. Apart from the possible impact on the international division of labor, on the development of local data resources, and on dependency and vulnerability, such centralization could also reduce the transparency of the operations of TNCs, affect the transfer-of-technology process within corporations, reduce the responsiveness of affiliates to local conditions, and limit their opportunities and freedom to pursue and develop particular activities. The last two possibilities, in particular, could mean that affiliates become only weakly linked to the overall development of the countries in which they are located.

2. Impact on foreign direct investment

Over the long term, TDF may contribute to far-reaching changes in the growth of FDI in both goods and service industries. If seen as a part of broader developments in microelectronics, the crucial factor in the *goods industries* is automation, an outgrowth of the use of data technologies. While automation is a development much broader than TDF, its internationalization as an ongoing interactive process depends on TDF. The accelerating automation of production may change the economics of production location and, in particular, erode one of the principal comparative advantages of most developing countries, the abundant supply of inexpensive labor. Some signs in this direction can perhaps already be detected. The introduction of data technologies is revitalizing industries which have been considered mature or declining. The telecommunication industry is one example, the automobile industry perhaps another. For the automobile industry, it has been predicted that all manual labor in car assembly and design (along with several layers of management) will disappear in the next 20 years with the introduction of new production technology; in this manner, a standardized technology and production process would be changed into a high-technology and production process.[88] A number of steps in this direction have already been taken. According to one estimate, the motor industry worldwide spent $340 million on CAD in 1984 and will spend $1.5 billion in 1989.[89] As discussed earlier, a number of automobile firms are even acquiring electronic companies to support their automation drive.

Even such an industry as textiles is experiencing changes that are making it competitive again in countries which were thought to have lost their comparative advantage in this regard. Thus, parts of the textile industry in the United Kingdom are being revitalized on the basis of, among other things, an increased use of automated processes. The principal reason is that the use of data technologies allows a better utilization of equipment (this is particularly obvious as regards robots), permits higher quality, and lowers labor costs. In spite of the capital intensity of automation, the last factor, in particular, has contributed significantly to a levelling of manufacturing costs between manual and automatic work processes in certain industries (see table II-32), a development which has induced some observers to conclude (in this specific case for the garment industry) that "although it has not happened yet, to a great extent, there is a feeling among the large producers that a large share of offshore production will be brought back" to the developed countries.[90] A study for the Federal Republic of Germany confirmed this feeling by suggesting that a large-scale back-deployment of production facilities to that country could take place when robots are introduced in clothing manufacturing on a larger scale—a development considered very likely before the end of the 1980s.[91]

In *service industries*, the crucial factor for the impact of TDF on FDI is the increasing tradeability of certain services brought about by the new information technologies. As was discussed in chapter I, in the internationalization of the service sector through trade and FDI the latter mode of delivering services to foreign markets has clearly been the more dynamic one, precisely because of the intangible and non-storable nature of most services. To the extent that data services increase the tradeability of certain other services, both sellers and buyers (companies as well as countries) have now two ways of providing or securing certain services. That the trade option is being increasingly used for certain services that have hitherto been traded internationally only to a limited extent has already been discussed. If more companies or countries take advantage of the new tradeability of certain services, this will particularly affect a number of services contained in the category "other private services". This is the category which, so far, has been the principal domain for services FDI. Increased tradeability may, therefore, decrease the need for FDI in services. For instance, if banks can increasingly deliver certain services to another country via trade (e.g., via automated teller machines), the need for foreign affiliates may decrease and the threshold at which it has to be decided whether a market should be served by trade or by FDI would be raised.

Such a development would not be without policy implications. For instance, banking is traditionally a highly regulated activity, and the entry and operations of foreign banks are tightly regulated in many countries. To the extent that banks take advantage of the new tradeability of banking products, the question arises, to what extent this new tradeability introduces a new dimension which is not only not captured by traditional FDI regulations, but many actually blunt their intentions. Entirely different approaches toward the regulation of banking may therefore be required, both as regards domestic and foreign banks and quasi-banks.

In any event, the result of the increased tradeability of certain services may well be, ceteris paribus, that the growth of FDI in certain services levels off in the future, if it does not decline. To the extent that this occurs, certain crucial services-FDI issues—such as right of establishment and nationalization and compensation—may lose their centrality in public-policy discussions, while certain service-trade issues—such as right of presence—gain in centrality. In other words, the underlying technological developments may not only lead to a shift in the pattern of trade and FDI in services, but also to a re-definition of the salient policy issues associated with both types of international transactions.

If increased tradeability is one factor that may contribute to a levelling off in the growth of FDI in services, another one would be the dismantling of restrictions to trade in services, hence decreasing the necessity to resort to FDI. As will be discussed later, this is in fact the main thrust of the current initiative to establish an international framework for trade in services. And finally, the scope for future expansion is bound to decrease once most of the large service TNCs are established in important markets, although diversification of services may generate new impulses.

The spreading use of data technologies could therefore affect the geographical location of economic activities, as the spread of electricity once did. If the processes described in the preceding paragraphs become more widespread and if automation changes the conditions of production to such an extent that older industries in developed countries are rejuvenated, the question would have to be raised whether it would still remain attractive for certain FDI projects to be located in developing countries. In other words, certain FDI flows may slow down or even reverse themselves as TNCs find the locating of certain production facilities in developed countries economically more attractive than they did in the past. Thus, for instance, a number of US semiconductor TNCs have already shifted the production of chips back to their home country because certain formerly labor-intensive work processes (especially in the assembly stage) have been automated: Schlumberger's Fairchild Camera affiliate moved some of its production from Southeast Asia to an automated plant in Portland, Maine; and Advanced Micro Devices did not expand its production facilities in Singapore, but instead those of an automated plant in the US.[92] At the same time, it is conceivable that a growing range of functions in foreign affiliates is increasingly assisted by TDF, thus making it less urgent to develop certain skills locally. Independently of this, furthermore, barriers to entry into data-technology based manufacturing may become higher, thus narrowing the industrialization path in general.

On the other hand, the higher mobility of data resources made possible by TDF enables those that are presently disadvantaged (especially the developing countries) to obtain better access to these resources. The developments in informatics and telecommunications have substantially increased the ability to handle large amounts of data and, therefore, have improved the prospects for better-informed decision-making concerning virtually all matters. Particularly important in this context is access to a rapidly expanding pool of up-to-date knowledge stored in automated data bases. Thus, growing data networks may allow better management of natural resources (e.g., through the use of on-line commodity-quotation data bases) and facilitate access to important information for export and import purposes, for financial transactions, and the like. Equally important, TDF may facilitate considerably the transfer of technology, not only because of increased transparency, but also because they offer better opportunities to secure and to coordinate R&D and even to undertake it in cooperation, perhaps on a division-of-labor or specialization basis. Greater knowledge in these areas may strengthen the bargaining capacity of developing countries. Increased information flows are also the precondition for more intense economic and technical cooperation among developing countries—they are, so to speak, the informational infrastructure for such cooperation. Furthermore, since the new information technologies incorporate knowledge into equipment, they may often save on specialized skills scarce in developing countries. For some of these countries it may also be easier to introduce micro-electronics-based systems since they, unlike developed countries, have fewer old capacities to adapt or to protect. In sum, if these benefits can be realized, TDF can make an important contribution to development and in particular play a catalyst role in industrialization. It may therefore be easier than in the past to improve the situation of the developing countries provided, of course, that they have the required infrastructure and are able to use data technologies productively.

Whether any of these contradictory trends will actually acquire any significance and which of them will prevail is impossible to predict. But given the importance of the changes initiated by data technologies, it is clear that TDF will affect the ability, especially of those countries that lack an adequate telematic infrastructure, to industrialize successfully and remain competitive in world markets, altering patterns of international investment and trade in goods and services. This must be kept in mind *today*, especially by developing countries, when planning or building the industries of *tomorrow*. If one wants these industries to be internationally competitive when they come on stream (or if one wants present industries to remain competitive), one cannot ignore the profound technical changes that are now unfolding. Clearly, therefore, care must be taken to ensure that TDF do not merely lead to an accentuation of existing international imbalances or to the emergence of a *new* set of imbalances between developed and developing countries and that all countries can benefit as much as possible from the new information technologies and their applications.

Notes

[1] Data are symbols that can be handled and transmitted through computers; information is the combination of data into messages intelligible to human beings, i.e., it is the processed form of the raw material, data.

² It has been calculated that "computer networks bring the cost of point-to-point electronic communication down to the point at which messages can be delivered at prices close to those of mass media and yet be addressed to individual receivers"; see Ithiel de Sola Pool, *et al.*, *Communications Flows: A Census in the United States and Japan* (Amsterdam: North-Holland, 1984), p. 30.

³ *Ibid.*, p. 33. The other three are writing, printing and telegraphy.

⁴ *Ibid.*, pp. 27 and 120, respectively.

⁵ See *ibid*. As the authors point out (p. 32), this is being done "by generating the growing overhead of computer-to-computer messages which the human user never sees. Consequently, the volume of words flowing in the message stream may continue to expand (both in the information base and also in the overhead of messages for information processing) while the volume of words ultimately consumed remains confined to the capacity of the human receivers."

⁶ See *New York Times*, 5 February 1985, and *Financial Times*, 21 June 1985.

⁷ In Brazil, one of the developing countries with the biggest computer industry, data-processing services (including computer power, software, consultant services and training) amounted to $580 million in 1980; see UNCTC, *Transborder Data Flows and Brazil: Brazilian Case Study* (New York: UN, 1983), Sales No. E.83.II.A.3 (also available from North-Holland, Amsterdam).

⁸ See Karl P. Sauvant, *Trade and Foreign Direct Investment in Data Services* (Boulder: Westview, 1986).

⁹ See footnote ⁷. A few countries, like India and Mexico, are however, developing a software industry.

¹⁰ See, also for the following data in this paragraph, UNCTC, *Transborder Data Flows: Access to the International On-line Data-base Market* (New York: UN, 1983), Sales No. 83.II.A.1 (also available from North-Holland, Amsterdam).

¹¹ The perhaps best source for on-line data bases is Cuadra Associates, *Directory of Online Databases* (Santa Monica: Cuadra Associates, semi-annually).

¹² See, for instance, UNCTC, *Brazilian Case Study, op. cit.*, and UNCTC, *Transborder Data Flows and Poland: Polish Case Study* (New York: UN, 1984), Sales No. E.84.II.A.8 (also available from North-Holland, Amsterdam).

¹³ See US, International Trade Commission (ITC), "The Relationship of Exports in Selected U.S. Service Industries to U.S. Merchandise Exports" (Washington, D.C.: ITC, 1982), mimeo., p. 13. Telephone and telegraph services account for about 80% of total communication revenues.

¹⁴ See Eurodata Foundation, *Data Communications in Europe 1981–1987: Management Summary* (London: Eurodata Foundation, 1983), p. 10.

¹⁵ *Ibid.*, p. 11.

¹⁶ See OECD, *Telecommunications: Pressures and Policies for Change* (Paris: OECD, 1983), pp. 20, 21.

¹⁷ See US, Congress, Office of Technology Assessment (OTA), *International Competitiveness in Electronics* (Washington, D.C.: OTA, 1984), p. 86. This is largely the result of decreasing hardware costs and increasing software costs.

¹⁸ See Sauvant, *Trade and Foreign Direct Investment, op. cit.*

¹⁹ See, for instance, Seev Hirsch, "Reindustrialisation of Western Economies: Is It Desirable or Feasible?", *The World Economy*, 7 (September 1984), p. 353: ". . . manufacturing itself has a growing 'services content'. The micro-electronics revolution and other technological developments are rapidly changing the structure of industrial manufacturing and the role

of production workers, transforming manufacturing into a human capital-intensive process. Thus the service economy . . . is also an economy where the output of the industrial sector itself has a growing services content".

²⁰ See Michael J. Piore and Charles F. Sabel, *The Second Industrial Divide: Possibilities for Prosperity* (New York: Basic Books, 1984).

²¹ See in the context also Juan Rada, "Advanced Technologies and Development: Are Conventional Ideas about Comparative Advantage Obsolete?" *Trade and Development: An UNCTAD Review,* 5 (1984), pp. 275–296, and Dieter Ernst, "Die Auswirkungen der Mikroelektronik auf die weltweite Neustrukturierung der Elektronikindustrie: Implikationen fuer die Dritte Welt", *Peripherie,* 15/16 (Winter/Spring 1984), pp. 53–73.

²² See Badiul A. Majumdar, "Technology Transfers and International Competitiveness: The Case of Electronic Calculators", *Journal of International Business Studies,* 11 (Fall 1980), p. 106.

²³ See Electronic Services Unlimited (ESU), "Telecommuting: The State of the Art and Market Trends" (New York: ESU, 1984), mimeo. The percentage is estimated to be larger if all forms of geographically independent work are included, such as the use of portable computers on the road. Jobs that offer themselves particularly to telecommuting are word processing, data-entry work, market research, financial analysis, statistical work, computer programing, software development, and banking, insurance and financial services. The benefits that are seen to be associated with telecommuting include increased productivity, both managerial and clerical; improved retention of highly trained employees; access to a wider labor pool and additional recruitment incentives; reduction in real estate costs; better utilization of investments in electronic media; and greater work flexibility through time and location independence.

²⁴ See, for instance, Raphael Kaplinsky, *Automation: The Technology and Society* (Harlow: Longman, 1984).

²⁵ US corporations hold nearly 100% of the US market for CAD/CAM products, 90% of the Western European market and 70% of the Japanese market. Apparently, the most important reason for this market dominance is the strength of software development in the US. See US, Department of Commerce, International Trade Administration (ITA), *A Competitive Assessment of the U.S. Manufacturing Automation Equipment Industries* (Washington: ITA, 1984), p. IX. The rapid growth of CAD applications is fueled by falling prices of CAD/CAM systems. The price of large systems was expected to fall from $400,000 in 1980 to $250,000 in 1985, with smaller, stand-alone systems already available in the $10,000 price range. The CAD market alone was $2 billion in 1983 and is projected to reach $9 billion by 1987. See *ibid.,* p. 34.

²⁶ This is one of the main points of Piore and Sabel, *op. cit.*

²⁷ OECD, *Software: An Emerging Industry* (Paris: OECD, 1985), p. 101.

²⁸ *Financial Times,* 28 January 1985.

²⁹ See *Financial Times,* 18 October 1984. The same article reported that it is estimated that for every British pound spent on robots, at least two pounds will be spent on related work such as installation and training.

³⁰ *Financial Times,* 6 June 1985, and *The Economist,* 12 October 1985, p. 36.

³¹ See *New York Times,* 10 May 1985.

³² *Financial Times,* 7 July 1985.

³³ See GM, *Public Affairs Newsletter,* 14 (September 1984), p. 1, and GM, "MAP Information Packet", mimeo.

³⁴ See George Leopold, "Factory Nets Follow a Map", *Electronics Week,* 17 December 1984, p. 20.

[35] For a general discussion of TDF, see UNCTC, *Transnational Corporations and Transborder Data Flows: Background and Overview* (Amsterdam, North-Holland, 1984).

[36] The term transnational computer-communication "system" refers here to the set of transnational computer-communication "links" of a given organization. In other words, one organization can have more than one link, although, as a rule, most organizations have only one. In the case of the data for Brazil quoted below, there were 23 systems installed in the country in March 1982, consisting of 29 links.

[37] See US, ITC, *op. cit.*, p. 23. Here, as in other statistics pertaining to international transactions in data services (and, for that matter, services in general), it is often not quite clear to what extent revenue figures reported by firms combine both exports and sales by foreign affiliates.

[38] See France, Ministère du Redéploiement Industriel et du Commerce Extérieur, Direction des Industries Electroniques et de l'Informatique (DIELI), "Les sociétés de service et de conseil en informatique: Résultats 1983" (Paris: DIELI, 1985), p. 15.

[39] It should be noted that software normally is not yet traded via telecommunication links; however, increasingly this seems to be occurring.

[40] See Sauvant, *Trade and Foreign Direct Investment, op. cit.*

[41] For the data in this paragraph and a further elaboration of the subject see UNCTC, *Transnational Corporations and Remote-sensing Data: A Technical Paper* (New York: UN, 1984), Sales No. E.84.II.A.11.

[42] See US, Department of Commerce, International Trade Administration (ITA), "A Comprehensive Assessment of the US Information Services Industry" (Washington: ITA, 1984), mimeo., p. 41.

[43] See Sweden, Ministry of Public Administration, *Sweden and Transborder Data Flows* (Stockholm: Liber Allmaenna Foerlaget, 1985), pp. 11–14.

[44] See M. Malek Asghar, Y. Senuma and R. Pinez, "Work of the World Plan Committee for the Development of Telecommunications, Paris 1980, and the Evolution of Telephone Traffic", *Telecommunication Journal*, 47 (September 1980), p. 559.

[45] These figures measure settlement transactions, not the value of transmissions from a point of origin to a point of destination. For instance, when a person in the US telephones a person in France, the message is being sent by a US carrier to the French PTT, which delivers the message to its destination. The US carrier receives payment for the entire transmission and then remits part of the payment to the French PTT. Only the payment to the French PTT is measured here.

[46] It should be noted that this discussion has only dealt with public or quasi-public data networks, not with corporate networks.

[47] See for these and the following data Eurodata Foundation, "Eurodata '79: Study Synopsis" (London: Eurodata Foundation, n.d.) and T. Johnson and D. Lewin, "International Data Communications: Volumes and Applications" (London: Logica Ltd., n.d.).

[48] See Hans Bergendorff, "International Data Communication in the OECD Area 1976 and 1981", in Henry Ergas and Jun Okayama, eds., *Changing Market Structures in Telecommunications* (Amsterdam: North-Holland, 1984), pp. 71–88.

[49] See *Financial Times*, 22 October 1984, p. 14.

[50] OECD, *Telecommunications, op. cit.*, p. 24.

[51] SITA, *Annual Report*, 1984.

[52] See UN, Economic Commission for Europe, "A Preliminary Survey of Intra-Regional Trade in Services", TRADE/R.423 of 26 October 1981, p. 9.

[53] See Kiyoshi Kojima and Terutomo Ozawa, *Japan's General Trading Companies: Merchants of Economic Development* (Paris: OECD, 1984), p. 25.

54 *Ibid.*

55 See in this context Edward J. Regan, "Emerging Transborder Data Flow Issues and Their Impacts on International Banking" (New York: Manufacturers Hanover Trust Company, 1984), mimeo., especially chapters 7 and 9.

56 The required investments in information technology are, however, large, as the figures for Citicorp's network indicate (see below). In fact, it has been suggested that few of the large diversified transnational banks "will survive the next round of necessary capital investment in information technology. . . . The costs and risks of such investment are enormous and will only be undertaken by the very largest and most confident enterprises. Such investment may not even best be undertaken by banks but rather by communications enterprises, or through joint ventures." See Neil Coulbeck, *The Multinational Banking Industry* (New York: New York University Press, 1984), p. 16.

57 Not surprisingly, the Bank for International Settlements (BIS) has initiated a study on the impact of electronic banking, especially as regards implications for monetary policy. See *Financial Times*, 11 December 1984. See also BIS, *Payment Systems in Eleven Developed Countries* (Basel: Bank Administration Institute, 1980).

58 UNCTC, *Trends and Issues in Foreign Direct Investment and Related Flows* (New York: UN, 1985), Sales No. E.85.II.A.15.

59 See Group of Thirty, *Foreign Direct Investment 1973–87* (New York: Group of Thirty, 1984), p. 2.

60 See UNCTC, *Transnational Corporations in World Development: Third Survey* (New York: United Nations, 1983), Sales No. E.83.II.A.14, p. 6.

61 See UNCTC, "Recent Developments Related to Transnational Corporations and International Economic Relations", E/C.10/1985/2 of 26 February 1985, table 5.

62 See Henry Ergas and Ann Reid, "Transborder Data Flows in International Enterprises: The Results of a Joint BIAC/OECD Survey and Interviews with Firms. A Background Report", in OECD, *Transborder Data Flows: Proceedings of an OECD Conference* (Amsterdam: North Holland, 1985), pp. 213–250, IBI, "IBI World Survey of National Policies and Company Practices Concerning Transborder Data Flows" (Rome: IBI, 1983), mimeo., and Business International (BI), *Transborder Data Flow: Issues, Barriers and Corporate Responses* (New York: BI, 1983). The BI study, one of the most comprehensive in the field, was written by Therese R. Revesz, Managing Editor of *Business International*.

63 Business International, *op. cit.*, p. 275.

64 US, Congress, Senate, Committee on Commerce, Science and Transportation, "Long-range Goals in International Telecommunications and Information: An Outline for United States Policy" (Washington, D.C.: Government Printing Office, 1983), Committee print, p. 168.

65 Business International, *op. cit.*, p. 8.

66 Joan E. Spero, "International Trade and the Information Revolution" (Cambridge: Harvard University Center for Information Policy Research, 1985), mimeo., pp. 6–7.

67 *Business Week*, 18 October 1982, p. 50.

68 See Ergas and Reid, "Transborder Data Flows in International Enterprises", *op. cit.*

69 See Rada, *op. cit.*

70 *International Herald Tribune*, 26 March 1984, p. 7.

71 For these and the following figures, see *International Herald Tribune*, 26 March 1984, p. 7, *Financial Times*, 22 November 1985, p. III, and *Neue Züricher Zeitung*, 19–20 May 1984, p. 18.

72 See *Financial Times*, 29 January 1985. The three principal payments systems are Visa (which includes Barclaycard and Carte Bleu), Eurocard (Access and MasterCard) and

Eurocheque (an association of Western European banks which offers uniform credit cards and cheques).

[73] See *Financial Times*, 21 October 1985, p. III, and Touche Ross International, "The Impact of Technology on Banking" (New York: Touche Ross, 1985), p. 3.

[74] See Salomon Brothers, Inc., *Technology in Banking: A Path to Competitive Advantage* (New York: Salomon Brothers, 1985), p. 65.

[75] *Ibid.*, p. 66.

[76] *Financial Times*, 11 June 1985.

[77] *New York Times*, 19 March 1986. As Harold Malmgren put it in "Negotiating International Rules for Services" (Washington: Malmgren Inc., 1983), mimeo., p. 7: "A few institutions have carried their strategic reasoning to a broad conclusion: a global computer-telecommunications- information process network can enable them to provide a comprehensive, all-purpose services capability. This conception for some of them involves over the next five to ten years a gradual extension of the range of services offered far beyond the traditional boundaries of banking. For example, leading banks have started to offer use of their grids to other institutions, including customers as well as other banks. It is a short step further to offer technical and engineering services to help other institutions, whether customers or competitors, to build their own network."

[78] *Ibid.*, p. 6.

[79] OECD, *Interfuture: Facing the Future. Mastering the Probable and Managing the Unpredictable* (Paris: OECD, 1979), pp. 114 and 336, respectively.

[80] Alain Madec, *Les flux transfrontières de données: vers une économie internationale de l'information?* (Paris: La documentation française, 1982), p. 83.

[81] Diane Lady Dougan, "Keynote Address", in OECD, *Transborder Data Flows, op. cit.*, p. 55.

[82] See Hans-Peter Gassmann, "Data Networks: New Information Infrastructure", *OECD Observer*, No. 95 (November 1978), p. 15.

[83] See Peter Robinson, "Dimensions of TBDF: Some Economic Implications", in IBI, *Transborder Data Flow Policies* (New York: UNIPUB, 1983), p. 230.

[84] Business International, *op. cit.*

[85] *Ibid.*

[86] *Ibid.*, p. 200.

[87] "Will Transborder Data Flow Concentrate Decision-Making at Corporate Headquarters?", *Business International*, 30 (14 October 1983), p. 322.

[88] See James Womack, *The Future of the Automobile* (London: Allen and Unwin, 1984).

[89] *Financial Times*, 7 July 1985.

[90] K. Hoffman and H. Rush, "Microelectronics and the Garment Industry: Not Yet a Perfect Fit", *IDS Bulletin*, 13 (March 1982), p. 40.

[91] The study was undertaken in 1984 by the IFO Research Institute. See Ulrich Adler and Michael Breitenacher, "Bekleidungsgewerbe: Immer noch Produktionsverlagerung ins Ausland", *IFO-Schnelldienst*, 25–26 (1984), p. 20.

[92] See Raj Aggarwal, "The Orientation of the U.S. Semiconductor Industry", *Global Perspective* (A publication of The International Business Institute of The University of Toledo), 4 (Winter 1986), pp. 1, 3.

Table II-1. The blurring of the boundaries within the data industry, 1984

Firm	Peripherals/ components	Small computers	Medium computers	Large computers	Software	Communications
ATT	Telectron (1)	In house, Convergent Technologies (4), Olivetti (2,8)	In house	No plans Intel (5), Zilog Digital Research (7), others	In house, Philips (3,8) (5), Motorola (5),	In house, Gold Star (3)
Bull	Trilogy Systems (2,5), Magnetic Peripherals (2)	In house, Fortune Systems (2,6,8)	In house, Convergent Technologies (4), Ridge Computers (5,8)	In house, NEC (5,8), Honeywell (6)	In house	In house
Burroughs	Memorex (1), Peripheral Components (2), Qume (4), Canon (4), Intel (9)	Convergent Technologies (4)	In house, Graphics Technology (1)	In house Technology (1), others	In house, Midwest Systems Group (1) Graphics	In house Systems Research (1)
Control Data	Centronics (2), Magnetic Peripherals (2), Trilogy Systems (2,5)	In house, Columbia Data Products (4)	In house Microelectronics & Computer Technology (5)	In house, Chrysler Corp. (5), Northrop Electronics (7)	In house, United Tele-communications (2)	The Source(2),
DEC	In house, Trilogy Systems (2,5)	In house	In house Microelectronics & Computer Technology (5)	In house, agreements	Third-party Telecom (5), Xerox (5), Voice Mail Inc'l (8)	Northern
Honeywell	Magnetic Peripherals (2), Synertek (1)	In house, Columbia Data Products (4)	In house, Bull (2,6) & Computer Technology (5), NEC (5,6,8,9)	In house, Microelectronics	Third-party agreements L.M. Ericsson (3, 5,8), Keycom (3)	Action Communication Systems (1)
ICL	In house, Fujitsu (4)	In house, Logica (4), PERQ Systems (5,9), RAIR (8,9)	In house	In house, Fujitsu (5,8)	In house, third-party agreements	In house, ATT (6,8), Mitel (8)
IBM	In house, Intel (2)	In house	In house	In house Comshare (8), others (4,7,8)	Microsoft (4), Merrill Lynch (3), SBS (2) Sears and CBS (3)	Rolm (2),

(Table II-1 cont'd)

Firm	Peripherals/ components	Small computers	Medium computers	Large computers	Software	Communications
NCR	In house, Magnetic Peripherals (2)	In house, Convergent Technologies (4)	In house Microelectronics & Computer Technology (5)	In house, third-party agreements	In house, (2), Intel (8)	Comten (1), Zzel
Nixdorf	In house, LSI Logic (4)	In house	Spartacus Computers (6) Systems (5)	In house, Auragen Computers (6)	In house, Spartacus	In house
Olivetti	In house, Hermes Precisa Int'l (1) Lee Data (2,8) Ithaca (2,8)	In house, Corona (2,8), Kyocera (4)	In house, Stratus Computer (2,8), AT&T (8)	IPL (2,8) Hitachi (8) Financial Systems (2,8)	In house, Digital Research (2,8), Shared Bolt Beranek Newman (8)	In house, ATT (8), Northern Telecom (8,9),
Siemens	In house, IBM (4), Furukawa (3), Intel (4), Xerox (6,8)	In house	In house	Fujitsu (3)	In house Corning Glass (3)	In house,
Sperry	Magnetic Peripherals (2), Trilogy Systems (2,5)	Mitsubishi (7)	In house Microelectronics & Computer Technology (5), Mitsubishi (7)	In house, third-party agreements	In house, Northern Telecom (7)	In house,

Source: Business Week, 16 July 1984.

Key: (1) Acquisition. (2) Equity position. (3) Joint venture. (4) Original-equipment-manufacturer agreement. (5) Technology development. (6) Technology exchange or licensing. (7) Joint product development. (8) Marketing agreement. (9) Manufacturing agreement.

Table II-2. International software and data-processing services,
by country and region, 1980, 1984
(Billion dollars)

| Country, region | 1980 | | 1984 a/ | |
	Software	Data processing	Software	Data processing
Japan	.7	2.1	2.4	...
United States	.4	11.8	6.6	22.3
Western Europe	1.1	7.0	4.0	14.0
TOTAL	4.2	20.9	13	...

Source: Report by INPUT.

Note: These estimates exclude sales of software included in the sales of
hardware manufacturers and software developed by firms using computers and
other automated devices (robots, automated teller machines, etc.).

a/ Estimated.

Table II-3. Estimated revenues for the on-line data-base market,
United States and Western European countries, 1980, 1985
(Millions of dollars)

| Country | Year | | Average annual growth rate, 1980-85 (Percentage) |
	1980	1985 (estimated)	
United States	1 170	4 227	30
Western Europe	124	1 398	62
United Kingdom	54	397	49
France	12	305	91
Italy	10	110	61
Germany, Federal Rep.	7	149	84
Other	41	437	61
TOTAL	1 294	5 625	34

Source: UNCTC, Transborder Data Flows: Access to the International
On-line Data-base Market (New York: United Nations, 1983).

Table II-4. The growth of the number of on-line
data bases worldwide, 1979-1985

Year	Number of data bases a/	Number of data-base producers
Fall 1979	400	221
Spring 1980	450	269
Fall 1980	600	340
Spring 1981	770	411
Fall 1981	965	512
Spring 1982	1 133	612
Fall 1982	1 350	718
Spring 1983	1 600	820
Fall 1983	1 878	927
Spring 1984	2 225	1 069
Fall 1984	2 453	1 189
Spring 1985	2 764	1 316

Source: Cuadra Associates, Directory of Online Databases (Santa Monica: Cuadra Associates, 1985), p. 5.

a/ Distinctly named files within data-base families.

Table II-5. Network-termination points in Western Europe,
1981, 1987[a]

Country	Number of NTPs		NTPs per 1,000 working population	
	1981	1987	1981	1987
UK	162 700	350 000	7.2	15.6
FRG	103 500	312 000	4.8	14.5
France	79 700	260 000	4.4	13.4
Italy	71 200	229 000	4.9	15.9
Sweden	42 000	126 000	11.9	36.2
Spain	41 300	128 000	4.6	14.2
Netherlands	25 100	64 200	6.3	16.2
Denmark	17 600	44 400	6.6	15.4
Switzerland	15 400	41 600	6.8	19.2
Finland	13 700	38 300	6.2	16.9
Belgium	13 500	40 000	4.5	13.3
Norway	11 100	38 600	6.0	19.6
Austria	9 970	37 200	3.6	12.0
Ireland	1 910	11 300	2.6	15.2
Greece	1 450	15 100	1.0	9.1
Luxembourg	1 280	2 300	10.2	19.0
Portugal	850	4 100	0.3	1.6
TOTAL	612 260	1 742 100	5.4	15.0

Source: Eurodata Foundation, Data Communications in Europe, 1981-87
(London: Eurodata Foundation, 1983), p. 11.

a/ Forecast.

Table II-6. Telecommunication-equipment sales of market economies,
by product line, 1980, 1985

(Billion dollars and per cent)

Product line	Value of sales		Share of total	
	1980	1985[a]	1980	1985[a]
Switching	12.6	18.4	32	32
Transmission	12.2	17.4	31	30
Terminals	5.8	8.0	15	14
Private systems	4.3	6.4	11	11
Mobile radio	3.8	4.9	10	8
Other	0.7	2.9	2	5
TOTAL	39.4	58.0	100	100

Source: OECD, Telecommunications: Pressures and Policies for Change
(Paris: OECD, 1983), p. 20.

a/ Estimated.

Table II-7. The market-economies market for data-processing
equipment, by market segment, 1982

Market segment	Value (Billion dollars)	Per cent	Estimated annual growth rate a/ 1982-1987	1987-1992
Computers	35	45	10-12	5-8
Peripherals	30	38	8-11	7-9
Terminals	13	17	6-11	3-9
TOTAL b/	78	100	10-13	8-12

Source: Financial Times, 21 March 1983.

a/ Based on constant dollars.
b/ Including software.

Table II-8. The market-economies market for data-processing equipment,
by region and market segment, 1982
(Per cent)

Country/region	Market segment			
	Computers	Peripherals	Terminals	TOTAL
United States	50.1	50.5	58.5	51.7
Western Europe	31.1	32.7	21.5	30.1
Japan	12.8	10.6	15.4	12.4
Other	6	6.3	4.6	5.8
TOTAL				
Per cent	100	100	100	100
Billion dollars	35	30	13	78

Source: Same as table II-7.

Table II-9. The world's 50 largest data corporations, 1984

Rank	Corporation	Country	Data-processing revenues (Million dollars)	Foreign as per cent of total DP-revenues (1983)
1	International Business Machines	US	44 292	38
2	Digital Equipment Corporation	US	6 230	36
3	Burroughs Corporation	US	4 500	40
4	Control Data Corporation	US	3 756	33
5	NCR Corporation	US	3 670	46
6	Fujitsu Ltd.	J	3 499	...
7	Sperry Corporation	US	3 474	33
8	Hewlett-Packard Corporation	US	3 400	41
9	NEC Corp	J	2 799	...
10	Siemens	FRG	2 790	...
11	Wang Laboratories Inc.	US	2 421	33
12	Hitachi Ltd.	J	2 200	...
13	Olivetti	Italy	2 012	20
14	Apple Computer Corp.	US	1 898	25
15	Honeywell Inc.	US	1 825	26
16	Groupe Bull	France	1 556	10
17	Xerox Corporation	US	1 518	42
18	American Telephone & Telegraph	US	1 340	...
19	Data General Corporation	US	1 230	34
20	ICL	UK	1 223	23
21	Nixdorf	FRG	1 147	14
22	Toshiba Corp.	J	1 139	...
23	Commodore International Ltd.	US	1 130	35
24	L. M. Ericsson	Sweden	1 123	27
25	TRW Inc.	US	1 105	24
26	Philipps	Netherl.	1 090	26
27	Northern Telecom Inc.	Can	1 050	...
28	McDonnell Douglas Corp.	US	983	14
29	Automatic Data Processing Inc.	US	958	...
30	Oki Electric Ind. Co. Ltd.	J	899	...

(Table II-9 cont'd)

Rank	Corporation	Country	Data-processing revenues (Million dollars)	Foreign as per cent of total DP-revenues (1983)
31	General Electric Co.	US	865	40
32	Texas Instruments Inc.	US	860	31
33	Mitsubishi Electric Co.	J	817	...
34	Storage Technology Corporation	US	808	20
35	General Motors Corp.	US	786	...
36	Amdahl Corporation	US	779	...
37	Harris Corporation	US	730	30
38	Tandy Corporation	US	719	17
39	Computer Sciences Corporation	US	709	...
40	Prime Computer Inc.	US	643	43
41	ITT Corporation	US	640	11
42	Triumph Adler AG	FRG	632	...
43	Motorola Inc.	US	618	33
44	Datapoint Corporation	US	589	...
45	Tandem Computers Inc.	US	566	31
46	Computervision Corporation	US	556	45
47	National Semiconductor	US	550	...
48	Dataproducts Corporation	US	485	20
49	C.Itoh Electronics Inc.a/	US	443	45
50	Telex Corp.	US	443	...

Sources: "The Datamation 100: The Leading Worldwide DP Companies", Datamation, 4 June 1984, 1 June 1985, p. 50, "The Datamation 100: The Leading U.S. DP Companies", Datamation, 4 June 1984, pp. 60–61, and "Crowning Europe's DP Royalty", Datamation, 1 September 1984, pp. 160–161.

a/ US corporation only.

Table II-10. Selected applications of computer capabilities

Example	Usual type of computer
DATA PROCESSING	
Business records (accounting, order processing and billing, production control, inventories, taxes, banking)	Mainframes, minis, or micros, depending on size of business
Government records and statistics (census and other data bases, tax records, social security, economic data)	Mainframes
Scientific and technical (social science data bases, engineering calculations, modeling of complex systems)	Mainframes for batch and interactive processing; micros and minis for laboratory automation as well as specialized applications such as modeling chemical reactions
Medical records	Minis or mainframes
Airline reservations	Minis or mainframes
Point-of-sale terminals, electronic cash registers	Micros, but may be part of distributed system
COMMUNICATIONS AND CONTROL	
Multiplexing and transmission of voice and alphanumeric data	Varies
Telephone exchanges	Mainframes
Private exchanges (PBX, PABX)	Micros and minis
Facsimile transmission	Minis and micros
Teletext, viewdata	Micros
Air traffic control	Mainframes
MILITARY SYSTEMS	
Signal processing (radar, sonar)	Mainframes or minis, depending on need for portability
Navigation	As above, or micros
Fire control	As above, or micros
Flight control	Micros
INDUSTRIAL SYSTEMS	
Batch process control (machine tools, assembly robots, heat treating, materials handling, steelmaking, typesetting)	Minis and micros

(Table II-10 cont'd)

Example	Usual type of computer
Continuous process control (petroleum refining, rubber and synthetic fibers, basic chemicals, paper products, foods)	Mainframes and minis
Computer-aided design	Mainframes and minis
Energy production, conservation and control (turbine startup, electric utility load management, process heat, building heating, ventilation, and air-conditioning)	Varies
Environmental monitoring and pollution control	Minis and micros
Education and training (computer-assisted instruction)	Varies
Measurement and testing (medical diagnostics, nondestructive inspection, chemical analysis)	Minis and micros

OFFICE AUTOMATION

Example	Usual type of computer
Word processors	Micros and minis
Copiers	Micros
Calculators and accounting machines	Micros

CONSUMER PRODUCTS

Example		Usual type of computer
Automobiles (engine control, driver information, diagnostics)	))	
Home entertainment (electronic and video games, personal computers)	))	
Appliances (refrigerators, microwave ovens, sewing machines)	))	
Thermostats and environmental controls	))	Micros
Calculators	)	
Cameras	)	
Electronic watches	)	

Source: United States, Congress, Office of Technology Assessment, International Competitiveness in Electronics (Washington, D.C.: Office of Technology Assessment, 1983), p. 91.

Table II-11. Number of robots in use in market economies,
by country, 1978-1982

(Units)

Country	1978	1979	1980	1981	1982
Japan	10 095	11 533	14 246	21 684	31 900
United States	2 831	3 340	3 849	4 700	7 232
Germany, Fed. Rep. of	450	...	823	2 301	3 500
Sweden	800	...	1 133	1 700	...
France	...	...	200	620	993
United Kingdom	125	...	371	713	977
Italy	...	...	400	450	600
Belgium	...	...	...	44	305
Canada	...	...	...	214	273
Switzerland	...	...	...	...	200
Finland	...	...	40	...	75
Austria	...	...	...	...	70
Norway	...	...	...	...	20
Taiwan	...	...	...	...	11
All others	...	...	...	...	2 000[a]/
TOTAL	16 000	19 000	24 000	35 000	50 000

Source: US, Department of Commerce, International Trade Administration
(ITA), A Competitive Assessment of the US Manufacturing Automation Equipment
Industries (Washington: ITA, 1984), p. 7.

a/ Estimated

Table II-12. Estimated size of the CAD market in Japan and
the US, 1980-1983

(100 million yen)

Country	1980	1982	1983	Growth rate (Per cent)
Japan	220	690	1 100	71
US	1 300	2 260	3 520	39

Source: "Japan's CAD Market: The Growth Phase Begins", Quarterly
Survey (Industrial Bank of Japan), 60 (October-December 1984), pp. 2,3.

Table II-13. Basic characteristics of the manufacturing
environment

Traditional technology	CAD/CAM environment
Economy of scale	Economy of scope
Experience curve	Truncated (or expanded) product life cycle
Task specialization	Multi-mission firms
Work as a social activity	Unmanned systems
Separable variable costs	Joint costs
Standardization	Variety
Flexibility and variety are expensive	Flexibility and variety create profits

Source: Mariam Jelinek and Joel D. Golhar, "The Interface between Strategy and Manufacturing Technology", Columbia Journal of World Business, 18 (Spring 1983), p. 27.

Table II-14. The introduction of electronic controls in
gasoline-powered engines by means of microprocessors

Main control function	1977	1978	1979	1980	1981
Fuel injection			x	x	x
Carburator			x	x	x
Ignition timing	x	x	x	x	x
Anti-knocking					x
EGR		x	x	x	x
Engine idling			x	x	x
Cruising speed					x
Torque converter, transmission					x
Engine displacement, etc.					x

Source: "Innovations in Automotive Electronics", Quarterly Survey (Industrial Bank of Japan), 61 (January-March 1985), p. 3.

Table II-15. The use of microelectronics in the manufacturing
industry of France, the FRG and the UK, 1984
(Weighted by employment of establishments
employing more than 20 people)
(Per cent)

Application	France	FRG	UK
Product applications	6	13	10
Process applications	35	47	43
All applications	38	51	47
No applications	62	49	53

Source: Jim Northcott, et al., Microelectronics in Industry. An
International Comparison: Britain, Germany, France (London: Policy Studies
Institute, 1985), p. 16.

Table II-16. Transnational computer-communication links
of Brazil and Austria, by type of user
(Number)

| User group | Brazil | | Austria |
	March 1982	December 1983	1985
Manufacturing	12	24	16
Data-processing equipment	4	6	a/
Other	8	18	...
Services	15	31	101
Banking	1	10	19b/
Trading	1	1	22c/
Computer services	2	5	32d/
Airlinese/	9	9	7
Petroleum distribution	2	4	...
Other	-	2	21f/
Government	2	2	29g/
TOTAL	29	57	146

Sources: UNCTC, "The Role of Transnational Corporations in Transborder
Data Flows", E/C.10/1984/14 of 24 January 1984, p. 8, and E/C.10/1986/16 of
12 February 1986, p. 12.

a/ Included in computer services.
b/ Including insurance (6 links).
c/ Including 4 that are trade and industry.
d/ Computer companies.
e/ Including closed user group.
f/ Including some government.
g/ Including 26 links of international organizations.

Table II-17. Transnational computer-communication systems in Japan,
by type of user, 1974-1983[a]/
(Number)

User group	1974	1975	1976	1977	1978	1979	1980	1981	1982	1983
Manufacturing	13	14	13	17	23	33	48	54	67	121
Services	23	25	31	40	54	80	99	131	152	240
Banking	2	2	4	7	13	22	31	47	53	67
Securities	1	1	1	1	1	3	4	5	8	12
Trade	10	10	11	14	16	25	30	32	40	90
Transport	6	8	10	10	15	18	24	29	32	41
Computer services	2	2	3	5	6	9	7	11	11	12
Communications, publishing and other services[b]/	2	2	2	3	3	3	3	7	8	18
Government	3	3	3	3	3	3	3	4	4	4
Kokusai Denshin Denwa (KDD)	1	1	2	2	4	5	6	6	6	7
TOTAL	40	43	49	62	84	121	156	195	229	372

Source: Government of Japan, Ministry of Posts and Telecommunications, White Paper on
Communications (Tokyo: Ministry of Posts and Telecommunications, various years).

a/ All figures are for March of the year given.
b/ For instance hotel reservations.

Table II-18. Foreign transactions of French computer-service firms, 1978-1983

(Million francs and per cent)

Item	Year						Growth rate 1982-1983 (Per cent)
	1978	1979	1980	1981	1982	1983	
Total revenues	5 400	6 900	8 500	10 600	13 000	15 800	22
Of which:							
Revenues by							
foreign affiliates	657	900	1 070	1 450	1 960	2 300	17
Exports	440	510	10	800	840	900	7

Source: France, Ministère du Redéploiement Industriel et du Commerce Extérieur, Direction des Industries Electroniques et de l'Informatique (DIELI), "Les sociétes de service et de conseil en informatique" (Paris: DIELI, various years).

Table II-19. Foreign revenues of US computer-service corporations, by service mode, 1980, 1981 a/

(Million dollars and per cent)

Service mode	Foreign revenue		Per cent of total revenue		Revenue growth 1980-1981 (Per cent)
	1980	1981	1980	1981	
Processing services	1 005	1 127	10	10	12
Software products	933	1 141	24	22	22
Professional services	353	428	8	8	21
Integrated sytems	158	267	7	8	69
TOTAL	2 449	2 963	12	12	21

Source: ADAPSO, Annual Reports.

a/ 243 corporations with over $10 million in US revenue.

Table II-20. The internationalization of the US information-
service industry, 1981, 1982
(Millions of dollars and per cent)

Area	Revenues		Growth rates		
	1981	1982	1981	1983	1987a/
US	9 759	11 004	13	14	14
Europe	1 815	1 990	10	9	9
All other	544	612	12	17	8
TOTAL	12 118	13 606	12	13	11

Source: US, Department of Commerce, International Trade Administration
(ITA), "A Comprehensive Assessment of the US Information Services Industry"
(Washington: ITA, 1984), mimeo., p. 39.

a/ Projected compounded average annual growth rates 1982-1987.

Table II-21. US telecommunication receipts and payments, 1970-1980

(Millions of dollars)

Item	1970	1973	1974	1975	1976	1977	1978	1979	1980
Receipts	304	498	551	648	777	865	978	1 109	1 337
Payments	291	494	555	647	827	894	1 043	1 266	1 476

Source: Anthony J. DiLullo, "Service Transactions in the U.S. International Accounts, 1970-80", Survey of Current Business, 61 (November 1981),
p. 39. U.S. Department of Commerce, Bureau of Economic Analysis, Balance
of Payments Division.

Table II-22. International data-transmission networks, 1986

Country	TELENET[a]	TYMNET	UNINET[a]	INFONET	AUTONET	MARKNET	IPSS	GLOBEDAT
Developed countries								
Australia	X	X	X	X	X	X	X	X
Austria	X	X	X	X	X	X	X	X
Belgium	X	X	X	X	X	X	X	X
Canada	X	X	X	X		X	X	0
Denmark	X	X	X	X	X	X	X	X
Finland	X	X	X	X	X	X	X	X
France	X	X	X	X	X	X	X	X
FRG	X	X	X	X	X	X	X	X
Greece	X	X	X	X	X	X	X	X
Iceland		X		X	X			
Ireland	X	X	X	X	X	X	X	X
Israel	X	X	X	X	X		X	X
Italy	X	X	X	X	X	X	X	X
Japan	X	X	X	X	X	X	X	X
Luxembourg	X	X	X	X	X	X	X	X
Netherlands	X	X	X	X	X	X	X	X
New Zealand	X	X	X	X	X	X	X	X
Norway	X	X	X	X	X	X	X	X
Portugal	X	X	X	X	X	X	X	X
South Africa	X	X	X	X	X	X	X	X
Spain	X	X	X	X	X	X	X	X
Sweden	X	X	X	X	X	X	X	X
Switzerland	X	X	X	X	X	X	X	X
United Kingdom	X	X	X	X	X	X	0	X
United States	0	0	0	0	0	0	X	X
Socialist countries								
Hungary	X	X	X	X	X	X		
USSR				X				
Developing countries								
Africa								
Egypt	X	X		X		X		
Gabon	X	X	X	X	X	X	X	
Gambia		X						
Ivory Coast	X	X	X	X	X	X	X	
Réunion	X			X	X	X		X

(Table II-22 cont'd)

Country	TELENET [a/]	TYMNET	UNINET [a/]	INFONET	AUTONET	MARKNET	IPSS	GLOBEDAT
Asia								
Bahrain	X	X	X	X	X	X	X	X
China	X	X		X	X	X		
Dubai								X
Fiji				X				
French Polynesia		X	X					X
Guam	X	X	X	X	X			
Hong Kong	X	X	X	X	X	X	X	X
Indonesia	X	X		X	X	X	X	
Iraq		X		X	X			
Korea, Rep. of	X	X	X	X	X	X	X	X
Kuwait	X	X	X	X	X	X		X
Malaysia	X	X		X			X	
Oman							X	
Philippines	X	X	X	X	X	X	X	X
Qatar	X	X	X	X	X	X		X
Saudi Arabia	X	X	X	X	X			X
Singapore	X	X	X	X	X	X	X	X
Taiwan	X	X	X	X	X	X	X	X
Thailand	X	X		X		X	X	
United Arab Emi.	X	X	X	X	X	X	X	X
Latin America								
Antigua		X						
Argentina	X	X	X	X	X	X	X	
Bahamas	X	X		X	X	X	X	
Barbados	X	X	X	X	X	X	X	X
Bermuda	X	X	X	X	X	X	X	X
Brazil	X	X	X	X	X	X	X	
Cayman Islands	X	X		X			X	
Chile	X	X		X	X	X		X
Colombia	X	X	X	X	X	X		
Costa Rica	X	X		X		X	X	
Netherlands Ant.	X			X	X			
Dominican Republic		X	X	X	X	X	X	
El Salvador				X				
French Antilles	X	X	X	X	X	X		
French Guyana	X	X					X	

(Table II-22 cont'd)

Country	TELENET[a]	TYMNET	UNINET[a]	INFONET	AUTONET	MARKNET	IPSS	GLOBEDAT
Latin America (cont'd)								
Guadeloupe		X	X		X	X	X	
Guatemala	X	X		X		X		
Honduras	X	X		X		X	X	
Jamaica	X	X		X		X		
Martinique		X	X		X	X	X	
Mexico	X	X	X	X	X	X	X	
Panama	X	X		X		X		
Peru	X	X		X				
Trinidad	X	X		X		X		

Source: Annual reports and other sources.

a/ To merge in 1986.

Key: X Countries served.
0 Country of legal incorporation.

Table II-23. Trade in data-processing equipment, 1978-1982
(Billion of dollars and per cent)

Region	Year				
	1978	1979	1980	1981	1982
Developed market economies					
Imports					
Billion dollars	7.0	9.3	12.0	12.8	13.9
Per cent	91	91	91	89	88
Exports					
Billion dollars	7.0	9.2	12.3	12.7	14.1
Per cent	99	99	98	97	97
Developing countries					
Imports					
Billion dollars	.7	.9	1.3	1.5	1.8
Per cent	9	9	10	11	11
Exports					
Billion dollars	.1	.1	.2	.4	.4
Per cent	1	1	2	3	3

Source: United Nations, 1982 United Nations Yearbook of International Trade Statistics (New York: United Nations, 1984), p. 194.

Table II-24. The share of numerically controlled machine tools in total
machine-tool exports, selected countries, 1976-1982
(Per cent)

Country	Year			
	1976	1980	1981	1982
Germany, Fed. Rep. of	14.2	18.1	19.9	25.2
France	11.8	19.4	20.2	19.4
Italy	18.1	22.5	23.7	22.5
Japan b/	23.8	64.1	70.5	...
United Kingdom	9.3 a/	10.9	15.6	22.7
United States b/	...	23.5	20.1	25.5

Source: OECD, "Trade in High Technology Products: An Examination of Trade Related Issues in the Machine-Tool Industry", DSTI/SPR/83.102 of 22 March 1984, p. 18.

a/ 1977.
b/ Metal-cutting machines only.

Table II-25. Communication expenditures of the nine
leading sogo shosha, 1978
(Millions of yen)

Name	Communication expenditures	Communication expenses as per cent of total sales
Mitsubishi Corporation	4 337	3.0
Mitsui & Co.	11 936a/	9.6a/
C. Itoh & Co.	3 528	3.9
Marubeni Corporation	3 593	3.8
Sumitomo Corporation	3 528	4.3
Nissho Iwai	3 386	4.7
Tomen	685b/	1.9b/
Kanematsu Gosho	1 494	4.5
Nichimen Jitsugyo	1 474	3.8

Source: Kiyoshi Kojima and Terutomo Ozawa, Japan's General Trading
Companies: Merchants of Economic Development (Paris: OECD, 1984), p. 90.

a/ Including computer expenses estimated at 6 billion yen.
b/ Expenses at headquarters only.

Table II-26. Membership and traffic evolution of SWIFT, 1977-1985

Year	Members (number)		Traffic evolution (Million messages)			Peak day (1000 messages)
	Member banks	Member countriesa/	Annual volume	Cumulative volume	Growth rate (Per cent)	
1977b/	518	15	3.2	3.2	...	...
1978	586	16	21.4	24.6	572	...
1979	683	16	34.4	59.0	61	...
1980	768	21	47.2	106.2	37	...
1981	900	26	65.5	171.7	33	319
1982	1 017	32	79.9	251.6	28	385
1983	1 104	37	104.1	355.7	30	490
1984	1 188	39	129.9	485.6	25	610
1985	1 275	46	157.2	642.8	21	733

Source: SWIFT, Annual Reports, various years.

a/ Countries in which SWIFT is operational.
b/ August-December only.

Table II-27. Assessment of the importance of transborder data flows
by corporate activity and region, 1983, 1988 a/
(Per cent)

Corporate activity	1983				1988			
	United States	Western Europe	Other	TOTAL	United States	Western Europe	Other	TOTAL
Financial functions								
Financial management	64	58	45	60	71	81	64	73
Invoicing	31	35	27	32	35	46	36	38
Paying	29	31	18	28	31	39	27	32
Portfolio management	15	23	–	16	23	27	–	21
Foreign exchange management	14	8	5	11	17	15	9	16
Marketing and distribution								
Ordering	37	31	45	36	42	35	45	40
Marketing and distrib.	35	31	45	35	40	54	55	46
After-sales services	21	19	36	23	27	19	36	26
Customer services b/	12	23	18	16	12	23	18	16
Pricing information	4	4	–	3	4	12	–	6
Production								
Inventory control	39	27	27	34	44	46	36	44
Manufacturing	35	23	18	30	44	35	18	39
Sourcing	19	8	27	17	35	12	27	27
CAD/CAM/CAE	17	8	–	12	31	12	9	23
Product quality testing	14	8	–	10	15	12	18	15
Management								
Strategic planning	31	15	18	25	44	27	27	37
Management info.	15	27	18	19	25	31	18	26
Electronic mail	10	–	9	7	14	–	18	10
Research and development								
Research and development	23	27	9	23	33	39	18	33
Design engineering	21	8	–	15	25	12	–	15
Personnel								
Payroll, personnel	23	12	9	18	29	15	9	23
TOTAL no. of firms	52	26	11	89	52	26	11	89

Sources: Business International, Transborder Data Flow, op. cit., pp. 11 and 14.
a/ Percentage of companies that consider TDF to be important or very important for specified corporate activities.
b/ Applies to banking/finance, transportation and information services companies.

Table II-28.   The increased tradeability of services

Service	Change
Shipping (freight)	Partial substitution of transport of goods by services by substituting the shipped printed matter and sending it through telecommunications.
Other transport (air, rail, road, inland waterways)	As above. New logistic systems are emerging where the goods themselves are transferred through telecommunications. This trend will be reinforced through cellular radio.
Travel (passenger transport)	Partial substitution especially of business travelling through the use of teleconferencing.
Tourism (counselling, advertising, tour operations, hotel/motel services)	New systems incorporating videodisc and inter-active routines are becoming available. Long-distance and international toll-free services will be widely used. Hotel/motel reservations are already, as for airlines, highly computerized. This industry will be far more internationalized. Some hotels are now offering teleconferencing services between their different locations. Videotext already allows bookings to be made directly for some services in this area.
Insurance and reinsurance	Customers will be able to order directly specific insurance through retailing points or terminals, as it is the case in many airports with flight insurance.
Banking and other financial services	The use of automatic teller machines can reach many different places while providing a 24-hour service. Telebanking is done now at corporate level and experiments are being conducted in households. Internationally, SWIFT will evolve into a world bank-trading network. Banks are also increasingly becoming information suppliers in finance, trade and investment.
Construction engineering (management, consulting, design/architecture)	The use of CAD systems and remote entry for calculations in centralized systems will increase the tradeability of services.
Professional services	Remote access is the key in this sector.
– Legal	More data bases of a national (e.g., Lexis) or of an international nature will come into existence. Legal professionals, as well as people seeking advice, will interrogate bases directly.

(Table II-28 cont'd)

Service	Change
- Economic	A large number of data bases, both national and international, exist. This area is expanding greatly.
- Medical	Remote diagnosis for some types of illness is already being tested. The results of medical exams can now be transmitted in some cases to specialist clinics within or outside the country. This is analogous to the processing of data abroad.
- Technical	Technicians operating in different places can work on the same problem as is now the case with the design of chips. Access to technical data bases has been possible since the late 1960s and developed rapidly during the 1970s. Specific technical data bases are being developed for new manufacturing processes, such as machining data bases.
- Education	This is normally a non-marketable service. The use of educational software, teaching machines, interactive programmes and video cassettes is converting a large proportion of this activity into a marketable service, at least as far as "instruction" is concerned.
Brokerage	This service is heavily based on the availability of information. It will become even more international in the future when it will be possible for non-specialists to intervene through terminals, thereby eliminating middle-persons in many cases.
Accounting	This was one of the first applications of electronic data processing and is used by many TNCs on an international basis. Many small and medium-sized enterprises will internalize this service rather than buy it from specialist firms. This is possible because of microcomputers with programs combining accounting, billing and management-reporting systems.
Advertising	Tradeability will increase especially with direct satellite broadcasting starting operations in Europe in 1985-86; DSB is already operational in Canada and parts of the US.

150

(Table II-28 cont'd)

Service	Change
Films and TV features	Direct satellite broadcasting will increase transportability while the existence of video tapes will make enforcement of copyright laws practically impossible.
Wholesaling and retailing	Easy access to price information and services could increase competition in this sector. Complex delivery systems are likely to be developed. In large supermarket chains, the trend may be to offer also a "supermarket of services".
Repairs and maintenance	As equipment increasingly includes electronics and self-diagnosis, maintenance and interaction for repair can be done remotely, as well as the running of recovery routines. Repairs as such have to be done in situ, but the instructions can come long distance, unless redundancy capacity can be switched on. Modular repairs are increasing the self-service aspects of this activity.
Data processing	The key in this sector is the ease of data communications. Data can be processed within or outside a country.
- Software	Software can be developed and maintained by teams at distant locations. It can be distributed using telecommunication lines.
- Remote data entry	There is a growing trend to use cheap skilled clerical labor for remote data entry.
Information services	
- Newspapers	Newspapers are considered to be "goods". However, TDF permit, e.g., that the International Herald Tribune is edited in Paris and printed in Zürich, Paris, London, and Hong Kong. Videotext will partly make hard copies obsolete.
- On-line systems	Commodity, stock and financial information. These systems will develop to provide a more analytical type of format with graphics included.

    Source: Partly adapted from Juan Rada, "Development, Telecommunications and the Emerging Service Economy" (Geneva: International Management Institute, 1984), mimeo., pp. 16-20.

Table II-29. Automated teller networks in the US, 1985

Network	Number of ATMs		Access-card base (millions)	
	Dec. 1984	Aug. 1985	Dec. 1984	Aug. 1985
Cirrus	6 471	8 119	27.3	30.8
Plus	4 675	5 617	26.6	48.6
Express Cash	3 200	5 294	2.1	2.9
Visa	2 240	4 500	20.0	45.0
Citishare	2 400	2 900	8.5	8.5
The Exchange	1 690	2 787	3.4	6.1
Nationet	1 434	2 400	12.0	10.0
Master Teller	1 000	2 000	3.0	6.0
TOTAL	23 110	33 617	102.9	157.9

Source: Financial Times, 21 October 1985.

152

Table II-30. The status of consumer banking technology, 1985

Country	ATM networks	EFT/POS	In-home banking
Australia	1	3	4
Belgium	1	3	5
Brazil	1	3	4
Canada	1	3	3
France	1	2	2
Germany, Fed. Rep. of	2	3	3
Hong Kong	1	2	2
Indonesia	5	5	5
Ireland	1	3	3
Italy	2	3	4
Japan	1	3	3
Luxembourg	1	3	5
Malaysia	2	4	4
Mexico	2	5	3
Netherlands	2	3	5
New Zealand	1	3	3
Norway	1	2	4
Panama	1	4	5
Philippines	1	4	4
Singapore	1	4	3
South Africa	2	3	3
Spain	1	2	3
Sweden	1	3	2
Switzerland	1	3	3
United Kingdom	1	3	3
United States	1	3	3

Source: Touche Ross International, "The Impact of Technology on Banking" (New York: Touche Ross, 1985), p. 9.
Key:

1 = Widespread penetration of technology among large/small banks. Growth rate slowed.
2 = Limited penetration primarily among large banks. Acceptance on widescale basis expected within 3 to 5 years.
3 = Current experience limited to testing mode. Broader acceptance possible over the next 5 years.
4 = Not operational even on test basis-conceptual phase. Acceptance 5+ years away.
5 = No plans or discussion among major banks. Acceptance not likely before mid-1990s.

Table II-31. Telecommunication plant gross investment and construction
             expenditures, selected countries, 1981, 1982

Region and country	Plant gross investment, 1981		Construction expenditures			
	Total (Million dollars)	Per capita (Dollars)	Total (Million dollars)		Per capita (Dollars)	
			1981	1982a/	1981	1982a/
Developed market economies						
US	186 543	804	23 297	24 700	100	106
Japan	39 300	333	7 695	...	65	...
Italy	13 170	230	1 803	2 174	32	33
FRG	4 700	76	3 974	4 335	64	70
Developing countries						
Brasil	200	2	1 241	1 844	10	16
Philippines	545	39	288	...	6	...
Egypt	200	5	203	285	5	7
Papua New Guinea	94	31	21	29	7	10

Source: "International Telecom Spending Slows Down", Telephony, 22 February
1982, pp. 74-86.

a/ Estimated.

Table II-32. Manufacturing cost per electronic device
             (Dollars)

Process	Hong Kong	United States
Manual	.0248	.0752
Semi-automatic	.0183	.0293
Automatic	.0163	.0178

Source: Global Electronics Information Newsletter, (October 1982), as
cited by Rada, op. cit.

III

The Interest Constellation

Data services, as we saw in the last chapter, have become important as industries in their own right. Furthermore, as we also saw, they have manifold implications for other economic activities, in the domestic as much as in the international context. As a crucial component of data resources in general, they have acquired strategic economic importance and have become central to economic development; and as a core service, they are obviously central to a discussion of all other services. As has been observed from the particular vantage point of restricting data flows:

> Restricting the transmission of data across national borders is a nontariff measure that has impact far beyond the industry itself: it touches on spectra of service and non-service industries dependent on such data. In fact, the spectra of industries and issues touched by the general area of service activity are limitless. It is strikingly illustrative of how a service function can so directly link to the functioning of international commerce. Constructing rules governing this activity is vital.[1]

The role of data services as a core service is the principal reason why the data-services discussion must be seen in the framework of the general discussion on trade and FDI in services. And, of course, any framework adopted for services in general will also apply to data services.

Before examining the interest situations shaping the search for an appropriate framework for trade and FDI in data services, a brief excursion into transborder flows of personal data is in order, because it was here that the TDF discussion had its genesis and it was on the matter of personal data that the first international agreements were reached.

A. Prelude: privacy protection

The TDF discussions originated in privacy concerns in the national context. Spurred by the growing conversion of name-linked files into machine-readable data and the subsequent interlinking of the resulting data bases during the 1970s, many OECD countries began to adopt privacy-protection laws. Since it became quickly obvious that the laws of a particular country could be evaded by locating data bases in a country providing less data protection, efforts were initiated to harmonize national policies in this respect. The results were Guidelines adopted by the OECD and a Convention ratified by members of the Council of Europe.

Both instruments deal exclusively with the transborder flow of personal (or name-linked) data and thus have a focus quite different from that of the present volume. There are three reasons, however, why they are briefly reviewed here. First, they are international instruments specifically dealing with TDF. Second, by dealing with one specific aspect of the subject, privacy protection in the context of the transborder flow of personal data, they provide, so to speak, the prelude to a broader international framework for TDF. And third, their adoption shows that it is possible to reconcile two important competing public-policy objectives in this area: protection of privacy and free flow of information.

The increased use of computers for the storage and processing of data about individuals magnified the concerns inherent in any form of personal record-keeping systems. Personal data files contain a wide range of data on such matters as an individual's financial, economic, educational, welfare, business and insurance status; medical and criminal history; membership in various organizations; and political and religious associations and beliefs. In comparison to traditional filing methods, the increasing application of computer technology to data manipulation gives the concern for individual privacy a new intensity.

Computerized personal data systems may have adverse effects on the right to privacy for a variety of reasons. First, they increase vastly the potential quantity and range of data stored on the private life of an individual. Furthermore, they allow information to be disseminated more easily and to a wider audience than the individual may have anticipated when originally surrendering the information. In particular, data may be shared—to an unpredictable extent—by normally separate organizations (including branches of government) and by an unidentifiable range of users. Since present computer technology permits the centralization of data collected from various sources and their merger into a single file, it also permits speedy access to large quantities of personal data gathered over time to obtain composite profiles of individuals. And, finally, they increase the risks of inaccuracies in reporting, recording and indexing of personal data files and the possibility of unauthorized access to personal information. All these factors are not only important for reasons of privacy per se but also because many of these data may be used for decisions pertaining to an individual's qualifications, creditworthiness, health, insurance, and the like.

In response to these developments, a number of governments—almost exclusively in developed market economies—have begun to deal with the issue in actions that range from constitutional provisions to the preparation of pertinent governmental reports (see table III-1).[2] Where a regulatory framework has been established, it is usually aimed at ensuring the individual's right to privacy by defining basic rules for the handling of personal information. Generally, these data-protection laws apply to name-linked data in both public and private computerized files and treat most personal data as sensitive data. They require the licensing or registration of systems for the processing of personal data; require the adoption of specific procedures that ensure accurate and fair collection, processing and distribution of data for clearly defined purposes; foresee procedures through which individuals can have access to data collected about them and can request the correction of wrong information; provide for the creation of a follow-up machinery

Table III-1. Status of data-protection and privacy legislation,
January 1986

Country	National	Sub-national
Australia	(P),R	L
Austria	C,L<u>a</u>/	
Belgium	P,R	
Brazil	P	
Canada	L	L
Colombia	P	
Cyprus	RP	
Denmark	L<u>a</u>/	
Finland	P,R	
France	L	
Germany, Fed. Rep. of	L<u>a</u>/,(P),R	L
Greece	RP	
Hong Kong	RP	
Hungary	L	
Iceland	L<u>a</u>/	
Ireland	RP	
Israel	L	
Italy	P,R	
Japan	R	
Luxembourg	L	
Netherlands	C,P,R	
New Zealand	L	
Norway	L<u>a</u>/,R	
Portugal	C,P	
Spain	C,P,R	
Sweden	L,R	
Switzerland	(P),R	L
Turkey	RP	
United Kingdom	L,R	
United States	L,P,R	L
Yugoslavia	RP	

Sources: G. Russell Pipe and Chris Brown, *International Information Economy Handbook* (Washington: Transnational Data Report, 1985), p. XI, and *Transnational Data and Communications Report*, 9 (January 1986), p. 29.

Key:
L	Law adopted.	R	Government report prepared.
C	Constitutional provision.	P	Legislation in parliament.
(P)	Draft legislation prepared.	RP	Government report in preparation.

a/ Under revision.

with varying degrees of competence; and use criminal sanctions in cases of violation of the applicable law.

An important feature of some laws—those of Austria, Denmark, Luxembourg, and Norway—is that they pertain not only to natural but also to legal persons. The inclusion of legal persons in data-protection laws makes it possible to extend restrictions on the transmission of data on natural persons to the transmission of data on legal persons (e.g., industrial firms or financial institutions). This issue arose when, in the preparation of data-protection laws, the applicability of these laws had to be determined. In defining "person", a country like Austria took the position that no difference in principle should be made between natural and legal persons, while a country like Denmark took the position that natural persons often find themselves parts of legal persons (e.g., in associations); in both cases, the result was that legal persons were covered by data-protection laws. The countries that restricted these laws to natural persons usually took the view that the problem in the case of legal persons is different and that, in addition, the public trend in the case of legal persons was not toward greater protection of data but rather toward greater transparency.[3]

The advent of TDF meant that privacy concerns could not be confined to the geographical limits of national jurisdictions alone but were bound to acquire a transnational dimension. In these circumstances, an adequate protection of the individual is guaranteed only if either national data-protection laws apply specifically to the transborder flow of name-linked data, or if the same data-protection standards are recognized in all countries to which data could be transmitted. If neither of these conditions is fulfilled, data-protection standards can easily be evaded by shifting data bases or data processing to data havens.

Most of the existing data-protection laws or regulations do, therefore, address the transborder flow of personal data. But even if a country does not have, in its data-protection laws, specific provisions applying to TDF, laws are frequently interpreted in a manner that takes TDF into account. The underlying philosophy is that the outflow of name-linked data into countries with comparable data-protection standards remains unrestricted, while limitations are applied to flows into countries in which compliance with domestic standards is not ensured. Thus, the principal objective of data-protection laws is not to control data flows per se but rather to ensure that data originating in a given country are subject to the country's data-protection standards regardless of the location of the processing, storage and retrieval equipment. Regulatory actions are thus aimed principally at those flows that may lead to an evasion of these standards. The possibility remains nonetheless that data-protection laws could be used as an indirect mechanism to protect the domestic data industry. This could be the case, for instance, if data-protection standards were formulated or administered so restrictively that data exports become virtually impossible or if the laws were used to regulate the type of equipment to be used. The principal exporters and users of data services, in particular, fear such protectionist applications.[4]

The fears of possible violations of privacy protection through TDF—balanced by fears that an international regulation of transborder flows of personal data may be used for more general restrictive purposes—led to two instruments aimed at harmonizing data-protection standards among countries: the "Guidelines Governing the Protection of Privacy and Transborder Flows of Personal Data", adopted by the Council of the OECD on 23 September 1980 as an annex to a recommendation on the same subject, and the "Convention for the Protection of Individuals with Regard to Automatic Processing of Personal Data", which was opened for signature by the Committee of Ministers of the Council of Europe on 21 January 1981.[5] (The texts of both instruments are reprinted as annexes I and II, respectively.)

The basic principles of privacy protection and the provisions concerning personal TDF are the center-pieces of the Convention and the Guidelines. Specifically, personal data should be collected, stored and communicated only for specified and legitimate purposes and with the authority of the data subject or the authority of law. Furthermore, these data should be accurate, up-to-date, relevant and not excessive for the uses for which they are required. Upon request, data subjects should be entitled to be informed by a data controller whether data related to them have been collected and (with certain exceptions) to have access to those data. Finally, both instruments recognize that data protection has an international dimension, even if the regulation of international data flows raises a number of difficulties. The main differences between the two instruments concern the legal nature (the Guidelines are voluntary, the Convention is legally binding), their scope (the Guidelines apply to the privacy of personal data irrespective of the manner in which they are handled, the Convention focuses on automatic processing), and their follow-up machinery (the Guidelines do not contain institutional provisions, the Convention envisages a Consultative Committee). Since the Guidelines are voluntary and the amendment process of the Convention is difficult, it is conceivable that the two instruments will develop differently and that, therefore, inconsistencies between them may emerge. This suggests that continued efforts at harmonization between the Convention and the Guidelines will be needed.

1. The OECD Guidelines

The OECD's TDF work has its origin in computer-utilization studies which began in 1969 through a Data Bank Panel. This Panel organized the First OECD Symposium on Transborder Data Flows in Vienna in 1977, at which potential international implications of privacy-protection issues were examined.[6] On the basis of the results of the Symposium, an ad hoc Group of Experts on Transborder Data Barriers and Privacy Protection was set up to develop guidelines on basic rules governing the transborder flow of personel data and the protection of privacy, in order to facilitate a harmonization of national legislations.

The basic objective of the Guidelines is to establish a set of fundamental principles of privacy protection acceptable to all OECD member countries and thus to ensure at least a minimum level of homogeneity in this respect throughout the OECD area. Except for Ireland (which is, however, not opposed to the Guidelines), all OECD member countries have indicated that they intend to adhere to the Guidelines. The OECD has decided to examine compliance with the Guidelines regularly. For this purpose, meetings were originally convened every 18–24 months, bringing together senior officials involved in privacy legislation and TDF. In 1985, however, no further meeting was scheduled because no real problems seemed to have surfaced.

The instrument consists of a recommendation which, in an annex, sets out the Guidelines in five parts.[7] The Preamble of the recommendation indicates the reasons for the adoption of the Guidelines. Specifically, the Council recognized:

> that, although national laws and policies may differ, Member countries have a common interest in protecting privacy and individual liberties, and in reconciling fundamental but competing values such as privacy and the free flow of information;
>
> that automatic processing and transborder flows of personal data create new forms of relationships among countries and require the development of compatible rules and practices;

that transborder flows of personal data contribute to economic and social development;

that domestic legislation concerning privacy protection and transborder flows of personal data may hinder such transborder flows.

Furthermore, the Council expressed its determination:

to advance the free flow of information between Member countries and to avoid the creation of unjustified obstacles to the development of economic and social relations among Member countries.

Part one, paragraph 4, of the Guidelines contains definitions and deals with the scope of the instrument. As regards the latter, it is specified that:

Exceptions to the Principles contained in Parts Two and Three of these Guidelines, including those relating to national sovereignty, national security and public policy (*ordre public*) should be: (a) as few as possible, and (b) made known to the public.

In addition, the Guidelines are described as minimum standards which can be supplemented by member countries. "Basic principles of national application" are enumerated in part two. They deal with collection limitation, data quality, purpose specification, use limitation, security safeguards, openness, individual participation, and accountability. Part three addresses itself to the "basic principles of international application: free flow and legitimate restrictions". In it, the relationships of the members of the OECD in regard to the Guidelines are spelled out; in paragraph 17, it is stated that:

A Member country should refrain from restricting transborder data flows of personal data between itself and another Member country except where the latter does not yet substantially observe these Guidelines or where the re-export of such data would circumvent its domestic privacy legislation.

The question of "national implementation" is the subject of part four. Its thrust is that appropriate measures should be taken by member countries to implement the principles set forth in parts two and three. Finally, part five takes up the question of "international co-operation". In particular, it encourages compatible national procedures for the protection of transborder flows of personal data and the exchange of relevant information.

2. The Council of Europe Convention

The Council of Europe, an international organization that brings together 21 Western European States, has been among the first to deal with the consequences that scientific and technological progress, particularly in the field of data processing, has for individuals.

In 1968, the Consultative Assembly of the Council of Europe addressed recommendation 509[8] to the Committee of Ministers, asking it to examine whether the European Convention on Human Rights and the domestic law of the member states offered adequate protection to the right of personal privacy vis-à-vis modern science and technology. A study showed that legislation at that time gave insufficient protection to individual privacy and to other rights and interests of individuals. On the basis of these findings, the Committee of Ministers adopted in 1973 and 1974 two resolutions on the protection of the privacy of individuals vis-à-vis electronic data banks in the private sector (resolution (73) 22) and in the public sector (resolution (74) 29).[9] The principles enunciated in these two resolutions were of a general nature:

- data must not be collected or processed by unfair or illegal methods;
- the accuracy and up-to-dateness of the data recorded must be assured;
- the objective of the recording must be made clear so that it is possible to verify whether the data recorded are consistent with the objective, whether they have been used for a purpose other than the specified objective and whether the length of storage of the data is excessive given the objective pursued;
- sensitive data must only be recorded if special safeguards have been adopted;
- the establishment of data bases must be made public;
- all persons must be able to know about the data recorded on them and, in case of error, be able to correct them; and
- the security of data bases must be assured. Although these resolutions left the member states of the Council of Europe free to decide how to give effect to the principles set out, the majority decided to do so by way of legislative action (see table III-1).

With the proliferation of such national actions, the need for harmonization of national laws became more urgent for the reasons discussed earlier, and the Committee of Ministers of the Council of Europe decided, in 1976, to entrust a Committee of Experts with the task of preparing a convention for the protection of privacy in relation to transborder data processing. This task was accomplished by the end of 1980. The Convention's aim is to reinforce and supplement national data-protection legislation on the basis of the organization's resolutions (73) 22 and (74) 29 and to strike a balance between the information needs of society and the individual's right to the protection of personal data.

The principal components of the Convention are substantive legal provisions in the form of basic principles, special rules on TDF, and mechanisms for mutual assistance and consultation between the contracting parties. These are spelled out in a preamble followed by seven chapters.

The preamble recognizes, inter alia, that it is necessary to reconcile the fundamental value of the free circulation of information with the equally fundamental value of the protection of privacy. "General provisions" pertaining to the Convention are set out in chapter I, including the purpose and scope of the instrument and relevant definitions. Chapter II contains the "basic principles for data protection" which constitute the core of the Convention and which the contracting parties are to give effect to in their domestic legislation. They deal with the duties of the parties, the quality of data, special categories of data, data security, additional safeguards for the data subject, exceptions and restrictions, sanctions and remedies, and extended protection. "Transborder data flows" are the subject of chapter III. The sole article in this chapter reads as follows:

Article 12
Tranborder flows of personal data and domestic law

1. The following provisions shall apply to the transfer across national borders, by whatever medium, of personal data undergoing automatic processing or collected with a view to their being automatically processed.
2. A Party shall not, for the sole purpose of the protection of privacy, prohibit or subject to special authorisation transborder flows of personal data going to the territory of another Party.
3. Nevertheless, each Party shall be entitled to derogate from the provisions of paragraph 2:
   a. insofar as its legislation includes specific regulations for certain categories of personal data or of automated personal data files, because of the nature of those data or those files, except where the regulations of the other Party provide an equivalent protection;
   b. when the transfer is made from its territory to the territory of a non-Contracting State through the intermediary of the territory of another Party, in order to avoid such transfers resulting in circumvention of the legislation of the Party referred to at the beginning of this paragraph.

In order to implement the Convention, the contracting parties agreed, in chapter IV, to render each other "mutual assistance", principally in the form of cooperation among themselves and through assistance to data subjects habitually residing abroad. Cooperation with respect to the Convention as a whole is taken up separately in chapter V, which established a "Consultative Committee" for this purpose. Chapter VI deals with "amendments". The last chapter, VII, contains "final clauses"; they specify, inter alia, that the Convention enters into force as a binding treaty three months after ratification by at least five members.

The Convention was opened for signature on 28 January 1981. Having been ratified by France, the FRG, Norway, Spain, and Sweden, the Convention entered into force on 1 October 1985. By that time, it had also been signed by Austria, Belgium, Denmark, Greece, Iceland, Italy, Luxembourg, Portugal, Switzerland, Turkey, and the United Kingdom. (In a recommendation adopted on 29 July 1981, the Commission of the European Community had urged the Community's member states to sign and ratify the Convention.) Any state not a member of the organization may accede to the Convention with the approval of the Committee of Ministers of the Council of Europe. A Consultative Committee (mandated under Article 19 of the Convention) was scheduled to hold its first meeting in June 1986. It is composed of representatives of each contracting party to the Convention. According to Article 19 of the Convention, it (a) may make proposals with a view to facilitating or improving the application of the Convention; (b) may make proposals for amendment of the Convention in accordance with its Article 21; (c) shall formulate its opinions on any proposal for amendment of the Convention which is referred to it in accordance with Article 21, paragraph 3; and (d) may, at the request of a party, express an opinion on any question concerning the Convention's application. Member states of the Council of Europe that have not yet ratified the instrument can be represented on the Committee by an observer; non-members may be invited as observers on an ad hoc basis.

While an important achievement, the Convention is only one stage in the work on data protection being carried out within the Council of Europe. In particular, efforts have been initiated to extend the application of the basic principles

The complexities involved in some of these matters can perhaps best be illustrated for an issue, choice of law, that has implications for many other issues. The following quote indicates some of its dimensions:

> When an electronic message is generated in country A, switched in country B and C, transits country E, F, G and H, processed in country I and J, stored in country K and involves entities residing in or operating in yet other countries, it is debatable whether existing choice of law and conflict of law doctrines are adequate. What law applies to data processing carried out by computer aboard a synchronous orbit satellite? Do we need new forms of remedy for information theft, for information mishandling? Do we need new rules on commerical entities' information rights and obligations? New fora in which to prosecute these matters? New law-making institutions? If so, how do we get there? Bilateral arrangements; multilateral arrangements; private contract law; world conference?[16]

This problem was also recognized in the discussions of the OECD Guidelines. The "Explanatory Memorandum" accompanying the Guidelines stated:

> As regards the question of choice of law, one way of approaching these problems is to identify one or more connecting factors which, at best, indicate one applicable law. That is particularly difficult in the case of international computer networks where, because of dispersed locations and rapid movement of data, and geographically dispersed data processing activity, several connecting factors could occur in a complex manner involving elements of legal novelty. Moreover, it is not evident what value should presently be attributed to rules which by mechanistic application establish the specific national law to be applied.[17]

In fact, the Guidelines themselves end with a call that "Member countries should work towards the development of principles, domestic and international, to govern the applicable law in the case of transborder flows of personal data."[18] Naturally, these observations do not apply only to personal but also to economic data, and they are of increasing concern as trade in data services grows.

These and other issues will eventually have to be addressed in an international legal framework for TDF. Such a framework will have to be much broader than these legal questions suggest, because it would have to deal, first and foremost, with the trade and FDI aspects of TDF.[19] The need for such a framework has been stressed most notably by developed market economies and business organizations from these economies. The principal reasons for this, the interests that shape the present discussions about the establishment of an international regime for trade and FDI in data services, and the policy orientations to which these interests give rise are examined in the following section.

C. Competing values and approaches

Given the strategic economic importance of data resources, those countries which, in their opinion, do not have sufficient data resources increasingly consider their acquisition as crucial. For instance, it has been observed for the semiconductor industry in the developed countries that "[a]pparently, most Governments have concluded that a significant national presence in this sub-sector, combined with a ready acceptance of the new electronic innovations by the users of capital goods, are essential to the preservation of technological independence."[20] Similarly, the Ministry of Posts and Telecommunications of Japan noted that "together with energy and food, the data base is taking on the character of an important resource. It is necessary for this country to improve the existing data bases . . . so as to be self-sufficient in information resources."[21] Developing countries, in particular, see in this situation a new dimension of dependence. And so do some developed ones: as the Ministry of Posts and Telecommunications of Japan put it: "Today information is vital for any country for its socioeconomic development; excessive dependency on one country for information needs to be reexamined".[22] One can rest assured that the result of this reexamination will be an internationally competitive Japanese data-service industry.

Those countries, on the other hand, that possess well-developed data resources (whether in all or some data industries) see their future development as dependent on the international growth of their data resources. As a study prepared by the US National Telecommunications and Information Administration (NTIA) put it: "Mature countries such as the United States increasingly rely on these industries [telecommunications and data-processing services] to offset the decline of low-technology sectors, and it has become virtually a requirement of U.S. economic health for such industries to expand abroad."[23] This observation is also relevant in a broader context, since the free-trade potential of the "sun-rise" industries can help to offset, to a certain extent, the protectionist pressures of the declining "smoke stack" industries.

The distinction between "countries that lack sufficient data resources" and "countries that possess well-developed data resources" is, of course, an artificial one, as many countries are in mixed situations. This dichotomy has been chosen for analytical purposes, to facilitate the identification of the principal policy objectives, policy rationales and policy instruments associated with the approaches chosen by countries. As will be seen, given the nature of the competing values at stake, these approaches essentially counterpose *national* and *international* strategies.

1. Acquiring data resources

For countries that see themselves as having insufficient data resources, the question of how to acquire such resources naturally arises. Two basic options present themselves: *physical* acquisition and *functional* acquisition.

a. Strengthening domestic data resources: physical acquisition

The physical acquisition of data resources aims at building up national resources, with or without the participation of foreign capital. The *principal objective* of such a national acquisition approach is to obtain competitive capabilities in as many data resources as possible. This, in turn, would enable the country:

- to have a maximum of economic resources central to future development located on the national territory;
- to capture the direct and indirect benefits (including skills) associated with the development of such industries;
- to stimulate the development of other industries because of the close links of data resources with the rest of the economy; and

• to establish a basis for foreign-exchange-saving import substitution and foreign-exchange-generating exports, as well as for a participation in the world market for data resources.

The *rationale* for such a national approach lies in the belief that—in spite of the immediate costs of an infant-industry policy—the realization of hitherto underdeveloped domestic capabilities adds to national and international welfare in the longer run. This strategy is particularly attractive because of the strategic importance of data resources for development and because distance-insensitive transport costs and the homogeneity of certain data services may offer specialization advantages that facilitate the growth of internationally competitive industries.

The main *policy instruments* of this approach include subsidies, performance requirements, procurement policies and the favoring of national champions (i.e., chosen domestic corporations to advance national objectives) through which the growth of domestic data resources can be stimulated, as well as the wide range of traditional protectionist measures through which fledgling domestic industries can be sheltered against overwhelming international competition. Also crucial in the context of this approach are various forms of control of TDF. The principal reason (as discussed earlier) is that *transborder data flows permit international access to data resources and may thus inhibit local development of such resources, either because there is no longer any need for such development or it is made difficult.* In other words, since TDF can have an influence on the location of data resources, any comprehensive national policy aimed at strengthening domestic data resources has to pay attention to these flows. Often, furthermore, it is also considered important that the data resources to be built up are not only located on national territory but also domestically controlled (i.e., not by TNCs headquartered elsewhere). Under these circumstances, the countries involved may discriminate (e.g., in procurement policy) against foreign affiliates.

Developed (e.g., Canada, the European Community, France)[24] and developing (e.g., Brazil, India, Mexico) countries alike pursue policies that contain some of the policy elements just mentioned. Many of these policies, especially in the developed market economies, begin with support for research and development in the data-goods sector and center (partly for defense, partly for core-industry reasons) on support for the semiconductor industry; considerable amounts of money are committed for this purpose (see table III-2). But policy intervention addresses data services as well. The Canadian Foreign Investment Review Agency, for instance, disallowed 5 out of 26 applications for FDI in software and 6 out of 15 applications in other data services between 1976 and 1983 (see table III-3). Better known is the Canadian Banking Act which requires that all banks operating in Canada maintain a minimum set of records related to their Canadian transactions in Canada (although *copies* of the set may be exported). This ensures that the Inspector General of Banks can have access to the records she needs to carry out her statutory duties. If such data left the country they would no longer be under Canadian enforcement jurisdiction; this would entail a sovereignty risk. The preparation of the minimum set of records requires, of course, data processing in Canada. While sovereignty concerns may well have been the primary considerations informing the adoption of this Act, it certainly has the (side?) benefit of strengthening data resources in Canada. An example of a different kind may be the UK government's veto (in October 1984) of British Telecom's agreement with IBM to launch jointly

Table III-2. Government assistance for research and
development in the semiconductor industry

Country	Date	Project	Million dollars	Comments
Australia	1983-84	CSIRO research[a]	0.6	
Canada	1981	Gallium-arsenide devices	1.7	
US	1978-84	VHSIC phase 1 and	341.4	
	1978-82	non-VHSIC R&D[b]	200.5	
	1985-89	VHSIC phase 2	340.3	
Japan	1975-81	LSI ICs for computer, telecommunications and microwave[c]	180.0	
	1976-79	VLSI[d]	121.2	Repayment required
	1980-91	Optoelectronics	77.5	Consigment payment (no refunding)
	1982-90	Supercomputer	92.3	
	1982-89	New function elements	100.4	
EC	1983-84	ESPRIT pilot projects[e]	11.4	
	1982-85	Microelectronics program	32.0	EC share
	1984-89	ESPRIT	744.0	EC share
France	1982-86	2nd components plan	487.0	
Germany, Fed. Rep. of	1974-78	BMFT electronic components[f]	157.0	R&D assistance to industry and institutions
	1981-82	BMFT electronic components	110.0	
	1981-84	VDI R&D[g]	0.9	
	1984-88	Submicron technology	196.0	
UK	1983-88	Advanced information technology program	308.5	
Finland	1982-85	C-MOS progress technology[h]	7.0	Funds for equipment and salaries
Sweden	1980-85	National Board for Technical Development	47.3	Grants to technical schools

Source: Dimitri Ypsilanti, "The Semiconductor Industry", *The OECD Observer*, 132 (January 1985), p. 18.
Note: Data are not strictly comparable in that assistance can be in the form of loans or grants, and assistance may be directly to firms or to universities and technical institutions; some projects are also part of larger programs and include other elements which may be only of indirect relevance to semiconductor R&D (e.g., software, CAD, computer architecture). Levels of funding for projects after 1983 are subject to change. Data are also incomplete in that details of all countries' R&D programs are not known.
a/ CSIRO: Commonwealth Scientific and Industrial Research Organisation.
b/ VHSIC: Very-High-Speed-Integrated-Circuits Program.
c/ LSI: Large-Scale Integration.
d/ VLSI: Very Large-Scale Integration.
e/ ESPRIT: European Strategic Programme for Research and Development in Information Technologies.
f/ BMFT: Ministry of Technology and Research.
g/ VDI: Association of German Engineers' Technology Centre.
h/ C-MOS: Complementary Metal-Oxide Semiconductors.

a sophisticated electronic data network in the UK for such purposes as electronic ordering, billing and payments systems. Although possible negative effects on domestic competition were cited as the principal reason, it would not be surprising if the consideration that this venture would significantly reinforce a foreign company's hold on the UK's computer market had also played a role. Not surprisingly, ICL, the largest UK-owned computer supplier, welcomed the decision.[25] The incidence of such policies is likely to increase considerably as awareness of the importance of data resources rises. At the same time, however, only a few countries have the

Table III-3. Applications for data-services FDI in Canada, 1976-1983<u>a</u>/
(Number)

Fiscal year	Software		Other data services	
	Allowed	Disallowed	Allowed	Disallowed
1976/1977	3	-	-	-
1977/1978	3	-	1	2
1978/1979	-	1	3	2
1979/1980	4	1	4	-
1980/1981	2	2	-	1
1981/1982	-	-	-	1
1982/1983	9	1	1	-
TOTAL	21	5	9	6

Source: Canada, Foreign Investment Review Agency, Annual Report, various years.

a/ Applications reviewed under the Foreign Investment Review Act of Canada. It should be noted that this table does not capture applications that were withdrawn or that were not made because of the expectation that they would not be granted.

capacity to develop the full range of data resources—most will have to place emphasis on selective import replacement, infrastructure development and improving access to international data resources.[26]

At the regional level, the European Community has taken a number of initiatives which are also, and at times prominently so, geared toward strengthening the Community's data resources. Perhaps the three most important recent programs are ESPRIT, RACE and EUREKA.[27]

After two years of preparation, the Community's Council of Ministers approved, in December 1982, the initiation of 16 pilot projects in the framework of a broad-based "European Strategic Programme for Research and Development in Information Technologies" (ESPRIT). The actual program began in 1984. Its principal objective is "to assist European industry to develop the indigenous technological capability needed to design, manufacture and use profitable and highly competitive information products, systems and services able within 10 years to compete successfully and profitably with the USA and Japan."[28] To achieve this objective, Community-wide cooperation between industry, software houses, research institutes and universities is encouraged. The resources earmarked for ESPRIT amount to over $1 billion for the first five-year period of a 10-year program, of which the Community will provide 50%. As of June 1985, support had been requested in the amount of ECU $565 million (almost three times more than the Community had allocated for this purpose), of which 30% was for advanced information processing, 23% for office automation, 19% for microelectronics, 16% for computer-integrated manufacturing, and 12% for software technology.[29]

In the area of telecommunication, the EC decided in June 1985 to set in motion the first stage of a program of "Research and Development in Advanced Communications Technologies for Europe" (RACE). For the first phase of 18 months, the Community had budgeted nearly $20 million for the effort, with at least a matching amount expected from corporations and research organizations.[30] The objective of the program is to create, within 10 years, an integrated broadbased communication network for Western Europe, capable of carrying voice, data and video communications.

The idea of a "European Research Co-ordinating Agency" (EUREKA)` was launched by France in Spring 1985 as a response to the US Strategic Defense Initiative (SDI) announced in March 1985. SDI's purpose is to examine the extent to which new technologies can provide effective defense against ballistic missiles of all ranges. Perhaps as much as $20–$30 billion may be spent on this program, perhaps half of it for data resources required for the effort. In other words, the US high-technology industry in general and the data industry in particular can be expected to receive a major boost from the public funds injected into them. Although the effort is directed toward military applications, it will certainly have important civilian spin-offs. In the face of this challenge, a conference of ministers from 17 Western European states created EUREKA formally on 17 July 1985. A second conference, attended by ministers from 18 countries and meeting on 5–6 November 1985, adopted a Declaration of Principles governing the operations of the project and agreed on the first ten multilateral research projects to be conducted within its framework. It is expected that a small secretariat will be created to act, among other things, as a clearing house for information and to assist firms and research institutes to find partners for EUREKA projects. As in the case of ESPRIT, EUREKA projects are to be implemented by the private sector and research institutes, although governments have committed themselves to facilitate these efforts as far as possible. EUREKA's principal purpose is to strengthen the productivity and competitiveness of the European economies in the world market through the increased cooperation of firms and research institutes in the area of high technology. EUREKA is meant to put Europe in a position to master and exploit the technologies that are important for its future.[31] The areas covered are products, processes and services in the areas of information and telecommunication, computers, robotics, laser and marine technologies, manufacturing, new materials, environmental protection and transport technologies, and biotechnology—nearly all areas that directly or indirectly involve data resources.

All these projects—ESPRIT, RACE, EUREKA—are major efforts to inject public funds and organization into new technologies, and especially data technologies, with a view to strengthening domestic—or regional—data resources.

Brazil is the country which has most clearly recognized, formulated and pursued this approach. It is an approach based on the recognition of the importance of data technologies for development and the role that TDF can play in influencing the location of data resources. Therefore, within the framework of Brazil's industrialization program, special attention is being given to the strengthening of domestic data resources. Virtually all policy elements mentioned earlier are utilized, including the explicit reservation of the production of certain data goods and services for domestic enterprises. An integral part of this policy, implemented by the powerful Special Secretariat of Informatics (SEI),[32] is a series of regulations that govern the establishment and use of transnational computer-communication systems in a manner ensuring that their usage does not conflict with national interests—particularly economic development—and, in fact, actually serves these interests where possible. The declared objectives of this policy are to maximize data resources located in Brazil, regardless of whether these are owned by national or foreign corporations; to acquire and maintain national control over the decisions and technologies relating to Brazilian industries where this is threatened through

Figure III-1. Brazil's industrial informatics strategy

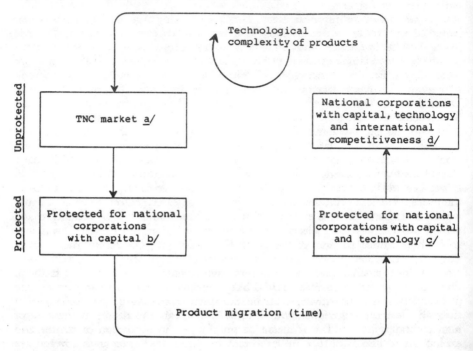

Source: Transborder Data Flows and Brazil, op. cit.

ᵃ Not protected (TNCs are welcome if they export and use state-of-the-art technology) because national corporations are not yet able to enter production.

ᵇ Protected for national corporations (which can use foreign technologies) because they are able to invest, but do not yet have their own technology.

ᶜ Protected for those national corporations that have their own capital and technology, but are not yet fully competitive in the international market.

ᵈ Protected barriers are lowered because national corporations are competitive in the international market. Local technology is still required and preventive measures are being taken to maintain control of the national industry.

TDF; to ensure the broadest possible access to data; and to administer data resources in such a manner that they enhance the country's cultural and political standing. These four objectives have led to considerable efforts to build the necessary infrastructure—an appropriate telecommunication network and a viable informatics sector—and they have given rise to clearly defined policies regarding telematics and TDF. The ultimate aim is to create data industries and links that contribute positively to Brazil's over all development within the context of the country's industrial policy.

With a view to serving these objectives, SEI has pursued a strategy to enhance the capabilities of national industry to manufacture increasingly complex data technologies (see fig. III-1). As part of this policy, foreign affiliates are encouraged to exercise their comparative advantage and to produce advanced state-of-the-art data goods and services, both for local consumption and export; they are also encouraged to improve local research-and-development facilities. Once a product can be manufactured with national capital, the respective market segments are reserved to domestic corporations so as to give the infant industry an opportunity to develop, while foreign affiliates are encouraged to shift toward more sophisticated products (instead of upgrading products in the same segment). The degree and type of protection is a function of the technological stage of the products involved. It is envisaged that as soon as international competitiveness is achieved, protective barriers can be lowered, although some measures may still be necessary to ensure the continued improvement of local technologies and the permanence of national ownership of the country's informatics industries.

To protect this informatics policy against international leakages, SEI has adopted specific measures dealing with TDF. Most importantly, it was decided that the establishment of international data-communication links would require SEI's prior approval to ensure that such links are set up in accordance with the guidelines of the national informatics policy. (The content of messages, however, is not supervised.) Such links are approved for specific purposes only and for fixed periods of time, which may be extended for up to three years.

This regulation is based on the principle that data and the means to treat them are economic resources, subject to trade and crucial to socio-economic development. Furthermore, data structuring is considered an activity closely related to national security. That any country has the right to regulate the nature of TDF is therefore a policy position supported by Brazil. The government of Brazil is of the view that the establishment of any link should not jeopardize the operations of the local units of a transnational corporate system in case of an interruption of the link; it should not lead to an outflow but rather an inflow of data resources; and it should not affect negatively the country's balance of payments.

Brazil's TDF policy consists, therefore, primarily of the application of criteria to evaluate the conditions under which, and the extent to which, individual applications for links fit with these overall and specific objectives and, hence, merit approval. The criteria are based on two dimensions of TDF: the *categories* of TDF (commercial and corporate) and the *types* of use to which information resources are being put in their transnational computer-communication systems (person-to-person data communication, data-base access, and data processing). Approval of transnational computer-communication systems for data processing, data communication and information storage and retrieval depends on which intersection of these dimensions is involved (see fig. III-2).

This policy extends also into the area of software where, as of September 1985, over 60% of the 7,437 software programs registered by SEI had been registered by US companies.[33] With the objectives of strengthening the competitive position of national hardware producers, encouraging technological development, improving the balance of payments, and, of course, fostering the establishment of a local software industry, Brazil's policies for nourishing a software industry are centered on the establishment of a national software registry.[34] Three categories of software are distinguished. The first category involves those software programs developed in Brazil by persons physically resident or software programs developed in Brazil by persons physically resident or domiciled in the country or by corporations owned by citizens of Brazil residing in the country. The second category includes those software programs for which no national alternatives exist, but which are

Figure III-2. Brazilian transborder data flow policies

| | | Category of on-line transborder data flows | |
		Corporate	Commercial
On-line use of transborder data flows	Data communications	Person-to-person communications are not restricted.	Brazilian PTT only; co-operation agreements possible.
	Data-base access	Copy of data base in Brazil, whenever reasonable.	Encouraged, but in co-operation with Brazilian institutions, preferably with copy of data base in Brazil. If no local copy, services are provided by the PTT, although co-operation agreements are possible.
	Data processing (including use of software)	Not favoured abroad if reasonable local alternative exists.	Not allowed abroad, except in exceptional circumstances.

Source: *Transborder Data Flows and Brazil, op. cit.,* p. 135.

of economic interest to Brazil; however, the technology and proprietary rights related to these programs have to be transferred to a national corporation (open packages). The third category includes all other software programs. Registration in this last category is temporary; it would not be renewed when comparable category-one software has been developed. (At the end of 1985, SEI was in the process of introducing a fourth category which includes the programs produced by the government for its own use. These are not to be commercialized.) The government of Brazil gives highest priority to the use of software from the first category, and all government agencies are required to use programs from that category whenever possible. Unregistered programs cannot be sold commercially and cannot take advantage of tax reductions available to buyers of registered software and to local software houses. Since the government is one of the most important users of data goods and services, the registry enables it to exert some control over the marketing of software products in the country and to encourage local production of them while reducing redundant imports. Software-import contracts are subject to approval of both SEI and the National Institute for Industrial Property. In implementing this policy, SEI scrutinizes all requests for registry and approves only those conforming to its general guidelines and to its overall objective of encouraging local software generation.[35] An interesting example in this context is the acquisition of UNIX from ATT, including the source codes, the development tools, the continued regular support by ATT and the license of the program for Brazil. Most Brazilian computer manufacturers and most Brazilian software houses joined together to establish a company which in turn negotiated on their behalf with ATT about the acquisition of UNIX. Faced with this unified approach, ATT agreed after two years of negotiations to the principal Brazilian conditions.

The government of Brazil believes that its TDF policy has neutralized a number of those impacts of transnational data links that would otherwise have been negative. This has been achieved through the rearrangement of some corporate data networks in the interest of enhancing the data resources of foreign affiliates in Brazil, be these affiliates in data industries or in other industries. In relation to Brazil's general objectives in this area, the country's TDF policy is seen by the government to have led to the increased location of computers, software, data bases and skilled human resources in the country and to better national control over them. As a result of its policy, the government believes that TDF links are not being used to export data resources and they are not thought to increase the country's vulnerability since most foreign affiliates of TNCs are seen to have a reasonable degree of autonomy. In the few cases in which Brazil's objectives were at stake, negotiations between the applicants and SEI seem to have led to mutually satisfactory results. In addition, the country's TDF policy is seen to have contributed positively to the emergence of a national data industry, especially its data-base and software segments. By 1985, over 600 software houses had been established, of which one-fifth produced local software.[36] A national catalogue of data bases had also been compiled, including a detailed list of governmental data bases. To encourage the diffusion of data, all data bases were expected to be made accessible on-line in 1986.

Since the same policy has also strengthened data resources in other sectors of the economy, the government of Brazil sees its policy as having contributed to the country's overall socio-economic development. The conclusion was, therefore, that "transborder-data-flow policies can be important instruments for the support of national development objectives. They can be used in a manner similar to that of a customs tariff policy to promote the growth of infant industries and to strengthen local industrialization in general".[37] Thus, the policies have been used to ensure that the country's efforts to strengthen its domestic data-resources cannot be evaded through TDF (hence data processing abroad is, as a rule, not allowed) and to ensure that transborder data flows are used to the advantage of the country when no reasonable local alternative exists (e.g., access to certain international data bases is permitted). Moreover, the country has made great efforts to strengthen its intellectual and technical data-resource infrastructure.

Until 1984, this policy was implemented through regulations. On 3 October 1984, however, the Brazilian Congress approved nearly unanimously an informatics law which codified and extended the country's informatics policy and gave it a higher standing.[38] The principles furnishing the basis of the law are:

- the government has to set priorities and give direction to the national data industry[39] and the application of data resources;
- infant data industries need protection;
- economic concentration or monopoly in data industries must be avoided;
- informatics is not mainly a commercial, but rather a strategic and political issue;
- the development of data resources should be subordinated to the welfare of the Brazilian society;
- the right of privacy (to know what data are stored and to correct them if necessary) must be respected;
- a certain balance must be achieved between increased productivity and employment in light of increasing automation; and
- Brazil's technological capabilities ought to be strengthened.[40]

The scope of the law extends to the research, development, production, trading, and operation of electronic components; digital data collection, processing, structuring, storage, switching, retrieval, and presentation; software; data bases; and data services in general. Through this broad definition of its scope, the law brings together industrial policies related to informatics and telecommunication and, thereby, substantially increases the applicability of SEI's pre-1984 policies. In fact, virtually any product which embodies digital components is covered by the law, including computers, electronic telecommunication equipment, terminals, peripheral equipment, scientific instruments, software and, in principle, any high-technology industry using digital components. As far as policy instruments are concerned, the cornerstone of the law's implementation is the market reservation scheme mentioned above for a wide range of products (see table III-4). Its main instrument is a mechanism through which the import of certain data resources is restricted. This instrument has been extended for eight years and is being administered by SEI. Also important is the required disclosure of certain technical standards and norms. Most importantly, technical information on subscriber-line unit infaces of SPC (stored program control) switching systems must be disclosed by manufacturers in order to permit the connection of equipment produced by other manufacturers. In addition, government procurement is made so as to support the country's informatics law, and certain (mostly tax) incentives are offered to encourage the development of a domestic data industry.

To oversee the implementation of the informatics law, a National Council for Informatics and Automation (CONIN) has been established, chaired by the President of Brazil. It is composed of a number of ministers as well as representatives of Brazilian informatics associations, industry associations, employees and the academic community (see fig. III-3). CONIN's functions cover all aspects of informatics and explicitly include the task of "setting norms for the control of transborder data flows and for granting channels and means for the transmission

Table III-4. The evolution of market reservation in Brazil, 1975-1986

1975	1981	1983	1984	1986a/
Minicomputers, microcomputers	Electronic cash registers	Microelectronic and opticelectronic components	Industrial robots	Software
Data-entry equipment	Electronic accounting machines	Digital instruments	Electronic PABX	Selected strategic materials, e.g., quartz
	Financial terminals and controls	Government procurement of data services	Optical fibers	
	Electronic authenticators, ticket preparers and optical scanners		CAD/CAM systems	
	Modems			
	Remote access terminals for data banks			
	Electronic communication processers			
	Digital multiplexors for data communication			
	Digital concentrators for data communication			
	Teleprinters			
	Facsimile equipment			
	Process-control instruments, programmable controllers			
	Numerical control equipment			
	Secrecy and crypto-technological equipment			
	Process-control projects			

a/ Predicted.

Figure III-3. Brazil's policy structure in informatics, 1985

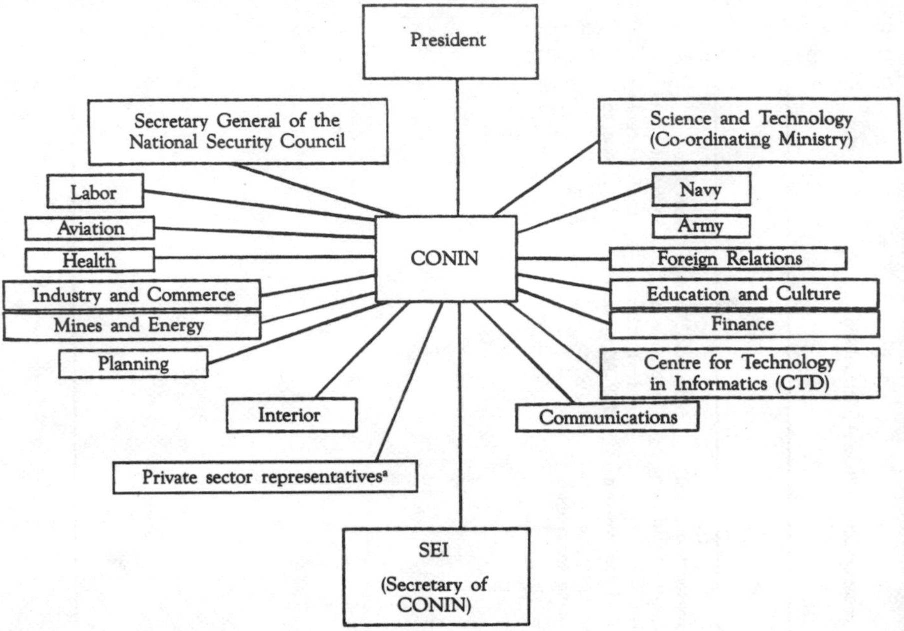

Source: Brazil's Informatics Law.

ᵃ Consisting of the following organizations: (1) Informatics associations: Brazilian Association of Computer and Peripherals Industry, Brazilian Association of Informatics Service Companies, Brazilian Association of Computer and Subsidiary Equipment Users, Association of Data Processing Professionals (each one representative). (2) Industry associations: National Industrial Confederation, National Commercial Confederation, National Confederation of Credit Companies (together one representative). (3) Workers/employees: National Confederation of Industrial Workers, National Confederation of Commercial Workers, National Confederation of Credit Company Workers (together one representative). (4) Academic community: Brazilian Society for Scientific Progress and Brazilian Computer Society (together one representative); and a noted informatics expert nominated by the Association of Brazilian Lawyers and the Institute of Brazilian Lawyers.

of data to effect a link with data bases and networks abroad" (art. 7[x]). The principal vehicle through which CONIN implements its policy is a National Informatics Plan. By the end of 1985, the draft of such a plan had been submitted to Congress for legislation. Formulated for a period of three years, its provisions require that foreign informatics affiliates dedicate at least 5% of their sales revenues to R & D and that government investments in informatics R & D and education during the plan's duration amount to $360 million, approximately one-third of what the private sector is expected to spend during that period. The plan gives direction for the development of microelectronics, software, data processing, industrial automation, teleinformatics, digital instruments, office automation, and informatics services in general. In short, it is a blueprint for the further development of Brazil's data resources.

To be sure, to date Brazil is the only country which has such a well-developed, detailed policy on data resources and which implements and monitors it vigorously. However, if data resources are as important for economic development as they are generally believed to be, it is only a question of time until other countries emulate the Brazilian example, even if they are more selective in choosing the industries in which they can develop national capacities.

b. Securing access to international data resources: functional acquisition

The second way to acquire data resources (and especially data services) is to rely on transborder data flows. In other words, *data resources are not physically but only functionally acquired*. While the actual resources remain located abroad, access to them is gained via transnational computer-communication systems. For instance, instead of creating local data bases or having copies of data bases located in the country, it is considered sufficient to have access to data bases located elsewhere.

Under such an access-oriented data-resource acquisition approach, the *principal objective* is to have the widest possible access to the use of data resources located elsewhere. This, in turn, requires an environment in which:

- uninterrupted access to international data resources is guaranteed (this is, in fact, the precondition for this approach); and
- barriers to trade in data services and other measures that could disrupt TDF are reduced or eliminated (barriers to FDI in data service would be of little interest, however, because presumably no important domestic data-resource firms exist).

Beyond this, and to the extent to which data resources are needed for international transactions (e.g., banking), the objectives are in many respects similar to those of countries that possess well-developed data resources (see below), especially with regard to the desire to benefit fully from the application of data services in international transactions.

The *rationale* for such an international acquisition approach is the desire to avoid the opportunity costs entailed in the development of domestic capacities and to benefit from international specialization by utilizing imported data resources for other economic activities in which the country is considered to have a comparative advantage. The principal costs of this approach are dependence on critical resources located elsewhere and the learning benefits and spin-off effects foregone in the development of domestic data resources.

The main *policy instrument* is to secure international agreement guaranteeing access to data resources.

This option has not yet received much attention as a separate and distinct approach to acquiring data resources, although Canada initiated a discussion on some of the relevant issues at the Second OECD Symposium on Transborder Data Flows in London in December 1983: "we do not believe that, in general, 'flow' per se is an issue. Instead, what we are dealing with is the right of access to data, information, and related services and the circumstances or conditions which may apply to limit access. We are concerned with individual access, corporate access and multi-national corporate access. . . . In our view, 'user access'—or denial of that access—is an overriding element in any discussion on transborder data flow".[41] This theme was picked up at the Symposium, as witnessed by the report on session 1 which stated, among other things, that "to secure free trade, the free access and use approach may be more effective than the traditional free flow approach."[42] The aim here is to establish an *obligation* for countries having data resources to *permit access* to these resources by parties located in other countries. This matter has been put into focus by such developments as the Dresser case, the prohibition of access to certain commercial data bases by socialist countries[43] and tendencies in the US administration to limit the export of certain technological data and data goods. It has found its expression in the "Communiqué" adopted in April 1985 by the OECD Council of Ministers which observed that "Initial conclusions from ongoing work show that access to markets for high technology products and access to high technology itself are both important. Open markets and free access provide the same advantages in this domain as in all other areas of trade."[44] As will be discussed below, the OECD Declaration on TDF also made reference to access. Furthermore, France has seized this concept and made it a centerpiece of a proposal presented at a meeting of the OECD Working Party on Transborder Data Flows in November 1985 to develop "a certain number of principles which could constitute a start for international negotiation."[45] "Access to information" and "guaranteed continuous access to sources" are two of the four elements specifically mentioned in this context. The concept has also received support from the FRG which seems to advocate an "international right of access to data bases" by improving the scope of access "in the spirit of the 'free-flow-of-information' principle."[46]

However, this issue is not without its complexities. At the micro level, a right of access is particularly important when it concerns, for instance, the location of data within a corporate transnational computer-communication system (precisely the Dresser case). In a sense, the "right of access" complements the "right of presence" (and especially one of its components, the right of non-establishment): unless access is guaranteed, a right of presence—which implies that critical data resources may be located elsewhere and are merely available via telecommunication lines—may become a risky undertaking for countries. In fact, TNCs may increasingly have to locate (for security reasons) critical data resources in several countries to maintain the functioning of their corporate systems in cases of (political) disruption (again the Dresser case). More general considerations of vulnerability[47]—for example, a disruption of critical data flows because of a breakdown of computer systems, strikes, natural disasters, acts of terrorism—may have the same effect. For the same reasons (further accentuated by fears of dependence) countries may well increasingly require that critical resources be located on their own territories (the Canadian Banking Act, mentioned earlier, was also inspired by considerations of this sort), although countries may also pursue broader developmental objectives with such requirements, as in the case of Brazil. Furthermore, the lines between security and developmental considerations may blur, as is perhaps the case with the Canadian Banking Act.

Another set of issues concerns the actual meaning of such a right of access. For instance, should—can?—access be permitted to the increasing number of specialized private or quasi-private computer-communication systems and the data bases associated with them, most of which are of an intra-firm or closed-user-group nature? If, for example, an airline establishes a reservation system, should other airlines be permitted to list their flights on it as well? And, if so, in which order? For instance, about three-quarters of the 21,000 US travel agents participated in computerized reservation systems in 1984 (compared to 4,000 in 1980). Five of the six most important on-line reservation systems are provided by airlines and four of the six have a bias in what they show on the terminal screen in terms of the order in which flights are listed. The economic importance of this can be seen in the fact that agents make about 85% of their bookings on flights from the first screen, 50%, in fact, on the flights shown on the first line.[48]

Finally, on a general level, such a right of access is a sine qua non for all those countries that are willing to forego the development of domestic data resources and/or are willing to rely on TDF for obtaining access to such resources. This holds true regardless of whether the countries involved are developed or developing countries, and regardless of whether they are pursuing this strategy because they do not wish to build up local data resources or because certain data resources cannot reasonably be developed locally. In a sense, right of access is actually an integral part of the concept of unrestricted flow of data; for without a right of access data flows are actually restricted. The concept also draws attention to the fact that, while barriers to trade are traditionally established on the *import* side, in the case of data resources barriers can effectively be established at the *export* side. A concern with access is therefore fully compatible with an interest in unrestricted data trade—it is just that the emphasis is on the export side.

It is on the basis of considerations of this sort (including the implications that uncertainty in this area may have for the prospects of US data-service exports) that an important business group in the US concluded that "the development of internationally acceptable terms of access to information and information-based services is therefore clearly in the U.S. interest. Such terms of access would likely include: (i) well defined conditions for denial, disruption, or termination of access; (ii) procedures for appeal; and (iii) sanctity for contracts between private parties."[49] While right of access is, in any case, a constituent element of the unrestricted flow of data and thus not necessarily a major trade-off (unless protectionist tendencies in the US grow stronger), a codification of this right and guarantees in this respect could be an important step toward alleviating the concerns of a great number of data-resource-poor countries. And it would be of particular interest to those countries that wish, for instance, to become regional TDF centers or to build export-oriented information-intensive service industries (e.g., banking), including in particular data-service industries (e.g., data bases, software). However, it must be kept in mind that right of access is no solution for those countries which, for broader reasons, want to strengthen the data resources located on their territories; for them, "right of access" only makes data flows (and perhaps dependence) a little more tolerable.

Before turning to the next strategy, it is important to note that both data-resource acquisition options have one common denominator: the need for an adequate national physical and intellectual data infrastructure (telecommunications, informatics and skills) to place the country in the best position to use data resources. Countries whose infrastructure is inadequate may have to put at least initial emphasis on the development of such an infrastructure. At the same time, there may be room for import substitution and/or the very selective application of data resources, be they produced locally or imported. Countries with a reasonably developed infrastructure may be in a position to embark on broader import replacement and/or broader efforts to diffuse data technology for domestic applications and use. Import substitution can, of course, also become the basis for exports. And the diffusion of data services—be they produced locally or imported—can strengthen the competitiveness of established industries.

2. Maintaining an open international environment

Countries that possess well developed data resources are, of course, in a different interest situation from those lacking them. They are the first to be affected by a legal void which permits governments to take any (especially restrictive) action they deem desirable as regards trade and FDI in data services. Their approach to this subject flows from their desire to benefit as much as possible from their technological and commercial lead in data industries.

Accordingly, their *principal objective* is to promote an international environment in which:

- barriers to trade and FDI in data services and other measures that could disrupt TDF are reduced or eliminated;
- data-service transactions and applications can take place as freely and securely and in as non-discriminatory a fashion as possible so that data industries can grow internationally through exports and FDI;
- other international transactions (especially trade in goods and services) can benefit fully from the application of data services;
- corporations can develop trade in services based on data technology;
- the functioning of corporate transnational computer-communication systems (i.e., the operation of TNCs) is not hampered; and
- the worldwide technical infrastructure for TDF is as efficient as possible to permit smooth transactions in data services.

Most of these objectives are also shared by the major users of TDF, especially TNCs.

The *rationale* for this approach lies in the conviction that an agreed-upon international framework will increase the stability and predictability which is required for a rapid and smooth growth of international transactions in data services and which is so important for long-term corporate decision-making, particularly in an area which involves capital-intensive expenditures with possible fundamental implications for corporate organization (e.g., the extent of centralization or decentralization). Furthermore, the proponents of this approach believe that—as with trade in goods—the world as a whole gains from growing trade and FDI in data services because such trade contributes to a more efficient international allocation of resources and increases the efficiency of doing transnational business and because trade in data services, like trade in goods, is an engine of growth.[50] It is an approach that highlights a classic dilemma in international political economy in that it places more emphasis on the efficient increase of global production and less (at least initially) on the appropriate distribution of production.

The objective of this approach cannot be obtained in a national context but requires rather an international approach: other countries have to be persuaded not to establish barriers to international transactions in data services. Accordingly, the main *policy instrument* is to seek the adoption of an enforceable liberal international regime that specifies the responsibilities of countries as regards trade and FDI in data services or, short of that, the conclusion of appropriate bilateral and regional agreements. The latter, in any event, are seen to bring about immediate improvements of the situation and, in addition, encourage multilateral negotiations.

3. Mixed interest situations

The strategies described so far are, in their pure form, ideal types seldom to be found in the real world. Even the US, as the exponent of an open international environment for data flows, restricts the outflow of certain data. Similarly, the country that comes closest to the first option, Brazil, pursues a mixture of strengthening domestic data resources and seeking access to international data resources. Thus, Brazil's market-reservation scheme applies to the micro and mini computer sectors only, and is limited to eight years. Furthermore, as discussed earlier, data processing within corporate systems is allowed abroad if no reasonable local alternative exists, and even commercial data processing is permitted abroad in exceptional circumstances. As regards information storage and retrieval, the Brazilian preference is to have copies of data bases located in the country although, as this formulation indicates, exceptions are certainly not unknown. Finally, as regards software, the Brazilian policy clearly recognizes that for some software no reasonable national alternative exists, which therefore must be imported. In other words, while the Brazilian policy is clearly aimed at strengthening national data resources, it relies on access to the international data market where no reasonable domestic alternatives exist and where a strict implementation of the national policy would be too costly.

This indicates that a number of mixed strategies are possible. A country may, for example, try to strengthen its domestic capacities for certain segments of an industry (e.g., microcomputers) or for an entire industry (e.g., data bases), but rely on access to international data resources for other segments (e.g., mainframes) or other industries (e.g., software). There are, of course, links among these strategies. For instance, a country that wishes to develop an export-oriented software industry may have difficulties in forbidding imports of certain computers, because state-of-the-art hardware is required to develop competitive software.

India has pursued such a policy mix and has begun to build up a rather successful software industry.[51] Since the mid-1960s, imports of computers had been closely controlled and were tied to certain export performance requirements regarding software. Since 1981, these requirements include the provision that at least one-third of the operating time of imported equipment must be used for the development of software for export. More specifically, if equipment is imported by an Indian company in order to develop software for exports, the company has to export software in the amount equivalent to 300% of the c.i.f. value of the imported equipment. Indian software exports increased from $0.7 million in 1975–76 to $24 million in 1982/83. It appears, however, that this strict control has hampered the development of the software industry. This factor, apart from the broader desire to strengthen the country's automation base, played a role in India's switch, in early 1985, to a more liberal policy on equipment imports.

Another mix of interests arises if a country desires to strengthen its domestic data resources, but one of the country's industries (e.g., banking) needs state-of-the-art data resources and, independently of that, needs an open international system for TDF to remain (or become) internationally competitive. In this case, a data-resource acquisition approach based on physical acquisition could be disadvantageous for maintaining the competitiveness of the industry involved; at the same time, an approach based on functional acquisition could be disadvantageous for building a domestic data-resource industry.

Many countries are likely to be in mixed-interest situations of this sort. This is all the more likely to be the case when countries already have other industries that are dependent on data services, i.e., especially countries that have information-intensive, internationally oriented service industries and countries that are the headquarters of TNCs. Most developed market economies fall in this category. France, for instance, is a relatively important exporter of software and Canada has a few strong computer-service corporations (e.g., I.P. Sharp). Most OECD countries, furthermore, have one or more important internationally active service industries which depend on data services as a core service. Thus, in shipping, such a service as the Reuters Dry Cargo and Tanker Service provides up-to-date shipping information. In air transportation, SITA has become indispensable. In tourism, the closed user-group network HOLIDEX, for instance, allows the world-wide making of hotel reservations and credit-card companies depend on central authorization systems. And in the whole range of "other private services", the new forms of international trade discussed in chapter II depend entirely on TDF. Countries that, in general, lack sufficient data resources may nevertheless play a leading role in these services and depend therefore to a certain degree on access to the international data market. There is also the fact that the major service exporters are also the home countries of most TNCs, for which transborder data flows are becoming the operational infrastructure. While these countries have, therefore, an interest in maintaining an open international environment for data flows, they have at the same time little interest in letting these flows impair the growth of their data industries as *independent* economic activities of central importance to their economic development. This dilemma arises precisely because of the position of data services as a core service.

It also arises for developing countries, although the situation of most of them appears to be simpler. Few of them are the headquarters of TNCs with transnational computer-communication systems, the overwhelming majority have no information-intensive service industries that are active internationally and hardly any have internationally competitive data-service industries. These countries can therefore pursue national acquisition policies for data resources more easily. However, even here, a number of countries are exceptions and some general caveats have to be made. For one, a number of developing countries participate actively in some information-intensive service industries, e.g., most countries in the airline industry and such countries as Bahrain, Panama and Singapore in banking. Second, a few developing countries have certain export-oriented data-service industries, e.g., India in software and Barbados in certain aspects of data processing. Third, data resources, as discussed in chapter II, are increasingly incorporated into other products and processes, and developing countries that wish to remain competitive on the international market for goods and services in general are likely to require data resources.

These conditions place virtually all OECD countries and a number of developing countries into mixed-interest situations. This places constraints on efforts to pursue strategies that are either directed strictly toward the strengthening of domestic data resources or founded entirely on access to international data resources. These constraints may be stronger for most developed market economies than for most developing countries, but in either case the situation calls for differentiated policies. Countries that lack sufficient data resources have to weigh carefully the advantages that one set of policies can bring in one area against the disadvantages that they may entail in other areas. Furthermore, countries also have to be somewhat concerned about the acceptability of their policies to other countries. For instance, a policy mix that is obviously restrictive in one data-service industry but relies on international access in another data-service industry may create credible liberalization pressures from countries that are excluded from the first industry but relied upon in the second industry. Finally, the mix of interest situations is further complicated, especially for the developed market economies, by the fact that the discussion of data services is embedded in the general discussion of the need for a multilateral framework for trade in services and that data services, as pointed out earlier, are a core service which provides the infrastructure for many other service activities.

D. The quest for an international framework

Since this volume focuses on the international politics of TDF, the strategy that aims at maintaining an open international environment for trade and FDI in data services is, of course, of special interest. The principal proponents of this strategy are the international business community (most notably in the US) and the US government. Accordingly, the following discussion focuses on their positions. They are furthermore part and parcel of the broader quest for an enforceable liberal regime for international transactions in services in general. For this reason, the domestic US policy and regulatory framework for international transactions in services in general is laid out first, while the narrower and more detailed objectives for an international regime for data services are reviewed in subsequent sections.

1. The US policy and regulatory framework for international service transactions

The principal policy instruments that are at the basis of US policies on services are the "U.S. National Study on Trade in Services" and a Statement by the President on "International Investment Policy". Their objectives are largely embodied in the subsequent "Trade and Tariff Act of 1984".[52] This section outlines their main features.

As to trade in services, the original policy objectives of the US administration were spelled out in the "U.S. National Study", prepared in 1983 by the Office of the US Trade Representative. It was the first national study submitted to GATT as that organization was beginning work on services. (Its Executive Summary is contained in annex III.) It examined in great detail a number of issues central to trade in services and set out the broad objectives of the US administration in this regard. Since the US trade position will be reviewed in great detail in chapter V, it is sufficient here to concentrate on the main thrust of the policy approach characterizing it. Thus, the "U.S. National Study" stated specifically that the US objective is to establish a "common framework applicable to all [service] sectors with specific rules set out for individual sectors".[53] The principles that the US wishes to be considered for inclusion in such a multilateral framework for services (which would also cover trade in data services) include: "national treatment, minimization of distortions to trade, nondiscrimination, the right to sell"; and the procedures include "transparency, due process, formal dispute-settlement procedures and provisions establishing the relationship of the framework agreement to other existing or future agreements, particularly those applicable to individual sectors."[54]

As to FDI (both in goods and services), the broad objectives of the US administration were set out in a Statement by the President on "International Investment Policy." It was developed by a Senior Interdepartmental Group on International Economic Policy and released on 9 September 1983, to replace a Statement made in 1977. The Statement encompasses the administration's views on international direct investment. (The text of the Statement is contained in annex IV.)

The statement underlined the importance attributed to services FDI: "*The United States is particularly concerned with foreign investment rules that prohibit service industries from doing business abroad.* Service sectors are among the most dynamic in today's economy, but there exists a number of limitations that inhibit export opportunities. For many service sectors, there is a universal requirement of establishment in host countries, with the competitive success of these industries heavily dependent upon the presence of branches to meet peculiar regulatory requirements. Thus, the investment policies of foreign countries have special importance to the service sector."[55] The statement specified further:

> The United States believes that an open international investment system responding to market forces provides the best and most efficient mechanisms to promote global economic development. . . . The basic tenet for treatment of investment is the national treatment principle: foreign investors should be treated no less favorably than domestic investors in like situations. . . . The United States opposes the use of . . . trade-related and other performance requirements . . . fiscal or financial incentives. . . . In this regard, the United States will make a particular effort to prevent the introduction by other countries of new measures of this type. . . . The United States will continue to work for the reduction or elimination of unreasonable and discriminatory barriers to entry of investment. The United States believes that foreign investors should be able to make the same kinds of investment, under the same conditions, as nationals of the host country.[56]

In addition, it noted that the US "reserves the right to take unilateral action against the use of performance requirements and similar policies, consistent with our international obligations".[57] In other words, "the Reagan Administration is pursuing an activist international investment policy in an effort to create an international environment conducive to [FDI] flows",[58] be they in services, data services or other sectors.

These broad service-trade-and-FDI objectives were combined in the "Trade and Tariff Act of 1984", adopted by the US Congress in the autumn of 1984. Especially through its Title III, "International Trade and Investment", the US Congress added its support to the service-trade-and-FDI objectives of the administration, clarified the government's authority in this respect and gave it a mandate for a wide range of actions. The 1984 Trade and Tariff Act is actually the third in a trilogy and completes a sequence of efforts designed to bring services fully into the framework of trade policy and to anchor services in legislative programs. The Trade Act of 1974 had recognized services for the first time but only to the extent that services were traded in conjunction with goods. The Trade Agreements Act of 1979 recognized services traded independently of goods. And, finally, the 1984 Trade and Tariff Act (which amends the Trade Act of 1974) gave services status equal to goods in every respect and, to a large extent, also covered FDI.

The 1984 Act provides the mandate, objectives, instruments, and resources for the government's service policy for at least the remainder of the 1980s. While advocating bilaterally and multilaterally negotiated solutions, it also provides the administration with several instruments to make its trading partners more amenable to US objectives and it empowers the administration to take certain unilateral measures if need arises. In particular, the Act gives broad authority to the administration to retaliate against what it considers unfair trade practices and investment restrictions and to use the Generalized System of Preferences as a negotiating tool.

The Act defines[59] "international trade" to include trade in both goods and services as well as FDI by US persons, especially if such investment has implications for trade in goods and services. "Services" are furthermore defined to include transfers of information, and they comprise services incidental to goods as well as services in and by themselves. (The definition of "services" had not changed from that in the 1979 Trade Agreements Act, except that the 1984 Act specified that "transfers of information" are to be included under this definition.[60]) This legislative evolution has a number of important implications. First, it establishes fully and clearly equal treatment for trade in services, trade in goods and certain forms of FDI under US trade law. Services, furthermore, are specifically understood to include data services—data services receive, so to speak, legal status. Second, since most if not all FDI has (or can be seen as having) implications for trade, FDI has effectively been brought under the purview of the US trade law. This, in turn, significantly expands the meaning of trade and can make such issues as right of establishment and performance requirements trade-policy issues for the US. Third, the scope of the remedial measures available to the administration is clarified and expanded. In other words, such measures can not only be used to remove barriers to trade in goods (which was permitted in the past) but also to remove barriers to service trade and trade-related FDI. Finally this change may have implications, in the long run, for US policy in an organization like GATT, where it may well seek an increasing coverage of FDI issues. It is noteworthy in this context, that the Commission on Industrial Competitiveness, formed by President Reagan in June 1983, recommended in its report that a future round of GATT negotiations ought to include FDI and performance requirements among its priority items.[61] As will be seen in chapter V, the US position is, in fact, that a number of FDI issues ought to be placed on the agenda of the new GATT round of multilateral trade negotiations.

Against this background, the broad purposes of Title III of the 1984 Trade and Tariff Act are:[62]

- to improve the ability of the US President to identify, analyse and eliminate barriers to US trade and investment;
- to encourage the expansion of international trade in services through the reduction or elimination of barriers to this trade;

- to encourage the role of US service industries in foreign commerce; and
- to enhance the free flow of FDI through the reduction or elimination of the trade-distorting effects of certain investment-related measures.

The emphasis of Title III is clearly on the reduction or elimination of barriers and other distortions. The principal manner in which this is sought is through the negotiation of bilateral and multilateral agreements which include dispute-settlement procedures. Accordingly, the Act provides the administration with the required negotiating authority. It is the first time that the President receives specific negotiating authority with respect to trade in services, US FDI and export-performance requirements, and trade and investment in high technology products and related services (i.e., mostly data services). Furthermore, the Act provides legislative guidance as regards the objectives of negotiations:[63]

- to reduce or to eliminate barriers to, or other distortions of, international trade in services (particularly US service-sector trade in foreign markets), including barriers that deny national treatment and restrictions on establishment and operation in such markets;
- to develop internationally agreed rules (including dispute-settlement procedures) in order to reduce or eliminate such barriers or distortions and help ensure open international trade in services;
- to reduce or to eliminate artificial or trade-distorting barriers to FDI, to expand the principle of national treatment, and to reduce unreasonable barriers to establishment;
- to develop internationally agreed rules, including dispute-settlement procedures, which help to ensure a free flow of FDI and reduce or eliminate the trade-distorting effects of certain investment-related measures; and
- to obtain and preserve maximum openness with respect to international trade and investment in high technology products and related services.

The high technology products mentioned in the last of these objectives include integrated circuits, parts of semiconductors and parts of automatic data-processing machines and units thereof. They are of particular interest in the context of this volume because the services related to them include, most importantly, data services. Apparently, high technology products and services were singled out in the 1984 Act because of the special importance attached to them by the business community. The negotiating objectives provided here are spelled out in great detail to include the following:

- to obtain the elimination or reduction of, or compensation for, the significantly distorting effects of foreign government acts, policies or practices . . . , with particular consideration given to the nature and extent of foreign government intervention affecting United States exports of high technology products or investments in high technology industries . . . ;
- to obtain commitments that official policy of foreign countries or instrumentalities will not discourage government or private procurement of foreign high technology products and related services;

- to obtain the reduction or elimination of all tariffs on, and other barriers to, United States exports of high technology products and related services;
- to obtain commitments to foster national treatment;
  . . .
- to provide effective minimum safeguards for the acquisition and enforcement of intellectual property rights and the property value of proprietary data.[64]

In other words, the main thrust of the 1984 Act—to obtain a maximum of freedom for trade and FDI flows in services—applies fully to data services.

The barriers to, and other distortions of, international trade in services specifically cover restrictions on information transfers and data processing since they include, but are not limited to[65]

- barriers to establishment in foreign markets;
- restrictions on the operation of enterprises in foreign markets, including
  - direct or indirect restrictions on the transfer of information into, or out of, the country or instrumentality concerned, and
  - restrictions on the use of data-processing facilities within or outside of such country or instrumentality.

To achieve these objectives, the Act invests the US administration with a range of powers to entice or pressure other governments to alter certain policies.

Perhaps one of the most important instruments in this respect is Section 301 of the 1974 Trade Act, as amended by the 1984 Trade and Tariff Act. It gives the administration broad discretionary powers to negotiate for the reduction or elimination of barriers to US service exports and FDI flows, and to take punitive actions against countries that do not reduce or remove such barriers.[66]

Section 301 gives the US administration the authority to take appropriate action to obtain the removal of foreign barriers to trade in goods and services and trade-related FDI. Cases arise under Section 301 when a domestic party files a complaint with the US Trade Representative alleging that a foreign government has erected import restrictions or has otherwise limited sales in its market. The US Trade Representative then has a short period available to determine whether to initiate an investigation. If the decision is positive, the US Trade Representative investigates the matter and simultaneously consults with the foreign government on the issues raised in the petition. If the consultations do not produce an agreement, the US Trade Representative is required to request proceedings under dispute-settlement arrangements. These procedures are followed under the auspices of GATT if the issue in question is covered by that organization. A panel hears the arguments of both sides, and issues a report on its findings. While these multilateral proceedings are taking place, the US and the foreign government may resolve the issue through bilateral discussions.

If neither the multilateral proceedings nor the bilateral discussions result in an acceptable solution, the administration may take unilateral action. If the President determines that an act, policy or practice of a foreign country

(i) is inconsistent with the provisions of, or otherwise denies benefits to the United States under, any trade agreement, or

(ii) is unjustifiable, unreasonable, or discriminatory and burdens or restricts
United States commerce,

the President shall take all appropriate and feasible actions within his power to
enforce such rights or to obtain the elimination of such act, policy or practice.[67]

The interpretation of these rather broad rules depends, of course, to a large
extent on the definitions of key criteria used to determine whether or not Section
301 is applicable. The term "unjustifiable" is defined to mean "any act, policy, or
practice which is in violation of, or inconsistent with, the international legal rights
of the United States. . . . [It] includes, but is not limited to, any act, policy, or
practice . . . which denies national or most-favored nation treatment, the right
of establishment, or protection of intellectual property rights". The term "unreasonable" is defined to mean "any act, policy, or practice which, while not necessarily
in violation of or inconsistent with the international legal rights of the United
States, is otherwise deemed to be unfair and inequitable. The term includes, but
is not limited to, any act, policy, or practice which denies fair and equitable (i)
market opportunities; (ii) opportunities for the establishment of an enterprise; or
(iii) provision of adequate and effective protection of intellectual property rights".
Finally, the term "discriminatory" is defined to include, "where appropriate, any
act, policy, or practice which denies national or most-favored nation treatment to
United States goods, services, or investment."[68] Clearly, these definitions are very
broad. In fact, the definition of "unreasonable" applies even to acts that are "not
necessarily in violation of or inconsistent with the international legal rights of the
United States". In other words, the perceived interests of the US are placed above
the strict letter of international agreements. Apart from that, this definition acquires
special importance with the administration's emphasis on international service
transactions and trade-related FDI. There are currently no internationally recognized
standards to govern these activities. Unless and until such standards are established,
the US will be able to determine and apply its own concept of "unreasonable".

If a foreign trade practice is determined to be in violation of these rather
broad rules, then the President may "suspend, withdraw, or prevent the application
of, or may refrain from proclaiming, benefits of trade agreement concessions to
carry out a trade agreement" with the foreign country or instrumentality involved,
and may "impose duties or other import restrictions on the products of such
foreign country or instrumentality, and may impose fees or restrictions on the
services of such foreign country or instrumentality, for such time as he deems
appropriate".[69] The President can exercise this authority with respect to any goods
or sector on a non-discriminatory basis or solely against the foreign country or
instrumentality involved and without regard to whether or not such goods or
sector were involved in the undesirable foreign trade practice.[70]

The 1984 Act furthermore clarified that the authorities granted by Section
301 apply to trade in services as well—and, for that matter, FDI with implications
for trade in goods and services. In other words, service exports now have the
same rights as goods exports in regard to remedies for practices considered unfair
by the US government. In fact, the Act adds to this authority by permitting
additional actions on services by authorizing the President to restrict, under certain
conditions, the terms and conditions of any service-sector access authorizations,
or to deny the issuance of such an authorization. These powers pertain to any
license, permit, order or other authorization issued under the authority of federal

law that permit a foreign supplier of services access to the US market in a given service sector[71] and they appear to permit the President to override the decisions of certain regulatory agencies.

Finally, the powers of the US Trade Representative regarding the initiation of investigations under Section 301 have been strengthened. The original Section 301 directed the Trade Representative to initiate investigations upon petition from domestic parties. Now, the Office of the Trade Representative may initiate such investigations on its own authority in order to advise the President on a particular matter.[72] This allows the Office of the Trade Representative to pursue US policy objectives more forcefully, and to file cases on behalf of firms that have grievances but do not wish openly to antagonize foreign governments. In fact, the Trade Representative self-initiated three cases in 1985 under this provision, involving Brazil, Japan and the Republic of Korea.

The 1984 Act also directs the US Trade Representative to identify and analyze acts, policies or practices which constitute significant barriers to, or distortion of, US exports of goods or services and US FDI and to estimate the trade-distorting impact of these barriers.[73] This analysis is to be updated annually, and to be submitted (together with information about what actions have been taken) to Congress. These reports are likely to increase the pressure for action against foreign trade barriers by focusing US attention on them and their effects. They will also render indirect assistance to those who wish to use Section 301 by doing some of the background work.

Section 301, as revised, is probably the most important instrument that can be used to further US trade and FDI objectives. But the 1984 Act also grants additional powers. One of these pertains to *new* export-performance requirements. If the Office of the Trade Representative determines that any new export performance requirements of any foreign country or instrumentality adversely affect the economic interests of the US, it can seek to reduce or eliminate these requirements through consultations and negotiations. In addition, the "United States Trade Representative may impose duties or other import restrictions on the products or services of such foreign country or instrumentality for such time as he determines appropriate, including the exclusion from entry into the United States of products subject to such requirements".[74] This is a rather sweeping authorization, although it is limited in that sanctions may not be applied to exports produced by US foreign affiliates established *before* the provision's date of enactment.

Specific customs-duty powers are granted in the area of high technology industries. In order to carry out any agreements concluded in this context, the administration has the authority to modify, eliminate or continue any existing duty, duty-free or excise treatment or to proclaim additional duties as it deems appropriate.[75] However, this authority is limited for a period of 5 years beginning with the date of the enactment of the 1984 Act.

Finally, the 1984 Act renews the Generalized System of Preferences (GSP) in such a way that it can be used as an instrument for the country's service policy as well.[76] One of the current purposes of granting GSP status is to encourage developing countries to eliminate or reduce significant barriers to trade in goods and services and to investment.[77] Accordingly, the administration is directed to consider, when designating beneficiary countries, the extent to which a country has taken action (a) to reduce or eliminate barriers to trade in services and (b) to reduce distorting investment practices and policies (including export-performance requirements).[78] If a country fails to take adequate measures in this respect, the President can withdraw, suspend or limit the application of the GSP.[79] At the same time, a country which is no longer treated as a beneficiary country can be redesignated as such if (among other things) it has taken adequate measures regarding services trade and FDI.[80] In other words, to a certain extent the GSP has become a negotiating tool with which developing countries can be enticed or pressured to accept US objectives regarding trade in services and FDI flows.

To provide the necessary resources for the government's more active role in international service transactions, the Act empowers[81] the Secretary of Commerce to establish a service-industries development program designed to develop policies that increase the competitiveness of US service industries in foreign commerce; to establish a service data base; to collect and analyse information pertaining to the international operations and competitiveness of US service industries;[82] to conduct research on service-related issues and problems; and to undertake sectoral studies of domestic service industries.

This review of the 1984 Trade and Tariff Act shows that the US government has now the mandate to negotiate bilaterally and multilaterally as regards trade in services (including data services) and trade-related FDI. The Act also specifies the principal purpose of these negotiations, namely the reduction or elimination of barriers to services trade and trade-related FDI. And it provides the government with the necessary administrative infrastructure to support its more active role in this field. Equally important, the Act strengthens considerably the bargaining power of the US government by giving it a number of instruments with which it can entice or pressure other governments to be more amenable to US objectives.

Naturally, the availability of these instruments does not necessarily mean that they will be used—partly because their very existence may have a deterrent effect, partly because the US may be reluctant to bring overt pressure to bear on its trading partners. At the same time, however, the application of punitive measures has become more likely than in the past, because the administration considers services a priority area. Therefore, it may utilize the powers it has more readily than in the past, if only to set examples. Section 301, in particular—and some of the other instruments—may well be at the center of a number of emerging service-trade and FDI disputes.[83] The readiness of the US to pursue a more forceful policy in this area can be seen from the fact that five of the total of ten 301 cases initiated in service industries since the enactment of the Trade Act of 1974 fall in the period 1983–1985; the last two were initiated by the US Trade Representative (see table III-5). In fact five of the total of thirteen 301 cases initiated during the period 1983–1985 were in services, compared to five of a total of 38 cases during the period 1975–1982.

In sum, the US has put services trade on the same footing as goods trade and certain forms of FDI under US trade law and it recognizes the interrelationships between trade in services, trade in high-technology goods, and FDI; it has placed the government's initiatives regarding transactions in services on a legislative basis; it has provided the mandate, objectives and resources for international negotiations; and its expanded version of Section 301 of the Trade Act of 1974 and its revision of the GSP Act have given the government tools to counter what it considers unfair trade practices and to put pressure on countries with a restrictive services policy. The government of the US is, therefore, fully and thoroughly prepared for international discussions and negotiations on services.

Table III-5. Cases in service industries brought under
Section 301 of the US Trade and Tariff Act,
1975-1985

Date of complaint or action	Petitioner/industry	Complaint	Status
1 July 1975	Delta Steamship Lines, Inc.	Notice of complaint alleging that Guatemala's requirement mandating certain cargo to Guatemala or associated line carriers constituted a discriminatory shipping practice.	Public hearings were completed on 20 September 1975. Following bilateral negotiations the petitioner withdrew the complaint since an accord had been reached between petitioner and the National Shipping Line of Guatemala. Investigation terminated 29 June 1976.
10 November 1977	American Institute of Marine Underwriters	Petition alleging that the USSR unreasonably required that marine insurance on all trade between the US and the USSR be placed with a Soviet state insurance monopoly.	In June 1978, the President determined that the Soviet practice was unreasonable. On 12 July 1979, the USTR suspended the investigation, pending review of the operation of the US-Soviet agreement. The suspension remains in effect until the USTR can conduct a thorough review and assessment.
29 August 1978	Certain US television licensees	Petition alleging that certain provisions of the Canadian Income Tax Act were unreasonable in denying tax deduction to any Canadian taxpayer for advertising time purchased from a US broadcaster for advertising aimed at the Canadian market when deductions were granted for the purchase of advertising time from a Canadian broadcaster.	Public hearings were held in November 1978 and July 1980. The President determined on 1 August 1980 that the most appropriate response was legislation which would mirror in US law the Canadian practice. Legislation was enacted on 30 October 1984.

(Table III-5 cont'd)

Date of complaint or action	Petitioner/industry	Complaint	Status
25 May 1979	American Institute of Marine Underwriters	Petition alleging that an Argentine requirement that marine insurance on trade with Argentina be placed with Argentine insurance firms is unreasonable and burdens US commerce.	Public hearings were conducted in August 1979. Upon an Argentine commitment to participate in multilateral negotiations, a goal of which was the elimination of restrictive practices in the insurance sector, the USTR suspended the investigation on July 25 1980.
5 November 1979	American Home Assurance Company	Petition alleging that the Republic of Korea was discriminating against the petitioner by failing to issue a license permitting petitioner to write insurance policies covering marine risks; not permitting petitioner to participate in joint venture fire insurance; and failing to grant retrocessions from Korea Reinsurance Corp. to petitioner on the same basis as Korean Insurance firms.	Beginning in June 1980, the US and the Republic of Korea held several rounds of consultations, resulting in the Republic of Korea's commitment to promote more open competition in the insurance market. Upon withdrawal of the petition, the investigation was terminated in December 1980.
21 September 1983	Air Courier Conference of America	Petition alleging that Argentina acted unreasonably in granting exclusive control over the international air transportation of time-sensitive commercial documents to the Argentine postal system.	On 7 Nov. 1983, the USTR decided to initiate an investigation and requested consultations. On 16 Nov. 1984, the President determined that Argentine practices were an unreasonable restriction on US commerce. He directed the USTR to hold another consultation, as requested by Argentina, and to submit proposals for action under

Date of complaint or action	Petitioner/industry	Complaint	Status
			301 within 30 days. Prior to the 30-day period, Argentina lifted its prohibition for a 90-day period. In March 1985, the restrictions were lifted permanently.
19 December 1983	Motion Picture Exporters Assoc. of America	Petition alleging that Taiwan discriminates against foreign film distributors.	On 30 January 1984, the USTR decided to initiate an investigation. The petition was withdrawn and the USTR terminated the investigation on 26 April 1984.
25 May 1984	Transpace Carriers Inc.	Petition alleging that the member government of the European Space Agency (ESA) and their space-related instrumentalities subsidize satellite launching services offered by Arianespace.	On 9 July 1984, the USTR decided to initiate an investigation and requested consultations with the European Space Agency. On 9 July 1985, the USTR submitted his recommendation to the President. On 17 July 1985, the President found that ESA's practices were not unreasonable.
16 September 1985	USTR on Brazil's informatics policy	The USTR self-initiated an investigation into all aspects of Brazil's informatics policy, including investment restrictions, subsidies, and import restrictions.	After extensive discussions with US industry, consultations were held with Brazil 1-5 February 1986. Recommendations to the President were to be submitted on or before 15 September 1986.
16 September 1985	USTR on the insurance practices of the Republic of Korea	The USTR self-initiated an investigation of the practices of the Republic of Korea which restrict the ability of US insurers to provide insurance services in the Korean market.	Consultations with the Republic of Korea were held in November and December 1985 and February 1986. Recommendations must be submitted to the President on or before 3 November 1986.

Source: Material supplied by the Office of the US Trade Representative.

2. The TDF focus

This preparedness extends also to the area of data services. There, the business community and the US government have given considerable thought to the elements of a future international arrangement.

a. The business community

In the case of the business community, TDF *users* (and especially TNCs) from developed and developing countries[84] have, for the reasons discussed earlier, a particular stake in this matter. This is especially the case for certain service industries for which TDF have become an integral part—indeed the lifeblood— of their operations. (On the other hand, data service *providers* outside the US may have a different interest, depending on their degree of competitiveness with foreign providers.)

The US business community took the lead in this matter because TNCs from that country were the first to use TDF on a larger scale, to become in certain circumstances dependent on them, to be confronted with obstacles to TDF, and to seek action to forestall the spread of such obstacles.[85] Prompted by service corporations like American Express, the US business community began to formulate and pursue its interests in TDF matters, both on the national and international levels (see table III-6).

In the US, work crystallized in the following organizations, in most of which a few individuals from service corporations (and especially data-service corporations) play a prominent role.

• The *Subcommittee on Transborder Data Flows of the Advisory Committee on International Investment, Technology and Development.* The Advisory Committee (whose meetings are open to the public) was established in 1975 to provide a private-sector input to the US government in all matters related to the subjects specified in its title. Its approximately 100 members represent business, labor and academia as well as public-interest groups, although business views are particularly influential. Two years after the establishment of the Advisory Committee, a Subcommittee on Transborder Data Flows was established under it.[86] Its meetings are held 4–6 times a year (mostly in reference to relevant OECD sessions) and are open to all members of the parent body. Its sessions were attended by 40–70 persons in 1985. The Subcommittee's function is to advise the US government in all matters relating to TDF and telecommunication issues. In that function, it is, first of all, a sounding board for ideas generated elsewhere (e.g., the US government, OECD), but over the years it has assumed a more active role. For instance, it contributed indirectly to the development of the OECD TDF Guidelines. Most recently, in fact, it has taken the initiative by proposing projects that should be undertaken. The Subcommittee's sessions are strictly for consultative purposes and no reports or papers are issued. It maintains close relations with the Interagency Working Group on Transborder Data Flow chaired by the Department of State (see below).

• The *Committee on Transborder Data Flows of the US Council for International Business.*[87] The US Council for International Business represents American business interests on international economic-policy issues to the executive and legislative branches of the US government and to major international economic organizations. Its principal objective is to promote an open system for world trade, finance and investment. It is the US member of the International Chamber of Commerce

Table III-6. Principal US and international business organizations
dealing with TDF, January 1986

Name	Year of establish- ment	Chair
United States		
Subcommittee on TDF of the Advisory Committee on International Investment, Technology and Development	1977	Hugh P. Donaghue, Control Data
Committee on TDF of the US Council for International Business	1979	Joan E. Spero, American Express
Committee on International Telecommunications Policy of the US Council for International Business	1980	Richard C. Mills, Consulting Services
West Coast Committee on International Information and Telecommunications Policies of the US Council for International Business	...	Bill C. Burgess, GTE Sprint
Ad Hoc Policy Group of the USA BIAC Committee on International Information Flows and the National Committee of the US organization for the CCITT of the ITU	1983	Hugh P. Donaghue, Control Data
International Relations Committee of ADAPSO	1969	Phillip Onstadt, Control Data
International Information and Telecommunications Issues Sub-Committee of CBEMA	1975	David Zarb, AII
Staff Committee of the International Trade and Investment Task Force of The Business Roundtable	1984	Richard Kahler, Caterpillar
Committee on TDF of the Bankers Association for Foreign Trade	1981	Edward Regan, Manufacturers Trust Hanover
International Telecommunications Committee of the American Bar Association	1980	Thomas J. Ramsey, Department of State
International		
Commission on Computing, Telecommunications and Information Policies (CCTIP) of the ICC	1981	Alfred Hartmann, Rothschild Bank
Working Party on TDF of the CCTIP	1981	Colin Preston, Sandoz
Working Party on Telecommunications of CCTIP	1981	Richard Mills, Consulting Services
Committee on Information, Computer and Communications Policies of BIAC	1980	Thomas Glueck, Skandinaviska Enskilda Banken
International Telecommunication Users Group	1974	Ernst O. Weiss

(ICC) and the International Organization of Employers. The Council's Committee on Transborder Data Flows was established in 1979 as a Working Group (which was upgraded to committee status in 1980). The Committee meets approximately three times a year and is attended by 30–40 persons. It was created to define the positions of US business in matters relating to TDF and to represent the views and needs of the business community both in the US and elsewhere, in particular regarding the growing body of data-protection legislation. In this regard, it presents its concerns to its counterparts within the ICC and works together with other national committees toward mutually acceptable positions and actions. In addition, the Committee is involved in such issues as market access, TDF/telecommunication-trade principles, standard-setting, copyright issues for software and data bases, and computer crime. The Committee on TDF also speaks for the US section of the Business and Industry Advisory Committee (BIAC) to the OECD. At the beginning of 1986, it appeared that this committee would merge with the Council's Committee on International Telecommunications Policy (see next paragraph), although separate working groups would remain for the TDF and telecommunication components.

• The *Committee on International Telecommunications Policy of the US Council for International Business*.[88] Established in 1980 as a Working Group (and upgraded to committee status in 1981), it meets about three times a year and is attended by 15–20 persons. Its principal function is to assemble the views, opinions and needs of US business in matters relating to international telecommunication policies, laws, regulations, services and facilities for the purpose of defining and expressing to appropriate organizations positions on existing, planned and required services. To meet these objectives, the Committee seeks to ensure, among other things, that business is given the maximum opportunity to participate in fora that decide or influence international telecommunication policy.

• The *West Coast Committee on International Information and Telecommunications Policies of the US Council for International Business*.[89] This committee meets about three times a year and is attended on the average by 15 persons. It deals with the same issues as the aforementioned Committees of the US Council for International Business.

• The *Ad Hoc Policy Group of the USA BIAC Committee on International Information Flows and the National Committee of the US Organization for the International Telegraph and Telephone Consultative Committee (the CCITT of the ITU)*.[90] The USA BIAC Committee exists no longer as a separate entity. Rather, it has merged with the TDF Committee of the US Council for International Business. An Ad Hoc Group on Telecommunications Development Issues meets under the auspices of the National Committee of the US Organization for the CCITT. Its mandate is chiefly to assess and monitor telecommunication development issues, especially as regards developing countries. After several informal meetings, it convened officially for the first time in October 1983, with about 20–25 persons attending the first two meetings. In December 1983, both organizations established the Ad Hoc Policy Group, which meets about 6–8 times a year in sessions attended by a dozen members. In an effort to encourage an active business stance in the area of TDF, its principal purpose was to develop objectives and principles for an assertive and coherent US policy on telecommunication and information issues (see below).

• The *International Relations Committee of the Association of Data Processing Service Organizations (ADAPSO)*.[91] ADAPSO, which has a membership of about

800 companies, represents the computer-service industry in the US. Its International Relations Committee was established in 1969 and has a membership of about 40–60 of the largest US computer and software firms. It monitors national' and international developments that hamper free trade, particularly those dealing with TDF and related issues. The Committee deals with such issues as private leased lines, relevant US government agencies involved in international communications, relevant OECD activities (especially the TDF Guidelines), the changing role of PTTs, and issues involved in discussions of CCITT.

• The *International Information and Telecommunications Issues Sub-Committee of the Computer and Business Equipment Manufacturers Association (CBEMA).*[92] CBEMA represents over 90% of US manufacturers of computers and computer equipment; it is primarily concerned with issues of national and international telecommunication laws and regulations as they relate to international service activities. A TDF sub-committee formed by CBEMA in 1975 became, by the end of the decade, the International Information Flows Sub-Committee which, in turn, became the International Information and Telecommunications Issues Sub-Committee in 1985. It is one of the four sub-committees under CBEMA's International Issues Committee, meeting approximately once a month with an average attendance of 5–7 members. Its basic purpose is to monitor issues in the TDF and telecommunication field as they may affect CBEMA. The Sub-Committee is composed of all members of CBEMA, including about 40 of the largest computer-manufacturing companies. The Committee is particularly concerned with the problems of tariff and non-tariff barriers faced by its members in international trade.

• The *International Trade and Investment Task Force of The Business Roundtable.*[93] This organization is composed of the chief executive officers of some 200 major US TNCs. Founded in 1972, its objective is to have an input into the policy process on issues which have a broad impact on the business community. Its International Trade and Investment Task Force is primarily responsible for keeping its members informed about developments in legislative issues relating to trade and investment. The Task Force's meetings have an average attendance of about 15–20 chief executive officers, who prepare position papers on relevant issues, including services and TDF. The Task Force is backed up by a staff committee which examines problems in greater detail. The meetings of the staff committee, which can take place every few weeks, are attended by an average of 30–40 persons.

• The *Committee on Transborder Data Flows of the Bankers Association for Foreign Trade.*[94] The Committee was created in 1981, has a membership of about ten bankers, and meets about four times a year. It concerns itself with a wide range of TDF issues, including privacy laws, PTT issues, local processing requirements, and non-tariff barriers and their impact on banking. Its principal purpose is to monitor developments in these areas as they affect member banks and recommend courses of action and official positions where appropriate.

• The *International Telecommunications Committee of the Science and Technology Section of the American Bar Association.*[95] It is composed of about 100 attorneys interested in international communication law. Formed in 1980, it meets 2–3 times per year and has an attendance of 20–40 persons. Its mandate is to monitor relevant international developments, including TDF.

• The *International Communications Association* (ICA) was established in 1948 and represents about 550 of the largest telecommunication-service users in the US. Its Public Policy Committee—which has about 20 members and meets four times a year—examines public-policy issues relevant to members in such areas as domestic competition, PTTs, private lines, and various aspects of commercial TDF. The ICA represents INTUG in the US.

• The *International Investment and Finance Committee (IIFC) and the International Trade Committee (ITC) of the National Association of Manufacturers.* The IIFC monitors issues which have an impact upon the overseas operations of US companies. Having a membership of 200, it meets 2–3 times a year, with an average attendance of 50. It deals with TDF issues as they emerge as a concern for the membership. Insofar as TDF issues involve telecommunication trade, GATT and US trade laws, they are dealt with by the ITC. This committee meets 4–6 times a year, with an attendance of 50–70 persons.

Internationally, a number of business organizations also undertake work on TDF, often with leading input from US bodies. The most important among them are the following ones.

• The *Commission on Computing, Telecommunications and Information Policies (CCTIP) of the International Chamber of Commerce (ICC).*[96] The ICC represents the interests of the international business community, drawing its membership from enterprises in over 100 countries. Its main objectives are to support the market economy, to help expand international trade and to make that trade easier. The ICC works through national committees and technical commissions. One of these technical commissions is the CCTIP which was established in 1981 and meets 2 times a year. Its meetings are attended by 35–45 persons. It provides a forum for suppliers and business users of data goods and services and focuses its work on TDF and telecommunications. Its overall objective is to promote an international environment for the optimal growth and development of computer-communications and information systems, to deal with the economic and social impact of information technology on business and to respond to issues arising from it in any way appropriate. More specifically, its terms of reference are to represent the interests of the international business community on trade issues arising from the increasing business use of, and dependence on, data services. These issues include the impact of national policies (including data-protection laws) and administrative practices on data flows; other social and governmental concerns which could lead to regulation; trade-related problems; and telecommunication issues. The Commission is to ensure that the needs of international business are adequately understood by decision-makers involved in regulatory efforts. It monitors developments, keeps interested ICC members informed, encourages national committees to follow policy developments at the national level, and attempts to ensure that the interpretation and implementation of regulatory instruments relating to data services is not broadened beyond the original intent to the detriment of the international free flow of business information. Finally, the Committee formulates ICC positions on the main issues and presents these to appropriate intergovernmental organizations, and it encourages national committees to seek to have the ICC positions taken into account at the national level. Several national committees have set up computing, telecommunications and information policies committees to support and extend the work of the Paris-based Commission.

• The *Working Party on Transborder Data Flows of the CCTIP of the ICC.*[97] Established in 1981, it met about 3 times a year and was attended by 15–20 persons. The tasks of the Working Party included ensuring that the information needs of international business were adequately understood by decision-makers; monitoring developments concerning TDF; defining issues of importance; encouraging national committees to follow developments in their countries; developing or updating analyses on relevant issues; and establishing liaison with appropriate organizations operating in this and related fields. The Working Party was dissolved during the autumn of 1985. The purpose of this was apparently not to de-emphasize TDF, but rather to recognize the way in which this term has become an umbrella term for issues concerning the application of information technologies. The responsibility for tracking developments in the TDF area was distributed among the individual members of the Commission.

• The *Working Party on Telecommunications of the CCTIP of the ICC.*[98] Established in 1981, it meets about 4 times a year and is attended by 25–40 persons. Its objective is to represent the international business community in matters relating to telecommunication plans and policies, services, facilities and tariffs. Its terms of reference are broadly patterned on those of the Committee on International Telecommunications Policy of the US Council for International Business.

• The *Committee on Information, Computer and Communications Policies of BIAC.*[99] BIAC represents the interests of the business community in the OECD. Members of BIAC committees are nominated by national federations of industry to represent national business communities. In 1980, BIAC established a Working Group on Information, Computer and Communications Policies, which was upgraded to committee status in 1982. It meets about 3 times a year and is attended by 15–20 persons. It is responsible for providing liaison with the OECD secretariat in matters relating to the mandate of the Committee; giving advice and comment to the OECD ICCP and monitoring the activities of its working groups; and following the reactions of governments and the response of business to the OECD TDF Guidelines. It also decides whether studies ought to be undertaken and positions and comments formulated which represent the views of business. The Committee participates in meetings and conferences with the OECD ICCP and the working groups functioning under its auspices. The Committee was involved in an advisory capacity in the formulation of the OECD Guidelines on Privacy and TDF.

• The *International Telecommunication Users Group (INTUG).*[100] Established in 1974 as a collective voice of telecommunication user associations (particularly from Western Europe), its principal purpose is to represent its members' interests in international telecommunication affairs. In particular, it seeks to ensure that business users' views are taken into account in the adoption of new technology facilities and the formulation of tariffs and standards. Its mandate is to pursue the introduction of new facilities, oppose excessive regulation and encourage the rapid adoption of new technology. INTUG co-operates with the ICC in the drafting and promulgation of position papers.

Although working groups on TDF have also been established by the business community in countries other than the US,[101] the level of awareness and concern in countries other than the US is generally nowhere nearly as high as in the US. In the US—as the brief review in the preceding pages indicates—the business community has, indeed, created for itself a sophisticated organizational infrastructure through which its interests can be identified, formulated and promoted. The same applies to the international level. The business community is further aided by the fact that some of its representatives play a key role in the international TDF discussions, thus ensuring a certain degree of consistency of views and coordination of policy. Developments since the beginning of the 1980s indicate, furthermore, that awareness, organization and policies have broadened from a focus on TDF and information flows to encompass telecommunication issues as well—thus reflecting the merging of the underlying technologies.

The principal specific aims of the business community—especially as concerns the trade aspects of data services—are perhaps best expressed in a document adopted in March 1983 by the US Chamber of Commerce after two years of internal discussions.[102] Emphasizing the importance of TDF as an integral part of world trade, the Chamber of Commerce underlined that "the freest flow of information across national borders is essential, and application of a progressive, liberal and comprehensive set of principles to such flow is timely and necessary to address present distortions and to prevent the emergence of new distorting practices". The Chamber of Commerce further suggested that such a set of liberalizing principles—which are seen as stimulating trade on the basis of market considerations and as contributing to global economic efficiency and growth— would consist of the following:

i)   That information trade should be conducted according to the principles of fair and open competition and the right to own, buy and sell information;
ii) That information originating from any country be subject to equal and nondiscriminatory treatment by the recipient nation (the most-favored-nation principle);
iii) That information originating from a foreign country be subject to treatment no less favorable than information originating in the recipient country (the national treatment principle);
iv) The transmittal of information be made in the most efficient way as determined by the parties to any information exchange or transaction;
v)   Government restrictions upon such transmittal should be only those necessary for legitimate technical reasons as opposed to being used to disguise protectionism and when government facilities or services are required for transmittal they should be provided upon a non-discriminatory basis and any fees or charges if levied should reasonably reflect the value of the service provided;
vi) That existing restrictions on the ability to obtain and to transmit information across national borders be reduced in as far-reaching a manner as possible;
vii) That new limits to the international movement of information be avoided and a standstill observed; and
viii) That exceptions for public policy purposes such as national defense or security will arise to countermand the liberal trade principles above. Such exceptions should be transparent and subject to periodic review.[103]

The Chamber of Commerce also recommended that the US government as a whole should move ahead strongly in the information-policy area and should, specifically:

• recognize international information flows as an emerging topic of national policy with important ramifications for the security and well-being of the American people and for the foreign relations of the United States;

- settle upon the best possible organization of the Executive Branch for monitoring developments affecting international information flows and for coordination and consultation with the Congress and the private sector;
- establish a goal of improving the government's understanding of the operation of the global information system in all respects, including: economic, technological, national security, cultural, and individual rights;
- agree upon a work program on international information flow which at the outset would identify the barriers, issues, interests and public and private institutions involved in international information flows;
- establish a system for improved monitoring of domestic and international developments affecting international information flows with a view to qualitative and quantitative analysis;
- commence an internal governmental process by which the significance of such developments can be fully evaluated in the light of national interest and the preservation of the global information system;
- identify the most appropriate governmental response, if any, in the light of such developments; and
- determine what policy, if any, the United States should pursue with a view to maintaining and advancing the global information system, including the calling for a standstill on new limits to the international movement of information.[104]

In other words, the private sector in the US strongly urged the government to recognize the importance of TDF, to organize itself for action in this area, to have a clearly articulated position on the subject, and to advance the topic in international negotiations.

Building on this work—and, in fact, supporting it but emphasizing the users' perspective more strongly—a joint Ad Hoc Policy Group of the USA BIAC Committee on International Information Flows and the National Committee of the US Organization for the International Telegraph and Telephone Consultative Committee (of the ITU) formulated the following "fundamental principles" concerning "U.S. Objectives in International Telecommunications and Information Policies" (they are reprinted, together with accompanying explanatory comments, in annex V):

In order to promote the growth and efficiency of the telecommunications and information industries, as well as the telecommunication-dependent industries, the following principles should apply.

- Open international marketing of information processing and telecommunications equipment should be encouraged on a fair and competitive basis without restrictive trade barriers.
- Users should have freedom to choose among competitive suppliers, including telecommunications agencies, for the supply, installation, and maintenance of their customer premises equipment.
- There should be an unrestricted and competitive international market for value-added (enhanced) telecommunications and information services.
- The encouragement of innovation in and development and application of new products and services should be through competitive market forces.

- Recognizing that there will always be a requirement for efficient public telecommunications networks, it is essential to continue to encourage the development of high quality services in both developed and developing countries.
- To provide maximum interconnectability among national telecommunication networks and services, reasonable minimum standards should be established on an international basis with users' and suppliers' participation.
- Users should have the freedom to choose from available basic transmission services, such as full-period leased circuits, which provide users with the greatest flexibility and ease of use.
- Prices charged for regulated telecommunications services should normally be based on the cost of providing the services, including a fair and reasonable rate of return.
- While attention should be paid to the protection of individual privacy, proprietary information, and national security, the general and traditional free flow of information among nations should be preserved in the interests of the advancement of the world economy.[105]

By the end of 1985, these principles had been endorsed by the TDF Committee of the US Council for International Business, CBEMA, ADAPSO, the Bankers' Association for Foreign Trade, the International Communications Association (which submitted them to INTUG, which expressed support for them), the US Chamber of Commerce, and The Business Roundtable. In this manner, they had become the most comprehensive statement of the US business community regarding TDF and related matters by the middle of the 1980s. They were also submitted to the appropriate BIAC and ICC committees, where they are likely to influence strongly the position of the international business community as a whole. The principles were furthermore submitted, in September 1984, to the US government, with the hope that they would be formally incorporated into US policy and serve as guiding principles for the government. However, this may only happen once they have been reformulated in the framework of the ICC and have thus come to represent the preferences of the international business community as a whole. Accordingly, the ICC is following up this initiative by stimulating national committees to develop their own standpoints, with a view toward distilling eventually an international position. When that happens, the new principles are also likely to be presented to other governments, through the mechanisms of the ICC at the national level.

Another important business organization which has taken a major initiative in this area is The Business Roundtable.[106] Apart from supporting the principles outlined in the preceding paragraphs and endorsing most of those adopted by the US Chamber of Commerce in March 1983, The Business Roundtable elaborated a number of these principles—emphasizing especially the data-flow side—and made several additions dealing with market access, the need to have reasonable assurances that the storage and processing of data abroad does not represent an unacceptable risk to countries and companies, and the need to establish adequate international structures to keep such trade-distorting policies as government procurement, tariffs and subsidies at a minimum. (The executive summary and recommendations of this report are contained in annex VI.)

In the international arena, finally, the ICC adopted in 1983 a policy statement which summarized the views and needs of business regarding TDF. (The text of this statement is contained in annex VII.) It is based on four basic perceptions:

- The intrinsic importance of the efficient exchange of information in the development and growth of modern international trade and commerce.
- The right of a business to communicate freely within and outside its corporate structure.
- The right of business to access and freely utilize national and international communications facilities.
- The necessity of recognizing the worldwide interdependence of modern business communications.[107]

The ICC was particularly concerned that the application of data technologies is inhibited "by the introduction of unwarranted or untimely laws or restrictions", without however, denying that regulatory constraints may be warranted in the public interest "provided they are non-discriminatory, enforceable and do not add to the existing bureaucratic burden."[108]

To determine the need for additional legislation or regulation, the ICC urged that the following criteria should be applied:

- That significant harm be clearly demonstrable, not merely a technical possibility. Regulations should focus on abuse of the information itself and not on the media of transmission.
- That only specific problems be addressed and interference with other parts of the information sector be avoided. An example of the latter has been the inappropriate inclusion of legal persons in the data protection laws of several European countries.
- That cost/benefit analysis of administration procedures demonstrate that neither unreasonable direct or indirect cost nor delays will be incurred by business.
- That in view of the dynamic state of information technology and the limited legal experience in this field, preference be given to the establishment of national and international codes or other means of ensuring flexibility and avoiding interference with growth and development.
- That regulatory measures be adopted only within an internationally harmonized framework. Due to the transnational character and importance of information flows, it is vital to reach an international consensus on their role.[109]

In conclusion, "the ICC urges governments and intergovernmental organizations to consult with business in order to promote policies which encourage the freedom of business communications and to review those that create barriers or hindrances."[110] Since the adoption of this statement, the ICC prepared a briefing paper on TDF, for the use of the Chamber's national committees in 57 countries.[111]

Thus, there is broad agreement among those parts of the business community which have dealt with the issue on the need to establish an international framework for TDF. It is generally seen as a separate agreement that could be adopted as part of a new round of multilateral trade negotiations under the umbrella of the trade-in-services negotiations. It is, furthermore, an agreement that is being sought with some urgency, at least by US business, because of the importance of data services in themselves as well as their importance as infrastructure for all other international transactions: "All segments of the American business community

have indentified international data flows as one of the top priorities for a new
round of trade negotiations. In fact, it is one of the few issues, along with the
importance of intellectual property, on which there was common agreement."[112]

This observation is based, among other things, on a survey conducted in
1985 at the request of the US Trade Representative by the chairpersons of the
private sector trade policy advisory committees on private sector views toward a
new round of GATT multilateral trade negotiations (MTN). The following organizations contributed to the survey: all policy advisory committees (Advisory
Committee for Trade Negotiations; Investment Policy Advisory Committee; Services
Policy Advisory Committee; Labor Policy Advisory Committee; Industry Policy
Advisory Committee; and Defense Policy Advisory Committee on Trade), the
American Retail Federation, The Business Roundtable, the Emergency Committee
for American Trade, the National Association of Manufacturers, the National
Foreign Trade Council, and the US Council for International Business. One of
the specific findings of the survey was that "the negotiation of a code on international
information flows is recommended by a number of private sector organizations for
inclusion on the agenda of any new MTN round."[113] Some of the individual
contributions to this survey made this point considerably stronger. Thus, the
National Foreign Trade Council observed that "emphasis should be placed upon
those service sectors, such as communications, which form the infrastructure of
services trade."[114] And the Services Policy Advisory Committee noted, in a special
section entitled "Centrality of Telecommunications": "Telecommunications plays a
central role in the international trade of all information based services because it
is the primary distribution channel for these services. . . . For this reason, policies
or practices that create barriers to the flow of information or to the use of
telecommunications services should be accorded a special priority in any trade in
services negotiations."[115]

These views and activities indicate how seriously the business community
takes the TDF issue and, especially, any restrictions on these flows. They are part
of a broad effort to define the interests of business in this matter, in order to
present a relatively unified position to governments. Since the members of the
relevant ICC and BIAC committees come from various countries, the business
community has a well-informed network of individuals who are often well-placed
to provide advice to governments.

b. The US government

The position of the US government is determined by the very strong position
that US firms have in all data industries, by the fact that the US is the principal
home country of TNCs and by the implications that TDF have for trade in services
in general. In addition, it reflects a commitment in principle to a liberal trade and
FDI regime. These considerations suggest that it is in the interest of the US to
have an open international system for trade and FDI in data services. It is the
same basic objective that the US has for trade and FDI in services in general, of
which data services are one component: "In terms of the trade implications of
domestic telecommunications and information policies, the U.S. considers these
to be part of the broader initiative now underway to develop disciplines over
international trade in services."[116] Accordingly, the broad objectives with regard to
trade and FDI in services in general (discussed earlier) are identical to those pursued
specifically with regard to data services.

Reflecting the interest and preference situation of the US, the overriding principles advocated to advance the objective of an open international system in the specific context of data services are unrestricted flow of information and marketplace competition in the context of a free-enterprise system. To quote a recent background paper prepared by an Interagency Working Group on Transborder Data Flow: "U.S. telecommunications and information policy is driven by a reliance on two broad principles: unrestricted flow of information and marketplace competition. Wherever possible, there has been a shift from regulation toward the promotion of competition, particularly by removing obstacles to market entry." And it continues: "In general, individual policy decisions concerning telecommunications and information reflect government efforts to: 1) enhance the free flow of information across national borders, and 2) promote an environment for the provision of telecommunications and information facilities, services and equipment where maximum reliance is placed on business enterprise, open and competitive markets and unrestricted trade with minimum government regulation."[117]

The broad goals derived from these principles are to:

- enhance the free flow of information and ideas among nations subject only to the most compelling national security and privacy limitations;
- promote harmonious international relations and contribute to world peace and understanding through communications;
- promote, in cooperation with other nations, the development of efficient, innovative and cost-effective international communications services responsive to the needs of users and supportive of the expanding requirements of commerce and trade by broadening opportunities for competition and investment;
- ensure efficient utilization of the geostationary orbit and electromagnetic frequency spectrum;
- expand information access and communications capabilities of developing countries to facilitate their economic development;
- ensure the flexibility and continuity of communications and information required to maintain national defense and international peace and security;
- promote competition and reliance on market mechanisms to ensure efficient prices, quality of services, and efficient resource utilization; and
- promote the continuing evolution of an international system of communication services that can meet the needs of all nations of the world, with attention directed toward providing such services to economically less-developed countries.[118]

At the operational level, the specific objectives of the US echo closely those of the business community. Foremost among them is the desire to reduce or eliminate any obstacles to trade and FDI in data services and to prevent the imposition of new ones. "Obstacles" are defined broadly to include any impediment to data flows—from restrictions on the use of leased lines to lack of competition because of state monopolies (e.g., PTTs). This policy has received endorsements on the highest political levels. Thus, as discussed earlier, the 1984 Trade and Tariff Act specifically identified restrictions on transfer of information (and the use of data-processing facilities) as barriers that ought to be reduced or eliminated. And the Presidential Statement on Investment Policy, also discussed earlier, pledged that the US will "continue to work in the OECD for a 'data pledge' which would assure that no new barriers to data flow will be imposed by developed countries and encourage all countries to join in adopting more open and liberal policies on transborder data flows."[119] Thus, the US position is in harmony with the interests of the country's business community[120] and, perhaps, TDF *users* worldwide.

On the policy level, the US government has been consistently and vigorously in the forefront of promoting an international environment in which data-service transactions and applications can take place as freely as possible. Leading agencies are the Office of the US Trade Representative (which is part of the White House and whose head has cabinet rank) and the Bureau of International Communications and Information Policy in the Department of State (whose head has ambassadorial rank).[121] The Bureau is responsible for the formulation, coordination, implementation and supervision of information policy. Coordination within the US government is ensured through an Interagency Working Group on Transborder Data Flow, whose members include representatives from some 20 federal agencies and which meets about 8–10 times a year.[122] US policy in this area is helped by the openness of the important US market for data goods and services, a fact which can provide leverage as and when needed to persuade others to open their (often closed) markets. One way in which this leverage can be exerted is through reciprocity legislation, i.e., legislation which links the opening of foreign markets to access to the US market. Efforts in this direction have already been made, especially as regards telecommunication equipment.[123]

Another way in which the US government could persuade other governments to adjust their policies is through the application of the powers given to it by the 1984 Trade and Tariff Act, especially through Section 301.[124] In fact, the use of Section 301 was advocated by the Senate Finance Committee with regard to Japan's telecommunication equipment trade. It also seemed to have been on the administration's mind as regards South Korea's computer-import policy and the FRG's policy on the international transmission of data via computer-communication systems.[125] In any case, on 11 July 1985 the US initiated an investigation under Section 301 into barriers to the sale of foreign semiconductors in Japan and, on 16 September 1985, into Brazil's trade and market-reserve practices in informatics. In the case of Brazil, such pressure is not new, it just reached a new level. As a report of the US Trade Representative observed:

> The United States has consistently objected to Brazil's informatics policy and warned Brazil of the likely effect of the [1984 informatics] law's passage and implementation on Brazil's development and U.S. economic interests. Since the law's approval, the United States has held bilateral consultations with Brazil under GATT Article XXII to learn more about the trade implications of the informatics policy.
>
> The United States also raised its investment-related concerns about this policy at the January 1985 meeting of the U.S.-Brazil Investment Working Group and at numerous cabinet-level meetings.[126]

Even if one of the objectives of initiating action under Section 301 may have been to forestall the enactment of protectionist trade legislation by the US Congress, it is clear that Section 301 is increasingly becoming an important policy instrument for an assertive US administration.

Table III-7. Regulation of data flows in Latin America, 1980/81

Country	Permissibility of third party use	Permissibility of connecting leased lines to public switched networks	Possibility of direct dialing between leased circuits	Restrictions on TDF
Argentina	No	Yes[a]	No	No restrictions for normal private users
Barbados	No	Yes	Yes	No policy
Bolivia	No	Yes	No	No policy
Brazil	No	Yes[a]	No	Restrictions on all users
Chile	No	Yes[a]	No	No policy
Colombia	No	Yes	Yes	No policy
Costa Rica	Yes	No	No	No policy
Dominica	...	Yes	Yes	No policy
Ecuador	No	Yes	No	No policy
El Salvador	Yes	Yes[a]	No	No policy
Grenada	Yes	Yes	Yes	No restrictions for normal private users
Guatemala	No	No	No	No policy
Guyana	No	No	No	No policy
Haiti	No	No	No	No policy
Honduras	No	No	No	No policy
Jamaica	No	Yes	Yes	No policy
Mexico	No	No	No	No de facto restrictions
Nicaragua	Yes	No	No	No policy
Panama	No	Yes[a]	No	No policy
Paraguay	No	Yes[a]	Yes	No policy
Peru	Yes	No	Yes	No policy
Saint Lucia	No	No policy	No	No policy
Uruguay	No	No	No	No restrictions for normal private users
Venezuela	No	Yes[a]	No	No policy

Source: United Nations Centre on Transnational Corporations, "Data Services in Latin America and the Caribbean", prepared for the Permanent Secretariat of the Latin American Economic System (New York: UNCTC, 1985), mimeo.

a/ With some restrictions.

As indicated, the principal targets of US policy are obstacles to trade in data services. There is general agreement that trade in data services has so far been relatively unimpeded by government action, even by the actions of developing countries (see table III-7).[127] However, there is concern that this situation may change considerably in the future and thus raise the costs of doing business internationally (because of such needs as having to maintain redundant data bases, acquire and maintain extra processing equipment and duplicate software) and introduce instability and unpredictability into corporate planning.[128] Thus, for instance, while 76% of the respondents in a survey conducted in 1983 by The Conference Board of mostly manufacturing companies in 16 countries reported that they had not encountered any obstacles or restrictions to the transborder transmission of internal data, 86% of those who addressed this issue expressed serious concern that any future restrictions by governments could have an adverse effect on their international business operations.[129] Increased transparency (e.g., in

Table III-8. Kinds of obstacles and restrictions encountered
by mostly manufacturing firms to the transborder
transmission of internal company data, 1983

Legal regulations
- Privacy and data-protection laws.
- Requirements to use locally manufactured EDP and telecommunication equipment and software.
- Requirements to process certain
  kinds of data locally.
- Requirements to maintain certain
  business records within a
  country-sometimes making it
  necessary to duplicate them.
- Requirement to send data abroad
  through a single border gateway.
- Prohibition on connections between
  leased lines and public telephone
  networks.
- Prohibitions of on-line connections for sending order and
  shipping information.
- Prohibition on the use of dial-up
  data transmission.
- Restrictions on intercompany
  exchange of exploratory data
  involving natural resources.
- Restrictions on technology
  transfer and export licenses
  for diskettes containing
  specified company information.
- Restrictions on using word-
  processing equipment for
  communications.
- Restrictions on using electronic
  mail systems.

PTT regulations and practices
- Refusal by some countries to
  accept certain kinds of mail,
  including diskettes and tapes.
- Restrictions and delays in
  making leased lines available
  to private companies.

- Tampering with mail containing tapes
  and diskettes.
- Tapes put through X-ray machines, thus
  corrupting the data.
- Martial-law restriction on telex and
  mail.
- Monitoring by governments of data sent
  through PTT facilities.
- Customs delay on diskettes sent through
  the mail facilities of PTTs.

Technical
- Incompatible equipment standards among
  countries.
- Delays caused by lack of adequate
  facilities.
- Garbled or slow transmission of data
  due to poor quality of equipment.

Miscellaneous
- Political restrictions on data transmission to proscribed areas.
- Linking government approval of unrelated business plans to company EDP
  and telecommunication policies and
  practices.
- Threats that governments may tax data
  transmission.
- Prohibitive costs, including high
  tariffs on leased lines, data-
  transmission services, EDP and
  communication equipment.
- Strikes, slowdowns and other labor
  difficulties at PTT and other
  transmission facilities.

Source: The Conference Board, Regulating International Data Transmission:
The Impact on Managing International Business (New York: The Conference Board,
1984), p. 8.

the form of an inventory) as regards restrictive measures is, therefore, an important
objective for the US since it would provide a basis from which to seek changes.

However, one important caveat is necessary: where the flow of data—specifically
the outflow of high-technology data from the US—threatens the country's technological lead, controls can be imposed. This is usually done with reference to
national security, especially in the East-West context.[130]

The kinds of obstacles to TDF that exist or can be established are wide-
ranging (see table III-8, which reports the results of the survey by The Conference

Board mentioned earlier). Many of them are of an indirect nature and include technical measures and regulatory and administrative practices. But measures geared directly to TDF also exist and are certainly conceivable. From the point of view of countries, the main virtues of such measures are that they permit domestic data industries to grow (infant-industry considerations) or protect existing industries, and that they broaden and increase the revenue base of the PTT or the government. From the point of view of data-service users and providers, their principal effects are that they impose higher costs for the users of data services; restrict business opportunities and the flexibility of users in terms of choosing among available services and making them available to others; and limit access to national markets.[131] The following discussion deals with some of the most important of these obstacles.

The introduction of taxes or tariffs on the value of data-service flows. Such action could be taken to raise revenues and/or to protect domestic data-service industries against competition from abroad. It would have the effect of raising costs for business and, depending on the manner in which it is done, could raise fears about confidentiality. The advent of public data networks gives the authorities the ability to monitor data flows and, if need arises, to sample those flows. Certain countries (e.g., Greece, South Korea, Taiwan) monitor for instance telex traffic completely and do not permit encryption. As with long-distance telephone traffic, taxes could be placed on the *volume* of data transmitted. Another and more difficult alternative is to tax the *value* of the data transmitted. As with shipments of goods across borders, for instance, tax authorities could request that a bill of lading or customs declaration be added to each economically relevant data package sent. Such a "data bill of lading" could indicate the nature and value of the data involved. The technology to administer volume-sensitive or value-sensitive rates appears to exist. It is worthwhile noting here that the GATT Valuation Code has set an international precedent on how certain services should be assessed. In fact, the GATT Committee on Customs Valuation decided at the end of 1984 that it is permissible to include the value of software in the calculations when determining the value of a carrier medium, e.g., a tape (as desired by developing countries), although it is also permissible to take only the cost or value of the carrier medium into account (as desired especially by the US). As the chairperson of the Committee remarked on that occasion: "Indeed, if the technical facilities are available to the parties to the transaction, the software can be transmitted by wire or satellite, in which case the question of customs duties does not arise."[132] It is precisely the increasing availability of these technical facilities and the possibility that customs authorities may place a tariff on TDF that are at stake, and it is probably only a question of time until taxes or tariffs are in fact placed on data flows. Not surprisingly, the business community has been strongly opposed to any moves in this direction.

This issue raises a fundamental question, a question which goes far beyond TDF: if national economies are increasingly information-based and an increasing proportion of the value of economic activities is generated by the production, processing, storage, retrieval, and dissemination of data and data services, how can governments maintain their tax base? The fact that the valuation of data and data services is usually very difficult is, in the final analysis, a poor argument for disregarding the matter because it fails to solve the underlying problem. It will probably require new and imaginative approaches to deal with this matter. At issue are not those data services for which established market values exist—e.g., commercially available software packages—but rather the wide range of intermediate data services whose economic value it is difficult to determine in isolation. Perhaps one approach is to let the parties to a data-service transaction themselves assign a value to the transaction, with the government auditing only on occasion. In any event, the problem is beginning to be recognized. The Business Roundtable, for instance, has recognized that, in principle, a country's interest in raising revenues in an information-based society is one of the considerations that may balance the free flow of information.[133]

Changed conditions for the operation of leased lines. Corporations that lease telecommunication lines from telecommunication authorities to establish private networks do so at a fixed rate for the lines involved, i.e., at rates independent of the extent to which the lines are used (as opposed to the usage-sensitive rates of the public systems which are based on call duration and distance); furthermore, they tailor these networks specifically to their needs. Telecommunication authorities could favor a switch from flat rates for such private leased lines to usage-sensitive rates (as discussed in the preceding paragraphs) or could introduce higher rates for international than for national traffic. The FRG, for example, has decided to charge volume-sensitive rates beginning in 1988, and other countries appear to be considering such a move. Depending on the actual rates that are being charged, such a change in the rate structure could increase PTT revenues, especially as the volume, speed and general use of data traffic increases. The effect on corporations, the main users of data traffic, depends, of course, on the actual rates that are being charged; business fears that such a switch in the rate structure would lead to an increase of operating costs.

Apart from changing the rate structure, PTTs could also decrease the supply of private leased lines or deny them altogether to ensure the viability of public data-transmission networks that have come into operation in virtually all developed market economies and are beginning to do so in a growing number of developing countries. An important argument for public data networks is that the proliferation of private networks can constitute a considerable waste of resources if regarded from a macroeconomic point of view. This is so because private systems are typically considerably underused, a fact exacerbated by the need to have back-up systems to ensure against failure. In addition, small and medium-sized users do not normally have the capital to establish their own networks. Denial of private lines reduces the flexibility with which users can establish networks tailored to their specific needs and, where the public network is less sophisticated, can impose constraints on the user's activities.[134] Flexibility is also reduced where the interconnection between private lines and the public system is restricted or prohibited; this could make it impossible for instance for bank customers to access the bank's private network. Equally important, where mandatory use of public networks is not accompanied by a willingness of the PTT to assume liability for, say, errors in the electronic transmission of funds, a special risk factor is introduced for users.

Finally, one widespread restriction is the prohibition of third-party use. As mentioned earlier, computer-communication systems are normally underutilized to a considerable extent—an incentive for the corporations involved to resell the unused capacity to other (third-party) users. This, however, places these corporations in direct competition with PTTs which do not wish to see the growing and profitable data traffic captured by private networks paying flat rates for leased lines. The interest of PTTs in their revenue base and in protecting their networks clashes here with the interest of private users in maximizing the use of their systems. Restrictions on shared use and resale of private lines also affect the competitiveness of smaller firms which do not have the financial strength—or need—for full-time private lines.

In order to deal with this situation, the US government has proposed an agreement in principle to the effect "that governmentally established user charges or taxes should not be so excessive as to constitute barriers to trade in services"[135] (i.e., that there be a reasonable relationship between the fees to be paid and the services rendered) and that private leased lines be made available to interested users.

National data-protection laws. As was documented at the beginning of this chapter, many developed market economies have enacted data-protection laws. Originally, parts of the business community and some governmental officials (especially in the US) feared that such laws could be used for protectionist purposes[136] (especially where they applied to legal persons), in so far as they restricted the transnational storage and transmission of name-linked data. While different and incompatible data-protection laws could, in fact, constitute barriers to trade, it has been generally acknowledged that their introduction served purposes other than protectionism and that they have not been abused. In addition, the adoption of the Convention for the Protection of Individuals with Regard to Automatic Processing of Personal Data by the Council of Europe and the Guidelines Governing the Protection of Privacy and Transborder Flows of Personal Data by the OECD have created a common framework within which relatively harmonized national laws and regulations can evolve.

Local-content requirements. As already indicated, some countries require that certain data-processing activities be carried out domestically and therefore prohibit TDF in these areas. Brazil is the most sweeping in this respect, but developed countries (e.g., Canada) also have such requirements. The principal reasons are infant-industry or vulnerability considerations. The former are dominant in the case of Brazil, the latter in the case of Canada's banking regulations. A variation of this approach is Brazil's requirement to have copies of data bases located on its territory.[137] Efforts to encourage domestic software production through various incentives or administrative practices fall also into this category. As the importance of data services for economic development becomes more recognized, local-content requirements of this sort may well become considerably more widespread.

Software protection. Given the importance of software and the rapidly rising volume of its trade, the protection of software has become a central concern for the principal software-producing and exporting country, the US. An indication of the importance that is attached to this issue is the intensity with which the US followed the 1984/1985 policy discussion of this matter in Japan. MITI had proposed in 1984 to remove software from the protection of the country's copyright law and place it under the patent law instead. The effect of such a move would have been to shorten the protection period for software from 50 to about 5-10 years. In addition, to stimulate software development, MITI was considering introducing compulsory licensing when this was in the national interest. In other words, a firm using software would have to license it to others interested in it, which implied that the software code, etc. would have to be made available. The US strongly objected to MITI's proposals because it considered such action an infringement on industrial property rights and because it feared that, after compulsory licensing, competitors would simply make small changes in existing software and then sell it as their own product. "Yielding to prevasive foreign pressure,"[138] MITI revised its stand in March 1985. New amendments to the Japanese copyright law were enacted on 14 June 1985 which unequivocally extended the standard 50-year statutory copyright protection to computer programs. Although the protection of software—and, for that matter, data bases—is not primarily a trade issue, it can be expected to become an increasingly important area of concern for the principal software-exporting countries and, therefore, to assume greater attention in their trade policy. The US Trade and Tariff Act of 1984, for instance, makes the enforcement of intellectual property rights one of the objectives of US trade policy. It would not be surprising if an international or regional (OECD) initiative were to be launched in this field.

Market access barriers. Many of the barriers described so far have the effect that they limit the access to markets or services, or make them available on a discriminatory basis only. Non-discriminatory access to and usage of national distribution systems—the telecommunication system—is of particular importance because otherwise data services cannot be provided through trade. As discussed in chapter I, it is in this context that the right of presence acquires its importance.

There is, however, a particular aspect to the right of access that is acquiring importance, namely access to specialized private or quasi-private networks and the data bases associated with them. This issue has already been discussed earlier in this chapter, and the example given concerned airline reservation systems. With the spread of data technologies as described in chapter II, more and more networks are bound to be created, involving virtually every economic and possibly even social activity. Automatic teller machine networks, point-of-sale networks and teletex networks are examples. Most of these are of a private, quasi-private or closed user-group nature, and they become important instruments to control certain markets. The extent to which non-participating (domestic and foreign) firms are to be allowed to connect with such networks is bound to become a matter of considerable policy debate. The US, for its part, favors an agreement "which would generally outline governmental commitments to open market access",[139] although it is not clear to what extent such an agreement should cover private, quasi-private and closed user-group networks alike.

Equipment policies. All data services require, of course, the use of equipment. In most countries, the telecommunication authorities play a major role in equipment questions, whether because they establish and enforce relevant technical standards and regulations as regards the equipment that can be connected with the tele-communication network (homologation procedures) or because of close relations with dominant suppliers (which are often national champions—like Phillips in the Netherlands—or foreign corporations that have a long tradition in supplying equipment). Where dominant suppliers are national champions, the temptation is particularly high to pursue procurement policies and to set standards that favor domestic firms over foreign ones in the supply of equipment. Some of these standards may well have the effect that independent users have to use (and hence buy) domestic equipment as well, even if better and less expensive compatible equipment is available elsewhere. This situation is further exacerbated if the domestic buyer takes advantage of its monopoly position and plays foreign suppliers off against one another when seeking certain imports. From the point of view of the country, equipment policies of this sort may be useful to foster its domestic data industry. From the point of the user, this approach can impose costs, reduce flexibility and make it difficult to create integrated transnational computer-communication systems. The US desires therefore the negotiation of "an international agreement which establishes a 'right to plug in' for equipment that meets agreed technical standards and allows firms to sell services that can be provided by using such equipment."[140] In other words, users should have the freedom to choose the customer-premises equipment (modems, terminals, cluster controllers, communications controllers, private branch exchanges [PABXs], etc.) which best suits their need, provided it meets certain minimum requirements for approval and does not harm the network, network personnel or other users.

Telecommunication monopoly. The equipment policies described in the preceding paragraph depend to a very large extent on the monopoly position of PTTs, and PTTs have in almost all OECD countries a monopoly over the provision of telecommunication services. PTTs contend that telecommunication is a natural monopoly which ought to be controlled closely as to investment, procurement, rate structure and the universal availability of services at a reasonable price. The last of these points is based on the desire to provide telecommunication services on the basis of equity and public-service considerations rather than market criteria. In many (especially small) countries, furthermore, it may not be efficient to permit more than one carrier. In addition, governments are hesitant to give up direct control over an industry that is vital to industrial and technological development, as well as to national security, and that can be used as an instrument through which they can implement part of their data-resource policies. Finally, PTTs are particularly interested in capturing the growing data traffic and the services associated with it and, conversely, in preventing this traffic and these services from being siphoned off into private computer-communication systems.[141]

For the reasons discussed earlier in this section, the monopoly position of the PTTs is not to the liking of international data-service users and export-oriented suppliers. The US administration, in particular, shares this view. The thrust of its policy has been to encourage the privatization of public telecommunication monopolies and the deregulation of the telecommunication market, with a view to creating competitive markets for telecommunication equipment and services, which, presumably, would be of benefit to users in general and US users and suppliers in particular. Privatization and deregulation in the UK and Japan were, therefore, very much welcomed by the US.[142] Where public monopolies continue to exist, the US would like to see the boundary between monopoly activity and competitive activity defined as narrowly as possible. Specifically, the US would like it to be the case that "monopolies and the governments under which they operate . . . compete with private firms on an arm's length competitive basis", that "service monopolies provide their services to all potential purchasers on an equivalent basis", and that "monopolies . . . agree to purchase services in a manner consistent with the principles laid down in the Governments Procurement Code."[143]

The export of the US deregulation model is not without friction. In particular, the pressures on Japan—a close political ally of the US—were extraordinary. As newspaper reports showed, this pressure built up almost daily during the period just before April 1985, when the Nippon Telegraph and Telephone Public Corporation (NTT) was scheduled to go public and new standards and requirements (especially covering market entry, equipment testing and certification procedures) for the import of telecommunication products were expected to be announced. Part of this pressure was the unanimous passing by the Senate of a (non-binding) resolution accusing Japan of unfair trade practices; the introduction of a bill barring Japanese companies from selling telecommunication equipment in the US until Japan opened its own market fully to similar US equipment; and approval (by a vote of 12 to 4) of a bill by the Senate Finance Committee which would give the President 90 days to respond to what it considered unfair trade practices of Japan by obtaining increased access for US products in Japan or to take action under Section 301 to ban imports from Japan. In addition, the House of Representatives passed (by a vote of 394-to-19) a non-binding resolution calling on the President to carry out a plan within 90 days to attack Japanese trade barriers and other causes of the US trade deficit. In view of these pressures, a trade adviser to the Japanese government was quoted in March 1985 as saying after a trip to Washington that "the sentiment in the United States is like that before the outbreak of a war."[144] Although this pressure has to be seen in the broader context of the US trade deficit with Japan, it clearly shows what political saliency certain data-resource—here: telecommunication equipment and services—have obtained.

The issue of monopoly raises also a broader question, namely that of the regulation or deregulation of certain services. As noted earlier, services in general and telecommunication services in particular are heavily regulated. Some tend to look at regulations primarily as barriers to trade. While it can certainly be the case that regulations have been adopted with protectionist purposes in mind, governments have equally certainly other (and legitimate) reasons for regulating services, including safety, health and environmental considerations; consumer and privacy protection; and defense, security and national independence interests. Naturally, there are border-line cases in which not all countries may agree whether or not regulations are legitimate—and infant-industry considerations are among them; in such situations, multilaterally agreed criteria may be the only solution. The point is that governments have well-founded public-interest reasons for regulation, and these have to be examined before specific regulations are declared to be protectionistic trade barriers or, more generally, before deregulation is sought.

The objectives of the US as regards telecommunications were further elaborated by the Counselor to the US Trade Representative in 1985. Placing the issue in the larger context of an umbrella agreement on trade in services in general and the principles that ought to apply to this trade, he suggested that:

> The negotiation of an umbrella agreement covering all trade in services would subject the practices of Postal Telephone and Telegraph (PTT) monopolies to full transparency. The national treatment principle would mean that countries could no longer exclude foreign manufacturers or service providers in the marketplace through domestic regulatory procedures, but would have to make such restrictions explicit. PTTs would have to follow open, non-discriminatory procedures for the procurement of equipment and services and for the estab-lishment of standards.
> The trade principle of transparency would build on current international cooperation activities in the telecommunications and information field. Trade relations among all countries could greatly benefit from common acceptance of a requirement to publish all laws, regulations and administrative rulings on telecommunications and information policy.

A consultation/dispute settlement provision would facilitate multilateral cooperation efforts in the telecommunications field. Governments would rely on a structured mechanism for resolving telecommunications trade disputes and setting telecommunications trade on a firmer footing. Application of these principles would reduce the likelihood that regulations could be used for protectionist ends and would increase cooperation in this field.

It is envisioned that the negotiation of an umbrella agreement would be followed, at a later stage, by negotiations designed to reduce existing barriers to trade in individual service sectors. It is too early to tell what kind of agreement might be developed to deal with the specific issues of telecommunications trade that would not be addressed by a general framework agreement. Four concepts that might serve as a basis for a future agreement on communication services are "the right to plug in telecommunications equipment into networks," "the right of access to a network," "the right to use a network" for transmitting various types of information, and the right to establish a value-added network.[145]

It is likely that the US would wish a similar approach to monopoly, national treatment, transparency, consultation and dispute settlement, and market access to govern other data services as well.

Overall, the most important objectives of the US are, therefore, the reduction or elimination of barriers to transactions in data services and the prevention of new barriers; the enhancement of conditions for market-place competition; the international recognition of the rights to sell, to be present in foreign markets and to establish foreign affiliates; and national treatment for foreign suppliers and foreign affiliates. Since the recognition of these objectives requires the agreement of other countries, the US seeks to negotiate a liberal multilateral regime which covers data services and which contains consultation and dispute-settlement provisions which ensure that the relevant international obligations are discharged. It is, of course, helpful for the US that its interests and those of transnational users and (many) suppliers of data services and equipment converge on a non-restrictive international environment for data flows. The reason is that this can counterbalance the data-policy influence of PTTs and that of internationally uncompetitive local data-service providers in those countries that aim at strengthening their national data resources.

At the same time, however, the US shares with all other countries an interest in strengthening the international infrastructure for TDF, especially as regards telecommunication, because this infrastructure is the precondition for TDF to take place. For this reason, the International Telecommunication Union remains an organization that enjoys the support of all countries. And for this reason, perhaps, the Maitland Commission could agree on recommending expanded technical assistance for telecommunication and the establishment of a Centre for Telecommunication Development.[146]

One should add one other point to understand the US position. The early discussion on information flows took place in UNESCO, in the context of the need for a New International Information Order. This discussion focused largely on *press* information flows and was perceived to lead to restrictions on such flows. The international information-flow discussion became, therefore, closely associated with freedom of the press and thus obtained high visibility in a value-laden context. Although news transmission is only a fraction of data flows, the free-flow-of-information approach has carried over to—and shaped—the TDF discussion to a certain extent, although increasingly data flows are seen in the ideologically less charged economic and trade context. As one observer put it: "While the free flow of information is a compelling position in debates on privacy and freedom of the press, this approach is less effective when confronting national economic prerogatives and aspirations. In a climate in which economics is increasingly the major concern of national information policies, many countries view free flow as simply good economics for the country in a strong or dominant position—namely the United States."[147]

In its efforts to promote an international framework for transactions in data services, the US can furthermore capitalize on the role of data services as a core service by embedding the discussion of this subject into the broader discussions about a liberal multilateral framework for service transactions in general: this defuses the position of the US as the dominant data-service supplier. In fact, by pursuing this approach, the US actually wins allies among those countries that are service exporters, be they developed or developing countries. At the same time, the most important part of these broader discussions remains the discussion on data services, precisely because data services are a core service. Nevertheless, this potentially strong alliance of the major exporters of services and service capital as well as users of data services is not without strain because of conflicting interests in the data-service area. This is reflected in the actual course of the discussions, which will be dealt with in the next chapter.

Notes

[1] Ronald K. Shelp, *Beyond Industrialization: Ascendancy of the Global Service Economy* (New York: Praeger, 1981), p. 171. Shelp is Vice-President of the Celanese Corporation. Until June 1985, he was Vice-President of American International Group (one of the largest insurance companies of the US), chairperson of the US Government Service Industry Sector Advisory Committee on Trade Policy, and chairperson of the Coordinating Committee of the Coalition of Service Industries.

[2] In 1970, the state of Hesse (Federal Republic of Germany) enacted the first data-protection law. See "Datenschutzgesetz des Landes Hessen", *Gesetz und Verordnungsblatt Hessen*, 1970, pp. 625ff. For an early compilation of privacy legislation in member countries of the OECD and a discussion of relevant issues, see, Rein Turn, ed., *Transborder Data Flows: Concerns in Privacy Protection and Free Flow of Information*, volume II, *Supporting Material on Transborder Data Flows* (Arlington, Va: American Federation of Information Processing Societies, 1979). For recent discussions of privacy protection, see, e.g., David H. Flaherty, *Protecting Privacy in Two-Way Electronic Services* (White Plains: Knowledge Industry Publications, 1985); Colin Mellors and David Pollitt, "Legislating for Privacy: Data Protection in Western Europe", *Parliamentary Affairs*, 37 (Spring 1984), pp. 199–215; Herbert Burkert, "Institutions of Data Protection: An Attempt at a Functional Explanation of European National Data Protection Laws", *The Computer/Law Journal*, 3 (1981–1982), pp. 167–188; George W. Coombe and Susan L. Kirk, "Privacy, Data Protection, and Transborder Data Flow: A Corporate Response to International Expectations", *The Business Lawyer*, 39 (November 1983), pp. 33–66; and Michael Bergmann, *Grenzueberschreitender Datenschutz* (Baden-Baden: Nomos, 1985). A general bibliography is contained in David H. Flaherty, ed., *Privacy and Data Protection: An International Bibliography* (White Plains: Knowledge Industry Publications, 1984).

[3] See, for instance, the "Proposal for a Council Directive on Procedures for Informing and Consulting the Employees of Undertakings with Complex Structures, in particular Transnational Undertakings" ("Vredeling initiative") of the Commission of the European Communities, *Bulletin of the European Communities*, Supplement 3/80, which requires that relevant data are transferred from headquarters to affiliates. For the view of the business communities on this issue see ICC, "Privacy Legislation, Data Protection and Legal Persons" (Paris: ICC, 1984), mimeo.

[4] See, e.g., John M. Eger, "Emerging Restrictions on Transborder Data Flow: Privacy Protection or Non-Tariff Trade Barriers", *Law and Policy in International Business*, 10 (1978), p. 1065.

[5] The person in charge of the Guidelines in the OECD is Hans-Peter Gassmann, Head, Information, Computer and Communications Policy Division; the person in charge of the Convention in the Council of Europe is T. L. Early, Division of Public Law, Directorate of Legal Affairs. For reviews of these instruments, see Martine Briat, "Synthesis Report on the Application of the Guidelines Governing the Protection of Privacy and Transborder Flows of Personal Data: Update as of December 1983", in OECD, *Transborder Data Flows: Proceedings of an OECD Conference held December 1983* (Amsterdam: North-Holland, 1985), pp. 351–392, H. Seip, "Results of a Survey on the Implementation of the OECD Guidelines Governing the Protection of Privacy and Transborder Flows of Personal Data" in *ibid.*, pp. 345–350, Martine Briat, "TNCs and the OECD TDF Guidelines", *The CTC Reporter*, 20 (Autumn 1985), pp. 43–44, and Craig T. Beling, "Transborder Data Flows: International Privacy Protection and the Free Flow of Information", *Boston College International and Comparative Law Review*, 6 (1983), pp. 591–622.

[6] See OECD, *Transborder Data Flows and the Protection of Privacy* (Paris: OECD, 1979), which contains the proceedings of the Symposium.

[7] An explanatory memorandum appended to the Recommendation deals with the general background of the OECD work in this area and the Guidelines themselves. See OECD, *Guidelines on the Protection of Privacy and Transborder Flows of Personal Data* (Paris: OECD, 1981).

[8] "On Human Rights and Modern Scientific and Technological Developments", *Annuaire Européen*, 6 (1968), p. 363.

[9] "On the Protection of the Privacy of Individuals vis-à-vis Electronic Data Banks in the Private Sector", *Resolutions 1973*, pp. 73–74, and "On the Protection of the Privacy of Individuals vis-à-vis Electronic Data Banks in the Public Sector", *Resolutions*, 1974, pp. 87–89.

[10] See, respectively, Council of Europe, Recommendation No. (81) 1, Recommendation No. (83) 3, Recommendation No. (83) 10, Recommendation No. (85) 20, and Recommendation No. (86) 6.

[11] See in this context the very instructive discussion by M. D. Kirby, "Legal Aspects of Information Technology", in OECD, *An Exploration of Legal Issues in Information and Communication Technologies* (Paris: OECD, 1983), pp. 10–57. See also Bernard Hanotiau, "Les flux trasfrontières de données, et la problematique du droit international privé", in *La telematique: Aspects techniques, juridiques et socio-politiques* (Gand: E. Story-Scientia, 1985), pp. 175–193, and Anne W. Branscomb, ed., *Toward a Law of Global Communications Networks* (New York: Longman, 1986).

[12] See for instance Allan Gottlieb, Charles M. Dalfen and Kenneth Katz, "The Transborder Transfer of Information by Communications and Computer Systems: Issues and Approaches to Guiding Principles", *American Journal of International Law*, 68 (1974), pp. 227–257.

¹³ As will be indicated later in this chapter, this is an issue of particular and increasing concern to the US.

¹⁴ See ICC, "Protection of Information in Electronic Systems: Operational Guidelines" (Paris: ICC, 1985).

¹⁵ The questions examined by UNCITRAL include when payments become final; liability for loss caused by delayed or incorrect payment instructions; and the evidential value of payment records kept in electronic form. See United Nations, "Electronic Funds Transfer", A/CN.9/221 of 17 May 1982. By the summer of 1984, the UNCITRAL Secretariat had prepared several parts of a Legal Guide on Electronic Funds Transfers (EFT) (see document A/CN.9/250 and Add. 1–4). The parts dealt with terminology; EFT systems in general; agreements to transfer funds; funds transfer instructions; and fraud, errors and improper handling of transfer instructions and related liability. During its summer 1985 session, the UNCITRAL Commission received the remaining draft chapters of the Legal Guide (see A/CN.9/266 and Add. 1 and 2 of 30 April 1985). Among the questions examined were whether major changes in law are required by the development of EFT, the principal types of financial transactions to which the law of funds transfer applies, whether internationally agreed rules on conflicts of law should be prepared for international funds transfers, and whether public telecommunication carriers, private data-communication EFT networks, and electronic clearing-houses should be responsible for losses arising out of errors or fraud in connection with a funds-transfer instruction. In addition, UNCITRAL continued to examine the problem of the applicability of rules to data-processing activities in domestic and international trade. The Commission at its June 1985 session submitted four recommendations to governments: to review the legal rules affecting the use of computer records as evidence; to review legal requirements that certain trade transactions or trade-related documents be in writing; to review legal requirements of hand-written signature or other paper-bases method of authentication; and to review legal requirements that documents submitted to governments be in writing and manually signed (see A/40/17, pp. 70, 71) . The person responsible for this work is Eric E. Bergsten, Chief of UNCITRAL's International Trade Law Branch.

¹⁶ "Testimony" of William L. Fishman, US, Senate, Banking Committee, Sub-Committee on International Finance and Monetary Policy, 9 November 1981, mimeo., pp. 10–11.

¹⁷ OECD, *Guidelines, op. cit.,* p. 36.

¹⁸ *Ibid.,* p. 12.

¹⁹ One interesting contribution toward such a framework—although not focusing on trade and FDI—is contained in Jon Bing, Petter Forsberg and Erik Nygaard, "Legal Problems Related to Transborder Data Flows", in OECD, *Exploration of Legal Issues, op. cit.,* pp. 61–135. In fact, this report "attempts to outline the possible basis for a legal régime for transborder flows of non-personal data" (p. 61). Examining especially existing international transport, telecommunication and intellectual property treaties, it extracts the following principles as being of particular relevance for an international TDF regime (pp. 97–98): national treatment; most-favored-nation treatment; the public's right to use equipment; innocent transit; custom free transit; free landing; secrecy of correspondence; and technical standards which facilitate TDF.

²⁰ UNIDO, *Industry in a Changing World* (New York: United Nations, 1983), p. 174.

²¹ *Report on Present State of Communications in Japan: Fiscal 1983* (Tokyo: Ministry of Posts and Telecommunications, n.d.), p. 33.

²² *Ibid.,* p. 29.

²³ US, Congress, Senate, Committee on Commerce, Science, and Transportation, "Long-range Goals in International Telecommunications and Information: An Outline for

United States Policy" (Washington: Government Printing Office, 1983), Committee print, p. 169.

[24] For a review of governmental involvement in the data goods industry in developed market economies, see UNIDO, *Industry in a Changing World*, *op. cit.*, pp. 170–175, and especially M. English and A. Watson Brown, "National Policies in Information Technology: Challenge and Responses", *Oxford Surveys in Information Technology*, 1 (1984), pp. 55–128, and UNIDO, "Survey of Government Policies in Informatics", UNIDO/IS.526 of 4 April 1985.

[25] See *Financial Times*, 16 October 1984.

[26] For a discussion of this approach, see Sauvant, *Trade and Foreign Direct Investment*, *op. cit.*, ch. V.

[27] These were not the first projects of the European Community in the data-resource area. Euronet-Diane is an earlier example. For a brief listing of these earlier projects, see English and Brown, "National Policies in Informatics Technology", *op. cit.*, pp. 117–118.

[28] See *ibid.*, p. 119. See also, "Forecasting and Assessment in the Field of Science and Technology" (FAST) and "European Strategic Programme for Research and Information Technologies" (ESPRIT), described briefly in Klaus W. Grewlich, "Die Informationsgesellschaft: Eine 'doppelte Herausforderung' fuer Europa", in Otto Ulrich, ed., *Die Informationsgesellschaft als Herausforderung an den Menschen* (Frankfurt: Haag and Herchen, 1984), pp. 33–54.

[29] See Commission of the European Communities (CEC) "The Mid-Term Review of ESPRIT" (Brussels: CEC, 1985), mimeo., and *Eurotech Forum*, 8 (June 1985), p. 3. These proportions do not reflect, however, the priorities preferred by the Commission. Of the ECU 205 million allocated, the respective distribution desired by the Commission was 20%, 16%, 19%, 15%, and 30%.

[30] See Commission of the European Communities, "Proposal for a Council Decision on a Preparatory Action for a Community Research and Development Programme in the Field of Telecommunications Technologies", COM(85) 113 final/2 of 1 April 1985, and "RACE", *Information Market*, 39 (April-June 1985), p. 3.

[31] See "EUREKA-Grundsatzerklaerung" (Hannover, 1985), mimeo., p. 1.

[32] See UNCTC, *Transborder Data Flows and Brazil: Brazilian Case Study* (New York: UN, 1983), Sales No. E.83.II.A.3, on which the following text draws. See also Paulo Bastos Tigre, *Technology and Competition in the Brasilian Computer Industry* (London: Frances Pinter, 1983). Since the beginning of 1985, the Informatics Secretary of SEI was Doria Porto, who followed Edison Dytz and Joubert de Oliveira Brízida.

[33] "Before the United States Trade Representative in the Matter of: The Government of Brazil's Informatics Policy. Rebuttal Comments on Behalf of ABICOMP" (Washington: USTR, 1985), mimeo., exhibit 19.

[34] See Normative Act 27, of 1 December 1983.

[35] Mexico has a similar instrument with its technology-transfer law. This law, originally promulgated in 1972 and restated in 1982, is designed to regulate contracts which involve transfer-of-technology (including software) contracts.- According to the law, whenever users purchase software products, they have to register the contracts with the National Registry of Technology Transfer. The only software products that are exempted from this regulation are operating systems and software games. During the first year of application of the restated law, 296 contracts were submitted for registration, of which 204 were approved and 92 denied (see TIES, *Newsletter*, No. 25 (April 1984), p. 12). The government of Mexico can reject a technology-transfer (including software) contract when a product equivalent to the one to be purchased has been produced in the country. The government is thus in a position to foster the emergence of a national software industry. On the other hand, the

government accepts the purchase of imported software if the product is not available in Mexico or if it would be very costly and lengthy to develop it locally. In cases in which users do not register software contracts, the law determines that the user will have to pay fines that can amount to 5,000 Mexican pesos; in addition, users are not able to treat payments for non-registered software as a deductible expense when calculating taxable income.

[36] See Ricardo Maciel, "Brazil's Policy for Informatics", speech delivered at a Friedrich Ebert Stiftung conference on TDF, Bonn, 11–13 November 1985.

[37] UNCTC, Brazilian Case Study, op. cit., p. 192.

[38] The bill was signed on 29 October 1984 by the President of Brazil, who vetoed, however, a number of items. Most important among them was a special fund for research. The original text wanted to empower the administration to allot annually in its fiscal budget an amount equalling 0.8% of its tax receipts to a special informatics and automation fund through which, among other things, R & D in informatics and automation technology was supposed to be financed. The discussion and adoption of the bill received widespread publicity. SEI has to draft the implementing regulations for the adopted law. A separate law is supposed to be drawn up to deal with software matters.

[39] A key variable is, of course, the definition of what constitutes a national firm. For the purpose of the law (art. 12), "national firms are corporations established and with their seat in Brazil, and which are under permanent, exclusive and unconditional direct and indirect control of individuals resident and domiciled in this country or of public entities." "Control" is understood to consist of de facto decision-making control, technological control and stock control. The last of these criteria refers to 100% of the voting shares and at least 70% of the company stock (66% in the case of corporations). A firm has to fulfill all these criteria to be regarded as a national firm.

[40] Maciel, op. cit.

[41] Speech of the Canadian representative, W. H. Montgomery, at the Second OECD Symposium on Transborder Data Flows in London, 30 November–2 December 1983, "Transborder Data Flow: Canadian Directions", in OECD, Transborder Data Flows, op. cit., p. 71.

[42] F. Vuilleumier, Rapporteur, "Session 1: Transborder Data Flows: (A) The Present Situation, (B) The International Firm", in ibid., p. 38.

[43] See UNCTC, Transborder Data Flows and Poland: Polish Case Study (New York: UN, 1984), Sales No. E.84.II.A.8.

[44] "Communiqué," PRESS/A(85) 31 of 12 April 1985, para. 14d. The discussion on access in the OECD is not only conducted in the framework of TDF, but also in the context of trade in services in general and in the context of trade in high-technology products.

[45] Raimundo Beca, "Codifying Information Access", Transnational Data and Communications Report, 9 (January 1986), p. 19. This article is based on the paper submitted to the OECD Working Party.

[46] See the summary of the country case study on TDF of the FRG, contained in "Transborder Data Flows and the Federal Republic of Germany", paper before the twelfth session of the Commission on Transnational Corporations, New York, 9–18 April 1986, mimeo.

[47] This issue has been particularly studied in Sweden and, perhaps not surprisingly, by that country's Ministry of Defence. See The Vulnerability of the Computerized Society (Stockholm: Ministry of Defence, 1978).

[48] See "A Choice of Brands", The Economist, 25 August 1984, p. 14.

⁴⁹ The Business Roundtable, *International Information Flow: A Plan for Action* (New York: The Business Roundtable, 1985), *op. cit.*, p. 33. See also Mark B. Feldman, "Commercial Speech, Transborder Data Flows and the Right to Communicate under International Law", *The International Lawyer*, 17 (Winter 1983), pp. 87–95, who also suggests that right of access should be part of an international regime for TDF.

⁵⁰ To quote US Secretary of State George P. Shultz, "Science and American Foreign Policy: The Spirit of Progress", speech delivered to the National Academy of Science, Washington, 6 March 1985, p. 9: ". . . any government that resorts to heavy-handed measures to control or regulate or tax the flow of electronic information will find itself stifling the growth of the world economy as well as its own progress. This is one of the reasons why the United States is pressing for a new round of trade negotiations in the services field, to break down barriers to the free flow of knowledge across borders."

⁵¹ See Sauvant, *Trade and Foreign Direct Investment, op. cit.*

⁵² See US, Office of the US Trade Representative, "U.S. National Study on Trade in Services" (Washington: USTR, 1983), mimeo., "Trade and Tariff Act of 1984", as amended in the "Conference Report", 98th Congress, 2nd Session, House of Representatives, Committee of Conference (Washington: Committee Print, 1984), mimeo., and "Statement by the President: International Investment Policy", reprinted in US, Department of Commerce, *International Direct Investment: Global Trends and the U.S. Role* (Washington: Superintendent of Documents, 1984), pp. 85–88 (and contained in annex IV of this volume). For a brief review of the origin of the service discussion in the US, see Raymond J. Krommenacker, *World-Traded Services: The Challenge for the Eighties* (Dedham: Artech House, 1984), ch. 6.

⁵³ "U.S. National Study", *op. cit.*, p. 8.

⁵⁴ *Ibid.* For an earlier exposition of the US position see William E. Brock, "A Simple Plan for Negotiating on Trade in Services", *The World Economy*, 5 (November 1982), pp. 229–240. Brock was the United States Trade Representative in President Reagan's cabinet between January 1981 and April 1985.

⁵⁵ "International Investment Policy", *op. cit.*, part II, emphasis added.

⁵⁶ *Ibid.*

⁵⁷ *Ibid.*, part V.

⁵⁸ William E. Brock, "Trade and Debt: The Vital Linkage", *Foreign Affairs*, 62 (Summer 1984), p. 1054.

⁵⁹ US, "Trade and Tariff Act of 1984", *op. cit.*, Title III, Sections 307(a) and 304(c).

⁶⁰ This is done in the context of amending Section 301 of the 1974 Trade Act. Elsewhere, in the context of the service-industry development program to be established by the Secretary of Commerce (Section 306(a)(5)), services are defined as "economic activities whose outputs are other than tangible goods". The illustrative list that follows includes banking, insurance, transport, communications and data processing, retail and wholesale trade, advertising, accounting, construction, design and engineering, management consulting, real estate, professional services, entertainment, education, and health care. Hence, there is no definitive definition of services. This gives the administration the flexibility to adapt it according to circumstances.

⁶¹ See *Global Competition: The New Reality* (Washington: Superintendent of Documents, 1985), vol. I, p. 44.

⁶² US, "Trade and Tariff Act of 1984", *op. cit.*, Section 302.

⁶³ *Ibid.*, Section 305(a)(1).

⁶⁴ *Ibid.* The acts, policies or practices referred to in the first of these objectives include: "(A) foreign industrial policies which distort international trade or investment; (B) measures which deny national treatment or otherwise discriminate in favor of domestic high

technology industries; (C) measures which fail to provide adequate and effective means for foreign nationals to secure, exercise, and enforce exclusive rights in intellectual property (including trademarks, patents and copyrights); (D) measures which impair access to domestic markets for key commodity products; and (E) measures which facilitate or encourage anticompetitive market practices or structures."

[65] *Ibid.*

[66] *Ibid.*, Section 304.

[67] *Ibid.*, Section 304(a).

[68] *Ibid.*, Section 304(f)(2).

[69] US, "Trade Act of 1974", Public Law 93-618, 3 January 1975, Sec. 301.

[70] US, "Trade and Tariff Act of 1984", *op. cit.*, Title III, Section 304(a).

[71] *Ibid.*, Section 304(c) and (f).

[72] *Ibid.*, Section 304(d).

[73] *Ibid.*, Section 303. The first such report was issued in 1985. See US Trade Representative, "Annual Report on National Trade Estimates 1985" (Washington: USTR, 1985), mimeo.

[74] US, "Trade and Tariff Act of 1984", *op. cit.*, Section 307(b).

[75] *Ibid.*, Section 308.

[76] *Ibid.*, "Title V: Generalized System of Preferences Renewal", Section 503(c).

[77] *Ibid.*, Section 501.

[78] *Ibid.*, Section 502.

[79] *Ibid.*, Section 505.

[80] *Ibid.*

[81] *Ibid.*, Title III, Section 306(a)(1).

[82] The information to be collected and analyzed includes (*ibid.*): "(i) policies of foreign governments toward foreign and United States service industries; (ii) Federal, State and local regulation of both foreign and United States suppliers of services, and the effect of such regulation on trade; (iii) the adequacy of current United States policies to strengthen the competitiveness of United States service industries in foreign commerce, including export promotion activities in the service sector; (iv) tax treatment of services, with particular emphasis on the effect of United States taxation on the international competitiveness of United States firms and exports; (v) treatment of services under international agreements of the United States; (vi) antitrust policies as such policies affect the competitiveness of United States firms; and (vii) treatment of services in international agreements of the United States."

[83] Observed the *Annual Report of the President of the United States on the Trade Agreements Program, 1983* (Washington: USTR, 1984), p. 100, prepared by the Office of the US Trade Representative: ". . . increasing attention has been given to Section 301 of the Trade Act as a means of providing appropriate action against unfair foreign trade practices in services sectors. While the trade remedies available do not always provide opportunity for relief to affect service industries, Section 301 remains an important tool for addressing unfair services trade practices in foreign countries, particularly in the absence of multilateral rules and principles governing services."

[84] More than 95% of all TNCs are, however, headquartered in developed market economies. It should be noted that one of the TNCs that had to make extensive adjustments to the Brazilian TDF policy was Brazilian.

[85] Originally, large segments of the business community in OECD countries were also suspicious of the privacy-protection instruments adopted by various countries and especially the Council of Europe and the OECD, for fear that they would be used to hinder

TDF. In the meantime, however, the legitimate concern of these instruments are widely recognized.

[86] Until January 1986, it was chaired by Hugh P. Donaghue, Vice President of Government Programs and International Trade Relations, Control Data Corporation.

[87] It is chaired by Joan E. Spero, Senior Vice-President, American Express Company. The Vice Chairperson is Hugh P. Donaghue, who is also responsible for BIAC-related questions.

[88] It is chaired by Richard C. Mills, Managing Principal, Consulting Services (formerly Vice-President, Citibank). The Vice Chairperson is Lowell Ravesloot, Director of Telecommunications Relations, IBM. See also US Council for International Business, "Committee on International Telecommunications Policy: Terms of Reference", mimeo.

[89] It is chaired by Bill C. Burgess, Director, Major and National Accounts, GTE Sprint (formerly Vice-President, Public Affairs, Bank of America).

[90] It is chaired by Hugh P. Donaghue.

[91] It is chaired by Phillip Onstadt, Director of Telecommunications, Control Data Corporation.

[92] It is chaired by David Zarb, Manager, International ATT Communications.

[93] It is chaired by Edeson Spencer, Chief Executive Officer, Honeywell. The chairperson of the staff committee is Richard Kahler, Manager, Governmental Affairs, Caterpillar Tractor Co.

[94] It is chaired by Edward Regan, Vice-President, Manufacturers Hanover Trust Co.; its vice chairperson is H. William Anderson, Executive Vice-President, First Bank Minneapolis.

[95] It is chaired by Thomas J. Ramsey, Deputy Coordinator and Deputy Director, International Communications and Information Policy, Department of State.

[96] It is chaired by Alfred Hartmann, Director-General, Rothschild Bank (Zuerich). Its rapporteur is Ray Austin, International Advisor to Unilever on Informatics Legislation and Regulations. See "Commission on Computing, Telecommunications and Information Policies: Terms of Reference for the Commission", document No. 373–20/5, Rev. 3 of 8 April 1981, mimeo.

[97] It was chaired by Colin Preston, Corporate Advisor, International Economic Relations Department, Sandoz S.A. (Switzerland). See also ICC, "Working Party 'Transborder Data Flows': Terms of Reference of the Working Party", document No. 373–22/2 of 25 May 1982, mimeo.

[98] It is chaired by Richard Mills. See also ICC, "Revised Terms of Reference for Working Party on Telecommunications", document No. 373/INT.36 Rev. bis of 21 May 1984, mimeo.

[99] It is chaired by Thomas Glueck, Senior Vice-President, Head of EDP and Marketing, Skandinaviska Enskilda Banken. The Vice Chairperson is L. John Rankin, Director of Standards and Data Security, IBM.

[100] Its president is Ernst O. Weiss.

[101] For instance, a working group has been established in the UK, and LOTIS was also undertaking work on TDF in 1984.

[102] See "Findings and Recommendations Regarding the Flow of Information Across National Borders" (Washington: Chamber of Commerce of the United States, March 1983), mimeo. This text was subsequently submitted to the ICC Working Party on Transborder Data Flows, which took it into consideration when formulating the position of the international business community on this subject.

[103] *Ibid.*, pp. 3–4.

[104] *Ibid.*, pp. 5–6.

[105] New York: US Council for International Business, 1984, mimeo.

[106] See The Business Roundtable, *op. cit.* The draft of this document was prepared by Arthur Bushkin and Jacqueline Hess, Telemation Associates, Inc., Washington, D.C.

[107] ICC, "Information Flows: An International Business Perspective" (Paris: ICC, 1983), mimeo., p. 2.

[108] *Ibid.*

[109] *Ibid.*, p. 3.

[110] *Ibid.*, p. 4.

[111] "Information Flows: Analysis of Issues for Business" (Paris: ICC, 1984), mimeo.

[112] Geza Feketekuty, "The Telecommunications and Services Market Worldwide: A US View" (Washington: Office of the USTR, 1985), mimeo., p. 10. Feketekuty is counselor to the US Trade Representative.

[113] "Chairmen's Report on a New Round of Multilateral Trade Negotiations. Submitted to the United States Trade Representative, May 15, 1985" (Washington: USTR, 1985), mimeo., p. 15.

[114] *Ibid.*, contribution by the National Foreign Trade Council, p. 7.

[115] *Ibid.*, contribution by the Services Policy Advisory Committee, p. 11.

[116] US, Interagency Working Group on Transborder Data Flow, "Communications and Transborder Data Flows in the United States: A Background Paper" (Washington: Interagency Working Group, 1985), mimeo., p. 127.

[117] *Ibid.*, p. 120. And one page later, the paper noted: "The fundamental principles underlying U.S. goals and policy in communications and information are free enterprise, open and competitive markets, and free trade with a minimum of direct government involvement or regulation."

[118] *Ibid.*, pp. 121–122.

[119] "International Investment Policy", *op. cit.*, part IV.

[120] This is not to say that there are no firms in the US in data services—or for that matter, in services in general—that would not face disadvantages from a liberal trading regime in services. However, those service industries that desire a liberal regime are certainly determining the agenda at the present time.

[121] Until the end of April 1985, the head of USTR was William E. Brock; since then it is Clayton K. Yeutter. The head of the Bureau is Diane Lady Dougan.

[122] The Interagency Working Group on Transborder Data Flow is chaired by Lucy Hummer, Department of State. Its members include the Department of Commerce (particularly the NTIA), the Office of the US Trade Representative, the Department of Labor, the Information Agency, the Department of Defense, and the FCC; the Treasury, the NASA Technical Information Service, the National Bureau of Standards, and the Department of Justice participate on a case-by-case basis. The Working Group is a subsidiary body of the Senior Interagency Group for International Communications and Information Policy established 1981 by the National Security Council. It is co-chaired by the Departments of State and Commerce and has 15 government agencies represented in it.

[123] Before the telecommunication deregulation in the US, Western Electric was virtually the sole supplier of the Bell System, the dominant telecommunication system of the US. After deregulation, the new regional telephone companies began to buy a share of their equipment from abroad (mainly Japan and Canada), which led to an influx of telecommunication equipment. Since the telecommunication markets in other developed countries are often closed (since the PTTs normally procure from local corporations), US suppliers are at a competitive disadvantage. The result was a bill in Congress (the Danforth bill, S. 168) which provided that if other markets did not open up the markets for telecommunication equipment

(which was defined to include services using such equipment) within three years of enactment of the bill, the US should introduce substantial tariff barriers to imports from those countries. Although the bill died in the 1984 session of Congress, some of its reciprocity ideas were incorporated into the Trade and Tariff Act of 1984. Nevertheless, a new "Bill to Promote Expansion of International Trade in Telecommunication Equipment and Services, and for Other Purposes" (S. 942) was introduced by Senator Danforth and others on 17 April 1985. Its purpose was to provide "a framework for negotiations to open foreign markets to U.S. exports and for aggressive enforcement of trade agreements related to telecommunications". (From this point of view, the unilateral divestiture of ATT represents a unilateral elimination of a major non-tariff barrier to imports of telecommunication equipment.) See the introduction of the Telecommunications Trade Act of 1985 by Sen. Danforth, *Congressional Record: Senate*, 17 April 1985, p. S4333. For a general discussion of the reciprocity discussion in the US, see William R. Cline, "'Reciprocity': A New Approach to World Trade Policy?", in William R. Cline, ed., *Trade Policy in the 1980s* (Washington: Institute for International Economics, 1983), pp. 121–158. On the other hand, reciprocity in such sectors as air transportation has traditionally been an important concept.

[124] Such an expansion of the application of Section 301 seems to be suggested, for instance, by Joan E. Spero, "Information: The Policy Void", *Foreign Policy*, 48 (Fall 1982), pp. 155–156. See also Michael Cohen and Thomas Morante, "Elimination of Nontariff Barriers to Trade in Services: Recommendation for Future Negotiation", *Law and Policy in International Business*, 13 (1981), p. 513.

[125] No actions were taken. Instead, the US arranged with the FRG bilateral talks in December 1985 during which the entire gamut of issues related to TDF (especially its telecommunication aspect) were reviewed. This was the first bilateral meeting of this sort that the US has had with a developed country, and more were to follow, including with the FRG. At the time of the bilateral talks, the government of the FRG announced that it would agree to let the Bundespost lease facilities for resellers to provide enhanced services (although not at flat rates). Commented Acting NTIA Director Rodney Joyce (one of the two heads of the 23-member delegation of the US to the talks): "It's clear that they have read our trade bills and are worried" (*Communications Daily*, 13 December 1985, p. 4).

[126] US Trade Representative, "Annual Report on National Trade Estimates 1985", *op. cit.*, pp. 35–36.

[127] See "U.S. National Study", *op. cit.*, p. 190, as well as Henry Ergas and Ann Reid, "Transborder Data Flows in International Enterprises: The Results of a Joint BIAC/OECD Survey and Interviews with Firms", in OECD, *Transborder Data Flows: Proceedings of an OECD Conference* (Amsterdam: North Holland, 1985), pp. 213–250.

[128] The "U.S. National Study", *op. cit.*, p. 191, suggests that, because of these reasons, some corporations have postponed investments in data services. As Shelp (*op. cit.*, p. 106) noted: "Problems confronting the communications, data processing, and information industry are proliferating at a rapid rate and are viewed by many as the major service industry problem. The dependence of numerous other industries, both service and nonservice, on this kind of service activity provides a striking example of the symbiotic relationship of many services to the functioning of the modern global economy."

[129] The Conference Board, *Regulating International Data Transmission: The Impact on Managing International Business* (New York: The Conference Board, 1984), p. 6. A survey conducted at the College of Business Administration of the University of South Carolina arrived at similar results; see Michael K. Kane, "The Impact of Transborder Data Flow Regulation on Change U.S.-Based Companies" (Columbia: University of South Carolina, 1985), mimeo.

¹³⁰ For a review of the types of restrictions and regulations that the US places on the transborder flow of scientific data, see Anne W. Branscomb, "Global Governance of Global Networks: A Survey of Transborder Data Flow in Transition", *Vanderbilt Law Review*, 36 (May 1983), pp. 1012–1017. See in this context especially "The Militarily Critical Technologies List" compiled by the US Department of Defense and containing primarily technologies that are considered to contribute to the development, production, or utilization of items being controlled for national security purposes. The list contains a wide range of data-service technologies.

¹³¹ See in this context also ICC, "The Liberalization of Telecommunication Services: Needs and Limits" (Paris: ICC, 1982); ICC, "An International Programme for Homologation/ Certification of Equipment Attached to Telecommunication Networks" (Paris: ICC, 1983), mimeo.; and ICC, "International Private Leased Circuits: The Business User's View" (Paris: ICC, 1984), mimeo.

¹³² See GATT, Committee on Customs Valuation, "Decision on the Valuation of Carrier Media Bearing Software for Data Processing Equipment, Adopted by the Committee on 24 September 1984", VAL/8, of 10 October 1984, and VAL/8/Add.1 of 21 November 1984.

¹³³ The Business Roundtable, *op. cit.*, p. 17.

¹³⁴ For example, American Express seems to have made the experience that if it had to use the public data network in the Federal Republic of Germany, it would suffer unacceptable delays in point-of-sale transmissions. See Joan E. Spero, "International Trade and the Information Revolution" (Cambridge: Harvard University Center for Information Policy Research, 1985), mimeo., p. 13.

¹³⁵ "U.S. National Study", *op. cit.*, p. 192.

¹³⁶ See, e.g., Eger, "Emerging Restrictions on Transborder Data Flow", *op. cit.*

¹³⁷ For instance, one US company has estimated that the need to duplicate data bases and other systems in Canada raised its operating costs by $150,000 a year; see *The Wall Street Journal*, 21 June 1985.

¹³⁸ Dario F. Robertson, "Copyright Protection for Computer Programs: The New Amendments", *East Asian Executive Records*, July 1985, p. 21.

¹³⁹ "U.S. National Study", *op. cit.*, p. 193.

¹⁴⁰ *Ibid.*, p. 192.

¹⁴¹ For a review of the issues in telecommunications (especially regulatory aspects) see OECD, *Telecommunications: Pressures and Policies for Change* (Paris: OECD, 1983), Henry Ergas and Jun Okayama, eds. *Changing Market Structures in Telecommunications* (Amsterdam: North-Holland, 1984), and Martin J. Kalin, *Telecommunications Policies in Ten Countries: Prospects for Future Competitive Access* (Washington: NTIA, 1985).

¹⁴² Deregulation in the UK and the signing of the GATT Procurement Code (to be discussed below) by the Nippon Telegraph and Telephone Public Corporation (NTT), however, appear to have had little effect so far on the actual buying pattern of British Telecom and NTT.

¹⁴³ "U.S. National Study", *op. cit.*, p. 106.

¹⁴⁴ Cited in *New York Times*, 6 April 1985.

¹⁴⁵ Geza Feketekuty, "Communications from the Perspective of Trade in Services Agreements." Remarks to the Washington Round of the World Telecommunications Forum, 19 April 1985, mimeo., pp. 9–10.

¹⁴⁶ See Independent Commission for World-wide Telecommunications Development, *The Missing Link* (Geneva: ITU, 1984). The basic objective of the Centre is to provide expert assistance.

¹⁴⁷ Spero, "The Policy Void", *op. cit.*, p. 149.

IV

The International
Policy Discussion:
Bilateral and Regional Fora

The policy discussion on trade and FDI in data services reflects, of course, the interest situations of the participating countries. In principle, it opposes the *national* approach of those countries that lack sufficient data resources to the *international* approach of those countries that have well-developed data resources. The discussion here focuses on the international rather than the national policy debate for several reasons. For one, most countries are not yet fully aware of the importance of data resources and therefore have no explicit policies in this respect. Secondly, to the extent that awareness increases, the likelihood of national approaches becoming more frequent also increases, given that most countries lack sufficient data resources. This, in turn, further increases the probability that data-service-exporting countries will seek to establish an international regime for TDF. Since such a regime would become the framework within which national policies have to evolve, it would have a crucial importance for national policies regarding data goods and services. And, finally, the US as the leader of the services discussion has made it clear that, in negotiations on an international regime, data services should have priority.[1]

The strategy pursued by the US administration was laid out by the US Trade Representative in an article published to coincide with the 1982 GATT Ministerial Meeting. Starting with the premise that "the challenge confronting governments is to find ways to ensure that trade in services is allowed to serve as a major engine of growth", the principal objectives are "to develop the means (i) for resisting the growth of new restrictions that could hamper trade in services and (ii) for removing long-standing barriers."[2] To achieve these objectives, a three-point program is suggested. First, a clear international commitment at the senior political level is sought to give trade in services high priority in order to improve international cooperation in this area and to facilitate the expansion of service trade. As will be seen in this chapter and the next, the OECD Council meeting at the ministerial level, the summit of the seven major industrialized countries and the GATT Ministerial Meeting all had the question of trade of services on their agenda. In a sense, the achievement of such a political commitment is of key importance because it generates the necessary impetus for the other two points of the program. Second, all available instruments should be used to prevent the

Table IV-1. Discussion fora for TDF, 1985

Level	Service trade in general and TDF	FDI
Bilateral	US - Canada US - Israel	Bilateral investment treaties
Regional	OECD, SELA, CALAI, IBI	OECD
International	GATT, UNCTAD, ITU, UNESCO, UN Commission on Transnational Corporations	UN Commission on Trans- national Corporations

creation of new barriers to trade in services. As will be seen in this chapter, this has been pursued most notably at the bilateral level and in the framework of the OECD. Third, "a comprehensive international framework of principles and rules for trade in services"[3] should be created. As will be seen in the next chapter, this point of the program has been vigorously pursued in GATT.

As this strategy envisages, discussions on services, including data services, are conducted at the bilateral, regional and international levels (see table IV-1). They are still held separately for trade and FDI, although there seems to be a growing recognition that the interrelationship between the two requires closer coordination, and a few developed countries are working simultaneously toward improving the environment for both. In the following, the principal contexts in which these discussions are being undertaken are described, dealing primarily with data services.[4] The focus is on the following questions: Why are these discussions taking place in a particular context? How are they shaped by the principal competing values? And what has been achieved so far?

A. Bilateral negotiations

At the bilateral level, a number of efforts are underway that may well set the agenda for—or even influence the actual outcome of—international discussions of data services. The US is the principal country favoring bilateral negotiations because discussions at that level can be initiated without delay, they can assist in clarifying issues and finding at least interim solutions, and because bilateral discussions can react more speedily than international organizations to the rapidly changing technological developments in this area. In addition, if they involve an important country like the US, they can serve to accelerate multilateral negotiations. As of the end of 1985, the most important discussions at the bilateral level involved bilateral investment treaties and the Israel-US and the Canada-US trade negotiations.

In addition, the US has included service issues in practically all its bilateral trade meetings in recent years. These meetings are not formal negotiations but rather discussions aimed at gaining a better understanding on bilateral issues relating to trade and are particularly conducted to investigate trade practices that are objected to by the US. Naturally, the results of such discussions can lead to changed behavior and may therefore make formal action on the part of the US (e.g., under Section 301 of the Trade Act) unnecessary. This, for instance, appears to have been the case as regards the FRG, when that country agreed to a bilateral meeting in December 1985, at which a wide range of issues related to TDF (especially telecommunication issues) were discussed. The mechanism of bilateral talks thus offers the US the opportunity to bring about changes without having to resort to formal action. Such meetings have taken place with such countries as Argentina, South Korea and Singapore. As already indicated, they are also beginning to take place with developed market economies. The first was held with the FRG in December 1985 and others are to follow, both with the FRG and with other Western European countries including, most probably, the Commission of the European Communities.

1. Bilateral investment treaties

While the OECD FDI instruments establish a multilateral framework for investment in the OECD area, no such framework exists for FDI outside that area, i.e., mostly in respect to the developing countries. To fill this void, many developed market economies have concluded bilateral investment treaties with developing countries; in fact, developing countries have concluded such treaties among themselves as well. Most of the over 200 treaties in force today are meant to protect foreign investors in the areas of fair and equitable treatment, national treatment, security of investment, nationalization and compensation, repatriation and remittances, subrogation, and dispute settlement. Capital-exporting countries regard these treaties as a useful tool for creating and maintaining a favorable investment climate and for protecting their investments. Developing countries, on the other hand, in general consider bilateral investment treaties unbalanced, in the sense that they only spell out obligations (based on traditional legal principles not always shared by developing countries) for host countries, while not spelling out the responsibilities of TNCs. A number of the principal host countries, especially in Latin America, have therefore refused to sign them. Bilateral treaties of this sort are hence unlikely to represent a long-term solution to the need for creating a stable and predictable investment climate. To a certain extent, this is also recognized in the "U.S. National Study" which observed that "questions remain as to the practical effect of these treaties against national laws and international rules that govern the same business practices."[5]

Nevertheless, bilateral investment treaties today represent the principal bilateral framework for FDI in developing countries. The definition of FDI contained in them clearly encompasses investments in both goods and services. Services are, therefore, not mentioned explicitly in the overwhelming majority of these treaties, and where they are, it is done mostly to encourage cooperation in specific industries or, as will be discussed below, to stipulate exceptions.[6] However, there seems to be a tendency for newer treaties involving the US to mention services explicitly. Recently, moreover, efforts have been made to include the right of establishment in these treaties and to deal with performance requirements. For example, the US had signed bilateral investment treaties with Egypt, Haiti, Morocco, Panama, Senegal, Turkey, and Zaire between 1982 and 1986, had initialed such treaties with Bangladesh,

Cameroon, Costa Rica, and Sri Lanka and, in January 1986, was negotiating treaties with Burundi, China, Gabon, Honduras, the Ivory Coast, Liberia, Malaysia, and Uruguay. These treaties grant a right of establishment to each other's corporations, subject to explicit reservations, most of which are in the service area. The US typically excludes air transport, ocean and coastal shipping, banking, insurance, custom-house brokerage, radio and television broadcasting, telephone and telegraph services, submarine cable services, and satellite communication.[7]

Moreover, most of the new US treaties explicitly prohibit performance requirements as a condition for the establishment—in some cases also for the maintenance and expansion—of foreign affiliates, which require, for instance, that goods or services specifically mentioned must be purchased locally.[8] (However, the treaties are silent about performance requirements linked to incentives, since corporations normally have the option to accept or not to accept them; besides, this is seen as a trade and not as an investment issue.) If these treaties were to be ratified, subsequent treaties entered into by either signatory and granting most-favored-nation treatment would generalize these provisions. US opposition to export-performance requirements and local-content requirements is also reflected in the Caribbean Basin Initiative: in determining whether to designate any country a beneficiary country, the President is supposed to take into account, among other things, the degree to which a given country imposes such requirements.[9] The clearest and most recent expression of this approach can be found in the US-Israel Free Trade Agreement, which was signed on 22 April 1985 and came into force in August 1985.[10] There, it is stated that

> Neither Party shall impose, as a condition of establishment, expansion or maintenance of investments by nationals or companies of the other Party, requirements to export any amount of production resulting from such investments or to purchase locally-produced goods and services. Moreover, neither Party shall impose requirements on investors to purchase locally-produced goods and services as a condition for receiving any type of governmental incentives.[11]

It is noteworthy that this provision concerning trade-related performance requirements is contained in a trade agreement and that even performance requirements linked to incentives are prohibited. This seems to signal that the US is adopting an even stronger attitude regarding performance requirements than in the past.

In any case, it is likely that future bilateral treaties will increasingly contain explicit and specific references to services, and in this manner establish important parameters for national data-resource policies. Under the recent US treaties, for instance, a data-resource policy such as that pursued by Brazil would not be permissible, since a number of the key policy elements typical of such an approach would be prohibited.

Developing countries have, therefore, to be particularly careful in concluding bilateral investment treaties containing certain service provisions. Many developing countries may be vulnerable in this respect because few of them currently accord high priority to services in general and to data services in particular, while needing FDI to advance industrialization. Capital exporters, on the other hand, attach great importance to such treaties because they regard them as giving a positive signal to foreign investors (in fact, in a number of OECD countries investors only qualify for FDI insurance programs if such treaties exist); this is all the more important because some of the biggest capital exporters favor FDI over other financial resources as avenues to channel financial resources to developing countries. In this cross-current of needs and interests, options for national data-resource policies may well be closed.

2. The US-Israel Free Trade Agreement

As already noted, an agreement between the US and Israel about the establishment of a comprehensive free-trade area between the two countries was concluded in 1985. Although the liberalization provisions of the Agreement itself deal only with goods, a separate article states that:

> The Parties recognize the importance of trade in services and the need to maintain an open system of services exports which would minimize restrictions on the flow of services between the two nations. To this end, the Parties agree to develop means for cooperation on trade in services pursuant to the provisions of a Declaration to be made by the Parties.[12]

In other words, the parties to the Agreement commit themselves to the establishment of a liberal framework for trade in services between themselves. The principles meant to be incorporated in this framework are already spelled out in a "Declaration on Trade in Services" attached to the Agreement, and both governments declared their intention to conduct their policies affecting trade in services between them in accordance with these principles. (The full text of the Declaration is contained in annex VIII of this volume.)

"Services" are defined in the Declaration as encompassing (but not being limited to) transport; travel and tourism services; communications; banking services; insurance; other financial activities; professional services, such as consulting in construction, engineering, accounting, medicine, education, and law and the provision of other professional services such as management consulting; computer services (which presumably also cover software and data-base services); motion pictures; and advertising. Among the principles meant to guide trade in these services, the greatest emphasis is placed on national treatment. The Declaration first establishes the general policy principle of national treatment by specifying (para. 3) that "each Party will endeavor to assure that trade in services with the other nation is governed by the principle of national treatment." This is then defined to mean that "each Party will endeavor to provide that a supplier of a service produced within the other nation is able to market or distribute that service under the same conditions as a like service produced within the first nation." More importantly, this traditional definition of national treatment is extended to include "situations where a commercial presence within the nation is necessary to facilitate the export of a service from the other nation or is required by that Party." What is meant here is that for certain services a minimal local presence is required to permit trade, perhaps because the importing country has established certain fiduciary requirements or because the nature of service trade demands a minimum local presence. In this context, the Declaration makes reference to commercial banking, for which "commercial presence" is understood as referring to the activities of representative offices, but not to agencies, branches or subsidiaries of commercial banks. Thus, the thrust of this paragraph is twofold. First it provides that trade in services ought to be governed by national treatment. Second, it extends trade in services to include "commercial presence." This is a significant extension, indeed, because it is the first time that the conceptual innovation of right of presence has been incorporated in an international instrument.

Apart from stipulating and extending the general policy principle of national treatment, the Declaration also provides (para. 5) that "each Party will endeavor to assure that its regulatory agencies will accord national treatment to suppliers of the service from the other nation. . . ." In this manner, the Declaration seeks to ensure that the principle of national treatment is, in fact, implemented, although the Declaration recognizes that statutory limitations and discretionary rights of regulatory agencies may constitute limitations. Also important in this context is a provision (para. 4) which stipulates that each party will make an effort to ensure that the regulations of political subdivisions (i.e., the states in the case of the US) are consistent with the principles of the Declaration.

In addition to these principles, the Declaration establishes the principles of "open market access" for trade in services (para. 2); non-discrimination of procurement in the case of public monopolies in areas outside their "reserved special rights" (para. 6) (this could mean, for instance, that while telecommunication can be considered a reserved special right, the provision of data services is a different matter); transparency of laws and regulations discriminating against service imports; access to established domestic review and judicial proceedings; and periodic consultations and review of existing regulatory regimes as they affect trade in services.

Although attached to the Agreement, the Declaration is non-binding. The principal reason appears to be that since an early trade agreement was sought, the time was not sufficient to lay the necessary political groundwork in an area in which little work had been done so far. This applies especially as regards the states of the US (which have considerable regulatory power for a number of services) and various US regulatory bodies in the service sector (which often enjoy a large measure of autonomy). At the same time, the Joint Committee to be set up under the Agreement to supervise the proper implementation of the Agreement and to review the trade relationship between the two countries has, as one of its responsibilities, the task of reviewing the Declaration. Independently of that, the parties commit themselves in the Declaration to review its effectiveness within 18 months from the date of its signature in April 1985, to "explore further opportunities to strengthen open trade in services between the two nations, including the possibility of transforming the provisions of this Declaration into legally binding rights and obligations" (para. 9). In fact, in the Declaration's preamble the two countries express their desire to work toward international acceptance of the principles laid down in it.

It can be expected that considerable efforts will be made over the 18-month period following the signing of the Declaration in April 1985 to transform it into a binding instrument. In the US, this requires, first of all, intensive and detailed discussions—on the basis of the text of the Declaration—with state and regulatory authorities, probably on an industry-by-industry basis. In the process, the general principles of the Declaration may well be operationalized in greater detail (for instance on a service-by-service basis) and, perhaps, new ones may be added to them (e.g., dispute settlement). By the end of 1985, however, the Joint Committee had not yet been set up, although informal consultations between the two parties had taken place in the framework of working groups which are likely to become part of the Joint Committee once it is established during 1986. Proceeding on a principle-by-principle basis, the discussions had started with travel and tourism and were envisaged for telecommunication services and, possibly, insurance.

Even in its original state as a best-effort instrument, the Declaration represents a considerable achievement for the proponents of a liberal international regime for trade in services. It is the first time that key elements of such a regime have been worked out in potential treaty language, incorporating the conceptual innovation of the right of presence in it. Furthermore, it is comprehensive in character because it covers all major services (although most trade in services between both countries is in tourism). Even if the Declaration should fail to become a binding instrument—and there is no reason to expect this—it is likely to be used as a model, be it in bilateral, regional or international negotiations.[13] In fact, it has been formulated to be GATT-consistent so that it may serve as a model for future multilateral discussions on services. In addition, it is an important sign-post for the services discussions as desired by the US, indicating the direction in which it wishes these discussions to progress and spelling out, for the first time, some of the principles that it wishes to see adopted. Furthermore, the negotiation of the Declaration, and the follow-up work to be expected, prepares the US thoroughly for international discussions on services, and places it in a favorable position as regards the determination of a detailed agenda for such discussions, the identification of possible trade-offs and the finding of solutions preferred by it.

3. US-Canada negotiations

Another important effort, dealing explicitly with data services as a separate and distinguishable sector, has been initiated between Canada and the US. The Royal Bank of Canada, an important intra-corporate user of data services within North America with strong links to the New York financial market (and hence a substantial interest in unrestricted data flows), proposed, in 1983, that Canada and the US negotiate a sectoral free trade agreement for computer services and other aspects of informatics.[14] In essence, such an agreement could affirm the relatively open border between the two countries as regards trade in data services; reduce or eliminate whatever tariff and non-tariff barriers there are; forbid the creation of new barriers; and establish a framework for consultation and dispute settlement should specific problems arise.

The proposal had a strong appeal to the users and exporters of data services in Canada since they have a high interest in assured access to data resources and the data market in the US. (At the same time, however, domestic suppliers could suffer.[15]) For them, "the public interest in the efficiency gains, particularly the gains arising from the effective use of computer facilities by major Canadian-based transnational firms for whom computer services are a vital operational, management and control service, is pervasive and overwhelming."[16] The US reacted very favorably to this proposal, since it would give the US assurances against future protectionist moves by Canada in this area and give US data-service firms an assured access to the Canadian market. In addition, the proposal gave the US a concrete opportunity to advance in a key area of interest to it. It was perhaps with this proposal in mind that the "U.S. National Study" suggested that "It may prove necessary and desirable for countries with similar trade and regulatory approaches to consider interim accords that will cover their needs until countries have an opportunity to consider the desirability of a broader multilateral approach."[17]

During the summer of 1984, the discussions focused on a free trade agreement covering computer services, information services, computer equipment and telecommunication equipment. What was explored was a reciprocal exchange of rights open to other countries to join, i.e., an arrangement in which any other country may acquire the same rights, but only on the condition that it makes substantially the same concessions (and assumes substantially the same obligations) as the original parties. However, it is questionable whether other potential participants would be satisfied simply to accede to the rules negotiated by the US and Canada or whether they would want to participate in the formulation of the rules themselves, to ensure that their special circumstances and interests are fully taken into account. Another possibility, therefore, was that third parties would be invited to join in the negotiations once they get beyond the preliminary discussion stage. Apart from this, an important question (in the light of most-favored-nation-treatment obligations under GATT) is how third countries not associated with any bilateral Canada-US agreement should be treated.

With the change of government in Canada, however, the discussions were on hold during the autumn of 1984, to give the new government an opportunity to define its position. It could discontinue these discussions, yielding essentially to the local providers of data services as well as to the domestic manufacturers of hardware which fear international competition. It could continue with this initiative and aim at an early conclusion of a bilateral agreement. It could also broaden discussions to create a free-trade area for other goods and services as well, an idea apparently favored by some business interests in Canada. Or it could put primary emphasis on multilateral negotiations, e.g., in the framework of a new GATT round. Naturally, some of these alternatives are not mutually exclusive. The discussions may have received new impetus by the meeting between the President of the US and the Prime Minister of Canada in March 1985. On that occasion, the two countries committed themselves to "halt protectionism in cross-border trade in goods and services" and to initiate action within a year to resolve specific impediments to trade in a number of areas. These include the "elimination or reduction of tariff and non-tariff barriers to trade in *high-technology goods and related services*, such as computers, data flow and computer-assisted design and manufacturing technology."[18] (This language echoes that of the 1984 US Trade and Tariff Act closely.) At the end of 1985, it appeared that these discussions would become part of a broader effort to negotiate a comprehensive free trade agreement between Canada and the US.

If the discussions between Canada and the US continue, they will serve to identify and define a good number of the relevant issues. In fact, they may lead to the first international (albeit bilateral) framework specifically designed for computer services, a framework which may acquire model character and be extended to include other parties—a possibility explicitly held open in the original proposal.

While bilateral discussions may have certain advantages, they run the risk of resulting in a patchwork of diverging rules which reflect the relative importance, special interests, philosophies, and market structures of the respective bilateral partners. Moreover, agreements reached in this manner can be changed relatively easily. It is, therefore, a widely shared view that "a myriad of bilateral understandings is not likely to produce a very desirable international regime."[19] Just as bilateral trade agreements are no substitutes for the multilateral GATT, bilateral arrangements on trade in data services are not likely to be adequate substitutes for a multilateral approach.

B. The Organisation for Economic Co-operation and Development

1. Work on services

After the prelude to the current trade-in-services discussion in GATT during the Tokyo Round (where services had been touched upon to the extent that they are incidental to trade in certain products), the actual international services discussions began in the OECD in the autumn of 1978, when the US put this topic on the agenda of that organization's Trade Committee, with the purpose "of beginning a low-key discussion so as to build an understanding of services and develop a consensus to deal with them within the OECD framework as a first step".[20] The thrust of this work was to identify and evaluate obstacles to trade in services in general, with a view to developing ways of removing unjustified impediments, improving international cooperation in this area, and establishing a general reference framework comprising principles and criteria for trade in services. Today, the OECD is the organization in which work and discussions on trade and FDI in services are furthest advanced.[21]

On the sectoral side, studies have been carried out (or are still being conducted) on insurance, banking, financial services (securities markets), tourism, maritime transport, construction and engineering consultancy, telecommunication services, computer and information services, and audiovisual and professional services. Their main focus is to identify and analyze obstacles to cross-border and establishment trade. Obstacles are generally defined to include discrimination against services provided by foreign firms, including discriminatory restrictions on market access, investment and the right of establishment; discriminatory treatment of established foreign-controlled service firms; regulations that are seen to have an excessively inhibiting effect; and lack of transparency of regulation and administrative practices. Parallel to this work, efforts are being undertaken to examine horizontal issues that are considered to be of interest to all or most service industries. These issues include right of presence, right of establishment, non-discrimination, national treatment, and transparency. Attention is also being given to the notion of distortions, exceptions, derogations and safeguards; regulation in federal states; private regulation; and competition arising out of the presence of strong state or private monopolies.[22] Finally, negotiations have been concluded in the specific area of TDF.

Although the US proposal to embark on a work program on services met with little enthusiasm, the OECD is an attractive forum for the supporters of an open international service system for a number of reasons. First, it assembles (in an organization in which the US wields considerable influence) all developed market economies, which include all major exporters of services and service capital. In the framework of this relatively like-minded group, positions can be harmonized and a consensus formed which covers most of the world's service trade and FDI. Secondly, any consensus reached is elevated to and endorsed at a high political level, the OECD Council of Ministers. Such endorsement transforms the attention and interests focusing on a given issue into an important political commitment which provides direction for future action, embeds specific agreements into other economic policies and cooperative efforts, and links issues and agreements to the economic summit process of the principal industrial countries. Thirdly, once agreement has been reached within the OECD, it strengthens the bargaining position of the group as a whole in any international negotiations. This is illustrated by the preparation for the Tokyo Round and the formulation of GATT's Procurement Code as well as by the negotiations on a code of conduct for TNCs, in which the OECD countries succeeded in adopting their own guidelines before the discussions on such guidelines began in the United Nations. Fourthly, since the OECD deals with both trade and FDI issues, the interrelationships between the two can be kept in mind by dealing with the relevant issues simultaneously in the OECD committees responsible for these matters. Fifthly, the basic philosophy of the OECD is to favor an open international economic system, an approach which, in the case of services, is of particular interest to the proponents of the services discussion. And finally, this philosophy is reflected in the past work undertaken by the organization on services and in the principal OECD instruments applicable to international service transactions: the Code of Liberalisation of Current Invisible Operations, the Code of Liberalisation of Capital Movements (both adopted in 1961), and the Declaration and Decisions on International Investment and Multinational Enterprises (which include a Decision on National Treatment).[23] Together, these instruments represent the most comprehensive framework currently applicable to trade and FDI in services, including data services.

On the FDI side, this framework was incomplete in an important respect until 1984. The Capital Movements Code provides that (subject to certain qualification) restrictions on the movement of capital among member countries should be abolished. The Investment Declaration provides that (subject to certain qualifications) member countries should accord national treatment to foreign affiliates *after* such enterprises had been established in their territories. The bridge between the two, the right of establishment, was, however, only built in April 1984, when the OECD Council decided to extend the Capital Movements Code to certain important aspects of the right of establishment. More specifically, the Code provides now that:

> the authorities of Members shall not maintain or introduce: Regulations or practices applying to the granting of licences, concessions, or similar authorizations, including conditions or requirements attaching to such authorizations and affecting the operations of enterprises, that raise special barriers or limitations with respect to non-resident (as compared to resident) investors, and that have the intent or the effect of preventing or significantly impeding inward direct investment by non-residents.[24]

During the same year, the National Treatment part of the Investment Declaration was strengthened, with a view to reducing the number of exceptions that can be made under the principle.[25] As far as the FDI mode of delivering data services to foreign markets is concerned, the two issues of central interest to capital exporters and TNCs—national treatment and right of establishment—have, at least in principle,[26] been now settled for and among the OECD countries, the area in which over two-thirds of all FDI activities take place. Work does, however, continue in the framework of the OECD's Committee on International Investment and Multinational Enterprises on the impact of TDF on the structure of TNCs.[27]

A framework exists also in the trade area, in the form of the Invisibles Code. It deals with a broad range of current invisible operations, including those in most service industries. Its general obligations cover liberalization, nondiscrimination and transparency as regards a number of specified service transactions and transfers; it also contains more specific obligations for individual service industries. However, this framework is inadequate in the eyes of a number of countries. The reasons are that, first, it does not apply to developing countries; second, it is very easy for countries to register farreaching reservations and limitations and to commit extensive derogations (and this has been done in many areas); third, there is no established apparatus for dispute settlement and particularly no sanctions for non-compliance; and fourth, the questions of the right of establishment, the right to conduct business, and national treatment for foreign-controlled affiliates are inadequately treated.[28] Furthermore, the Invisibles Code does not cover all services (including computer and telecommunication services) and, more generally, "some parts of the Code appear to require updating, mainly because of technological developments in recent years in many of the service sectors and the new current invisible operations to which these developments have given rise".[29] For these reasons, the US has sought to strengthen this code.[30] In fact, the OECD Council decided, in July 1979, that an overall updating and revision of the service sections of the Code should be undertaken, with a view to making it more effective as an instrument for the liberalization of international service operations. The work is being carried out mainly by the Committee for Capital Movements and Invisible Transactions (which also monitors the application of the Capital Movements Code). It has so far centered mostly on an updating of the insurance provisions in the light of recent technological and economic developments.Work is also under way on the provisions concerning tourism, maritime transport, financial services and audio-visual services, and some discussion has occurred on the coverage of telecommunications. At the same time, the Trade Committee has been examining the entire range of issues related to trade in services from both a general and a sectoral perspective.

2. The Declaration on Transborder Data Flows

Against this background, the US initiated, in the framework of the OECD's general work on services, a separate initiative aimed at establishing an appropriate framework for trade in data services. The forum was the Working Party on Transborder Data Flows and the vehicle the "Declaration on Transborder Data Flows". The Working Party, which meets three or four times a year, reports to the Committee on Information, Computer and Communications Policy (CICCP) which was raised to committee status only on 1 April 1982, an elevation indicating the importance the OECD attaches to the new information technologies in general and to TDF in particular.[31]

A forerunner of the Working Party, namely an Expert Group (with a different membership), prepared the OECD Guidelines Governing the Protection of Privacy and Transborder Flows of Personal Data (described in chapter III). Since the adoption of the Guidelines, the work of the OECD has shifted toward economic and legal questions relating to TDF as they affect the developed countries. Since

1984 telecommunication issues have also received considerable attention. To examine these issues, the Committee and the Working Party meet regularly and in special sessions, high-level conferences are organized, and a number of studies are being prepared.[32]

As part of this work, and in the broader context of the services discussion, the US formally tabled a draft text of a TDF Declaration in January 1982, patterned on the earlier OECD Declaration on Trade Policy and the OECD TDF Guidelines.[33] Conceptualized as an interim measure—a sort of stand-still until a firmer multilateral framework could be established—it was meant to be a statement of political will through which the OECD governments would commit themselves voluntarily but firmly to maintaining and improving an open system for international information flows and to avoiding restrictive measures which would disrupt these flows, impede trade in telecommunications, data processing and information services, and inhibit economic growth, productivity and technological innovation. The draft did not mention any competing policy objectives which could mitigate the flow of data. The Declaration was also intended to serve as a political signal which would set the tone for international discussions of TDF and indicate to the business community that the uncertainty in the data-service area (which could impede the establishment of corporate computer-communication systems and the development of new services) had been recognized.

The proposal met, for two main reasons, with "lukewarm support from most delegations and suspicions by some."[34] First, as one of the persons involved in the original drafting of the TDF Declaration observed, "many in Europe saw the data declaration as a strategy to preserve U.S. preeminence in communication and information services."[35] In other words, given US leadership in data services, a liberal regime governing international trade in such services was seen to benefit no one but the US, since it would make it very difficult for other countries to develop their own data services and to improve their position in the international trade in these services. The European Community made this explicit by saying that "asking Europe to adopt the Data Declaration was like asking Europe to fight with one hand tied behind its back."[36] More generally, there might have been a fear that a specific, strongly worded, high-level political commitment with narrowly defined exceptions and a liberal trade presumption would make it more difficult to use the entire range of policies that might be required in the pursuit of national data-resource objectives. Even a general commitment could become an obstacle in this respect since it could alter the existing bargaining situation. In the existing situation, countries were free—within their existing international commitments— to restrict data-service trade. However, with the adoption of a formal commitment, they would be put on the defensive, i.e., they would assume an obligation to justify their actions whenever they wished to take restrictive measures. Even more, the adoption of a commitment would give the promoters of unrestricted data-service trade a reference point against which they could urge the abolition of existing restrictions.

France in particular—which is building a broad-based data-resource industry and seems to be willing to give it a certain measure of protection during the launching stage—offered considerable resistance. France preferred a three-step approach.[37] The first step would center on the identification of the problems presented by TDF; in this context it was suggested that three types of flows be distinguished, since different issues were seen to arise for each of them: commercial flows; intra-company flows; and trade-accompanying flows.[38] The second step would then involve the identification of common interests among member countries. And the third step, finally, would consist of negotiations. Obviously, the adoption of this approach would have led to time-consuming research and considerably delayed the commencement of negotiations. In particular, the distinction of three types of flows—which in the eyes of proponents of a TDF Declaration was not necessary for the purpose of the general instrument envisaged—would have increased the complexity of the discussion. Besides, it also raised the possibility that one type of flows may be regulated (or taxed), while others remained unrestricted. In addition, the distinctions among various types of flows could have a bearing on the subsequent discussions in GATT on the establishment of a liberal framework for trade in services in that the introduction of these distinctions makes an en bloc consideration of those flows in GATT more difficult. In any case, France appeared to prefer broader multilateral negotiations, along the lines suggested by President François Mitterrand at the June 1982 summit of industrial countries, where he called for "common rules for international data exchanges."[39] This broader approach was, however, not pursued in subsequent discussions.

To defuse the suspicions of its partners, the US took a relatively low profile in the ensuing OECD debate, indicating that it was flexible on the formulation of the text and promoting its objectives in bilateral talks. Nevertheless, negotiations did not make much progress between January 1982 and December 1983.

In December 1983, then, the Second OECD Symposium on TDF took place. It brought together a large number of high-level policy makers and representatives of the private sector. The private-sector representatives made it very clear how important TDF had become for their international operations and how important it was, therefore, to establish an international framework for these activities. Perhaps none made that clearer than an officer of the Royal Bank of Canada, North America's fourth largest bank with operations in 47 countries:

> we . . . know that many transborder data flow issues can only be resolved through governmental agreement, and we greatly fear that, in the absence of such agreement, individual governments will move unilaterally, thereby causing an outbreak of information protectionism which could seriously threaten the prospects of economic recovery. More specifically, we not only fear that information protectionism will directly threaten the prospects for tertiary industries—it will indirectly damage the ability of primary and secondary industries to improve their productivity through the application of modern technology and know-how.[40]

From this perspective, he called for a "multilateral consensus" and "a start towards writing 'rules of the road' which will allow us to maintain the flow of information across borders, without endangering legitimate national interest." In this vein, he ended his speech by saying "I strongly recommend the OECD continue to discuss the broad issues, but also to start developing multinational negotiations governing trade in computer services."[41] It must be recalled, furthermore, that this statement expressed a consensus of the North American and especially the US business community that a set of international principles governing TDF was needed.

The government representatives gave little attention to the Data Declaration at the Symposium, although the US representative observed that "with the approach of 1984, it would be a fine counterpoint if we could present the world with a consensus on principles for an open international information system. . . . We urge the members of the OECD to move forward in attaining the objectives of our proposal."[42] More importantly for the future course of the negotiations was the introduction of the concept of "access" to data services in the debate. As mentioned earlier, the Canadian representative introduced it in his keynote speech, and it subsequently found its way into the report of one of the Symposium's sessions. It gave the Western European countries for the first time an angle from which they could see some benefit in a Declaration.

In the wake of the London Symposium, then, the chairperson of the Working Party on Transborder Data Flows galvanized the increased awareness of the strategic importance of non-personal TDF for international economic transactions and the concept of access to data services into a new effort to advance the idea of a TDF Declaration. He received support from the UK, where a deregulation of the telecommunication sector had taken place, awareness seemed to have risen about the importance of data services for the country's exports, and (as will be shown in the next chapter) LOTIS supported action on TDF on a priority basis. Support was also forthcoming from Switzerland (which has an important banking sector) and The Netherlands and Sweden (which are the home countries of important TNCs). The June 1984 Second IBI World Conference on Transborder Data Flow Policies further underlined the importance of non-personal TDF and offered an additional opportunity for consultations. A new text was prepared by the chairperson which, during the Working Party meeting in September 1984 and the CICCP meeting in October 1984, became the accepted basis of animated discussion.

Finally, during a further meeting of the Working Party in February 1985 and of the CICCP during 20–22 March 1985—and after the US and Switzerland expressed strong displeasure about the lack of progress in the negotiations and urged a successful conclusion of the three-year negotiation process—the Declaration on Transborder Data Flows in its final version found the support of all countries. It was formally adopted by the OECD Council of Ministers during its meeting on 11–12 April 1985.[43] A press release issued by the US Mission to the OECD marked this occasion with the following words: "With strong United States support, OECD Ministers adopted April 11 a Declaration on Transborder Data Flows (TDF). The Declaration is an important accomplishment by the OECD in the area of trade in services."[44]

Thus, after three years of negotiations, the promoters of the instrument, tempered especially by French reluctance, finally reached their principal objective. The other countries went along because the commitments contained in the Declaration are not too strong and seem to have become more flexible during the course of the negotiations. Besides, it was known that the US was very much interested in the Declaration and communicated this interest forcefully to its partners. Moreover, most countries probably perceived a need for rules of the road in this area and saw it as inevitable that such rules would eventually be adopted. The willingness of the US to include formulations on access to data resources helped in this respect since it introduced a certain measure of balance.[45] Above all, however, it was the consistent and continuing pressure of the US administration that assured the adoption of the Declaration. The US argued not only in the OECD in favor of the instrument but also bilaterally in the capitals of the most important OECD member countries—and it did so at the ministerial level. Considering that awareness about TDF matters was not exactly widespread at higher political levels, and considering that the draft text was relatively general and reasonable, the Declaration was simply not considered a major undertaking by most countries and not important enough to defy the US and expend political capital that might be more fruitfully used for the resolution of greater and more urgent economic and political problems in negotiations with the US. Thus, in spite of lack of enthusiasm on the part of Western European countries and the probable lack of conviction that a truly satisfactory text had been arrived at, the TDF Declaration was adopted. This was probably also helped by a certain ésprit de corps among the negotiators who felt that, after years of negotiation, they had to show results.

In any case, the Declaration became the first multilaterally agreed instrument dealing specifically with the transborder flow of non-personal data. In reads as follows:

Declaration on Transborder Data Flows

Rapid technological developments in the field of information, computers and communications are leading to significant structural changes in the economies of Member countries. Flows of computerised data and information are an important consequence of technological advances and are playing an increasing role in national economies. With the growing economic interdependence of Member countries, these flows acquire an international dimension, known as Transborder Data Flows. It is therefore appropriate for the OECD to pay attention to policy issues connected with these transborder data flows.

This declaration is intended to make clear the general spirit in which Member countries will address these issues.

In view of the above, the GOVERNMENTS OF OECD MEMBER COUNTRIES:

Acknowledging that computerised data and information now circulate, by and large, freely on an international scale;

Considering the OECD Guidelines on the Protection of Privacy and Transborder Flows of Personal Data and the significant progress that has been achieved in the area of privacy protection at national and international levels;

Recognising the diversity of participants in transborder data flows, such as commercial and non-commercial organisations, individuals and governments, and recognising the wide variety of computerised data and information, traded or exchanged across national borders, such as data and information related to trading activities, intra-corporate flows, computerised information services and scientific and technological exchanges;

Recognising the growing importance of transborder data flows and the benefits that can be derived from transborder data flows; and recognising that the ability of Member countries to reap such benefits may vary;

Recognising that investment and trade in this field cannot but benefit from transparency and stability of policies, regulations and practices;

Recognising that national policies which affect transborder data flows reflect a range of social and economic goals, and that governments may adopt different means to achieve their policy goals;

Aware of the social and economic benefits resulting from access to a variety of sources of information and of efficient and effective information services;

Recognising that Member countries have a common interest in facilitating transborder data flows, and in reconciling different policy objectives in this field;

Having due regard to their national laws, do hereby DECLARE THEIR INTENTION TO:

a) *Promote* access to data and information and related services, and avoid the creation of unjustified barriers to the international exchange of data and information;

b) *Seek* transparency in regulations and policies relating to information, computer and communications services affecting transborder data flows;

c) *Develop* common approaches for dealing with issues related to transborder data flows and, when appropriate, develop harmonized solutions;

d) *Consider* possible implications for other countries when dealing with issues related to transborder data flows.

Bearing in mind the intention expressed above, and taking into account the work being carried out in other international fora, the GOVERNMENTS OF OECD MEMBER COUNTRIES,

Agree that further work should be undertaken and that such work should concentrate at the outset on issues emerging from the following types of transborder data flows:

i) Flows of data accompanying international trade;

ii) Marketed computer services and computerised information services; and

iii) Intra-corporate data flows.

The GOVERNMENTS OF OECD MEMBER COUNTRIES AGREE to *co-operate* and *consult* with each other in carrying out this important work, and in furthering the objectives of this Declaration.[46]

Thus, the Declaration recognizes, first of all, the increasing *economic* importance of TDF, in distinction to the *privacy* aspects which had been the subject of the earlier guidelines on the transborder flow of personal data. In fact, the Declaration is specifically seen as "the first international effort to address economic issues raised by the information revolution."[47] It acknowledges that, to date, transborder flows of economic data are subject to few restrictions; it underlines the importance of transparency and stability of policies, regulations and practices for investment and trade in this field; and it draws attention to the social and economic benefits resulting from access to data. While recognizing the growing importance of TDF and the benefits they entail, the Declaration also notes that not all members of the OECD are in an equal position to reap these benefits (an observation that has even more validity in the North-South context). Nevertheless, it says that member countries have a common interest in facilitating TDF and in reconciling different policy objectives in this field. Differing policy objectives may derive from a range of social and economic goals, whose pursuit can involve a variety of means. In distinction to the first draft, therefore, the TDF Declaration specifically recognizes that the unrestricted flow of data is not an absolute value, but rather one that competes with others. Importantly, however, these competing values do not necessarily have to be of a fundamental nature—e.g., national sovereignty, national security, cultural identity, privacy protection, intellectual property, and consumer protection—as specified in an intervening draft,[48] but can be any aspect of national laws and policies. It is a formulation, therefore, which can be used as an escape clause for a wide range of national actions. This escape clause is further strengthened by the first clause in the "intention" part of the Declaration which provides— under the governing clause of "due regard to . . . national laws"—that only the creation of "unjustified" barriers should be avoided—implying that justified barriers (e.g., those erected by national law) are permissible. The effect of this escape clause is to tone down substantially the definite and clear-cut message of the original text, and to soften the force of the Declaration.

At the same time, however, the basic objective and general direction of the original US text to maintain and promote an environment with relatively few restrictions to data flows has been saved, despite French reluctance. In fact, the "intention" part of the Declaration establishes for the first time the principle that governments should avoid the creation of unjustified barriers to TDF—the central objective of the US. In addition, the OECD members have agreed to promote access to data services and to seek transparency as regards relevant regulations and policies. The access objective was particularly championed by Canada and it reflects the concern of a number of countries over their increasing dependency on data located elsewhere and the vulnerability that results from this situation, as exemplified by the Dresser case. (The importance attached to access is underlined by the attention given to this concept in the "Communiqué" adopted by the 1985 meeting of the OECD Council of Ministers; the relevant text was quoted in the preceding chapter.) The last objective is potentially very broad, because it could not only cover regulations and policies regarding the narrow area of TDF, but all areas that affect data flows, e.g., standards, tariffs and data-processing requirements. Furthermore, the OECD countries commit themselves to develop common approaches and solutions to issues posed by TDF, and to take into account the implications for other countries (which could include developing countries) when taking measures on TDF. With that, governments have recognized that they have certain responsibilities regarding TDF, even if these are tempered by other responsibilities arising out of competing social and economic goals.

In another concession to the French position, finally, the Declaration calls for further work on the various types of TDF, without, however, agreeing on an exhaustive list of such types. There is, however, a slight ambiguity in this formulation, because it does not specify that this work ought to be undertaken in the framework of the OECD. Since, at the time the Declaration was adopted, work on services had already begun in the framework of GATT, it is possible that the intention was to undertake this work there. Nevertheless, since the OECD members pledge themselves to cooperate and consult with each other in carrying out the work and in furthering the objectives of the Declaration, continuous activity of the OECD in this field is assured. It may, in any event, be desirable to monitor the implementation of the Declaration, to see whether it has any effect. It is, for instance, not inconceivable that individual countries may wish to raise, in the appropriate committee, specific restrictions to TDF which they feel are not in agreement with the general spirit of the TDF Declaration. (This had, however, not yet been done by the end of 1985, although the US can be expected to begin, sooner or later, to focus on the practices of individual countries.) In the process, the Declaration could become part of customary international law, i.e., it would acquire a higher standing than the parties to the Declaration may originally have envisaged. The logical body to undertake this follow-up and monitoring work would be the CICCP. However, since the CICCP is under the science committee (which, in the informal internal hierarchy of the OECD, has not the same standing as the economic committees) and since TDF is increasingly seen as a trade issue, the question may arise whether, for instance, the Trade Committee should get involved in this work as well.

The adoption of the Declaration on Transborder Data Flows is certainly a breakthrough for all those who seek a committment to maintain an open environment for TDF. Even if the Declaration is not as powerful as it was originally conceptualized but represents rather a "best efforts" understanding to keep TDF unrestricted unless other reasons require different action, it provides "a halfway base betweeen no international rules and fully developed international rules covering transborder data flows. It . . . provide[s] a pragmatic basis for solving problems. . . ."[49] Moreover, it can become the basis for elaborating more specific and detailed commitments if desired—and the present instrument provides the direction in which this work could progress. In any event, the Declaration is—because of the core nature of data services—a sectoral agreement with far-reaching implications for trade in other services and for the operations of TNCs. In fact, it is the first agreement reached in the context of the trade-in-services discussion. As such, it is a sign-post for the discussions on trade in services in general, affirming the direction desired for these discussions. Furthermore, the Declaration establishes a minimum platform— "a stepping stone toward more comprehensive future agreements"[50]—for the developed countries for the perhaps most important part of the international negotiations on services, a short time before such negotiations actually begin.

The difficulties encountered in negotiating the Declaration, the length of time required to reach agreement, and, above all, the softness of the final commitments suggest, however, that it has not been possible to reconcile completely the basic interests of a number of the countries involved. Essentially, the discussions appear to have pitted those that favor an open international environment for data flows against those that have a strong national interest in strengthening their domestic data resources, moderated by the mixed-interest situation of almost all other countries. To assume in this situation the obligations of a specific, strongly worded, high-level commitment with narrowly circumscribed exceptions requires a convincing quid pro quo. In the case of the OECD TNC Guidelines, the basic trade-off was between certain constraining guidelines for the operations of these corporations on the one hand and a commitment of states to the principle of national treatment on the other. In the case of the OECD Privacy Guidelines, the basic trade-off was between a commitment to the free flow of information on the one hand and the recognition that the protection of privacy is a justifiable reason to limit this flow. In the case of the TDF Declaration, the trade-off was not clear—hence the reluctance of countries to accept it and the eventual adoption of a rather soft instrument.

The search for trade-offs will have to continue if countries wish to improve on what has been achieved so far and/or if a similar commitment is sought at the international level. One possibility may involve limitations on the extra-territorial application of laws. Although this issue is considerably broader than data flows, the Dresser case has highlighted the extent to which the use of TDF has broadened the scope for such actions and the effects they can have. These effects cannot—as in other areas of extraterritorial applications of laws such as the cases in which authorities in one country request information from an entity in another country—be neutralized through blocking legislation. Thus, limitations on extraterritoriality may offer a quid pro quo, but this matter is so complicated that no immediate solution is in sight.[51] Finally, some room for trade-offs may be found when considerations of right of access to data resources, discussed in chapter III, are included in the equation. This is reflected to a certain extent in the Declaration on Transborder Data Flows because it expresses the intention of the OECD countries to promote access to data services. As discussed earlier, this may well be an area which is most promising as far as further and firmer commitments regarding TDF are concerned. The French initiative in the OECD Working Party on Transborder Data Flows in November 1985 to develop a number of principles which could constitute a start for international negotiations point in this direction: two of the four principles proposed in the initiative specifically mentioned access.[52]

In the final analysis, however, it may well be that strong specific commitments with relatively narrowly defined exceptions can only be obtained if some (at least implicit) recognition is given to the use of infant-industry and performance requirement considerations, because they are at the heart of the reluctance of many countries to make such committments. Perhaps this can be done by recognizing such considerations as valid reasons for exceptions, at least for a certain period in specific circumstances. Finally, the data-service debate can be embedded in the general service discussions, in the hope that trade-offs can be found across services. In any case, without a matching trade-off, it is not likely that a compromise can be reached which establishes stable rules and a predictable environment for TDF.

Discussions in the OECD on data services will continue as part of the expected further work on the TDF Declaration, as well as in the framework of the Organisation's general services work. The latter work received strong support from the May 1984 meeting of the OECD Ministerial Council which stated that

> Recognizing the importance of the issues raised by international trade in services, Ministers noted that as further analysis proceeds, the Organisation would increasingly focus its efforts on ways to remove unjustified impediments and improve international co-operation. They expressed support for the efforts, under the aegis of the Trade Committee, to relate broad concepts relevant to trade in services to the problems identified in specific sectors. They also encouraged continued work to strengthen existing OECD agreements applicable to services. Ministers requested the Secretary-General to submit a report including action proposals to Council within two years.[53]

It is very likely that, over the next few years, these discussions will lead to further concrete results covering directly or indirectly data services, either through changes in existing instruments or the adoption of new ones.

The principal limitation of the OECD is, of course, that it includes only one group of countries, although the differences among them often bring up positions that reflect concerns of other countries, including developing ones. Hence, whatever agreements are reached, they are limited, at least in principle, to the members of the Organisation only.[54] However, this does not imply that OECD instruments are unimportant. On the contrary, given the importance of the members of this Organisation, any instruments adopted by it—including the Declaration on Transborder Data Flows—would, at the very least, significantly influence any international public-policy framework that may eventually emerge in the service area. Furthermore, even if such instruments were non-binding they could well acquire, if applied by governments over time (e.g., through a review committee), the standing of customary international law.[55]

C. The Intergovernmental Bureau for Informatics

The Intergovernmental Bureau for Informatics (IBI) offers a broader framework than the OECD, but not a much broader one, since fewer than 40 countries are members of this organization.[56] Besides, whereas the members of the OECD are all developed market economies, all but two (Italy and Spain) members of the IBI are developing countries. Although more countries participate in IBI's principal conferences, its representativeness, like that of the OECD, is therefore limited.

Most developed market economies do not feel comfortable with IBI. One fundamental reason is that IBI is specialized in areas—informatics and TDF—for which most of them do not yet have explicit policies, regulatory frameworks or institutional focal points. In other words, except in such countries as France, Italy and Spain, the national counterpart (and hence a national constituency) does not exist. This makes it difficult for IBI to draw the developed market economies into its work, especially since the credibility of the organization has suffered on occasion from uneven preparations and follow-up of its substantive events (such as conferences and working-group meetings). Partly as a consequence, IBI is dominated by developing countries, a fact which in and by itself makes many developed countries suspicious of the organization. This suspicion is fueled by IBI's work on guidelines for TDF which, it is feared, would be restrictive and geared primarily to the interests of the developing countries. As a result, the overwhelming majority of the developed market economies have not become members of what they perceive to be a developing-country organization and have attended IBI's meetings only as observers—if at all.

Virtually all of IBI's activities—in informatics (the organization's principal area of concern) as in TDF—take place in developing countries. These countries are responsive to the IBI because informatics is increasingly considered by them a key area of economic development. This finds its expression for instance in the fact that a growing number of countries establish organizational entities responsible for informatics (often close to the head of government) and adopt policies in this area. IBI has, therefore, national counterparts, and it can strengthen them through concrete technical assistance projects. TDF, in turn, are considered by many developing countries to be an extention of informatics. Since these countries normally lack in-depth knowledge about the implications of these flows, IBI is a logical organization for them to turn to for advice and guidance. In this, IBI is strengthened by its readiness to deal both with the physical infrastructure for TDF (informatics, data networks) and the contents of these flows—in contradistinction, most importantly, to the International Telecommunication Union, which avoids dealing with content questions and the economic and social implications of data flows. Another aspect that makes IBI attractive for developing countries is that, given its membership and orientation, it is essentially an importers' organization: since virtually all developing countries are primarily importers of data goods and services, IBI offers a forum in which users can get together and, to a certain extent, consider problems they have in common vis-à-vis suppliers. In a sense, therefore, IBI is an institution which tries to counter-balance the OECD.

IBI's main method of work in the TDF area is the convening of conferences.[57] Since they normally reach far beyond IBI's membership, they play an important role in introducing developing countries to TDF matters and shaping their attitudes in this regard. The First Intergovernmental Conference on Strategies and Policies for Informatics (SPIN I), organized with UNESCO in 1978 and attended by 78 national delegations, focused almost exclusively on informatics, but a recommendation was adopted on that occasion which called for international agreements on the rights of states in respect to TDF.[58] As a follow-up, IBI organized a number of regional conferences at which resolutions concerning TDF and the desirability of international guidelines were adopted. These, in turn, became an input into the First World Conference on Transborder Data Flow Policies convened by IBI in June 1980.[59] This Conference decided to establish three working parties with the mandates to examine, respectively, the economic and commercial impact of TDF, issues related to data protection and international law, and the new international environment for TDF.[60] The products of these working parties, the resolutions of various regional conferences (Santiago de Chile, 19–20 November 1981; Dakar, 8–10 February 1982; Buenos Aires, 20 April 1983, and Buenos Aires, 28 May–2 June 1984) and the results of a world survey of the TDF policies and practices of governments, PTTs and TNCs[61] were then presented to the Second World Conference on Transborder Data Flow Policies on 26–29 June 1984, at which 56 countries and 32 governmental and nongovernmental international organizations were represented. The objectives of the Second World Conference were to promote a better knowledge of the TDF phenomenon; to begin a debate on possible general principles which could inspire future negotiations in a forum open to all developing countries; and to put into action a cooperation program in this field. The Conference adopted a series of recommendations[62] (most of which were subsequently embraced by the Director General of IBI) to strengthen the organization's work on TDF.

Specifically, IBI decided in December 1984 to establish a high-level International Consultative Commission on Transborder Data Flow Development, originally thought to be composed of leading individuals nominated by governments of 25 countries from every geographic region and open to the participation of concerned international institutions. This Consultative Commission (for whose creation and functioning $100,000 were allocated) is meant to coordinate and assist TDF policy research at the national level conducted by governmental, academic or other institutions by organizing a documentation clearing house on TDF and by preparing a directory of relevant research in progress; to provide liaison with intergovernmental and non-governmental organizations involved in TDF activities; to sensitize leaders of developing countries to TDF issues, opportunities and problems, in particular with regard to the preparation of national informatics policies on international data flows; to assist IBI with appropriate definitions and methodologies for classifying TDF along sectoral lines and conducting regional activities in this field; and to advise IBI on the design of telematics infrastructures, software, and data-base development projects for developing countries. To support the work of the Consultative Commission, a special unit is to be created within the IBI Secretariat.

The Consultative Commission held its first organization meeting from 18 to 20 September 1985.[63] It was attended by 20 members, of which 17 were developing countries, 2 developed countries (Italy and Spain) and 1 socialist country (Bulgaria). Several members could not attend. The Commission decided to set up four working groups to study the following aspects of TDF: (1) TDF and development; (2) international information protection measures; (3) sectoral and regional approaches and issues; and (4) technical standards and financial problems. The working groups are to report their findings to the full Commission in 1986. The Commission is also expected to meet in 1987. An interim report on the Commission's work, containing preliminary findings and recommendations, is expected to be submitted to the Third World Conference on Transborder Data Flow Policies, provisionally scheduled for 1987.[64]

An interesting question is to what extent the Commission will deal with guidelines for TDF. Various past conferences of IBI have called for such guidelines, one of the working parties established by the First TDF Conference dealt with relevant principles, one of the three secretariat background documents for the Second World Conference on TDF Policies was dedicated to "The legal framework of international data flows",[65] and one of the three principal objectives of the Conference itself was to begin a "debate on the possible general principles which could inspire future negotiations in a forum open to all developing countries."[66] In fact, it even appeared at one point that SPIN II (which was originally planned jointly with UNESCO to take place in Havana) would be able to consider principles and elements for international guidelines for the transborder flow of personal and economic data. The basic principles that IBI appears to have in mind seemed to be based on the following:

1. *Transborder data flows serving the interests of States.* Recognition of rights inherent to the sovereignty of States which foresee that transborder data flows serve their interests and objectives and contribute as far as possible to the development of nations and the welfare of peoples.
2. *Transborder-data-flow transit.* In crossing intermediate States, TDF shall not violate their sovereignty nor their constitutional and legal principles. Reciprocally, national authorities of the intermediate States shall facilitate the TDF which conform with such principles.
3. *Free flow of information.* The free flow of information is essential to the States' political, economic and social well-being, and since TDF are the practical expression of this free flow, TDF cannot be subject to restrictions other than those which may be imposed by legitimate interests and national objectives.
4. *Preservation of culture and language.* Flows of information across borders should be consistent with socio-cultural patterns and in particular employ the language of countries to which they are transmitted.
5. *Harmonization of transborder-data-flow regulations.* Rapid expansion of international data communications, bringing increasing interdependence among States, requires uniform and coordinated regulatory, technical and economic policies designed to lessen obstacles to the flow of information and reducing negative consequences.
6. *Establishment of international harmonization.* International harmonization in the field of TDF is essential for the free flow of information. States must therefore set up national techno-legal bodies with a view to:

- harmonizing at the international level the relevant legal systems which already exist,
- promoting and fostering the adoption of national objectives in connection with data transmission,
- drafting international technical norms covering TDF.

7. *Availability of information on data transmission research.* The dissemination of knowledge and research on the issue of data transmission cannot but favor the free flow of information, reducing doubts and fears about possible violations of national sovereignty.

8. *International information exchange must conform to the principles contained in the Universal Declaration of Human Rights* which recognizes everyone's right "to receive and import information . . . regardless of frontiers" (Article 19).[67]

Curiously, however, in spite of these preparations, and in spite of the fact that a number of speakers during the 1984 Conference referred to the need for rules of the road, the matter was not systematically discussed at the Conference, its conclusions did not mention them, and the terms of reference of the International Commission do not explicitly include them either. The last point does not, of course, prevent the Commission from dealing with the topic. In fact, it would be surprising, indeed, if this were not to occur. An International Commission of high-ranking individuals is not likely to concentrate its energies on research, coordination, technical assistance and the preparation of another conference, leaving aside the one topic on which preparatory work has already been undertaken by IBI, on which important discussions are taking place elsewhere, and which is worthy of examination at a high political level. This may, in fact, be a useful exercise if the composition of the Commission represents all interests involved, and if discussions are based on carefully gathered facts and well-prepared analyses.

The angle from which the subject should be approached would have to be clarified early in the discussions in the light of the likely addressees of guidelines (IBI members only?). At the present time, an omnibus approach dealing with personal and economic data appears to be preferred by IBI, but since the issues in each area are vastly different from one another (and become even more so if the FDI aspect is included), different approaches may be required. In spite of these and other questions, the basic fact remains that the IBI Commission is, apart from the OECD's CICCP, the only intergovernmental body dealing specifically with TDF and, because of its composition, would give the developing countries a specific opportunity to make their concerns heard internationally.

With the initiation of these activities, IBI is clearly in the position of assuming a leadership role in the international TDF discussion, which would be to the advantage of IBI's main constituency, the developing countries. Endowed with considerable resources and supported by its own secretariat, the Commission could direct IBI's policy discussion and research program, raise the awareness of developing countries in TDF matters, and influence (through IBI's technical assistance work) practical informatics, telecommunication and TDF industrialization decisions in developing countries. The informational and organizational advantage that the developed market economies currently have through their work in the OECD may thus be balanced to a certain extent through a body that provides the developing countries with an opportunity to intensify contacts, exchange information, define interests, formulate policies for national and regional application, and coordinate strategies at the international level.

D. The Latin American Economic System

The Latin American Economic System (SELA) is so far the only organization of developing countries that is systematically dealing with services, with a view to studying the role of services in the development process and the impact of the sector's international transactions on the economies of Latin American countries and to formulating policy options for consideration by member countries.[68] Within this program of work, the Permanent Secretariat of SELA has been paying special and increasing attention to trade and FDI in data services, as a core service. More specifically, SELA established a Working Group on Trade in Services during the Autumn of 1983 which, after several meetings, prepared a report on "Services and the Development of Latin America",[69] which was submitted to a High-level Latin American Co-ordination Meeting on Services, held 22–24 August 1984 in Caracas. The High-level Meeting—which also considered an extensive report prepared for it on TDF[70]—elaborated a services work program[71] which recognized the importance of data services and urged that national and sectoral studies on services, including data services, be undertaken in order to determine their role in the development process and to assist governments in taking appropriate actions.

The subsequent Tenth Regular Meeting of the Latin American Council, held in Caracas from 24 to 26 October 1984, took up the services question.[72] It underlined the need for approaching the subject from the perspective of the contribution of services to the development process and for actions aiming at strengthening indigenous national and regional capabilities with a view to improving the international trading position of the countries involved. With these considerations in mind, the Council decided to approve the work program formulated by the Co-ordination Meeting on Services and to request the Permanent Secretariat to carry it out. It also encouraged member states to undertake national studies on services on the basis of a methodology drawn up by the Permanent Secretariat. Futhermore, the Council reaffirmed that "any international discussion of the subject, whatever its scope, must seek to safeguard the economic development goals pursued by the developing countries and that a greater knowledge of services in the development and economies of the region is fundamental and must be a precondition of any decision about the expedience or otherwise of launching discussions on services"; it also reaffirmed that "the unity of developing countries is essential to co-ordinated action in international discussions on services, to which end it is necessary to strengthen actions relating to the adoption of a common stand at the regional level, in the Group of 77 and at other levels of interregional co-ordination."[73] On the basis of this, the SELA Permanent Secretariat initiated practical work on TDF, including an in-depth review of informatics, telecommunication and TDF policies of Latin American countries and practical policy options open to them.[74] In addition, the Council decided to create, in the framework of SELA, an "Action Committee on the Informatics and Electronics Industry"[75] to promote regional self-sufficiency in Latin American industries, share information on relevant national legislations, undertake industrial complementarity activities in the informatics and electronics fields, and examine possibilities of harmonizing national legislation in these fields.

The Eleventh Regular Meeting of the Latin American Council, held in Caracas from 27 November to 8 December 1985, considered again the issue of services and, on the basis of the material submitted to it by the Permanent Secretariat, adopted a resolution on this subject.[76] It reaffirmed the further need for work on this subject, especially in the light of the proposed GATT negotiations. For this purpose, the Council decided to hold, during the first half of 1986, a second High-level Latin American Co-ordination Meeting on Services, and to assist in the conduct of national studies on services. In this work, continued attention will be given to data services and, in addition, to the linkage between trade and FDI in services.

SELA includes, of course, only developing countries from the western hemisphere and its resources—compared with those of the OECD—are small. Nevertheless, SELA has undertaken valuable background work and has become the leading organization in the Third World as regards policy formulation in services at the national, regional and international levels. It can be expected that, in pursuance of the Decisions adopted by the Tenth and Eleventh Latin American Council, SELA will intensify its efforts to arrive at a common service position not only for Latin America but also for the developing countries as a whole, in the framework of the Group of 77. SELA has already made a special effort to coordinate the Latin American countries' policies in GATT and UNCTAD.[77] Its influence in the Third World is not unimportant because a number of the developing countries particularly interested in services are Latin American countries and they play a leading role in SELA's policy-formulation process. Furthermore, being so far the only developing-country organization examining the subject matter, the positions adopted by it strongly influence the positions taken by the Third World as a whole, i.e., those of the Group of 77. This manifested itself, for instance, during the November 1984 meeting of the GATT Contracting Parties— at which Latin American countries played a key role in slowing down the US services initiative—and in the twenty-ninth session of the UNCTAD Trade and Development Board (both to be discussed below)—at which the Latin American countries played a key role in preventing an indirect endorsement of service work in GATT.

In the Latin American region, finally, mention should also be made of another practical effort, the Conferencia de Autoridades Latinoamericanas de Informática (CALAI). It is an organization conceived to coordinate computer policies in the region and to share experiences in this field. Its work includes efforts to define common regulations. Thus, for instance, during the seventh CALAI meeting in Montevideo in November 1983, it was decided to constitute a working group to study the possibility of adopting standardized protocols for the different data communication networks in the region; this would facilitate access to telematics services for users throughout the area. CALAI is also surveying (at the initiative of Brazil) the entities that develop software, with the objective of establishing joint software development projects. In addition, the 1983 CALAI meeting agreed to stimulate joint software development by two or more countries in the region.[78] Finally, CALAI has studied the issue of regional trade in data goods and services, in order to consider the creation of a common regional market in this regard. The eighth CALAI in Mexico City, held on 12-16 November 1984, approved a program of action aimed at defining a strategy for informatics development in the region. On the basis of a report on transborder data flows, the Conference adopted a resolution[79] asking for further work in this area. Among other things, Mexico (together with IBI) was asked to analyze the strategies of TNCs in Latin America in the field of informatics in such areas as the production of hardware and software, research and development, trade and balance of payments, investment and reinvestment, transfer of technology, informatics contracts, and agreements with local institutions. Chile (together with Argentina and IBI) was asked to coordinate national studies to develop legislative policy measures with a view to adopting national policies and a regional position on TDF matters. To what extent these initiatives do in fact result in common policies remains to be seen. In any case, CALAI is certainly an important forum for exchanging information and learning from one another's experience.

Notes

[1] For a critical review of the services discussion, see Murray Gibbs, "Continuing the International Debate on Services", *Journal of World Trade Law*, 19 (May/June 1985), pp. 199-218.

[2] See William E. Brock, "A Simple Plan for Negotiating on Trade in Services", *The World Economy*, 5 (November 1982), p. 235.

[3] *Ibid.*

[4] For the trade-in-services discussion in general, see UNCTAD, "Services and the Development Process", TD/B/1008 of 2 August 1984.

[5] US, Office of the US Trade Representative, "U.S. National Study on Trade in Services" (Washington: USTR, 1983), mimeo., p. 77.

[6] For instance, tourism and transport in the case of Greece/Egypt, transport in the case of The Netherlands/Indonesia, tourism in the case of Switzerland/Sudan.

[7] See, for instance, "Treaty between the United States of America and the Republic of Panama Concerning the Treatment and Protection of Investment", mimeo., annex. Reservations by Panama include communication, distribution and sale of imported products, retail trade, insurance, and banking.

At least as regards the US, some of these reservations and exceptions are, however, more sweeping than they need to be. For instance, because foreigners are not permitted to own, operate or control broadcast facilities and common carriers in the US, the entire industry is excluded. It can be expected that exceptions in the future will be more refined.

[8] See, e.g., *ibid.*, art. 4, and the treaty between the US and Costa Rica, art. 7.

[9] See "Caribbean Basin Economic Act, Public Law 98-67 (5 August 1983), Title II: Caribbean Basin Initiative", in *International Legal Materials: Document Highlights*, 22 (1983), pp. 1381-1388.

[10] The US, "Trade and Tariff Act of 1984", as amended in the "Conference Report", 98th Congress, 2nd Session, House of Representatives, Committee of Conference (Washington: Committee print, 1984), "Title IV: Trade in Israel", provided that the Agreement could be submitted to expedited congressional ratification.

[11] "Agreement on the Establishment of a Free Trade Area between the Government of the United States of America and the Government of Israel" (Washington: USTR, 1985), mimeo., article 13. The provision contained in the last sentence appears to apply to investments made on and after 1 April 1985 only; see also the (binding) annex 4 of the Agreement, dealing with subsidies.

[12] *Ibid.*, art. 16.

[13] The text of the Declaration was formally made available to OECD's Trade Committee where it was considered by the Committee's Working Party at the end of April 1985.

[14] See Rowland C. Frazee, "Trade and Technology: It's Canada's Move" (Montréal: Royal Bank of Canada, 1983). Frazee is chairperson and chief executive officer of the Royal Bank of Canada. For the analytical underpinning and practical elaboration of the proposal see Rodney de C. Grey, "Traded Computer Services: An Analysis of a Proposal for Canada/U.S.A. Agreement" (Montréal: Royal Bank of Canada, 1983).

The Royal Bank has seven data-processing centres in Canada and operations in more than 40 countries. It spent $377 million in 1984 on technology (including hardware, software, telecommunications and salaries), which represented 20% of the Bank's non-interest expenses. See Jack Burnett, "A Common Market in Traded Computer Services", Computer Law, 1 (September-October 1984), p. 73.

[15] See W. H. Loewen, "Will Canadian Data be Processed in Canada?" (Winnipeg: Canadian Independent Computer Services Association, 1985), mimeo.

[16] Grey, "Traded Computer Services", op. cit., p. 5.

[17] US, Trade Representative, "U.S. National Study on Trade in Services" (Washington: USTR, 1983), mimeo., p. 78.

[18] "The Quebec Summit, March 17–18, 1985: Declaration by the Prime Minister of Canada and the President of the United States of America Regarding Trade in Goods and Services", mimeo., pp. 2 and 3, respectively. For a detailed discussion of this subject see Peter F. Cowhey and Jonathan David Aronson, "Canada-U.S. Trade in Communication Services: The Prospects for and Implications of Liberalization" (San Diego: University of California, 1984), mimeo.

[19] William Diebold, Jr., and Helena Stalson, "Negotiating Issues in International Services Transactions", in William R. Cline, ed., Trade Policy in the 1980s (Washington: Institute for International Economics, 1983), p. 588.

[20] Ronald K. Shelp, Beyond Industrialization: Ascendancy of the Global Service Economy (New York: Praeger, 1981), pp. 174–175.

[21] For a brief review of the OECD's work in this area, see Serge A. Devos, "Service Trade and the OECD", Journal of Japanese Trade and Industry, 4(1984), pp. 16–19.

[22] See ibid.

[23] See OECD, Code of Liberalisation of Capital Movements (Paris: OECD, 1982), OECD, Code of Liberalisation of Current Invisible Operations (Paris: OECD, 1973) and "Declaration on International Investment and Multinational Enterprises", The CTC Reporter, 18 (Autumn 1984), pp. 37–41. For a report on the review of these codes, see Bernard Hugonnier, "TNCs and the OECD Liberalisation Codes", The CTC Reporter, 16 (Autumn 1983), pp. 30–31.

[24] OECD, "Decision of the Council Amending Annex A to the Code of Liberalisation of Capital Movements (Adopted by the Council at its 600th meeting on 4th April 1984)", C (83) 106 (Final) of 19 April 1984. It remains to be seen, however, to what extent reservations will be lodged against this provision. This should become apparent during 1986.

[25] The revised text of the decision on National Treatment is reprinted in The CTC Reporter, 18 (Autumn 1984), p. 41.

[26] A number of OECD countries have, however, entered exceptions to the National Treatment Decision and the Capital Movements Code, including as regards telecommunication services.

[27] See OECD, Report on the 1984 Review of the 1976 OECD Declaration and Decisions on International Investment and Multinational Enterprises (Paris: OECD, 1985), especially paras. 46–52.

[28] "U.S. National Study", *op. cit.*, pp. 87 and 193.

[29] OECD, *International Trade in Services: Insurance. Identification and Analysis of Obstacles* (Paris: OECD, 1983), p. 7.

[30] See "U.S. National Study", *op. cit.*, p. 193. Consideration is also being given to cover telecommunications explicitly in the Code. The Subcommittee on Transborder Data Flows of the Advisory Committee on International Investment, Technology and Development in the US encouraged in January 1986, the US administration to expand the Invisibles Code to telecommunication and information services, based on OECD's TDF Declaration.

[31] Until the end of 1985, the chairperson of CICCP was Johan Martin-Loef, the chairperson of the Working Party on Transborder Data Flows Peter Robinson. During the March 1986 sessions of the CICCP and the Working Party, A. Stenman and F. Vuilleumier were elected for the respective chairs. The CICCP is serviced by OECD's Information, Computer and Communications Policy Division, whose head is Hans-Peter Gassmann.

[32] See, e.g., Hans-Peter Gassmann, ed., *Information, Computer and Communications Policies for the 80s: An OECD Report. Proceedings of the High Level Conference on Information, Computer and Communications Policies for the '80s, Paris, 6th–8th October, 1980* (Amsterdam: North-Holland, 1982); Henri Ergas and Jun Okayama, eds., *Changing Market Structures in Telecommunications* (Amsterdam: North Holland, 1984); and OECD, *Transborder Data Flows: Proceedings of an OECD Conference* (Amsterdam: North-Holland, 1985).

These publications contain the principal results of the OECD's work on TDF, including work on TDF in TNCs and the evolution of the international data-base market. The Secretariat has also worked, among other things, on software, the role of telecommunication as the infrastructure for trade, and the needs for expansion of the international computer-services industry. Considerable emphasis has moreover been given to legal aspects of TDF, where, in 1985, three projects were underway: the first concerned copyrights and computerized information and involved the formulation of principles acceptable to OECD member countries in order to facilitate the dissemination of protected work through networks. The second (based on a Canadian proposal) concerned conflictual legal situations and involved the collection of material on cases in which conflictual legal situations can arise from the use of TDF. And the third concerned computer crime and involved the definition of a consensus on what computer crime is and how international cooperation in the prosecution of such crime can be improved.

[33] Reprinted in Geza Feketekuty and Jonathan David Aronson, "Restrictions on Trade in Communication and Information Services", *The Information Society*, 2 (1984), pp. 233–234. The idea of such a Declaration had originally been introduced by the US in the OECD's Trade Committee in October 1981.

[34] George W. Coombe, "Transborder Data Flow Legal Issues: The Case for Economic Analysis. Remarks to the American Society of International Law" (San Francisco: Bank of America, 1985), mimeo., pp. 6–7. See also Klaus W. Grewlich, "Les flux transfrontières de donnés: Plaidoyer pour un effort de connaissance et de cooperation", *Revue Economique et Social*, 1 (1983), p. 23.

[35] Lucy A. Hummer, "The OECD Declaration on Transborder Data Flows and Beyond" (Washington: Department of State, 1985), mimeo., pp. 2–3.

[36] *Ibid.*, p. 3.

[37] See "France Asks TDF Trade Rules", *Transnational Data Report*, 7 (October/November 1984), pp. 368–369.

[38] The last type of flows is not seen to represent any problems. Corporate flows, however, are seen to be more difficult because they may, for instance, escape taxation; in addition, they raise the issue of the autonomy of foreign affiliates and the responsiveness

of these affiliates to the host country. Commercial flows, finally, are seen to be a potential subject for normal trade rules.

[39] See "Technology, Employment and Growth: Report by M. François Mitterrand, President of the French Republic at the Summit of the Industrialized Countries, Château de Versailles, June 5, 1982", mimeo, p. 13.

[40] J. C. Grant, "New Financial Services and Transborder Data Flows", in OECD, *Transborder Data Flows, op. cit.*, p. 338.

[41] *Ibid.*

[42] D. L. Dougan, "Keynote Address", in OECD, *Transborder Data Flows, op. cit.*, p. 58.

[43] See "Communiqué", PRESS/A(85) 31 of 12 April 1985, para. 14e: "The rapid growth of international computer communications has become an important feature of the international economy. The Governments of OECD Member countries therefore have adopted a Declaration on Transborder Data Flows."

[44] US Mission to the OECD, "Press Release: United States Supports OECD Adoption of Declaration on Transborder Data Flows", Paris, 11 April 1985, mimeo., p. 1.

[45] The US might also have accepted the access concept because it could be used as an argument to obtain access to the Japanese market, or, for that matter, other markets.

[46] OECD, "Declaration on Transborder Data Flows", PRESS/A(85) 30 of 11 April 1985.

[47] *Ibid.*, covering statement.

[48] See "Statement of Common Intent on TDF", *Transnational Data Report*, 8 (December 1984), pp. 470–471.

[49] Geza Feketekuty and Jonathan David Aronson, "Meeting the Challenges of the World Information Economy", *The World Economy*, 7 (March 1984), p. 81.

[50] Geza Feketekuty, "The Telecommunications and Services Market Worldwide: A US View" (Washington: Office of the USTR, 1985), mimeo., p. 16.

[51] Independently of the TDF discussion, the OECD's Committee on International Investment and Multinational Enterprises has examined the issue of extraterritoriality and is expected to continue to do so.

[52] See Raimundo Beca, "Codifying Information Access", *Transnational Data and Communications Report*, 9 (January 1986), pp. 19–20.

[53] OECD, "Press Release", PRESS/A (84) of 18 May 1984, para. 31. Earlier OECD Ministerial Meetings had also dealt with the service question. At the 1985 Ministerial Meeting, the OECD countries confirmed that "given the growing significance of trade in services, continuing efforts toward their liberalisation are important." See "Communiqué", *op. cit.*, p. 6.

[54] In some cases, provisions agreed among OECD member countries are meant to have a broader geographical application. For instance, the Investment Declaration declares that member countries will consider applying the national treatment principle in respect of countries other than member countries.

[55] The manner in which this can happen is discussed by Hans Baade, "The Legal Effects of Codes of Conduct on Multinational Enterprises", in Norbert Horn, ed., *Legal Problems of Codes of Conduct for Multinational Enterprises* (Deventer: Kluwer, 1980), pp. 3–38.

[56] The Director General of IBI is F. A. Bernasconi; the work on TDF is undertaken in the Department of Policies (whose Director is J. F. Soupizet) by Lucio Clavijo.

[57] For a summary review of IBI's work on TDF, see IBI, "Second World Conference on Transborder Data Flow Policies: Working Document" (Rome: IBI, 1984), mimeo., chapter

I. See also J. Conquy Beer-Gabel, *Informatisation du tiers monde et coopération internationale* (Paris: La documentation française, 1984), pp. 39–44.

58 See UNESCO, *Final Report of the Intergovernmental Conference on Strategies and Policies for Informatics, Torremolinos (Spain), 28 August–6 September 1978* (Paris: UNESCO, 1978).

59 The papers presented at this Conference are contained in IBI, *Transborder Data Flow Policies: Papers Presented at the IBI Conference on Transborder Data Flow Policies, Rome (Italy), 23–27 June 1980* (New York: UNIPUB, 1982).

60 See "Transborder Data Flows, Data Protection and International Law" (Rome: IBI, 1981), mimeo., "First Meeting of the International Working Group on Data Protection and International Law: Summary Records" (Rome: IBI, 1981), mimeo., "First Meeting of the International Working Group for the Analysis of Economic and Commercial Impacts of Transborder Data Flows: Summary Records" (Rome: IBI, 1981), mimeo., and "New Techniques in Informatics and Telecommunications: Their Consequences" (Rome: IBI, 1981), mimeo.

61 The results have been published in "IBI World Survey of National Policies and Company Practices Concerning Transborder Data Flows: Description and Tabulation of Results" (Rome: IBI, 1983). For a summary, see G. Russell Pipe, "IBI Survey on TNCs and TDF", *The CTC Reporter*, 17 (Spring 1984), pp. 42–43.

62 See IBI, "Proceedings of the Second World Conference on Transborder Data Flow Policies, Rome, 26–29 June 1984" (Rome: IBI, n.d.).

63 See IBI, "International Consultative Commission for TDF Development: Inaugural Meeting. Final Statement" (Rome: IBI, 1985), mimeo. The chairperson of the Commission is Amir Jamal (Tanzania); the vice chairpersons are Jorge Phillips (Colombia), Carlo Sarzana (Italy), André Silcox (Zimbabwe), and Aboud Taki (Iraq). As of January 1986, the members of the Commission came from the following countries: Argentina, Bulgaria, Chad, Colombia, Cuba, Dominican Republic, Ghana, Honduras, Iran, Iraq, Italy, Ivory Coast, Jordan, Madagascar, Spain, Syria, Tanzania, Thailand, Togo, and Zimbabwe.

64 In addition, IBI established (together with the government of Italy) an International Institute for the Development of Informatics, which took up its work during the summer of 1985. Its efforts are aimed at training and informing those reponsible for informatics policies in developing countries, particularly in IBI member countries. See, *IBI Newsletter*, 27 (October-December 1985), p. 2.

65 Rome, IBI, 1984, mimeo.

66 IBI, "Second World Conference on Transborder Data Flow Policies", *op. cit.*, p. 1.

67 See IBI, "Working Document", *op. cit.*, pp. 47–48. The text has been slightly edited.

68 See Decision 153 of the Ninth Latin American Council. The service work in the SELA Permanent Secretariat is undertaken under the direction of Miguel Rodriguez Mendoza, Director of Co-ordination, and Henry Gill.

69 SR/RCLA/SERV/DT No. 2/Rev.1 of 31 July 1984.

70 Later published as Karl P. Sauvant, *Trade and Foreign Direct Investment in Data Services* (Boulder: Westview Press, 1986).

71 SELA, "Conclusions and Recommendations of the High-level Latin American Co-ordination Meeting on Services, held at the Headquarters of the Latin American Economic System (SELA), Caracas, 22 to 24 August 1984", in SP/CL/X.10/DT No. 14 of 4 October 1984.

72 See Tenth Regular Meeting of the Latin American Council, Decision No. 192, "Services and the Development of Latin America" in "Final Report of the Tenth Regular Meeting of the Latin American Council", CL/X.0/DF No. 1 of 26 October 1984, mimeo.

[73] *Ibid.*, p. 83.

[74] See UNCTC, "Data Services in Latin America and the Caribbean" (New York: UNCTC, 1985), mimeo.

[75] Decision No. 221, in "Final Report of the Tenth Regular Meeting of the Latin American Council", *op. cit.*, pp. 271–272.

[76] Resolution 225, "Services and Development", *ibid.*

[77] SELA's "Conclusions and Recommendations", *op. cit.*, for instance, were distributed at the 29th session of the UNCTAD Trade and Development Board.

[78] See, respectively, Seventh CALAI, "Resolucion 4/83" (Montevideo, 1983), mimeo., "Informe de la Secretaria Permanente a cargo de la delegacion de Brasil" (Montevideo, 1983), mimeo.; and "Resolucion 4/83" (Montevideo, 1983), mimeo.

[79] Resolution 7/84 of CALAI VIII.

V

The International
Policy Discussion:
International Fora

A. The General Agreement on Tariffs and Trade

The General Agreement on Tariffs and Trade (GATT), with its 90 Contracting Parties (and a number of countries which apply the GATT rules on a de facto basis), offers, of course, a broader framework than the IBI or the OECD, even though many developing and socialist countries are not contracting parties, and even though GATT in its current form does not cover services: some exceptions aside (e.g., films), it is a general agreement relating to trade in goods, not services. The principal reason is that, when GATT was conceived, trade in services was relatively insignificant compared to trade in goods; besides, to the extent that trade in services took place, it was mostly seen as being incidental to trade in goods. Accordingly, GATT was set up to provide a set of rules for trade in goods and a forum in which concessions could be negotiated with the aim of liberalizing this trade.

1. The position of the developed countries

With trade in services having become as important as it has, it is not surprising that the principal service-exporting countries have initiated efforts to expand the GATT framework to trade in services to make this trade subject to a multilateral agreement which defines the rules of service trade and matters pertaining to it. For these countries—almost all of them developed countries— GATT is an attractive forum to pursue this objective because the industrialized countries have considerable influence in this organization. At the same time, many developing countries, particularly the newly industrializing countries, are also contracting parties, and consequently a minimum of representativeness exists. Furthermore, the GATT framework would permit an umbrella approach to services under which sectoral agreements could be negotiated. Alternatively, if not all members of GATT are interested in agreeing on a service framework, those which are, could act in the framework of a code for trade in services. (The code instrument—which does not require adherence by all contracting parties—was developed during the Tokyo Round; it is a flexible mechanism through which matters of interest to less than the full membership of GATT can be regulated.)

An important consideration for the developed countries may also have been that the inclusion of services in GATT would not only permit trade-offs between goods trade and service trade, but also the exercise of cross pressure. Developing countries are not very vulnerable to retaliatory pressure in the service area if they should take restrictive action, but they are vulnerable to pressure in the goods area.

The principal attractiveness of GATT for the proponents of the trade-in-services discussion, however, is that the free-trade persuasion underlying the institution's Articles of Agreement suits their interests perfectly: since probably all OECD countries are convinced that they—and world welfare in general—would benefit from a liberalization of trade in services, they favor the extension of this free-trade persuasion to internationally traded services. GATT is, therefore, seen by them as the proper forum to arrive at a contractual understanding on service-trade principles. OECD countries expect the liberalization of trade in services to yield the same benefits as the liberalization of trade in goods did; in particular, the liberalization of trade in services is regarded as a potential source of new growth in the world economy and the rapid expansion of this trade is seen as facilitating continued structural adjustment. The close relationship that exists between many traded goods and services further supports this approach. In fact, in the eyes of the supporters of this approach, most of the GATT principles could fruitfully be applied to services, as could GATT's ready-made mechanism for dispute settlement. However, before outlining this approach in greater detail, a few words must be said about the views of the private sector because these views shape to a considerable extent the domestic and international discussion on trade in services.

a. The business community

Before governments turned their attention to services, the private sector had undertaken considerable preparatory work. The focal points were most notably the International Insurance Advisory Council, the Chamber of Commerce, the Coalition of Service Industries, the Services Policy Advisory Committee and the Industry Sector Advisory Committee on Services and Trade Policy Matters in the US; the Liberalisation of Trade in Services Committee (LOTIS) in the UK; and the International Chamber of Commerce in Paris.

US service industries led the movement toward organizing the interests of the service sector. The phases through which the thinking of the US service industry went between the late 1960s and the early 1980s are aptly summarized in the following observation which, although made for the US insurance industry, applies to US service industries in general:

> The first [phase] was recognizing unfair treatment, defining it as discrimination, and expressing the injustice that results when insurers operating in foreign markets faced the imposition of conditions which favored local firms.
> The second phase was the building of a community with other U.S. service industries also facing foreign discrimination and with the U.S. government, thus creating the power base necessary to address the newly recognized problem at the domestic and international levels.
> The third phase is now emerging. It involves directing this power to eliminate discriminatory practices by trading partners and doing so in a fair, reasonable, and deliberate way through both bilateral and multilateral negotiation. The

expectation is that over time such a step-by-step process will lead to the reduction and elimination of unfair and discriminatory treatment.[1]

The organization of the US service sector began in the mid-1960s when US transnational insurance corporations established under the aegis of the US Chamber of Commerce the International Insurance Advisory Council (IIAC) in 1967 to discuss issues arising out of the increasing incidents of nationalizations of foreign insurers, as well as other insurance-trade matters.[2] The drafting of the 1974 Trade Act galvanized the US services sector when the US Chamber of Commerce, apparently on the prompting of the IIAC, called a series of meetings of US service industries in July 1974 and, eventually, convinced the Department of Commerce to prepare a study of the trade by 18 US service industries.[3] These meetings and increasing contacts with the administration continued and, in August 1978, led to the establishment of the International Service Industry Committee of the US Chamber of Commerce, which proposed "to act jointly to foster the freer flow of U.S. services into world markets."[4] The new Committee urged that greater attention be given to services in the Trade Act of 1979. It also encouraged the establishment of a service working party by the US Council of the ICC and sectoral studies on service trade in the OECD. For a number of reasons, the Committee was, however, disbanded in 1983. For one, the various trade associations responsible for individual service industries had, by that time, been sensitized to the trade issue to such an extent that they were now pursuing the matter independently. Secondly, key promoters of the trade-in-services discussion apparently felt that an independent group dedicated entirely to services and consisting of high-level participants was needed to give the issue a higher profile. As a result, the Coalition of Service Industries was established in 1982, a body consisting (at the end of 1985) of the chief executive officers of 26 major US transnational service corporations. The efforts of the Coalition "are directed toward shaping those aspects of domestic and foreign economic policy which affect the interests of the service sector, as well as increasing public awareness of the major role services play"[5] in the US economy. One of the Coalition's specific objectives is to combat barriers to international trade in services and to provide remedies for injured US service exporters.[6] Today, the Coalition is probably the single most important private-sector organization promoting the services discussion in the US. It claims among its achievements the Congressional passage of the US Trade and Tariff Act of 1984, Congressional passage of Export Import Bank legislation which mandated equal treatment for goods and services under Eximbank programs, the strong commitment of the 1984 London economic summit to reduce barriers to trade in services, and the completion of the U.S. National Study on Services.[7]

The principal official channels through which the private sector in the US makes its views known to the administration is the Services Policy Advisory Committee (SPAC) and the Industry Sector Advisory Committee on Services and Trade Policy Matters. SPAC was established in 1980 as part of the private sector advisory process mandated by the Trade Acts of 1974 and 1979.[8] It has over 30 members, all chief executive officers or senior vice-presidents primarily of major service corporations or presidents of service unions. The Committee's sessions—which are held 2–3 times a year—are attended by 20–30 individuals. Its mandate is to advise US government officials on service-trade matters, especially as regards GATT. Its addressee is the US Trade Representative.

The Industry Sector Advisory Committee on Services was also created in 1980, as part of the same advisory process.[9] It consists of approximately 50 members from the service-industry sector. They are appointed by the Secretary of Commerce and the US Trade Representative. In distinction to the broad policy mandate of the SPAC, the Committee advises the Secretary and the USTR on specific service-trade issues. Thus, it provides detailed policy and technical advice and information and recommendations on such matters as trade barriers and the implementation of certain trade agreements.

The views of the SPAC were expressed in April 1985 in a statement prepared to advise the US Trade Representative on the new GATT round. With the overwhelming support from its members, the SPAC recommended that the US should "seek to create, in this decade, a workable and effective international system of rules and dispute settlement designed to maintain and foster liberal trade in services."[10] To achieve this objective, the government is encouraged to utilize every possible means, including multilateral, bilateral and plurilateral negotiations in appropriate forums. In this context, the statement counsels that "the recalcitrance of some countries, particularly developing countries, should not be permitted to obstruct agreement among more developed countries for whom services trade may be more significant."[11] The statement continued:

> The new services trade system should take the form of an umbrella general agreement, forming a "constitution" of general services trade principles to which most developed nations should subscribe. In addition, there should be sectoral agreements, subsidiary to the general agreement, to which countries might subscribe *a la carte*. Emphasis should be placed upon those service sector agreements, which form the infrastructure of services trade. An effort should also be made to amend the existing GATT Non-Tariff Barrier (NTB) codes to deal with services where appropriate.
>
> Both the international general agreement on services and the subsidiary, sector agreements, should adopt certain general principles from the GATT. As discussed more fully below, contracting parties should commit to halting the introduction of new services trade barriers on the date of accession. In addition, they should commit themselves to reducing existing barriers in accordance with a set schedule. They should obligate themselves to maintain transparent systems in which the balance of their concessions is maintained and to redress any subsequent changes in the balance.
>
> The principles of transparency, balance of concessions, conditional Most Favored Nation treatment, and national treatment should be adapted and borrowed from the present GATT system. In addition, however, the United States should not allow the longstanding inhibitions of the present international economic system to prevent it from breaking *new* ground in negotiating international rules on services. For example, telecommunications forms the infrastructure for services trade, much in the way shipping serves as an essential infrastructure for merchandise trade. Therefore, emphasis should be placed on the negotiation of services trade principles by which countries agree not to create unnecessary, technical barriers to telecommunications services and to keep their regulation of telecommunications a political decision, potentially subject to international negotiation. In addition, the present system's lack of international rules on the right to market access is itself a major deficiency and inequity in the existing international regime. Accordingly, it is critical that a right of market access be recognized if a new system of international rules on services is to have any meaning whatsoever. Negotiating such principles,

even on a bilateral basis, will require a willingness on the part of the United States and its trading partners to make concessions. Although this effort is likely to be politically difficult and will raise international sensitivities, the long term economic benefit for the U.S. makes such an effort a necessity.[12]

   This brief review, and especially the recommendations of the Services Policy Advisory Committee, show that the service initiative of the US administration has the full support of the country's private sector.
   An important service exporter, and a supporter of the US in the international services discussions, is the UK. There, LOTIS has been the principal focal point of the private sector. LOTIS was formed by the British Committee on Invisible Exports (now the British Invisible Exports Council) in 1982.[13] Since that time, its principal aim has been to press for the removal of obstacles to trade in services since this "should be in the interest of the UK economy and to the net advantage of the UK in the longer term. . . . As a consequence LOTIS considers that it is logical as well as wise that the UK should support and be seen to support any initiative for the gradual removal of barriers to trade in services."[14] Since "many of the obstacles to trade in services are common to several service industries", LOTIS recommends that "the prime objective should be to seek the formulation of some general principles" and that "the GATT framework would be an appropriate forum within which to handle the subject."[15] The issues deserving priority attention were identified in 1982 as access to markets and right of establishment; the prevention of new restrictions in the service sector; the removal, as a first step, of restrictions to those services that are related to trade in goods; and international initiatives, on a priority basis, on TDF.[16] Later, these objectives were substantially endorsed (although TDF were not mentioned separately) and elaborated, with priority to be given to the adoption of general principles and, in particular, a standstill agreement.[17]
   On the international level, the ICC—as in the TDF discussion—plays the principal coordinating role of the private sector. The ICC established, at the end of the 1970s, a Working Group on Obstacles to Trade in Services under its Commission on International Trade Policy and Trade-Related Matters. In 1981, the Commission adopted a position paper on the liberalization of trade in services prepared by the Working Group in which most of the themes of the international services discussions were struck. Most importantly, the ICC called "upon all governments to accept that the principles espoused in the GATT systems for the regulation of world trade be extended to cover trade in services" and it urged governments "to begin preparations towards multilateral negotiations to reduce existing impediments to international trade in services and to create an accepted framework for the conduct of liberal trade in services."[18] The position paper was referred to the ICC specialized committees, with the purpose of encouraging the preparation of sectoral studies on the subject.[19] On the basis of the earlier work done in this area, the Council of the ICC reached interim conclusions on international trade in services in June 1984. (The text of the interim conclusions is contained in annex IX.) Among other things, they stated that it is now desirable to have an agreed framework of international rules in the service sector; the general principles of international trade are applicable to trade in services as well; GATT is the appropriate forum for the elaboration of a system of international obligations; service trade includes both cross-border trade and establishment trade;

rules about the "right of presence" should be evolved; transparency as regards national legislation and administrative measures is needed; and non-discrimination between domestic and foreign suppliers should be ensured.[20] The ultimate objective should be an "Agreement on Services" which might also have "some special arrangements for countries 'at an early stage of development of participation in international service trade'".[21] These conclusions were distributed to national governments and GATT, with a view to encouraging the adoption of a liberal international regime for trade in services.

The preceding paragraphs should not create the impression that the service sector *as a whole* is well organized in every country. While there are certainly strong service *industry* organizations (e.g., in banking and insurance) in many countries, *inter-service-industry* co-operation is in its infancy in most countries. The principal reason is that the service sector has simply not yet developed an identity of its own in most countries but rather has remained in the shadow of the manufacturing sector, which normally dominates national private-sector organizations. Partly this is so because the diversity of service activities has made it difficult for the producers of individual services to focus on their common interests. In addition, since many services are being produced by the manufacturing industry as auxiliary products, their representation as activities in their own right suffers. To the extent that an increased specialization in the production of services leads to the emergence of independent service companies, this situation can be expected to change. In any event, services as a sector have been considerably less well organized than industry. While this situation is changing (with new groups having been formed in Belgium, Canada, France, Japan and Sweden only during the past two years), it gives service organizations with their own organizational framework and articulated position an advantage in influencing the international services discussion.

It is furthermore noteworthy that no major segments of the business community appear to oppose the inclusion of services into a new GATT round — perhaps because all industries consider services (and especially data services) as their infrastructure and, therefore, benefit from its easy international availability. This is implied in the position of the ICC on this subject, and it is particularly clear in the US. There, the survey conducted in 1985 by the chairpersons of the private sector trade policy advisory committees on private sector views toward a new round of GATT negotiations (described in chapter III) dealt specifically with desirable US objectives and priorities for the new round and the disadvantages such a round could have for the US. In that survey, the participating organizations agreed to a large extent that any new round should focus on two sets of issues: (1) unfinished business of the Tokyo Round on non-tariff barrier codes (especially regarding the safeguards and anti-counterfeiting codes) and GATT framework issues (especially dispute-settlement procedures); and (2) new areas and issues affecting world trade flows that should be brought under GATT coverage (especially services, intellectual property and graduation).[22] Most groups contributing to this survey recommended in fact specifically that services ought to be included in the new round (although some believed that the US was not yet sufficiently prepared to enter multilateral negotiations on this subject at this time), and none of the participating organizations raised the possible inclusion of services as a major disadvantage of the new round.[23] Thus, at least at the end of 1985, those who desire a liberal framework for service transactions are clearly determining the views of the private sector.

Most of the organizations reviewed here—and those discussed in chapter III in the context of the role of the private sector in the TDF discussion—continue to influence the politics surrounding international transactions in services. And they do a considerable amount of the preparatory work on the basis of which governments formulate their policies.

b. The US position

Against the background of the views of the private sector described here and in chapter III, and on the basis of its domestic policy and regulatory framework, the US developed its position on an appropriate framework for international transactions in services. The tone was set, and the direction indicated, by an article which the US Trade Representative published on the eve of the 1982 GATT Ministerial Meeting, at which the services discussion began in that organization. It set out the principles and procedures which the US had in mind. Since they have shaped the subsequent discussions, they deserve being quoted in full:

Objectives: The basic goal of any future negotiations should be to expand the opportunities for trade, making possible the economic gains that can be obtained from trade based on comparative advantage. A closely related objective should be to ensure that barriers to trade in services do not become a major obstacle to trade in goods. In order, then, to expand the opportunities for trade, such negotiations should focus on,

first, the development of a stable institutional environment for trade in services, providing 'predictability' in governmental actions and an orderly way for dealing with the problems that arise; and,

second, the development of a negotiating process for reducing or eliminating barriers to trade in services, which to a large extent means addressing government regulations that discriminate between domestic and foreign suppliers of services.

We should recognise the right of every government to establish its own social objectives for the regulation of services and the obligations of foreign suppliers of services to adhere to such regulations. At the same time, though, governments should assume an obligation to minimise the extent to which such regulations distort trade beyond the minimum necessary to achieve legitimate social objectives. Where such regulations are meant to protect domestic service industries, they should be clearly notified as trade restrictions.

Principles: Future negotiations might be guided by some of the following principles. Restriction on trade in services should be made explicit and should be negotiable. All government regulations that are not notified as barriers should be applied on a 'national treatment' basis. Where national treatment is difficult to apply for technical or regulatory reasons, governments should commit themselves to minimise the distortion of trade inherent in such regulations. Government monopolies should operate on a commercial basis where they are in competition with foreign commercial enterprises and they should offer foreign and domestic customers the same reliability, quality and prices; that is, they should observe the principle of national treatment.

Procedures: Governments should be willing to consult with each other when problems arise with respect to their mutual trade in services and if they cannot resolve their differences on the basis of such consultations they should have access to a dispute-settlement procedure. New regulations that offset foreign suppliers should be notified in a timely way and foreign suppliers should be given an opportunity to discuss technical problems related to the application of such new regulations. Foreign suppliers of services should have the same access to government officials and to local courts as domestic suppliers of services.

Rights and Obligations: Commitments entered into by governments as a result of negotiations should result in contractual rights and obligations. Governments should agree not to take other actions that would deny foreign countries the benefits of negotiated concessions, except under agreed circumstances. Where governments act in violation of their commitments, efforts should be made to reach a new understanding on the issues involved; otherwise, affected countries should have the right to take compensatory actions that would re-establish a balance of commitments.

Organisation of Future Negotiations: A considerable amount of staff work is needed before we can develop any concrete propositions for future negotiations. Within a common framework of principles, rules and procedures, negotiations could be organised either along sectoral lines or in terms of issue-oriented codes such as the GATT standards code negotiated in the Tokyo Round deliberations. We might be able to develop, for example, a regulatory code that could be patterned on the standards code.[21]

This has remained the basic US position. It was later formalized in the "US National Study" prepared for GATT (whose Executive Summary is contained in annex III). At the same time, the key elements of a possible framework for services have been elaborated in greater detail, and official recognition has been given to the priority that ought to be given to TDF. Naturally, the US also elaborated objectives for trade in goods, some of which also bear on data services. The basic US objectives for a new round of multinational trade negotiations, as they stood at the beginning of 1986, are outlined in the following paragraphs.[25]

The new round in general. The US supports strongly a new round of multilateral trade negotiations to strengthen and develop trading rules with a view to bringing them into greater harmony with the current and future trading environment; to expand the exchange of goods through the reduction of trade barriers; and to develop a set of rules applicable to trade in services. The negotiations ought to be conducted under the auspices of GATT and would be open to any contracting party wishing to participate in them.

Trade in goods. A first set of objectives relates to the *management of the GATT system*. The objectives sought here are:

- To *strengthen* considerably GATT's current mechanism for *dispute settlement* because otherwise, it is felt, governments and the international business community would lose confidence in the GATT system;
- To establish *effective discipline over import restrictions and export subsidies* in agriculture;
- To establish *effective discipline over* all actions taken to *restrain* imports (with agreement sought on the principles of transparency, surveillance,

limited duration and degressivity which are sought to apply to *import restrictions*, as a first step);
- To *improve the Codes negotiated during the Tokyo Round*, especially regarding non-tariff barriers;
- To *reach agreement* on actions and procedures which ensure that the practices of countries in the area of *intellectual property rights* do not constitute barriers to trade (a topic which could be directly relevant to data services if it covered software and data bases); and
- To find ways of dealing with trade in *counterfeit goods*.

A second set of objectives relates to the *expansion of market access*. Such expansion is sought to ensure that trade and related investment can grow, to facilitate economic growth and development, and to help ease the debt burden. *Non-tariff barriers* deserve special attention in this context, as do measures aimed at expanding market access for *high technology products*. Since high technology products involve, most importantly, products based on data technologies, this topic is of immediate relevance to the data-service discussion.

A third set of objectives, finally, relates to *foreign direct investment*. GATT discipline is sought for a number of practices which are seen to be an increasingly important source of trade distortions, especially local content rules and export performance requirements. As regards FDI in general, the US seeks agreement on practices that are seen to distort or restrict FDI flows, including barriers to FDI and other discriminating measures. All of these issues have an immediate bearing on services, including data services.

Trade in services. Here, the US seeks negotiations with as many interested GATT members as possible under the aegis of GATT, using the organization's administrative facilities and secretariat staff. (Apparently, the US does not insist on the participation of *all* contracting parties in these negotiations.) As already indicated, the result is meant to be a *general agreement on principles and procedures to ensure that trade in services is as open as possible.* What is sought is a legal framework of rules and procedures which would provide basic guidance on the rights and obligations of the countries that subscribe to it, with a view to ensuring free trade in services through a commitment to transparency of practices, the resolution of problems through consultation, and the reduction of trade barriers. More specifically, the principal elements of this legal framework are seen to be:

- *Transparency:* the parties to the agreement should notify each other about laws and regulations meant to protect domestic service industries.
- *National treatment:* certain well-defined exceptions apart, all laws and regulations should be subject to the obligations of national treatment. Where the total number of enterprises in an industry is limited by regulations, additional commitments may be required to ensure reasonable market access.
- *Open regulatory procedures:* all regulations and rules dealing with services should normally be made available prior to their implementation to give interested parties an opportunity to comment on them.
- *Public monopolies:* where a public monopoly enters into competition with other enterprises, it should be required to adopt an arms-length relationship between its own monopoly activities and its activities as an international

competitor, as a domestic competitor in other services, and as a supplier of services.

- *Dispute settlement*: any legally binding framework should contain procedures that allow parties to consult over specific problems arising under the framework and that provide for compensation by a party whose trade opportunities have been impaired because of foreign practices inconsistent with the framework.
- *Subsequent commitments*: binding provisions should be adopted regarding future commitments about the further reductions of trade barriers, including the rights and obligations of the parties in this respect.

The US also envisions that such a general agreement on services would be complemented by parallel discussions on FDI matters related to services, negotiations of a functional character, and negotiations of a sectoral character.

As to *FDI*, the US believes that corporations will not be able to take advantage of the full range of commercial opportunities until FDI questions are regulated in a framework similar to that sought for trade in services. The US seeks therefore an understanding dealing with investment issues in services and urges countries to begin examining how FDI issues affecting services could be managed in the context of an investment framework for services. Independently of that, however, a service framework should cover these activities, providing for the right of commercial presence for service TNCs for the purpose of marketing and facilitating a service imported into a country.

As to *functional negotiations*, the US would like to examine the applicability to trade in services of the basic concepts and principles in some of the GATT codes dealing with non-tariff barriers (e.g., standards and procurement). Intellectual property issues are also important in this context.

As to *sectoral negotiations*, the US proposes that—parallel to the negotiations on a general legal framework for services—a series of understandings would be reached which would be consistent with the overall framework and would deal with the specific problems affecting trade in individual service industries. Again, the thrust of these understandings would be to remove barriers to trade.

Trade in data services. In the context of such sectoral negotiations, the US advocates explicitly—and, as discussed in chapter III, with the full support of its business community—that *priority be given to developing a multilateral agreement on international information flows.*[26] The US feels that it is critical to address this particular area as soon as possible because of its crucial role in most service industries and its role in the technological change of all countries. In the same vein, a US background paper on "Communications and Transborder Data Flows in the United States" concluded:

> Transborder data flow issues are, of course, only a part of the broader telecommunications and information issues which are being actively discussed internationally. In terms of the trade implications of domestic telecommunications and information policies, the U.S. considers these to be part of the broader initiative now under way to develop disciplines over international trade in services. . . . The telecommunications and information services sector is certain to be a key component of future work on trade in services.[27]

For the US, it is furthermore a consideration that data services are an area in which the federal government has jurisdiction, as opposed, for instance, to banking and insurance, in which the individual states have far-reaching authority. This situation facilitates, as far as the US is concerned, speedy negotiations on a sectoral agreement on TDF.

Thus, the importance of TDF, and especially the nature of data services as a core service, are fully recognized. Not only are transborder data flows an integral part of international negotiations on trade and FDI in services, but it is very likely that they will receive priority attention in these negotiations. The priority accorded to TDF per se, especially if joined by the potential discussions of intellectual property rights (software, data bases), high technology products (data goods and, possibly, some data services associated with them) and certain FDI issues (including such matters as local-content requirements which are of immediate interest to data services), could give data services a truly prominent place on the agenda of GATT's next round of multilateral trade negotiations.

c. The position of other developed countries

The objectives of the US for the new GATT round as regards services are clearly formulated and, as discussed earlier, grounded in domestic legislation and extensive domestic consultations. In most other developed countries (with the most notable exception of the UK), the services—and especially the TDF—discussions were only beginning in 1985, mostly stimulated by the US interest in this matter and the preparation of national studies on services for GATT. (By the beginning of 1986, such studies had been prepared by Australia, Belgium, Canada, Denmark, the European Community, Finland, the FRG, France, Italy, Japan, The Netherlands, Norway, Sweden, Switzerland, the UK, and the US.) Although probably somewhat hazy about their specific negotiating objectives, all other developed countries supported the US in having services on the agenda of the next GATT round, and most of them expected that this would lead to the establishment of a liberal framework for trade in services. After all, the overwhelming majority of the developed countries are important exporters of services, and most of them have at least one service industry which is internationally competitive and would thus benefit from a liberal service-trade framework. Nevertheless, differences in support exist.[28]

Perhaps most supportive are Canada and Japan. Canada attaches considerable importance to the development of a new trading framework for trade in services. It holds that, in the process of negotiating it, the possible application of such basic principles as non-discrimination, national treatment and transparency in national regulations should be explored. Japan favors the adaptation of the General Agreement to deal adequately with trade in services and believes that new rules for this trade are needed; a GATT code is seen as possibly providing a transitional arrangement for this subject.

The Commission of the European Communities agrees that negotiations on services should take place in the framework of GATT because that organization's objectives and experiences are seen to be best suited to facilitate the expansion of international trade in services.[29] In addition, the introduction of this issue into GATT could revitalize the organization. The Community has, however, doubts whether the General Agreement as it stands can simply be extended to trade in services; the objective in its view should rather be to develop a framework of rules appropriate to trade in services, drawing on GATT principles where there is agreement that these are relevant. Finally, the Commission of the European Communities has an institutional interest in the negotiations because, under the Treaty of Rome, it (and not the individual member states) has the authority to negotiate trade matters. The Commission would, therefore, play a major role in any negotiations.

Within the European Community, attitudes differ from country to country. The UK is probably the most supportive of the US, reflecting the position of the country as a major service exporter and the preparatory work of LOTIS. Thus, the UK national study prepared for GATT observed:

> In the UK's view . . . any international approach to services problems should consider services as a whole rather than simply addressing the special problems of individual sectors. It will be necessary in particular to examine carefully the possible application to trade in services of existing international provisions governing trade in goods and the experience gained in preparing and operating those provisions. The UK Government believes that such an overall framework— while retaining, however, a flexibility of application to fit the particular circumstances of individual sectors—offers the best chance of progress towards genuine liberalisation of trade in services.[30]

Rather supportive also are The Netherlands, Denmark and Belgium. France appeared to be the developed country most reluctant to agree to the inclusion of services in the GATT agenda. It is, however, not quite clear why this seemed to be the case since France is a major service exporter. But perhaps France is not so much against the inclusion of services in the agenda as against the speedy commencement of the new round. The principal reason could well be that the new round is very likely to deal with trade of agricultural products and related issues. Once this occurs, the European Community would have to defend (and possibly amend) its Common Agricultural Policy (CAP), which is highly protectionist and, for many products, depends heavily on export subsidies and import restrictions. With France being one of CAP's principal beneficiaries, and the US having strongly criticized it for a considerable period of time, France may be playing for time to protect its agricultural sector. Furthermore, France may be seeking to use the service issue as a bargaining lever for possible trade-offs in the negotiations on agriculture.

Outside of the European Community, Switzerland and the Nordic countries have shown support for the US position. Switzerland, which fully supports the opening of negotiations with the aim of establishing a multilateral system designed to facilitate trade in services, places particular emphasis on the need to examine the nature and the underlying motives of existing national regulations in order to determine the conditions under which such regulations could be considered not to represent barriers to trade. The Nordic countries are also most interested in creating a multilateral framework which would be compatible with the rules governing trade in goods and which would counteract protectionist and arbitrary elements in regulations concerning trade in services. The agreement which is sought from the negotiations should provide for transparency and future liberalization of trade in services.

Finally, New Zealand and especially Australia, while not denying that services can appropriately be included in the agenda for the next GATT round, are giving priority to reducing barriers and distortions to trade in goods.

In spite of this broad support for the US position, it is also clear that most of the other developed countries do not show the same drive as the US in launching the new round, including services in its agenda, and establishing a comprehensive and legally binding framework for services. Partly this may reflect the lower level of awareness and public discussion noted earlier. Partly it may also reflect the fact that no country plays as important a role as the US in trade and FDI in services in general and a number of individual service industries in particular. As a result, the interest of other countries in a service-trade framework is less global and strong while, at the same time, there are fears that liberalization may create difficulties for domestic suppliers of services in some industries. Added to this must be the special importance of data services. (Except for the studies submitted by Belgium and the European Community, all of the 16 national studies on services prepared for GATT until the end of 1985 dealt separately with computer services; 13 of the 16 also dealt separately with telecommunications.) The interest situation here, as has been examined in chapter III, is mixed at best. To the extent that these factors play a role, they are not conducive to speedy negotiations and the adoption of a comprehensive and binding agreement, but rather to voluntary understandings on individual industries.

Countries for which these factors should balance the considerations of self-interest mentioned earlier may, however, not necessarily express their disagreement openly and strongly, given the intense interest shown by the US in this matter and the possible costs that may be associated with opposition, such as the possibility that the US may intensify bilateral negotiations. At the same time, such countries may not be too concerned about the reluctance of some developing countries to enter into services negotiations and about the delays that this may cause.

2. The position of the developing countries

Given their interest situation, the developing countries naturally insist that the focus of any international trade discussions ought to be on trade in goods because, for them, trade in goods is considerably more important than trade in services. In fact, the likelihood that trade in agricultural products will be covered by the negotiations is probably one of the single most important agenda items from the point of view of many developing countries. Furthermore, they point out that the 1982 GATT Ministerial Meeting had adopted a work program[31] which contained a wide range of commitments in such areas as safeguards, quantitative restrictions and other non-tariff measures, agriculture, tropical products, and textile and clothing. For the developing countries, the main task of the international trading community is precisely the completion of this work program even before a new round of negotiations begins or any new issues (such as services) are considered. The developing countries in GATT pointed out during a meeting of the GATT Council in May 1984: "Unless and until the work programme is fully implemented . . . , any initiative such as a new round of negotiations in GATT would be lacking in credibility and devoid of relevance particularly for developing countries".[32]

This approach was maintained during the November 1984 meeting of the contracting parties, during which the developing countries held that the US was jeopardizing a new round of GATT negotiations by sidetracking the organization's work toward the service area and it was further confirmed during the various rounds of discussions during 1985. It received important support from a report prepared on request of the Director-General of GATT by seven eminent persons on problems facing the international trading system. Among the fifteen "proposals for action" recommended by the group, one read: "Governments should be ready to examine ways and means of expanding trade in services, and to explore whether multilateral rules can appropriately be devised for this sector"; however, the group coupled this proposal with the observation that "we are also convinced that there will be no progress on services without substantial progress on trade in goods. There is no future for an effort to involve GATT in services while neglecting its central and essential responsibilities. An attempt to extend a rule-based approach to new areas of economic relations while permitting the rules for trade in goods to continue to decay would lack credibility".[33]

The basic position of the developing countries, as it stood at the beginning of 1986, is outlined in the following paragraphs.[34]

The new round in general. The developing countries recognize that they have a high stake in the preservation of the multilateral trading system. For them, the system's fundamental objective ought to be to remove the asymmetry in trade relations between developed and developing countries and to bring about genuine trade liberalization. In this view, if the developed countries were to comply with their undertakings, most notably those made during the 1982 Ministerial Meeting, an important step would be made toward this objective. In spite of lack of progress in the implementation of these undertakings, and responding to the pressures exercised by the developed countries, the developing countries are prepared to participate in a new GATT round, but it would have to be confined to trade in goods only. Such a round should cover manufactured and semi-processed goods, natural-resource products, and agriculture; liberalization in the trade of agricultural products, most notably, requires special attention. The negotiations ought furthermore to deal with all tariff and non-tariff barriers. Their concrete objectives ought to be to improve significantly the access of developing countries to the markets of developed countries in order to expand their capacity to absorb higher levels of imports from the developed countries and to ensure effective protection and enforcement of the rights of the developing countries under the multilateral trading regime.

Trade in goods. For the developing countries the emphasis of the new round is clearly meant to be on trade in goods. In response to the lack of action in areas long demanding it, the developing countries seek, in addition, agreement on the following actions *before* specific negotiations begin:

- A firm and credible commitment (supported by appropriate legislative sanctions where necessary) to *stop and reverse protectionism (stand-still and roll-back)*;
- A categorical and unconditional commitment by the importing countries to the full application of the rules and principles of the GATT in the area of textiles and clothing trade and hence a *recognition of the unsuitability of the Multi-Fibre Arrangement* as an instrument for the regulation of international trade in this area;
- The establishment of a short timetable for *liberalization in the area of tropical products*;

- Strict *observance of GATT discipline on the use of subsidies*, especially in the use of export subsidies for products which compete with the exports of developing countries;
- Utmost *restraint in the use of countervailing and anti-dumping procedures* against imports from developing countries;
- *Adoption of special rules for a more favorable treatment of developing countries*, including a confirmation of earlier commitments by developed countries not to expect (and, therefore, not to seek) reciprocity; and
- *Recognition of the linkage between development, trade, money, and finance* and, therefore, the commencement of a parallel process in appropriate fora to review and reform the international financial system and to examine in GATT the effects of exchange-rate fluctuation on international trade.

Whether these actions (or some of them) will be taken before the new round begins remains to be seen. Given the strong opposition of the developed countries against any preconditions and prior commitments for the beginning of the negotiations, it is more likely that most of the topics addressed in these points will become part of the agenda for the new round.

Trade in services. The position of the developing countries concerning the inclusion of trade in services in the new GATT round is determined, first of all, by their fear that the inclusion of any new issue in the negotiations would take attention away from what is most important to them, namely trade in goods. They have seen themselves confirmed in this view because, on the one hand, little progress has been made in the implementation of the (goods-oriented) 1982 Ministerial Meeting work program while, on the other hand, considerable attention has been paid to services. Even more, developing countries fear that a linkage is being made between progress in goods-related issues of interest to them and services-related issues of interest to other countries, and that such a linkage could be utilized to extract concessions from developing countries in the service area in exchange for progress in the goods area. Thus, the developing countries feel that new themes alien to the jurisdictional competence of GATT are being systematically promoted at the expense of the central area of responsibility of GATT, and that this puts them into a disadvantageous bargaining position.

The fear of the developing countries that the inclusion of new themes would direct GATT's attention away from issues of priority interest to them is coupled with another strong and substantive concern: the fear that a liberal service-trade regime could effectively hinder the growth of indigenous service industries in developing countries, because international competition could be overwhelming in many instances. For many countries, this is undesirable in and of itself, given the importance of this sector for long-term growth. And this is considered to be all the more serious because a number of developing countries are building service industries which, however, still require government support and participation, protection and preferences before they are internationally competitive. Infant-industry considerations, in other words, play an important role in the opposition of a number of developing countries as regards the establishment of a liberal service regime.[35]

In addition, the creation of such a regime could mean that domestic policies would have to be adapted to it (i.e., would have to be liberalized) and, in fact, would become, to a certain extent, subject to review by an international organization.

This could mean that governments could lose control over certain services (e.g., banking) which are crucial instruments for the promotion of economic development and the implementation of wider economic policies. In other words, services are not only seen purely from a commerical angle but rather as instruments which play a central role in promoting national development.

These concerns are exacerbated by the fear that a liberal regime, especially if it has a FDI component, could lead to a domination of the domestic service sector by TNCs. In fact, given the nature of services, some developing countries fear that the real argument is not about trade in services but rather about FDI in services and, particularly, about the right of establishment.[36] The inclusion of any FDI matters into the GATT framework is strongly resisted by the developing countries.

In addition, developing countries fear that their basic bargaining situation would be reversed. The argument has already been outlined in the context of the OECD TDF Declaration: at the present time, developing countries are free—within the limits of their international obligations—to protect and stimulate their service industries as they see fit. The moment they subscribe to a GATT-type regime, this freedom is taken from them: they would not be permitted to undertake certain steps and, if they do, they would have to justify them internationally. In fact (as already indicated), a GATT regime (especially one in which dispute-settlement proceedures are strengthened) could make certain national service legislation subject to international review and potential retaliation.

For all these reasons, a GATT involvement in services is perceived by developing countries as a basic threat to their economic interest and their development objectives. Many of them fear that agreeing to having GATT cover services could mean a permanently inferior position for their service industries in the emerging international service economy. (This applies, of course, primarily to those developing countries that could establish competitive service industries.) Furthermore, apart from the general assertion that a liberalization of trade in services is beneficial to world economic growth, it has not yet been shown to the satisfaction of the developing countries how they would benefit from it, apart from the general point that because many services are important intermediary inputs, they are crucial for the development process. In sum, most developing countries feel that, under the present circumstances, they have little to gain from establishing a liberal international service regime.

These fears have led a group of developing countries to oppose vehemently the consideration of trade (let alone FDI) in services by GATT. This opposition extends to all services and, therefore, includes data services as well. However, except for some work in SELA, and in a few individual countries, virtually the entire Third World has to date paid little attention to trade and FDI in data services.

Opposition is being voiced mainly on the following grounds. One, as already indicated, is that a work program exists and that it ought to be implemented before any other matter can be taken up. A forceful intervention by the representative of Brazil during the November 1984 meeting of the GATT contracting parties makes this point:

> we will be reluctant to lend our support to initiatives which do not inscribe themselves in the context of the full implementation of the 1982 work programme,

or which either focus disproportionately on themes of doubtful relevance to the GATT system or are alien to the specific interests of a group of Contracting Parties. . . . The attempts we have seen during our present session to place the complete Ministerial work programme at hostage to progress on items of questionable priority to whole segments of GATT membership are, in our view, entirely out of proportion.[37]

A second argument concerns the competence of GATT to deal with service issues. It is based both on the origin and actual coverage of GATT. As regards the latter, it has already been pointed out that the General Agreement does (with minor exceptions) address goods only. As regards the origin of the GATT, the resolution of the UN Economic and Social Council which convened the International Conference on Trade and Employment did so "for the purpose of promoting the expansion of production, exchange and consumption of goods";[38] the resolution did not mention services. It was this Conference which led to the Havana Charter for an International Trade Organisation and the GATT as an interim arrangement. Accordingly, developing countries have held that GATT is simply not competent to deal with services. This was, for instance, clearly expressed in the statement of the representative of India during the Special Session of GATT Contracting Parties in September/October 1985:

> It is the firm view of my Government that GATT has competence only in matters of trade in goods. . . . Services are a different specie. The treaty of GATT cannot be stretched to authorize consideration of or to deal with matters concerning services beyond its mandate. It is not a matter of procedure, but of law. It is not a question of amending one or the other article within the basic structure of GATT for a better implementation or better realization of the objectives. Extension of the treaty to another specie outside its framework can be only through plenipotentiary action or unanimous agreement of the Contracting Parties. We would like to place on record this fundamental legal aspect.[39]

This point has also been made on a number of occasions by various groups of developing countries. Thus, the Heads of State or Government of Non-Aligned Countries noted, at their seventh summit conference in New Delhi in March 1983: "The developing countries had exercised commendable vigilance and caution in countering the tendency to introduce subjects outside GATT's competence" into the 1982 GATT Ministerial Meeting.[40] Similarly, the Fifth Ministerial Meeting of the Group of 77 in Buenos Aires in March-April 1983 ". . . reaffirmed that the competence of GATT should be limited to the areas contained in the General Agreement and not be extended to the field of services".[41] And a high-level meeting of Latin American countries confirmed in 1984 that GATT "was conceived for the sole purpose of regulating the goods trade and, therefore, has no competence in the area of services".[42] This opinion was endorsed by the Tenth Regular Meeting of the Latin American Council (an organization which brings together representatives from almost all countries of the Latin American region) which declared categorically "that the GATT forum is exclusively restricted to regulating merchandise trade and, therefore, has no competence in the area of services."[43]

A related argument is that, in any event, the approach and concepts of GATT as regards goods cannot be simply transplanted to services. The principal reason is that, on the one hand, the GATT approach and concepts were developed for goods, while, on the other hand, the nature and characteristics of services are different from those of goods. Not only does the service sector cover a widely disparate set of activities but, most important, many services require for their delivery to other markets the establishment of foreign affiliates and/or the movement of people. And these are issues that lie far outside the trade domain. Thus, if an international regime for trade in services were to be created, it would require a new beginning—conceptually as well as politically and organizationally.

But such a new beginning, developing countries hold, is not necessary because a number of fully competent forums exist already which deal with the international aspects of particular services; and they do so not only (in most cases) with a larger membership than GATT, but also in the specific context and framework appropriate to these services. Examples are the International Telecommunication Union as regards telecommunication services; the World Intellectual Property Organization as regards intellectual property (including software); UNCTAD as regards shipping, transfer of technology and perhaps insurance; the International Civil Aviation Organization and the International Air Transport Association as regards air services; the International Maritime Organization regarding maritime services; the IMF as regards certain financial services; the World Tourism Organization as regards tourism; and the United Nations Commission on Transnational Corporations as regards FDI in services. Since each one of these organizations is fully competent in its own field and has accumulated considerable experience, it is not necessary to begin a new effort in GATT. And if the existing regimes are not satisfactory, they ought to be improved in the competent bodies.

A final set of considerations influencing the position of the developing countries deserves mention. Many developing countries are not members of GATT, and the cohesiveness of the Group of 77—the Third World's principal organ for articulating and promoting its collective economic interest in international organizations[11]—is not very high in GATT. Furthermore, international cooperation in development matters was at a low level during the mid-1980s and the bargaining position of the developing countries as a group was relatively weak during that period. All these factors complicate negotiations in GATT and do not augur well for a favorable negotiating outcome for the developing countries; rather, they suggest a preference for delaying negotiations and the choice of a different forum.

The developed countries agree that work in the framework of the 1982 work program should continue, but they feel that, at this stage, any substantial progress is not likely to occur outside formal negotiations in the context of a new round. As to the question of GATT's competence in the area of services, the developed countries do not disagree with the point that GATT had been established to deal with goods trade (although it has been argued that the Preamble of the General Agreement, read with its Article XXV, permits the contracting parties to deal with any issue); in fact, the US took this position at one point as well.[45] Rather, they argue that failure by GATT to tackle issues crucial for international trade and economic adjustment today and in the future would condemn the organization to increasing irrelevance and ultimate obsolescence—a fate all countries presumably wish to avoid. Their point is, therefore, that GATT needs to adjust to today's economic realities; it must evolve, if it wishes to maintain its relevance. Naturally, this will also involve conceptual adaptation and development. Since the GATT has unquestionably the greatest experience in trade matters and has a dispute-settlement procedure which permits the enforcement of agreements reached in its context, it is seen to offer the best prospects for the elaboration of a broad framework for trade in services in general. Ultimately it probably does not matter very much what GATT's practice has been over the years and whether, legally, GATT can take up services. What does matter is whether the interests of contracting parties are served by the organization. If not, countries are likely to lose interest in it and search for alternatives.

It remains to be seen how long the opposition of the developing countries is maintained and what changes it can bring about. In maintaining its opposition, the group of developing countries has the additional problem of preserving its unity—not a mean task considering that there are about 60 developing countries in GATT and nearly 130 in the Group of 77. Until the end of 1985, this unity has largely been preserved, but only at a very general level and in the sense that no developing country openly supported the inclusion of services in the next GATT round. Brazil and India, especially supported by Argentina, Egypt and Yugoslavia, took a leadership role. The opposition of the developing countries was most clearly expressed in a statement made in June 1985 by India on behalf of itself and 23 other developing countries in preparation of the July 1985 meeting of the GATT Council of Representatives. However, not even the majority of the developing countries in GATT supported this statement. Before that meeting, furthermore, the ASEAN countries (Indonesia, Malaysia, Philippines, Singapore, and Thailand) circulated a separate communication in which they welcomed the launching of the new round and called for expeditious preparations—a position much more forthcoming than that expressed by the group of 24 developing countries. The developing countries were, therefore, no longer united by mid-1985. Even within the Latin American region, the leading opponents had to compromise: as the resolution on services adopted by the December 1985 Eleventh Regular Meeting of the Latin American Council shows, the focus had shifted from opposition to the new round to an appeal that any international discussion of services must seek to safeguard the economic development goals of the developing countries.[46]

Thus, under the over-arching commonality of interests outlined earlier, the concrete interest situations of individual countries differ. Some—like Brazil, India, Argentina, Egypt, Yugoslavia—have a considerable potential for developing a wide range of service industries (if they have not already done so, e.g., in certain engineering and software services); they may, therefore, be interested in protecting their infant service industries against the competition a liberal regime would imply. (Brazil's position, in particular, appears to be strongly influenced by the pressures it experienced because of its informatics law.) Others may not have the preconditions (or the desire) to establish viable service industries; for them, agreement to a service regime may simply be a bargaining chip to achieve objectives related to trade in goods. At the same time, a number of them (e.g., African countries) are not interested in a continuing confrontation with developed countries in a matter in which they have no primary interest and which costs them only political capital. Others again—perhaps some of the ASEAN countries led by Singapore—may be in a mixed-interest situation; some of them may wish to have multilateral rules for certain services in which they are internationally competitive, but not for others. Yet others may be mostly interested in the data-service aspect of the entire discussion, because of the impact of these services on economic development in general. For some of these countries, therefore, a sectoral as opposed to an umbrella approach may be more interesting. These differences in concrete interests make it difficult to maintain the unity of the developing countries against a movement toward meaningful negotiations on services, especially if the developed countries continue to exercise a high level of pressure or if they should begin with negotiations on their own, inviting those developing countries that are interested to join them. In any event, a large middle ground seemed to have emerged among developing countries during 1985 which is ready to discuss services, with only an influential minority—consisting primarily of Argentina, Brazil, Egypt, India and Yugoslavia—remaining in strong opposition. Some developing countries (e.g., Singapore, South Korea and Uruguay, all countries with a relatively strong service sector) may in fact be more interested in such talks than some of the developed countries (e.g., Australia and New Zealand, countries much more interested in raw materials trade). This shift in opinion is underlined by the fact that the US had no major difficulty in obtaining the required majority of 46 countries to convene a special session of the GATT contracting parties in September 1985 to break the deadlock in the preparations of the new round. At the same time, this does not meant that all the developing countries that supported the US quest for a special session would also support the specific proposals this country has for the service area (and especially the extent to which FDI should be included)—it just means that these countries are prepared to discuss, in a manner still to be determined, services in the framework of GATT.

It is clear that the different views on services have put considerable strain on GATT and international negotiations on trade in general. For instance, during the November 1984 meeting of the GATT contracting parties it took (reportedly) a postponement of the review of the organizations' 1985 budget until after the adoption of the work program to ensure that services were included in that program—a highly unusual occurrence in GATT.[47] And in 1985, the US asked for (and obtained) a special session of the GATT contracting parties to break the deadlock on the new round and especially the service issue—the first time that a special session was held in GATT's history on the insistence of a member country. In fact, fears were being voiced that if GATT would not be able to deal with services, the role of the organization as the principal world trade body would be in jeopardy. As it appeared at the beginning of 1986, however, a compromise was likely to be worked out—a matter dealt with in the next section.

3. The preparatory process

The preceding two sections described the principal positions bearing on the new GATT round and especially the inclusion of services in it. Naturally, these are initial positions which are likely to be modified in the process of agreeing on the modalities for the negotiations and during the negotiations themselves, although it is obvious that some countries or groups of countries are in a better position to pursue their objectives than others. The course of the negotiations between 1982 and the end of 1985, to be traced in this section, bears this out. When the US set out to build support for its initiative—and in spite of doubts among other developed countries and fierce opposition from developing countries—the issue was soon no longer *if* negotiations on services should take place but rather *when* they ought to begin and *how* they should be conducted.

Peripheral services discussions in GATT began during the Tokyo Round (1973 to 1979), for which the US Trade Act of 1974 provided the US administration, for the first time, with wide-ranging authority on trade in services.[48] Little was made of this authority, however, because the Tokyo Round (like all preceding negotiations of this kind) focused on trade in goods and because awareness of the importance of service trade was lacking.[49]

However, four of the codes on non-tariff barriers developed during the Tokyo Round—the Agreement on Technical Barriers to Trade (Standards Code), the Customs Valuation Agreement, the Subsidy Code, and the Agreement on Government Procurement—are relevant to services, although they were not formulated to apply to services traded independently of goods.[50] The Standards Code provides that standards, technical regulations and testing and certification systems should not create unnecessary obstacles to trade. While the rules formulated for this purpose are not applicable to services, the Code could, in principle, be extended to cover certain aspects of services, including data services (e.g., telecommunication standards and protocols). The Customs Valuation Agreement, which defines the customs valuation treatment of goods, also covers certain services associated with goods. The principles used to assess these services could, conceivably, be of use in valuing services, for instance, for tariff purposes. Similarly, the Subsidy Code covers certain services, although not service exports as such. Since subsidies can play an important role for countries desiring to strengthen their service industries, the proponents of an open international trading regime for services could attempt to extend this Code to subsidies for services. Finally, the Procurement Code, which applies to the procurement of products by the entities signatory to the Agreement, "includes services incidental to the supply of products if the value of this incidental service does not exceed that of the products themselves" (Art. I). However, the Code specifically requires (Art. IX) that possibilities should be explored "of expanding the coverage of the Agreement to include service contracts." In compliance with this provision, discussions were initiated in November 1983 to improve the procedural aspects of the Code, expand the number of entities which it covers and examine possibilities of including services. As regards the last of these objectives, a series of pilot studies has been initiated to analyze the feasibility of covering services. Not much progress has been made to date, among other reasons, no doubt, because government procurement is one of the most difficult avenues through which market access can be improved.

An expansion of these Codes in the direction indicated would certainly be a step in the direction of a liberal international trade regime for services, but it would be a piecemeal approach.[51] A comprehensive approach would be to amend GATT's Articles of Agreement or to adopt a separate service code. It is with such a comprehensive approach in mind that the US (after the matter had been discussed for some time in the OECD) tabled the question of the role of GATT in service trade during the preparations of the 1982 GATT Ministerial Meeting.[52]

The US initiative met with little enthusiasm or outright opposition, and the US did not achieve what it had sought to achieve, namely the beginning of a work program on services in GATT. The main resistance came from the developing countries, but a number of developed countries were not more than lukewarm at best. After intense discussion, the Ministerial Meeting recommended that each contracting party with an interest in services undertake pertinent national studies and invited an exchange of information on the issues involved. Furthermore, the contracting parties decided to consider at their autumn 1984 session whether any multilateral action in this area was "appropriate and desirable".[53]

One of the reasons why the US was not successful at that meeting was that other countries, including its OECD partners, were not yet prepared to support a service initiative in GATT. Accordingly, the US set out after the Ministerial Meeting to generate the high-level political commitment that was required to make progress in this field. Within a short period of time, it succeeded in obtaining such a commitment from most of its OECD partners. They agreed to a service program in GATT, among other reasons because many of them discovered that they were (in one service industry or in several) net exporters; in fact, the European Community appears to have played a mediating role with the developing countries, with a view to convincing them to find a modus vivendi.[54] This found its expression at the 1984 London summit of the seven major industrialized countries and the European Community, where the participating heads of states or government agreed "to press forward with the work on trade in services . . . and to consult partners in the GATT with a view to decisions on an early date on the possible objectives, arrangements and timing for a new negotiating round."[55] While no firm dates were given (as the US desired), it is clear that the US and other developed countries were pressing for a new round of GATT trade negotiations, perhaps to be launched as early as 1985 or 1986.[56] Furthermore, the US followed up the recommendation of the 1982 GATT Ministerial Meeting to undertake pertinent national studies on services and submitted, in December 1983, its national study to GATT. By the beginning of 1986, this example had been followed by 15 other developed countries—but by no developing country.[57] In addition, a number of informal exchanges of views took place in GATT in accordance with the decision of the Ministerial Meeting.

At the 26-30 November 1984 meeting of the GATT contracting parties, then, the US, generally supported by Japan and a number of Western European countries, made another strong effort to establish a formal mechanism *within* GATT to examine service issues. Specifically, the US suggested that a working party on services (the traditional vehicle to examine questions of interest to members of the organization) be established to exchange information on a wide range of issues; that the working party be assisted by the GATT secretariat which, for this purpose, should receive a broad mandate; that interested members and the secretariat submit their views to the next session of the contracting parties on whether any multilateral action on trade in services is appropriate and desirable; that more national studies be prepared; and that the chairperson of the contracting parties keep the GATT Council informed about the progress made under these arrangements. While the US recognized that services were a new issue, it held that the GATT framework had to be dynamic and flexible, if it wanted to continue to provide an effective framework for international trade and if it wanted to prevent individual members from turning to other means to pursue their trade objectives. The developing countries, on the other hand, acting in unity and led by Brazil and India, opposed this proposal. For the reasons outlined earlier, they maintained that services do not belong on GATT's agenda and that the matter should therefore not be pressed.

The "Agreed Conclusions" eventually reached at the November 1984 meeting read as follows:

The CONTRACTING PARTIES,
Noting:

that a number of contracting parties with an interest in services have undertaken and circulated national examinations of the issues in this sector, and that other such examinations are recommended,

and that the process of carrying out the Ministerial Decision highlights the complexity of the issues involved,

In pursuance of the 1982 Ministerial Decision on services,

Agree to the following arrangements within GATT:

1. That the Chairman of the CONTRACTING PARTIES will organize the exchange of information provided for in the Ministerial Decision on issues in the services sector, essentially on the basis of national examinations, which could refer to any considerations in the area of services which appear relevant to the contracting party concerned, and the compilation and distribution of such information based on as uniform a format as possible;

2. The GATT secretariat will provide the support necessary for this process;

3. The Chairman of the CONTRACTING PARTIES will keep the Council informed of the progress made and report to the CONTRACTING PARTIES;

4. The CONTRACTING PARTIES decide to review the results of these examinations, along with the information and comments provided by relevant international organizations, at their next regular session and to consider whether any multilateral action in these matters is appropriate and desirable.[58]

These Agreed Conclusions represented a breakthrough for those who wanted GATT to deal with services, although they were less than what the US had hoped to achieve. Most importantly, the Agreed Conclusions specifically stated that the arrangements regarding services are to be undertaken "within GATT." In other words, the basic objective of the US to bring the services discussion into the GATT framework had been realized—a major procedural and conceptual success, considering that the developing countries had strongly argued that services do not belong into the GATT framework. In a sense, the remaining points of the Agreed Conclusions flow from this. First, the chairperson of the contracting parties was called upon to organize *formal* exchanges of information on services (as opposed to the informal exchanges provided for by the 1982 Ministerial Meeting); although the establishment of a formal working party was not approved, meetings open to all contracting parties were organized for the purpose of these exchanges, and took place between January and November 1985.[59] Second, the GATT secretariat received a clear—even if limited—mandate (which it did not have from the 1982 meeting) to provide the support necessary for this process, i.e., to perform the normal functions of a secretariat for its governing body. The secretariat's mandate was limited because the chairperson of the contracting parties interpreted it to consist (apart from servicing and keeping records of meetings) solely of the elaboration of a common format for the preparation and distribution of the national studies and the preparation of a summary of these studies and of the issues raised in the exchange of information.[60] Except and unless specifically agreed upon, the secretariat could not undertake any additional tasks. Third, the chairperson of the contracting parties was called upon to report to the November 1985 regular session of the contracting parties about the progress made. At that session, the service issue was to be examined again and it was to be considered whether there should be multilateral negotiations on trade in services. In sum, services had, in principle, been brought into the GATT framework and a formal work program on the subject had begun, although the speed with which the service issue was dealt with was not what the US would have liked.

Nevertheless, the opposition of the developing countries continued. As the representative of Brazil observed during the November 1984 meeting:

> We feel it necessary to acknowledge that, while capable of following a consensus on the agreed conclusions on services, which clearly remains at the stage of implementation of paragraph 2 of the Ministerial Decision on this item, we believe nevertheless that consideration of this issue has not reached any degree of the maturity required before decisions can effectively be taken. We doubt, in fact, that our perception of this matter will reach the maturity required for the adoption of an international decision on services for many years to come.[61]

This resistance found its expression in a statement of the chairperson of the contracting parties made before the adoption of the Agreed Conclusions, that "Nothing in these agreed conclusions shall be interpreted as prejudicing the rights or positions of any contracting party in these matters nor as prejudging the consideration by the Contracting Parties of whether any multilateral action in these matters is appropriate and desirable."[62]

Pressures for a new round of GATT negotiations continued to mount after the November 1984 meeting of the GATT contracting parties. Thus, the OECD Council of Ministers agreed in April 1985 to propose to the GATT contracting parties that a preparatory meeting of senior officials should take place before the end of the summer of 1985 to reach a broad consensus on the subjects and modalities for the new GATT round. In addition, OECD countries agreed that the round "should begin as soon as possible (some felt this should be in early 1986)."[63] (France, apparently with some support from Italy and Greece, ostensibly sought parallel negotiations on the international monetary system, and, without agreement on this issue, prevented full consensus on an early 1986 date.) Although the OECD countries considered the active participation of "a significant number of developed and developing countries" in such negotiations "essential",[64] this formulation seemed to suggest that the participation of *all* these countries was not a precondition for negotiations to commence. Less than one month later, the quest for a new GATT round was continued at the May 1985 Bonn summit of the seven major industrialized countries and the European Community. The discussions had narrowed down to the specific question of whether a date should be fixed for the launching of the round. The US, supported by most of the other countries, pressed for the explicit setting of an early date, preferably early 1986, to stem mounting protectionist sentiment in Congress; in fact, the US indicated that if multilateral negotiations were not possible, it would have to resort to bilateral discussions. France, on the other hand, insisted for the reasons mentioned earlier that the new round had to be prepared carefully, even if that meant a delay in its beginning. In addition, France, along with other countries, wanted to ensure that the developing countries participated fully in negotiations.[65] Because of France's objection, and in spite of intense discussions, the meeting failed to set a date to start the new trade round. Instead, the heads of state or government resolved to "strongly endorse the agreement reached by the OECD Ministerial Council that a new GATT round should begin as soon as possible"; in what the US regarded as an improvement of the OECD language, the Declaration then continued that "most" of the countries supported the effort, as opposed to the "some" in the OECD text.[66] As in the OECD text, the summit also called for a GATT preparatory meeting of senior officials before the end of the summer of 1985 and the active participation of a significant number of developed and developing countries.

The outlines of a compromise began to emerge during an informal meeting of 20 trade and finance ministers in Stockholm in June 1985. At that meeting, Brazil made the proposal of twin-track negotiations during which those on trade in services would be conducted separately from, but parallel with, those on trade in goods. Later, however, this proposal was clarified to mean that there should be no formal links and trade-offs between the negotiations and that it would be understood from the outset that GATT rules would not apply to the talks on services.[67] While these conditions were unacceptable to the US and, for that matter, to the developed countries in general, a formula had been introduced in the discussions which offered possibilities of a compromise.

The discussions reached a new climax during the meeting of the GATT Council of Representatives, 17 to 18 July 1985. By that time, it had come to be accepted by the developing countries that a new GATT round would take place. The only crucial outstanding issues concerned its date and scope. The focus of the Council was therefore on procedural matters. The European Community proposed a meeting of senior officials of GATT contracting parties in September 1985 to discuss the preparations of the new round. Implicitly, this proposal (which was also supported by a number of developing countries) would have permitted discussions on services as well. Brazil, on the other hand, proposed a clear separation of future GATT talks. Accordingly, it supported a September 1985 meeting of senior officials dealing with trade in goods, and it considered the possibility of a similar meeting in October of that year to deal with trade in services.[68] In spite of intense late-night negotiations it was, however, not possible to reach agreement. Brazil (supported most importantly by India, Argentina, Egypt, and Yugoslavia) insisted that the preparatory process for the new round could only be initiated if prior agreement was reached that talks about trade in services would be kept separate from the new round of negotiations about trade in goods. The Council meeting was suspended without having resolved the issue.

This continuing opposition and the insistence of the countries led by Brazil on certain preconditions before actual discussions could begin, prompted the US to take dramatic action: it announced that it would request a special session of the GATT contracting parties for September 1985 to break the deadlock. It was the first time in GATT's history that this mechanism had been used on the insistence of a member country and it was a break with GATT tradition, which requires consensus. The US move was quickly supported by the European Community, Canada and Japan. Over the following weeks, 65 contracting parties agreed to the special session—19 more than were required to convene it.[69]

The special session of the GATT contracting parties took place 30 September to 2 October 1985. Its task was to examine "the subject matter and modalities of a proposed new round of multilateral trade negotiations in the light of the

GATT Work Programme and priorities for the 1980s as contained in the Ministerial Declaration of 1982 and the continuing consideration of changes in the trading environment so as to ensure that the GATT is responsive to these changes."[70] The unprecedented US action, combined with intensive consultations prior to the session and continuing pressure on the developing countries during the session, resulted in a formal agreement by consensus to initiate the preparatory process for the new round and, to further this process, to establish a group of senior officials which would examine the subjects to be negotiated and the working methods to be used. The senior officials, in turn, were to report to the regular November 1985 session of the contracting parties, at which occasion a decision was to be taken on the establishment of a formal Preparatory Committee which would lay the basis for the launching of the new round. It was understood that the work of the senior officials would not prejudice GATT's ongoing work on the 1982 Work Program and that it would also not prejudice the ongoing work on services. The senior officials group began its work in a first session between 14 and 16 October 1985 at which virtually all GATT members took part; it met again 22 to 23 October and 30 October to 1 November 1985.

The full text of the agreement of the special session reads as follows:
The Contracting Parties agreed as follows:

- a preparatory process on the proposed new round of multilateral trade negotiations has now been initiated;
- in order to further this process, a group of senior officials, open to all contracting parties, is established; it will meet for the first time on 14 October;
- this group will report to the Contracting Parties at their November session;
- at that session of the Contracting Parties, a decision will be taken on the establishment of a Preparatory Committee to prepare the basis for the launching of a new round.

It is understood that:

- the senior officials' group will examine the subject matter and modalities of the proposed negotiations in the light of the GATT Work Programme and priorities of the 1980s as contained in the Ministerial Declaration of 1982 and the continuing consideration of changes in the trading environment so as to ensure that the GATT is responsive to these changes;
- the work of the senior officials' group will not prejudice the ongoing work of the GATT in terms of the 1982 Work Programme, and will not prejudice the work on services in terms of the 1982 and 1984 decisions and agreed conclusions of the Contracting Parties; the November session will also receive reports on this ongoing work.[71]

Thus, the special session brought the procedural breakthrough sought by the developed countries, although, formally speaking, nothing had been settled as far as the substance of the negotiations was concerned. However, the session marked the beginning of a speedy preparatory process for the new round and, in that sense, gave the starting signal for the round itself. Furthermore, given the facts that the session took place upon the request of the US and that, for the US, there could be no new round without services it was clear, for all intents and purposes, that services would be discussed under the aegis of GATT. It only remained to be settled how this would be done and when the actual negotiations would begin.

The latter point may have been resolved during the regular annual session of the GATT contracting parties, which took place 25 to 28 November 1985. In the weeks preceding this session, difficulties had continued in the group of senior officials regarding the treatment of services. At the same time, the US maintained its pressure. It indicated, for instance, that it was prepared to break with the GATT tradition of consensus and would seek a vote at the annual session if countries insisted on imposing conditions on the establishment of the Preparatory Committee and on the start of negotiations. Furthermore, the US Trade Representative warned in November 1985 in a statement in a Senate Finance Committee hearing that "we are prepared to use alternative ways of bringing about a more free and open trading system"; he continued: "We could, for example, convene a conference here in Washington to negotiate on trade matters of interest to the participants only. Those attending would be countries which share our objectives of seeing trade disciplines and codes of conduct established in such areas as services, intellectual property and other mutually-agreed subject matters. Nonparticipants *would not* enjoy any of the benefits of such international agreements."[72] At the session itself, the following decision was taken by consensus:

The Contracting Parties decide that:

1. The Preparatory Committee is established to determine the objectives, subject matter, modalities for and participation in the multilateral trade negotiations, taking into account the elements of the 1982 Ministerial Work Programme and the views expressed in the Group of Senior Officials;
2. The Preparatory Committee is open to any contracting party or country which has acceded provisionally to the GATT;
3. The Preparatory Committee will prepare by mid-July 1986 recommendations for the programme of negotiations for adoption at a Ministerial Meeting to be held in September 1986.[73]

At the same time, the following decision was reached on the question of GATT's work related to trade in services:

The Contracting Parties,

In pursuance of the 1982 Ministerial Decision on Services, and

In accordance with the agreed conclusions adopted by the Contracting Parties on 30 November 1984,

Decide to invite contracting parties to continue the exchange of information undertaken in pursuance of the agreed conclusions of 30 November 1984, and to prepare recommendations for consideration by the Contracting Parties at their next session.[74]

Thus, the Preparatory Committee was established—and the formal preparatory process set into motion—without any preconditions as regards the objectives of the round, the scope of its negotiations, or the manner in which the negotiations should be conducted. In particular, the precondition of the developing countries for a standstill and roll-back of protectionist measures was dropped. These matters, as well as those relating to safeguards and the treatment of developing countries, will be among the principal issues to be considered by the Preparatory Committee.[75] The speed desired particularly by the US is reflected in the decision thàt the Preparatory Committee would begin meeting in January 1986 and have a report ready by mid-July of the same year. The launching of the round itself could then be decided by a ministerial meeting which was scheduled to take place in Punta del Este (Uruguay) in mid-September 1986.

The principal compromise that made the agreement on this time-table possible involved, not surprisingly, the treatment of services. Essentially, the twin-track approach introduced by Brazil earlier that year had become, at least for the time being, the accepted approach. Apart from the Preparatory Committee, a separate committee was to continue to examine services and also prepare recommendations for the contracting parties. This means that services can continue to be considered separately, an approach which takes into account the views of the developing countries. This structure remains in place until the launching of the round itself, whose structure still has to be determined.

On the other hand, the decision taken by the contracting parties in November 1985 was again a merely procedural one. No decision on *what* precisely ought to be the subject of negotiations had been taken at that time. Proposals in that respect were to be made by the Preparatory Committee. It is very likely, therefore, that the discussions on how to deal with services will continue in the framework at the Preparatory Committee. In addition, the controversy surrounding services had deflected attention from the fact that a number of other issues proposed for the new round are very controversial as well. Among them are most notably trade in agricultural products, FDI-related issues, non-tariff trade barriers, counterfeit goods, and intellectual property rights. To draw up an agenda under these circumstances is not an easy task—especially considering the short time the Committee has at its disposal.

It may well be that the twin-track approach of the preparatory process will be adopted for the round itself. If so, it may reflect no more than the procedural convenience of having two quasi sub-committees beginning and ending their work simultaneously under the same umbrella and as an integral part of the same process. A variation of this approach would be to leave it open whether the results of the negotiations would be implemented by GATT or be given effect in some other manner. It is also conceivable that services would be negotiated in a separate diplomatic conference, an approach favored by some developing countries; if this were to occur, it is further conceivable that these negotiations would not only be serviced by the GATT secretariat but also, for instance, by the UNCTAD secretariat. Since this approach would, however, diffuse GATT's role considerably, it is very likely to encounter strong opposition from developed countries. Be that as it may, it is clear that a formula has to be found which accommodates both the resistance of developing countries to have the GATT framework applied to services, and the insistence of the developed countries to have service-trade matters negotiated in GATT. Indications are that a face-saving formula will be found which permits GATT to negotiate a framework for trade in services. It would not be surprising if this matter were only to be resolved in dramatic final moments of the preparatory process, and if it were to be facilitated by a number of concessions on the part of developed countries (e.g., standstill, the inclusions of agriculture in the round and perhaps even a commitment to phase out voluntary export restraint agreements).

Whatever the formula, it is not likely that the US (and, for that matter, other developed contries) will agree to any package reached in the goods area before agreement has been reached on services. Such a linkage need not be formally established—it is sufficient that all participating parties are aware of its existence.

At the end of 1985 the stage was set for the eighth round of multilateral trade negotiations under the aegis of GATT. It may well become a round which extends GATT's influence into a number of new subject areas. It would be launched because all countries can expect a number of benefits from it. But ultimately it was the determination of the US and the benefits which this country expected from the new round which were largely responsible for setting the preparatory process in motion and determining the direction which it took.

4. Negotiations on services

The launching of a new round does not necessarily mean that actual negotiations begin immediately or progress rapidly, particularly if the resistance of key developing countries does not diminish. For one, most countries (including developed ones) need time to work out the implications of a liberal framework for international transactions in services for their own economies, to define their precise interests in this regard, and to identify trade-offs they may be willing to consider. Second, the scope of the service negotiations has to be worked out. Should they focus just on trade (inter- and intra-firm trade, intermediate products, or only final outputs?) or also on FDI? The US maintains that the framework should cover only the trade aspect of services. But, as discussed earlier, the interrelationships between service trade and (service) FDI are becoming increasingly important and, except for FDI-related trade, GATT has clearly no competence in FDI matters as such. (The fact that FDI-related trade is being discussed in GATT is an indication of the blurring of the boundaries between trade and FDI discussed in chapter I.)

A perhaps even thornier issue concerns the international migration of labor, or at least the entry or temporary visits of professional personnel. For many service industries, the use of expatriate professional personnel (managers, technical experts, software specialists, salespersons) is critically important. It becomes even more so, to the extent that the negotiations cover right of presence and FDI issues. The sale of services through the movement of persons at the professional level is, furthermore, of particular importance for TNCs. But in some categories it could also be of interest to developing countries. The sale of services through the movement of other persons (e.g., hospital personnel, construction workers) may be of particular importance for developing countries and could, indeed, be one of the areas in which these countries could gain considerably from a liberal service regime.The US believes that since it would be impossible to reach a general agreement permitting the free flow of persons in a general way, this matter ought to be left to bilateral negotiations.[76] In fact, the 1984 model US bilateral investment treaty contains a sweeping clause specifying that "Companies . . . shall be permitted to engage top managerial personnel of their choice, regardless of nationality."[77] Language along these lines was incorporated in a number of bilateral investment treaties signed by the US. The effect of this language is generalized to the extent that the host countries involved grant most-favored-nation treatment. From a balance-of-payments perspective, it is furthermore argued that categories under the "services" heading that relate to labor—and, for that matter, capital—should not be included in a framework for service trade because labor and capital are factors of production in both goods and services.

All this suggests that the new round would probably begin with intense discussions of the nature of services, their definition and measurement, boundaries to FDI, the role of services in development, the issues that are most relevant from an international point of view, and the services that could conceivably become subject of an international agreement. At the same time, an intensive research program would probably take place, e.g., further national service studies and the discussion of these studies. For the proponents of the trade-in-services negotiations, important objectives in this research program would probably include the compilation of a list of restrictions to service trade, the examination of the effect of these restrictions on trade, and the acceptance of the idea that the GATT framework can apply (or be made applicable) to service trade. Only then could actual negotiations commence which, if the last negotiating round is an indication, could require several years before they are concluded. As one observer summarized this approach: "first, a cease-fire; second, a determination of the why and how of service regulation; and third, a major negotiating round to minimize restraints."[78]

The negotiations themselves would, in all likelihood, be a gradual, step-by-step process, and one in which progress would be linked to roughly equivalent concessions by all involved. Even in the goods sector, it took seven rounds of tariff negotiations to achieve the current level of liberalization.One difficulty in dealing with service trade is that it may be rather difficult to measure the equivalence of concessions because of the inadequacy of the service-trade statistics discussed earlier and the fact that trade in services is normally not subject to tariffs; in the goods sector, trade flows and tariffs provided useful, even if rough, measuring rods. Perhaps more relevant, therefore, is the experience gained with the reduction of non-tariff barriers. Generally speaking, agreement could be reached on an increase of transparency as regards barriers to service trade. Transparency can be increased if governments notify each other (or a central institution) about the regulatory and administrative practices in the service sector which have an impact on international trade. (The Declaration on Trade in Services, annexed to the US-Israel Free Trade Agreement, foresees that the parties notify each other of restrictions.) Such notification could be given by the country originating such regulations or practices or by countries that consider themselves affected by them; the latter approach would require a mediation process through which the need for such barriers could be established and mutual agreement on existing barriers could be reached. These barriers could then become subject to negotiations. In its broadest sense, this approach could also include regulatory regimes. In other words, one could work toward roughly similar regulatory regimes and, in this manner, make competitive opportunities more similar as well. The US administration is laying the groundwork for this approach by emphasizing the need for transparency and deregulation.

To reach agreement on services in the framework of GATT is both harder and easier than reaching agreement on a Declaration on Transborder Data Flows in the framework of the OECD. It is more difficult because negotiations become more complex as the number of participants and the range of service industries increases and, indeed, other matters are considered as well. But it may also become easier to find trade-offs. Data services, for instance, become only one service and the dominating position that the US enjoys in them may be balanced by advantageous positions other countries have in other services (e.g., banking) and their need to support a relatively unrestricted data flow in the interest of these services. Mixed-interest situations, in other words, may facilitate agreement.

To a large extent, these considerations apply primarily to developed market economies and a few developing countries because not many developing countries have internationally competitive service industries or are interested in trade-offs between service industries (a country benefitting from tourism, for instance, may have only very limited objectives in these negotiations). For these countries, the same question must be asked that was raised in the context of the OECD Declaration on TDF: why should they give up the status quo for an agreement that ties their hands as regards the means they can use to build up their own service industries?

One answer is they may have no alternative. If developing countries—or, for that matter, other countries—should not agree to include services in a formal GATT round, the main service and capital-exporting countries could always fall back on the framework of the OECD (where negotiations are continuing in any case) or, alternatively, could assemble a group of interested (developed and developing) countries to negotiate a separate, plurilateral understanding. The latter alternative also exists if the topic is included in a formal GATT round but negotiations become dead-locked. Should this happen, the GATT-code approach may offer a solution since GATT codes bind only signatories.[79] Naturally, in this case those countries that do not participate have little opportunity to influence the outcome of any negotiations. Finally, countries could resort to bilateral negotiations along the lines outlined above. (The possibility of negotiating outside the GATT framework was raised by the US on several occasions.) In bilateral discussions, weak countries are normally at a considerable disadvantage, with the result that unbalanced and discriminatory rules could evolve. Conversely, a system based on multilaterally agreed rules provides a certain measure of restraint and insurance against arbitrary, discriminatory and unilateral action. But such a system normally also implies obligations and the sanctions associated with them. Thus, the advantages of a rule of law have to be weighted against the disadvantages of having to submit to the discipline of a particular framework. Considerations of this sort were, in fact, one of the principal reasons for which the Leutwiler Report recommended that governments should explore the possibility of multilateral rules for services: "We recommend this partly because of the obvious importance of the service sector, and partly because we fear that, if multilateral rules are not developed for services, discriminatory bilateral or regional rules will be developed instead."[80] There is, however, a balancing consideration to take into account: since one of the principal reasons for moving the discussions from the 24-member-countries OECD to the 90-member-countries GATT is to establish a *broad* multilateral framework (which is particularly important regarding TDF in TNCs, because a substantial part of FDI is located in developing countries), negotiations in the GATT context become less interesting as fewer developing (and socialist) countries participate in them. If the developed countries were not interested in including the developing countries in a service framework, they could simply concentrate their efforts on a strengthening of the relevant OECD instruments. It is precisely the interest of the developed countries to make the developing countries party to an agreement which gives the latter a certain bargaining leverage.

Another answer is that developing countries can find trade-offs outside the service sector. Reference has already been made to the fact that most developing countries are more interested in manufacturing trade than in service trade. The interest of developed countries in a broad multilateral framework for service trade could, therefore, be used as a bargaining lever to obtain concessions in manufacturing trade, especially in areas in which concessions are difficult to obtain in the present (goods) GATT framework. Such a strategy may encourage developed market economies not to agree to any further manufacturing-trade concessions at the present time, with the intention of trading these off against service-trade concessions on the part of developing countries—but this may happen in any case since the principal developed market economies see trade increasingly as trade in goods *and* services. In fact, developed countries may actively seek such trade-offs. Thus, it has been suggested that "Because few developing countries can realistically make major advances as exporters of services to developed country markets, the developed countries may have to adopt a policy of making concessions that favour goods exported from developing nations in return for reductions of NTBs to services exports from developed nations"; to illustrate this point, the authors of this quote continue: "Mexico, for example, might be willing to eliminate a restriction on the use of non-Mexican personnel for foreign accounting firms operating in Mexico in return for a reduction by the United States of the duty on winter vegetables. . . ."[81] In this situation, it may well be more advantageous for many countries to make a virtue out of a necessity and discuss such trade-offs in a multilateral forum rather than in bilateral negotiations in which smaller countries are typically in a weak bargaining position.

Trade-offs of this type could be particularly interesting if they were to be extended to trade in agricultural products, an area which has largely remained outside GATT so far, but which is of great importance to many developing countries. Here, the interests of a number of developing countries are actually parallel to those of the US, a fact—if the stakes of a service agreement are added— that may add pressure on the European Community and Japan to agree to a package that could contain important advantages for the developing countries (e.g., access to markets, reduction of quotas). Another area in which developing countries could benefit substantially from trade-offs of this sort concerns voluntary export restraint agreements, trade restrictions which have proliferated in recent years. In this case, the developing countries could very likely count on the support of Japan which has also been the victim of a number of these agreements.

Naturally, if trade-offs of this sort are being sought, every effort has to be made to ensure that the service framework that is then established does not foreclose options for the future as far as the development of indigenous service industries in developing countries is concerned. In addition, developing countries may have to pay special attention to any linkages between trade in services and FDI. Since, as discussed in chapter I, the governing principle of the international FDI regime is different from that of the trade regime, it may be to the advantage of the developing countries to keep discussions about trade in services separate from those of FDI in services—both for services in general and for data services in particular.

Regardless of what trade-offs are being considered, and regardless of which (if any) linkages are being made between trade and FDI, any multilateral framework that seeks the support of the developing countries must give special consideration to the weakness of the service sector in most of these countries. The present

GATT framework already recognizes (in Art. XVIII) that developing countries may need to take recourse to protective measures to promote their development. Given the state of services industries in most developing countries, it may be all the more important to permit the use of certain protective measures by developing countries in the service sector as part of a framework governing trade and FDI in services. (As far as data services are concerned, it may well be that some developed countries would insist on a measure of minimum protection as well.) Foremost here is the need to recognize infant-industry and performance-requirement considerations and the need not to expect or demand reciprocity, and, perhaps, not to insist on graduation. Without strong special considerations for developing countries in this respect, it is very difficult indeed to imagine how these countries could agree to a liberal multilateral framework for trade in services. In addition, special efforts—perhaps in the form of a separate program—could be made to strengthen the service infrastructure of developing countries. In this context, particular attention could be given to the improvement of telecommunication services, an objective shared by all countries.[82]

The discussions in GATT have set in motion a process which, in all probability, will lead to a multilateral framework for trade in services, be it in the form of binding rules or a voluntary code. The US wishes to reach an umbrella framework under which "ideally all sectors should be moving in the same basic direction,"[83] namely liberalization. Alternatively, it is also possible that sectoral agreements (i.e., agreements for specific service industries) will be the result. Finally, a combination of both approaches is also conceivable, namely a general agreement supplemented by sectoral agreements which adapt the general agreement to the specific characteristics of individual industries. (An analogy can perhaps be drawn here to GATT's Articles of Agreements which formed the framework for the specific Codes negotiated during the Tokyo Round.) As in the OECD, data services—either as a whole or any of the components distinguished by France in the context of the OECD TDF Declaration—will probably receive priority attention, precisely because of their role as core services. The elements of such a framework for data services, as conceived by the proponents of a liberal regime for trade and FDI in data services, have been spelled out in chapter III. It will be a framework which will apply to one of the most dynamic components of international trade. It will strongly influence how the informational infrastructure for trade in goods and services will develop. It will provide the rules of the road for the increased tradeability of certain services. It will define the conditions for the operations of transnational corporations. It will become an important parameter for domestic policies on data resources. And, finally, it will be the central part of a more general framework for the development of the service sector in general, the most important economic sector in most countries.

*　　*　　*

In 1981, an influential early actor in the service field made the following observations:

A problem area termed by many as the service issue of first priority, the sine qua non of a service agenda . . . is in the data transmission area, often characterized more broadly as *telematique*. . . . To ensure that the extraordinary ramifications of this issue are weighted, . . . it must be discussed in a setting offering ample perspective. There are several reasons. First, it must be brought to the forefront of the international agenda. A forum that enhances that likelihood must be chosen. Second, it needs to be considered from a vantage point that supersedes the concerns of the various sectoral interests involved. Finally, it should be framed in a trade policy context. However, the outcry of alarm over this issue has yet to produce one of these results.[84]

There has been no "outcry of alarm" since then. However, many voices have combined to become strong enough to contribute to a new round of GATT negotiations on whose agenda transborder data flows are likely to occupy a central place.

B. The United Nations system

The OECD, IBI and GATT all fall short of universality. Since it is in the interest of the major exporters of services and service FDI to have as broad a multilateral framework as possible and, in any event, since the principle of universality is considered crucial by developing countries, it is unavoidable that international transactions in data services will sooner or later be dealt with in a comprehensive manner in the UN system. The possible bodies for this purpose are UNCTAD, the International Telecommunication Union, UNESCO, and the United Nations Commission and Centre on Transnational Corporations.

1. The United Nations Conference on Trade and Development

In UNCTAD—which, to a certain extent, is regarded by developing countries as a counterweight to GATT—the discussion of data services is, as in GATT, embedded in the general services discussion. The UNCTAD secretariat has, however, recognized the role of data services as a core service, describing TDF as "a new, revolutionary force in the evolution of national economies."[85]

For the developing countries, UNCTAD is an attractive forum. It offers a framework for discussion and has, within the UN system, primary responsibility for trade issues. In fact, service issues have been on UNCTAD's agenda since the organization's inception in 1964. Moreover, UNCTAD is sympathetic to developing countries, approaches the subject from a development-oriented framework, and has universal membership. Furthermore, the Group of 77 is firmly established in UNCTAD and is accustomed to acting there in unity. Finally, the work program of the secretariat focuses on furthering the understanding of the role of services through the preparation of national studies and does not envisage the creation of a legal framework for service transactions. Hence, it does not raise issues such as liberalizing trade in services, and it excludes the FDI angle. For all these reasons, the 1983 Seventh Conference of Heads of State or Government of Non-Aligned Countries recommended that "UNCTAD should undertake an examination of the issues related to services, bearing in mind the need to safeguard the present and future interests of non-aligned and other developing countries,"[86] and the 1983 Fifth Ministerial Meeting of the Group of 77 suggested that UNCTAD undertake studies on services and formulate recommendations "with respect to establishing mechanisms for multilateral co-operation in the field of services which may be of benefit to the developing countries."[87] The Group of 77, through its Intergovernmental Follow-up and Co-ordination Committee on Economic Co-operation among Developing Countries, further underlined its desire in September 1984 that UNCTAD be the forum in which negotiations relating to trade in services ought to take place.[88]

For mostly the same reasons (except universality), most developed market economies do not regard UNCTAD as an attractive forum. Their preference lies with GATT, for the reasons outlined earlier.

UNCTAD has, in fact, a tradition of work on services (e.g., shipping transport, insurance); the Liner Convention,[89] adopted under UNCTAD's auspices, has been one of the concrete results of this work. In 1982, then, the Trade and Development Board decided that attention needed to be given to the service sector as a whole.[90] Supported in particular by the Fifth Ministerial Meeting of the Group of 77, this led eventually to a resolution adopted in 1983 by UNCTAD VI, in which one part (which was adopted against the sole negative vote of the US) provided that "the Secretary-General of UNCTAD will continue his studies of the issues involved [in services] and UNCTAD will, inter alia, consider the role of the services sector in the development process."[91] On the basis of this mandate, the Secretariat prepared a report[92] which dealt with a whole range of service issues within a development-oriented framework and submitted it to the twenty-ninth session of the Trade and Development Board in September 1984. At that session, which was meant to consider appropriate future work by UNCTAD on services, delegations regarded the report a suitable basis for future work on services and agreed that UNCTAD's efforts in this field should continue. However, a formal decision laying out a work program could not be adopted.

The principal reason was the fear of the developing countries that the decision, as it was formulated, would prejudice their position for the meeting of the GATT contracting parties two months later. In spite of their reservations regarding UNCTAD, the developed market economies were, however, willing, for two reasons, to agree to an UNCTAD work program on services. For one, it would build further momentum for work on services in general, especially by inducing the developing countries to prepare their own national studies (which, of course, could also be used in the GATT context where, until the end of 1985, only developed countries had submitted studies). This was certainly aided by the fact that the secretariat's work program did not aim at rules of the road for service trade and hence did not pose a challenge to service negotiations in GATT—the only forum, in the eyes of the US, in which actual negotiations should take place. Besides, it was recognized that UNCTAD is the appropriate forum to study the developmental impact of services. The second reason for which the developed countries were willing to support an UNCTAD work program was that they wished to secure the acceptance of the developing countries for work on services in GATT. The US had originally (i.e., at UNCTAD VI) been the one country opposed to work on services in UNCTAD because it felt that the resolution in question had dealt inadequately with the issue of complementarity between UNCTAD and GATT work on services, especially since the Group of 77 had insisted that GATT has no role regarding services. The US agreement to a work program in UNCTAD was, therefore, an offer for a bargain: US support for service work in UNCTAD would be exchanged for developing countries support for service work in GATT. The vehicle for this offer was the decision in which the Board was to give the mandate to the secretariat to undertake work on services: the developed market economies insisted that the resolution encourage not only work in UNCTAD, but also in other international institutions (i.e., including GATT). The Group of 77 opposed this language (precisely because it would have been an implicit acceptance of services work in GATT), even at the cost of blocking, at least for the moment, the formal beginning of service work in UNCTAD.

As it turned out, however, this resistance could not prevent the contracting parties from adopting, two months later, a service program in GATT. Not surprisingly, therefore, the spring 1985 meeting of the UNCTAD Trade and Development Board approved an UNCTAD work program on services as well which, if the work done so far is an indication, will pay special attention to TDF. Specifically, it was agreed that UNCTAD's work (in addition to the ongoing work on specific service industries) should encompass:

(a) consideration of the definitional aspects of services; (b) strengthening and refining the data base at the national, regional and international levels, together with methodological improvement in this field; (c) further in-depth studies of the role of services in the development process to enable countries to analyse the role of the services sector in their economies and its contribution to all aspects of the development process; (d) assisting, upon request, within available resources, interested member States in their analysis of the role of services in their economies.[93]

Pursuant to (d) above, UNCTAD begun, at the beginning of 1986, to collaborate with some 20 developing countries in the preparation of country examinations of the service sector. In addition, UNCTAD participated in the GATT exchange of information on services to explain its views on these matters.

2. The International Telecommunication Union

The International Telecommunication Union (ITU) plays a key role in the establishment of the technological infrastructure required for TDF, the technical standards that guide them and the rates that apply to them. The various protocols adopted by the Union, its format prescriptions for data networks, and the regulations for international leased lines for data transmission are particularly important.[94] In fact, most of the basic technical and operational aspects connected with the telecommunication side of the application of TDF are the subject of ITU texts of a regulatory, quasi-regulatory or standard-setting kind. The leading role is played here by the ITU's International Telegraph and Telephone Consultative Committee (CCITT), in whose deliberations the PTTs and the private sector play an important role. The CCITT conducts a good part of its technical work through study groups on such questions as data-communication networks, terminal equipment for telematic services, transmission systems, data telecommunication over the telephone network, and digital networks. Some of its special autonomous groups, moreover, deal with somewhat broader questions, such as economic and technical aspects of the choice of transmission systems and economic and social problems relating to telecommunication development. In 1983, these groups revised 330 recommendations and drafted 255 new ones.[95] At ITU's Plenipotentiary World Administrative Telegraph and Telephone Conference (the supreme organ of ITU) in Nairobi in late 1982, furthermore, a special voluntary program for technical co-operation, based on financial contributions and the provision of training services or any other form of technical assistance was established. Furthermore, through resolution 20 of the Nairobi Conference, the International Commission for World-wide Telecommunications Development (the "Maitland Commission") was created to examine the totality of actual and potential future relationships among countries in the field of technical co-operation and the transfer of resources in telecommunications.[96]

An effort that may deserve special attention is the implementation of resolution 10 adopted by the Nairobi Conference. Considering "that it is advisable to establish, to the extent necessary, a broad international regulatory framework for all existing and foreseen new telecommunication services" and "that the introduction and utilization of the new telecommunication services have given rise to a series of new problems relating to telecommunications", it was resolved that "a World Administrative Telegraph and Telephone Conference shall be convened immediately after the CCITT Plenary Assembly in 1988 to consider proposals for a new regulatory framework to cater for the new situation in the field of new telecommunication services."[97] The results of the work related to the implementation of this resolution may well become the governing technical regulatory framework for TDF and the increased tradeability of services.

The developed countries value the ITU for the technical work it does— work which becomes all the more important as new technological developments increase the volume of telecommunication traffic, broaden the range of telecommunication applications, and make it increasingly necessary to establish minimum common technical standards in the interest of compatibility of equipment and services. In addition, the developed countries value very much the direct and intense participation of the private sector in the standard-setting work of ITU's organs. While the latter factor is of little concern to developing countries, they too value the organization's technical work and technical assistance.

Although ITU's activities continue to focus on the technical aspects of TDF, it is possible that the organization's mandate could be expanded to cover new tasks. Thus, INTUG has suggested that the ITU consider "the broader issues arising from the impact of telecommunications on trade, commerce, education and the information flow necessary to sustain them."[98] For that purpose, INTUG proposed the establishment of a new consultative committee on international telecommunication policies within the ITU. The explicit introduction of economic and political aspects of the subject into ITU's work would, of course, lead to a certain politicization of the ITU—which need not, however, be detrimental to its work.

3. The United Nations Educational, Scientific and Cultural Organization

Although the United Nations Educational, Scientific and Cultural Organization (UNESCO) has not yet dealt directly with TDF, its convening (with IBI) of SPIN I, its technical assistance activities in informatics and communications and its interest in technology questions in general give it a natural interest in TDF. The subject is also attractive to UNESCO because some of its aspects (e.g., news transmission) can be related to the efforts to establish a New International Information Order (NIIO).[99] The tendency, particularly on the part of the US, to think of

TDF in connection with news transmission naturally provides an additional reason for the interest of UNESCO in the subject.

UNESCO is also involved in the TDF debate because the Universal Declaration of Human Rights, adopted in 1948 by the General Assembly of the United Nations, established the right to communicate and the principle of free flow of information, issues at the heart of UNESCO's work. Article 19 of the Declaration provides: "Everyone has the right to freedom of opinion and expression; this right includes freedom to hold opinions without interference and to seek, receive and impart information and ideas through any media and regardless of frontiers."[100] This Article is sometimes taken by proponents of a liberal framework for trade in data services as the basis of precisely such a framework.[101] While the Declaration may govern mass media and press-information flows, it is not at all clear that it also governs *economic* data flows, e.g., the sending of software packages via telecommunication lines. Obviously, this is a question of boundaries, and a very important one at that. The general tendency is clearly *not* to regard economic data flows as the type of flows which in the US would be covered by the First Amendment, but rather as flows which are more properly dealt with in a trade context.

The work of the Interim Intergovernmental Committee on the Intergovernmental Informatics Programme, established by UNESCO's 1983 General Conference, may also become of relevance. It held its first meeting in Paris from 13 to 16 November 1984.[102] Among other things, the Committee reviewed main trends in informatics and their implications for development, considered proposals on the contents and possible lines of the Committee's action in the immediate future, and adopted recommendations on the nature and statutes of the Committee. On recommendation of the Interim Committee, the 1985 General Conference of UNESCO decided through Resolution 6.2 to establish an Intergovernmental Informatics Programme "aimed at strengthening international co-operation and national efforts, devoted to the training of specialists, the development of infrastructure, the definition of national policies, and the better recognition of the role of informatics."[103] The resolution also created an Intergovernmental Committee composed of 33 member states and adopted the Committee's statutes. To what extent the Informatics Programme will deal with TDF-issues proper—as against focusing only on informatics—remains to be seen. Finally, mention should be made of UNESCO's International Programme for the Development of Communication (mandated in 1980) through which the Organization finances technical assistance in the communication area.

Thus, the extent and nature of UNESCO's involvement in the TDF discussion is still open. The withdrawal of the US and the UK from the Organization and its internal efforts at reform may slow down the beginning of any new activities. But given the importance of this area, it is very likely that UNESCO will eventually make efforts to build on its past work and establish itself firmly in this area. As to the direction of this work, much will depend on whether it will build up its own infrastructure through the new Intergovernmental Committee, or whether it will leave this area primarily to IBI and participate only in a few major events. At the present time, the former approach seems more likely but not necessarily to the exclusion of the latter. Under the first approach, one would expect an orientation toward information flows, technical assistance, and the cultural and sovereignty implications of TDF. Under the second approach, all would depend on how UNESCO co-operates with IBI and what guidelines, if any, emerge from it.

For reasons related mostly to the NIIO debate, many developed market economies are not favorably inclined to UNESCO. Hence they are not likely to favor an expanded role of that organization in TDF. The developing countries, which support UNESCO, certainly stand to benefit from the Organization's technical assistance in this area. Moreover, they could quite conceivably be attracted by a broader role for UNESCO in TDF as their awareness of the importance of the subject increases and they seek a forum in which they can discuss broad TDF concerns, perhaps even from the perspective of guidelines not conceived on the basis of GATT principles.

4. The United Nations Commission and Centre
on Transnational Corporations

Lastly, the United Nations Commission and Centre on Transnational Corporations (UNCTC) have taken up the topic of TDF. They are, so far, the only organs in the UN system which deal specifically with TDF and, apart from the IBI, they are currently the only international bodies which specifically discuss TDF with the participation of the developing and socialist countries.

The Commission and the Centre are, within the UN system, the focal point for all questions related to TNCs. At its seventh session in August-September 1981, the Commission (which reports to the Economic and Social Council), having before it a report on "Transnational Corporations and Transborder Data Flows: An Overview", [104] decided to include in its agenda an item on TNCs and TDF. Since then, it has dealt regularly with this subject in its annual sessions. [105] The work of the Commission and the Centre has focused on research, especially regarding possible implications of TDF for developing countries, although broader issues have also been taken into account. The main purpose of this work is to examine carefully the importance and impact of TDF (paying special attention to TNCs and developing countries), with the purpose of facilitating an objective discussion of the issues raised by this new phenomenon.

Since the preparation of the initial overview study, UNCTC's work has focused on three priority areas: country case studies on TDF; access to the international data market; and TNCs and remote-sensing data. [106] In 1984, UNCTC initiated a study on international trade and foreign direct investment in data services. The study deals with a number of the conceptual issues relating to these transactions; their nature, volume and determinants; the obstacles facing them; the regimes most appropriate to them; the role of TNCs in them and their impact on the development process in general and on developing countries in particular. A number of these questions were addressed in a preliminary manner in a study prepared in 1984 for SELA. [107] In addition, work in TDF is closely linked with the Centre's work on services in general. The Centre has considerable experience in work on services, having prepared studies on banking, advertising, shipping, insurance, tourism, and engineering and consultancy services [108] and having undertaken work on FDI in services in general. [109]

Furthermore, the country case studies on TDF are continuing. On the basis of an examination of a country's telecommunication, informatics and telematics infrastructure, the country case studies aim at an empirical assessment of the role of TNCs in TDF, the economic impact of TDF (especially on developing countries), and policy responses to TDF. They are intended to enable countries to take stock of their capacity, especially infrastructure capacity, to utilize TDF; to serve as a vehicle for the exchange of views with other governments on issues related to TDF; and to provide governments with the empirical material needed to formulate appropriate national policies and to participate effectively in international discussions. As of the end of 1985, case studies by Brazil, Poland, the Federal Republic of Germany, and Austria had been completed,[110] while studies by Mexico, Argentina and Thailand were underway. It is envisaged that, eventually, a general analysis will be prepared on the basis of these case studies to review the experience of various countries, the policies adopted by them and the applicability of such policies to countries at different levels of development and in different circumstances.

The country case studies take the Centre's work into the area of technical assistance. The Commission very much encouraged this development when it decided in 1985 that a stronger link should be sought between the Centre's research on TDF and its technical assistance activities.[111] This technical-assistance work emphasizes especially the importance of an appropriate infrastructure for TDF. Thus, the Centre prepared, in 1985, a report for SELA which reviewed the status of the data-service industry in Latin America and the policies pursued in this regard, focusing on the role of TNCs and discussing policy options available to countries interested in data services.[112] The study was subsequently submitted to a meeting of the Latin American Council, held in Caracas in November-December 1985. The facility of the Centre to combine its research and technical-assistance capacities gives it an opportunity to be particularly relevant to the needs of developing countries.

As can be seen from the country case studies, all regions have participated in the Centre's work, which indicates that the Commission is being regarded as an appropriate and fair forum in which to discuss TDF issues. The deliberations of the Commission have dealt mostly with the issues raised in the studies prepared for it and have therefore focused on economic matters. Not being an expert forum, governments have used the Commission's sessions to underline the general importance of TDF and the need for more information and analysis in this respect.

To bring more expertise to in-depth discussions, the developing countries suggested the establishment of an ad hoc working group of experts during the ninth session of the Commission in 1983, and again during the tenth session in 1984. According to the proposal:

> The ad hoc working group shall consider issues relating to transborder data flows and the role of transnational corporations in these flows in order to study the importance and implications of transborder data flows and the role of transnational corporations in this regard, particularly in developing countries; review, on the basis of the foregoing studies, possibilities of maximizing the positive effects of transborder data flows and minimizing negative ones, in a manner that contributes to development and economic co-operation; and take into account the broader context of microelectronics, telecommunications and informatics, of which transborder data flows are an outgrowth.[113]

The terms of reference (which, of course, were open to negotiation) further suggested that the working group consult with all interested parties and elicit their views; meet for a period of one week not more than once a year; and report to the Commission. The Commission, in turn, was supposed to keep the mandate, terms of reference and achievements of the group under review, with a view to deciding on the advisability of its continuation. During the 1985 session, a few countries suggested that the TDF discussion be embedded in a broader discussion on international transactions in services, but the formal proposal to establish an *ad hoc* working group was not repeated.

During the 1983 and 1984 sessions of the Commssion, most developed market economies that addressed the issue were not against the establishment of a working group as such but argued that such an action was premature at the present time. (The socialist countries kept a low profile.) Since the Commission acts, as a rule, by consensus, the proposal was withdrawn by the Group of 77. This strengthens, of course, the prospect of UNCTAD and possibly UNESCO becoming the principal forum for UN discussions on TDF. These would by no means be inappropriate forums, since the trade, technology and information-order aspects of the discussion are at the moment the predominant themes.

For the developing countries, the reasons for wanting the Commission to pay greater attention to TDF were straightforward. They were beginning to realize the importance of these flows for their development effort and, naturally, wished to know more about them. Hence their desire to establish an ad hoc working group of experts of the classical sort: a group charged with illuminating a given subject. This desire was further strengthened by the knowledge that the OECD as an organization had been dealing with TDF for several years at both the working-group and committee levels, while the developing countries as a whole had no similar forum. While the Commission and Centre on Transnational Corporations may not be the ideal forum for this purpose, these two institutions do pay special attention to the developing countries and could therefore be expected to prepare materials relevant to them. In addition, since the Centre has a strong technical-assistance arm, it may be expected that developing countries could obtain practical assistance from it, especially as regards the strengthening of their infrastructure.

In any event, since the efforts of the developing countries to have the Commission pay more attention to this subject have been in vain, they have to turn to other bodies within the UN system or to pursue the matter on a regional basis. As to the first option, it has already been indicated that UNCTAD has received a mandate to work on TDF in the framework of work on services in general. As to the second option, it is not inconceivable that such an organization as SELA may upgrade its activities in this respect. The adoption of the OECD Declaration on TDF and the beginning of the GATT discussions on services make it imperative for the developing countries to find a forum, even if only on a regional basis, to further their understanding of the importance of TDF. In fact, there are indications that the developing countries may begin to prefer a forum which does not include the developed countries. During the 1985 session of the Commission on Transnational Corporations, for instance, the Group of 77 pursued the idea of establishing an ad hoc working group of experts with considerably less urgency than in the preceding sessions and, in fact, did not even make a formal proposal in this respect—among other reasons because it was thought that a more restrictive forum may be more desirable. Brazil in particular seemed to begin placing more emphasis on SELA. But ultimately it may well be that developing countries prefer to put national policies into place before returning to the international level.

For the developed market economies, the Commission on Transnational Corporations has proven itself to be a useful forum to articulate and discuss the whole range of issues relating to TNCs. Since TNCs play a key role in all aspects of TDF—from the production of the underlying equipment, to the construction of the necessary networks, to the application of TDF—the Commission offers itself as a place to examine questions related to TDF and to explore ways of ensuring that all countries benefit from these flows as much as possible. The advantage of this approach is that an early involvement of all countries in the international discussions on TDF contributes to the creation of a common body of knowledge and understanding of a phenomenon which presents all countries with a new challenge. In such a situation, it is more likely that countries will see not only the potential costs but also the potential benefits of TDF, and it is less likely that they will be surprised by developments in this area and react restrictively. One disadvantage of such a preparatory approach is that the results are not as tangible as in the case of the OECD (e.g., the guidelines on the transborder flow of personal data; the TDF Declaration). Another disadvantage (from the developed countries' point of view) is that developing and socialist countries would be involved in international discussions of the subject earlier than may be either necessary or desirable, although, with the adoption of the OECD TDF Declaration, the OECD countries now have a common approach. Added to this is perhaps a fear that the inclusion of the topic in the UN agenda could lead to a politicization of the subject along the lines, for instance, of the New International Information Order. In addition, the developed countries have little interest in focusing an international discussion on the role of TDF in TNCs, not only because this could lead to a focus which could pay too much attention to intra-firm flows but because the subject clearly transcends TNCs. In other words, the mandate of the Commission and the Centre is a restraining factor; but given the importance of the role of TNCs in TDF, it would be easy for the members of the Commission to interpret its mandate in a manner that covers general TDF issues as well.

The preceding discussion of the work of the UN Commission and Centre on Transnational Corporations has focused only on the TDF aspects of this work, although the Centre has also undertaken a number of studies on services in general. Furthermore, and most importantly, the highest priority in the work of the Commission and the Centre has the formulation and adoption of an international framework for FDI. This matter will be discussed in the conclusions of this volume.

Notes

[1] Gordon J. Cloney, "The American Connection" (Washington: IIAC, 1983), mimeo., p. 5.

[2] See *ibid.* Cloney is the Director of the IIAC, P. Herson (Senior Vice President of CIGNA Corporation) its chairperson.

[3] US, Department of Commerce, *U.S. Service Industries in World Markets: Current Problems and Future Policy Developments* (Washington: Department of Commerce, 1976).

[4] Chamber of Commerce of the US, International Service Industry Committee, *Report 1978-1980* (Washington: Chamber of Commerce, 1980), p. 15. The chairperson of the Committee was Ronald K. Shelp, the Executive Secretary Gordon J. Cloney. In other words,

the concern of the service industries had shifted toward promoting service trade liberalization. This is exemplified by Cloney's (*op. cit.*, p. 3) observation for the US insurance industry: "Thus, the 1966 reaction against LDC *nationalization* had evolved by 1978 to be an assertive concern with global insurance *liberalization*." He also describes (*ibid.*) the underlying attitudinal change: "Thus, as the 1970's closed, barriers and restrictions encountered in overseas markets had undergone a major transformation in the mind of the U.S. international insurance and reinsurance industry. Formerly, more or less tacitly accepted as unfortunate conditions associated with doing an international business, they were now seen as trade barriers, as unfair, and as proper subject for international trade discipline in the light of existing trade principles."

[5] "Coalition of Service Industries, Inc." (Washington: CSI, n.d.), mimeo. The chairperson of the CSI Board is Maurice R. Greenberg, President and Chief Executive Officer of the American International Group; the chairperson of the Coalition's Coordinating Committee was (until June 1985) Ronald K. Shelp. The Coalition undertakes its activities through five task forces: Data Collection and Statistical Improvement Task Force; Tax Task Force; Washington Legislative Task Force; Trade and Investment Task Force; and Measurement and Improvement of Productivity Task Force. A key person behind the Coalition (and one of its Vice Presidents) is Harry L. Freeman, Senior Vice President, American Express Co.

[6] It is interesting to note in this context that, according to a survey taken in August and September 1984 of the chief executive officers of the *Fortune* 500 Directors of Service Companies (response rate: 22%), 70% of the respondents expected their international trade in services to expand moderately in the next five years and 16% expected a great expansion of their international business; at the same time, 69% had encountered restriction on right of establishment or foreign ownership; 68% had encountered restrictions on repatriation of royalties, fees and profits; 43% had experienced discriminatory tax policies; and 38% had encountered barriers to TDF (this was particularly important for banks and diversified financial companies). In addition, while 67% believed that other countries were taking unfair advantage of the open service trade policies of the US, 94% also believed that other countries would retaliate if the US instituted new restrictions on services trade. See Price Waterhouse, "Business Views on Public Policy and International Trade in Services" (Washington: Price Waterhouse, 1985), mimeo.

[7] See Harry L. Freeman, "Some Thoughts on 'Things which can be Bought and Sold but which you cannot Drop on Your Feet'" (New York: American Express, 1985), mimeo., addendum.

[8] It is chaired by James Robinson, Chief Executive Officer of American Express.

[9] It is chaired by Peter J. Finnerty, Vice-President, Sea-Land Corporation, a major container-shipping and other ocean-overland freight-transport corporation; its vice-chairperson is Joan E. Spero.

[10] "Chairmen's Report on a New Round of Multilateral Trade Negotiations. Submitted to the United States Trade Representative, May 15, 1985" (Washington: USTR, 1985), mimeo., contribution by the Services Policy Advisory Committee, p. 1.

[11] *Ibid.*

[12] *Ibid.*, pp. 1-3.

[13] The terms of reference of LOTIS are "to take note of international developments in, and official moves towards, the liberalisation of trade in services, to analyse and comment on such developments and to make recommendations to the Committee on Invisible Exports and, where appropriate, through the Committee, to the Bank of England, the Department of Trade, the Treasury and other relevant bodies." See, LOTIS, "Liberalisation of Trade in Services: A United Kingdom Private Sector Assessment" (London: LOTIS, 1982), mimeo.,

p. 1. LOTIS is chaired by Sir Michael Palliser, Vice-Chairperson, Samuel Montagu & Co. Ltd.

[14] Ibid., p. 6. LOTIS also expressed its belief that liberalization will encourage economic development in all participating countries (ibid.).

[15] Ibid., p. 9. Similar in LOTIS, "Liberalisation of Trade in Services: An Assessment Paper" (London: LOTIS, 1984), mimeo., especially pp. 48 ff. (This paper is a response to the UK national study on services prepared for GATT in 1984.)

[16] See LOTIS, "A United Kingdom Private Sector Assessment", op. cit., pp. 7–8.

[17] See LOTIS, "An Assessment Paper", op. cit., pp. 48–54. The document suggested (pp. 48–49) that "if an international agreement on services were to become a reality, it should embody articles which would deal with the following issues of principle to be applied across all sectors: (a) a standstill agreement avoiding the creation of new restrictions except insofar as these might be permitted in strictly limited circumstances; (b) a most-favoured-nation provision, subject to defined exceptions such as those covering harmonisation agreements reached within common markets; (c) 'national treatment'—non-discrimination in respect of: (i) establishment of subsidiaries, branches, agencies, etc.; (ii) internal taxation; (iii) internal regulations and administrative barriers; (d) free access to markets without the need to set up local offices; (e) freedom of transit across borders (a particular problem for the transport industries and the electronic flow of data); (f) an equivalent for services of an 'anti-dumping clause' against unfair competition which would also need to consider the concept of measurement of damage and compensation; (g) valuation for customs purposes (a particular problem for the telematic sector); (h) freedom to employ and transfer skilled staff across frontiers; (i) balance of payments safeguards and the extent to which temporary and/or emergency action is permissible; (j) the level of subsidies, if any, which are permissible; (k) the position of state trading enterprises in respect of limiting free trade and competition; (l) general exceptions, concerned with social issues such as action necessary to protect religion, public morals and health."

[18] See, ICC, "Position Paper on Liberalisation of Trade in Services", document no. 103/34/Rev. 4, p. 4.

[19] A sectoral study, mentioned earlier, was produced on TDF.

[20] See ICC, "Services in International Trade: A Summary of Interim Conclusions by the ICC", document no. 103/70 of 17 June 1984, mimeo.

[21] Ibid., point 10.

[22] "Chairmen's Report", op. cit., pp. 8–9, 12–13.

[23] Ibid., p. 4.

[24] William E. Brock, "A Simple Plan for Negotiating on Trade in Services", The World Economy, 5 (November 1982), pp. 238–239. Similarly, the Deputy US Trade Representative, as quoted in "GATT: A Proposal for the Extension of the GATT to a Coverage of Services. The Case of Telecommunications Services. A Briefing Paper" (Washington: US National Committee of the International Institute of Communications, 1982), mimeo., p. 13, stated: "The work program that we would like to have the GATT undertake includes: (a) compilation of an inventory of barriers that countries experience in these sectors; (b) analyzing the GATT Articles as to their potential application to services; (c) examining the GATT codes as to their potential application to service industries. Such a program should lead to negotiations aimed at developing international rules to liberalize services trade. One of our aims is to frame a Code of Conduct that will incorporate a general set of principles applicable to a cross-section of service industries. We would also like to explore the possibility of sector specific agreements dealing with market access and related issues, where that proves

appropriate and desirable. We are convinced that it is in the interest of every country to establish fair markets for services."

[25] Based on material submitted by the US to GATT.

[26] In the GATT framework, this was apparently spelled out explicitly for the first time during a meeting of the GATT Consultative Group of 18 at the beginning of July 1985; see *Financial Times*, 11 July 1985. This objective was repeated during the subsequent meeting of the Council of Representatives, which took place 17–18 July 1985. Similarly, Assistant US Trade Representative Richard Self noted that "The U.S. wants priority attention devoted to data processing, point-to-point communication and TDF." See *Transnational Data and Communications Report*, 9 (January 1986), p. 4.

[27] US, Interagency Working Group on Transborder Data Flow, "Communications and Transborder Data Flows in the United States: A Background Paper" (Washington: Interagency Working Group, 1985), mimeo., p. 127.

[28] The following review is based mostly on material submitted by individual countries or groups of countries to GATT, and the national studies prepared by individual countries.

[29] The European Community, through a meeting of trade ministers, declared formally on 19 March 1985 its readiness to participate in the launching of a new GATT round. On that occasion, the EC also accepted formally that services would be a suitable subject for inclusion in the new round. See *Financial Times*, 20 March 1985.

[30] UK, Department of Trade and Industry, "UK National Study on Trade in Services" (London, 1984), mimeo., p. 19.

[31] For a brief discussion of the work program, see Bhagirath L. Das, "The GATT Ministerial Meeting, 1982: An Interpretive Note", *Journal of World Trade Law*, 18 (January–February 1984), pp. 3–15.

[32] Quoted in Tenth Regular Meeting of the Latin American Council, "Final Report of the Tenth Regular Meeting of the Latin American Council", CL/X.0/DF No. 1 of 26 October 1984, mimeo., pp. 81–83.

[33] GATT, *Trade Policies for a Better Future: Proposals for Action* (Geneva: GATT, 1985) (the "Leutwiler Report"), pp. 45, 46.

[34] Based on material submitted by a group of developing countries to GATT.

[35] See, for example, "Statement by India" at the Special Session of the GATT Contracting Parties, 30 September–2 October 1985, mimeo.

[36] This fear was, for instance, voiced by India's Commerce Secretary, Prem Kumar; see *Financial Times*, 20 October 1985.

[37] "Statement of Brazil" at the Meeting of the GATT Contracting Parties, 26–30 November 1984, mimeo.

[38] ECOSOC resolution 1/13 of 18 February 1946, para. 1.

[39] "Statement by India", *op. cit.*

[40] Seventh Conference of Heads of State or Government of Non-Aligned Countries, "Final Documents: Economic Declaration", p. 88, in Odette Jankowitsch and Karl P. Sauvant, eds., *The Third World Without Superpowers: The Collected Documents of the Non-Aligned Countries* (Dobbs Ferry, N. Y.: Oceana, 1986), vol. VII.

[41] "The Buenos Aires Platform: Ministerial Declaration on Individual Items of the Provincial Agenda for UNCTAD VI", p. 3., in Karl P. Sauvant, ed., *The Third World Without Superpowers*, 2nd series, *The Collected Documents of the Group of 77* (Dobbs Ferry, N. Y.: Oceana, forthcoming), vol. VII.

[42] See Latin American Economic System (SELA), "Conclusions and Recommendations of the High-level Latin American Co-ordination Meeting on Services, Held at the Headquarters

of the Latin American Economic System (SELA), Caracas, 22 to 24 August 1984", in SP/CL/X.0/DT No. 14 of 4 October 1984, p. 6.

[43] Tenth Regular Meeting of the Latin American Council, Decision No. 192, "Services and the Development of Latin America", in "Final Report of the Tenth Regular Meeting of the Latin American Council", CL/X.0/DF No. 1 of 26 October 1984, mimeo., pp. 81–83. Decision No. 25, entitled "Services and Development", adopted by the Eleventh Regular Meeting of the Latin American Council one year later, took, however, a different approach. It reaffirmed, in its article 1, that "the present and prospective economic importance of services indicates that any international discussion of the subject, whatever its scope, must seek to safeguard the economic development goals pursued by the developing countries." This indicates a shift in position since international discussions on services are no longer ruled out.

[44] On the Group of 77, see Karl P. Sauvant, The Group of 77: Evolution, Structure, Organization (Dobbs Ferry, N.Y: Oceana, 1981).

[45] As Ronald K. Shelp, Beyond Industrialization: Ascendancy of the Global Service Economy (New York: Praeger, 1981), p. 154, noted: "The Nixon and Ford Administrations strongly resisted introducing services into the Tokyo Round of multilateral trade negotiations because services were not traditionally included in GATT."

[46] See footnote 43 of this chapter.

[47] In the opinion of the Financial Times, 3 December 1984, p. 14, the US was "strong-arming a reluctant Third World in order to get the question put formally on the Gatt agenda."

[48] See Shelp, op. cit., pp. 153-154. Shelp reports that this legislation was mostly the result of the efforts of the aviation and insurance industries, which had become concerned about barriers facing them in international markets.

[49] For a review of the services discussion in GATT see Raymond J. Krommenacker, World-Traded Services: The Challenge for the Eighties (Dedham: Artech House, 1984), ch. 7.

[50] For the texts, see GATT, Basic Instruments and Selected Documents: Twenty-Sixth Supplement (Geneva: GATT, 1980).

[51] The Business Roundtable has recommended, for instance, that the Standards Code model would be the best way to deal with TDF. See The Business Roundtable, International Information Flow: A Plan for Action (New York: The Business Roundtable, 1985), p 12.

[52] In GATT, the Technical and Other Barriers to Trade Division, whose Director is Jacques Nusbaumer, is responsible for the organization's work on services.

[53] The relevant part of the GATT Declaration, as adopted on 29 November 1982, reads as follows: "Services: The Contracting Parties decide: • To recommend to each Contracting Party with an interest in services of different types to undertake, as far as it is able, national examination of the issues in this sector. • To invite Contracting Parties to exchange information on such matters among themselves, inter alia, through international organizations such as GATT. The compilation and distribution of such information should be based on as uniform a format as possible. • To review the results of these examinations, along with the information and comments provided by relevant international organizations, at their 1984 session and to consider whether any multilateral action in these matters is appropriate and desirable." (GATT, "Ministerial Declaration", Press Release, GATT 1328 of 29 November 1982)

[54] This occurred already during the 1982 GATT Ministerial Meeting. See Leslie Fielding (Director General for External Relations, Commission of the European Communities), "The Development of a Community View on International Trade in Services" (London:

Conference of the Chambers of Commerce of the North Sea Ports, 1983), mimeo., p. 3. It continued in 1985 when the EC launched a campaign to win over reluctant developing countries to support the new round; see *Financial Times*, 31 May 1985.

⁵⁵ See "London Economic Declaration", in UN document A/39/304 of 13 June 1984. In the relevant paragraph 9(x), it was agreed "to accelerate the completion of current trade liberalisation programmes, particularly the 1982 GATT work programme, in co-operation with other trading partners; to press forward with the work on trade in services in the international organizations; to reaffirm the agreement reached at the OECD Ministerial Meeting in May 1984 on the important contribution which a new round of multilateral trade negotiations would make to strengthening the open multilateral trading system for the mutual benefit of all economies, industrial and developing; and, building on the 1982 GATT work programme, to consult partners in the GATT with a view to decisions at an early date on the possible objectives, arrangements and timing for a new negotiating round." At the preceding year's summit in Williamsburg, the service issue had been on the agenda for the first time.

⁵⁶ See William E. Brock, "Trade and Debt: The Vital Linkage", *Foreign Affairs*, 62 (Summer 1984), p. 1050.

⁵⁷ Because no developing country had submitted national examinations to GATT, UNCTAD was invited in 1986 to participate in GATT's informal service discussions to illuminate service questions related to the development process of the developing countries.

⁵⁸ L/5762 of 20 December 1984.

⁵⁹ The dates of the meetings were 24 January 1985, 1–2 April 1985, 2 May 1985, 7 June 1985, 15 July 1985, 18 September 1985, 17 October 1985, and 11 November 1985.

⁶⁰ After the adoption of the "Agreed Conclusions", the chairperson made the following statement, of which the contracting parties took note (L/5762): "With reference to the arrangements just agreed by the CONTRACTING PARTIES which provide for the organization of the exchange of information on issues in the sector of services, it is understood that in addition to servicing and keeping records of meetings, the secretariat would prepare an analytical summary of national examinations together with information made available by relevant international organizations and a summary of issues raised in the exchange of information. Concurrently the secretariat would propose a format, for the compilation and distribution by it of the information exchanged among contracting parties, to be progressively elaborated in order to make it as uniform as possible. It is also understood that the secretariat could, on an agreed basis, undertake additional tasks as required."

⁶¹ "Statement by Brazil" at the Meeting of the GATT Contracting Parties, 26–30 November 1984, mimeo.

⁶² "Agreed Conclusions", *op. cit.*

⁶³ OECD Council of Ministers, "Communiqué", *op. cit.*, para. 11. The full text of the paragraph reads as follows: "Ministers reaffirmed their commitment to the open multilateral trading system and their determination to strengthen it by further liberalisation. A new round of trade negotiations in GATT would contribute significantly to achieving this objective. There was therefore agreement that such a round of negotiations should begin as soon as possible (some felt this should be in early 1986). Ministers agreed to propose to the Contracting Parties that a preparatory meeting of senior officials should take place in GATT before the end of the summer to reach a broad consensus on subject matter and modalities for such negotiations. Active participation of a significant number of developed and developing countries in such negotiations is considered essential. The various actions recorded in this Communiqué insofar as they lead to a better international economic, financial, monetary and investment environment, will contribute to the success of this process."

[64] Ibid.

[65] Since it had already been decided that the question of a monetary conference would be examined by the finance ministers of the Group of 10, this issue was no longer an argument. France held that the principal reason for the growing US trade deficit was the overvalued dollar: if appropriate and stable relations for exchange rates were established, there would be no trade problem. France's concern in this matter was further decreased when, in September 1985, the US, UK, FRG, France, and Japan agreed to realign the dollar's value by increasing intervention in currency markets.

[66] "The Bonn Economic Declaration Toward Sustained Growth and Higher Employment", New York Times, 5 May 1985, para 10. The full text of that paragraph reads as follows: "Protectionism does not solve problems; it creates them. Further tangible progress in relaxing and dismantling existing trade restrictions is essential. We need new initiatives for strengthening the open multilateral trading system. We strongly endorse the agreement reached by the O.E.C.D. Ministerial Council that a new GATT round should begin as soon as possible. Most of us think that this should be in 1986. We agree that it would be useful that a preparatory meeting of senior officials should take place in the GATT before the end of the summer to reach a broad consensus on subject matter and modalities for such negotiations. We also agree that active participation of a significant number of developed and developing countries in such negotiations is essential. We are looking to a balanced package for negotiations."

[67] See Financial Times, 8 July 1985.

[68] See Neue Zuericher Zeitung, 18 July 1985.

[69] See IFDA/IPS, SUNS, no. 1392, 28 September 1985, p. 3.

[70] As quoted in GATT Focus, October-November 1985, p. 1.

[71] GATT Focus, October-November 1985, p. 1.

[72] Clayton Yeutter, "Testimony on U.S. Trade Policy and Unfair Trade Practices before the Committee on Finance, United States Senate, November 14, 1985" (Washington: USTR, 1985), mimeo., p. 14.

[73] GATT Focus, October 1985-January 1986, p. 1.

[74] Ibid.

[75] This understanding was part of the session's compromise and was announced by the chairperson of the contracting parties after the adoption of the decision establishing the Preparatory Committee. See ibid.

[76] See, US, Trade Representative, "U.S. National Study on Trade in Services" (Washington: USTR, 1983), mimeo., pp. 73-74. Naturally, other governments may have a different view, if only for bargaining purposes.

[77] US, "Treaty between the United States of America and . . . Concerning the Reciprocal Encouragement and Protection of Investment" (Model Treaty), 24 February 1984, Art. II, para. 4. This language was for instance included verbatim (Art. II, para. 5) in the US-Turkey bilateral investment treaty, signed December 1985.

[78] Shelp, op. cit., p. 187.

[79] However, an argument could be made that under Article I of the General Agreement (which enshrines most-favored-nation treatment, the cornerstone of GATT), any concessions negotiated in the framework of such a code would have to be extended to all other contracting parties.

[80] GATT, Trade Policies for a Better Future, op. cit., p. 46.

[81] Michael Cohen and Thomas Morante, "Elimination of Nontariff Barriers to Trade in Services: Recommendation for Future Negotiation", Law and Policy in International Business, 13 (1981), p. 514.

[82] It should be pointed out that various multilateral institutions are already funding projects to strenghen the developing countries' telecommunication infrastructure. Reference has already been made to the Maitland Commission Report. Noteworthy here is also the Technical Information Pilot System (TIPS) implemented by the UN Financing System for Science and Technology for Development in consultation with UNDP and other UN organizations. TIPS is designed to respond to the need for a user-oriented mechanism that strengthens information flows in science and technology among developing countries and facilitates the utilization of current information for development purposes.

[83] "U.S. National Study", op. cit., p. 8.

[84] Shelp, op. cit., pp. 190–191.

[85] See UNCTAD, "Services and the Development Process", TD/B/1008 of 2 August 1984, p. 28 and passim. UNCTAD's work pays special attention to the role of TDF in TNCs. In this respect, the report observed (p. 37), among other things, that TDF "serve to reduce the autonomy of foreign-controlled subsidiaries" since the advent of sophisticated computer-communication links permits "an abrupt increase in the scope for control from one central point." The study continued (ibid.): "The sharp increase in centralization raises a number of policy issues. It raises a practical question of whether manufacturing or service industry subsidiaries of parent firms located in other countries can realistically be expected to exercise independent functions, such as research, product design and development and marketing decisions. As described in more detail below, it can also lead to inter-firm division of labour according the less sophisticated tasks to developing countries. The increasing centralization clearly reinforces situations of dependence, including those of access to computer links with the parent company. The centralization of control derived from the increasing use of computer-communication systems will inevitably heighten dependence and could lead to attempts to insulate the peripheral economy from access to vital information."

[86] "Economic Declaration", op. cit., p. 88.

[87] "The Buenos Aires Platform: Action on Items 8 to 13 of the Provisional Agenda for UNCTAD VI", in Sauvant, op. cit., p. 26. The full text of this passage, which is part of a draft resolution on "Services" for UNCTAD VI, read: "The United Nations Conference on Trade and Development . . . Decides: (a) The UNCTAD secretariat should carry out studies to identify and establish priorities regarding services of particular importance to developing countries and to devise programmes which would enable the developing countries to have greater participation in international trade in services. These studies should also cover those services which do not fall within the specific competence of international organizations. (b) These studies by the UNCTAD secretariat should also make recommendations with respect to establishing mechanisms for multilateral co-operation in the field of services which may be of benefit to the developing countries."

[88] See Group of 77, "Report of the Third Meeting of the Intergovernmental Follow-up and Co-ordination Committee on Economic Co-operation among Developing Countries", IFCC-III/G-77/84/ Rpt. 1, pp. 9–10, contained in Sauvant, op. cit. The Committee's recommendations were subsequently endorsed by the Eighth Meeting of Ministers for Foreign Affairs of the Group of 77, held in New York, 26–28 September 1984. See "Declaration", in Sauvant, op. cit., para. 29.

[89] UN publication, Sales No. E.75.II.D.12.

[90] Decision 250 (XXIV).

[91] UNCTAD resolution 195 (VI), contained in Sauvant, op. cit.

[92] UNCTAD, "Services and the Development Process", op. cit. The report was supplemented by background documents dealing with specific industries, namely "International Trade and Foreign Direct Investment in Data Services: Transborder Data Flows in the

Context of Services and the Development Process. Report by the United Nations Centre on Transnational Corporations" (TD/B/1016 of 27 August 1984), "Insurance in the Context of Services and the Development Process: Report by the UNCTAD Secretariat" (TD/B/1014 of 3 August 1984), "Technology in the Context of Services and the Development Process: Report by the UNCTAD Secretariat" (TD/B/1012 of 18 July 1984), and "Maritime Transport in the Context of Services and the Development Process: Report by the UNCTAD Secretariat" (TD/B/1013). Murray Gibbs, Chief of the International Trading System Section of the Manufactures Division is in charge of UNCTAD's work in this area.

⁹³ Draft decision TD/B/L.770 of 29 March 1985. The decision was almost identical to the draft resolution TD/B(XXIX)/CW/L.4 submitted by the Group of 77 on 19 September 1984.

⁹⁴ See, for instance, ITU, *Provisional Recommendations X.3, X.25, X.28, and X.29 on Packet-Switched Data Transmission Services* (Geneva: ITU, 1978), as well as the Series D Recommendations.

⁹⁵ See, ITU, *Report on the Activities of the International Telecommunication Union in 1983* (Geneva: ITU, 1984). Examples are recommendations D.3 and D.6 on the leasing of international circuits, recommendation X.10 on access categories to data bases, and draft recommendation S.90 on the linking of teletex with telex. See *ibid.*

⁹⁶ ITU, *International Telecommunication Convention: Final Protocol, Additional Protocols, Optional Protocol, Resolutions, Recommendation and Opinions, Nairobi, 1982* (Geneva: ITU, 1983), pp. 252–254 and 254–256, respectively. The report of the Maitland Commission was published in 1984 under the title *The Missing Link* (Geneva: ITU, 1984)

⁹⁷ *Ibid.*, pp. 238–239.

⁹⁸ Quoted from INTUG's submission to the OECD Second Symposium on Transborder Data Flows, as excerpted in *Transnational Data Report*, 6 (January-February 1983), p. 5.

⁹⁹ The report of the McBride Commission, the blueprint for the New International Information Order, deals in fact with many elements that also play a role in the TDF discussion. See UNESCO, *Many Voices, One World: Towards a New, More Just and More Efficient World Information and Communications Order* (Paris: UNESCO, 1980). For a brief review of the history of the NIIO see Reinhard Keune, *An International Information Order?* (Bonn: Friedrich Ebert Stiftung, 1984).

¹⁰⁰ General Assembly resolution 217A of 10 December 1948.

¹⁰¹ For example, after quoting article 19 of the Declaration, a US study on TDF observed: "The burden of proof should be on those who claim that a restriction on the free flow of information is necessary. Broad generalizations, such as the 'protection of cultural integrity', are not sufficient justification for information control, particularly as these may be a guise for economic protectionism or censorship. If the purpose of a restriction is the protection of individual privacy or property rights, or for genuine national security interests, those exceptions should be clearly stated. From the U.S. standpoint, the free flow principle embodies the objectives of the first amendment to the U.S. Constitution. Ongoing changes in communications and information technologies have great potential for fostering the growth of more open societies worldwide. Through greater openness, mutual understanding among nations can be improved and economic growth of all nations benefitted. More effective management of resources, beneficial trade policies, effective responses to global problems, and better maintenance of international peace and security are achievable." (See US, Interagency Working Group on Transborder Data Flow, *op. cit.*, p. 123)

¹⁰² See, "Main Working Document", SC-84/CONF.209/4 of 22 August 1984. The document declared (p. 1) informatics to be "a choice instrument for economic and social development" which "could enable developing countries to manage better and at less expense

their resources and improve the performance of their economies"; but the document went on to caution that "informatics contributes at present to widening the gap between the developing and the rich countries", a situation which is not likely to improve in the near future. Furthermore, the document suggested with respect to the developing countries (pp. 3–4) that "the competitivity of the products marketed by these countries will continually decrease. The international division of labour is likely to be more pronounced, with a concentration of higher value added activities in areas where technological know-how exists. . . . On the contrary, in most developing countries, the incipient nature of the informatics industry does not allow them to benefit from these economic advantages."

[103] *Records of the General Conference, Twenty-third Session, Sofia, 8 October to 9 November 1985*, vol. 1, *Resolutions*, p. 47. The proposals of the Director General of UNESCO are contained in his report to the General Conference, document 23 C/14.

[104] E/C.10/87 of 6 July 1981. The document was based on *Transnational Corporations and Transborder Data Flows* (New York: UN, 1982), Sales No. E.82.II.A.4.

[105] The progress reports prepared by UNCTC, the actions taken by the Commission, as well as various other materials prepared by the Centre are contained in *Transnational Corporations and Transborder Data Flows: Background and Overview* (Amsterdam: North Holland, 1984).

[106] See UNCTC, *Access to the International On-line Data-base Market* (New York: UN, 1983), Sales No. E.83.II.A.1, and UNCTC, *Transborder Data Flows: Transnational Corporations and Remote-sensing Data: A Technical Paper* (New York: UN, 1984), Sales No. E. 84.II.A.11.

[107] See Sauvant, *Trade and Foreign Direct Investment in Data Services* (Boulder: Westview, 1986).

[108] Most of these studies are summarized in GATT, "Summary of Information Made Available by Relevant International Organizations", MDF/17 and Add. 1 of 16 September 1985.

[109] See especially Karl P. Sauvant and Zbigniew Zimny, "FDI and TNCs in Services", *The CTC Reporter*, 20 (Autumn 1985), pp. 24–28. See also UNCTC, *Trends and Issues in Foreign Direct Investment and Related Flows* (New York: UN, 1985), Sales No. E.85.II.A.15, ch. IX, and UNCTC, "Recent Developments Related to Transnational Corporations and International Economic Relations", E/C.10/1986/2 of 6 February 1986.

[110] See UNCTC, *Transborder Data Flows and Brazil: Brazilian Case Study* (New York: UN, 1983), Sales No. E.83.II.A.3, and UNCTC, *Transborder Data Flows and Poland: Polish Case Study* (New York: UN, 1984), Sales No. E.84.II.A.8. The case studies on Austria and the FRG were scheduled to be published in 1986; they are summarized in "Transborder Data Flows", E/C.10/1986/16 of 12 February 1986, and "Transborder Data Flows and the Federal Republic of Germany", paper before the twelfth session of the Commission on Transnational Corporations, New York, 9–18 April 1986, mimeo. A case study prepared by the US was eventually not submitted to the UN; it is available from the US Department of State. See Interagency Working Group on Transborder Data Flow, *op. cit.*

[111] See *Commission on Transnational Corporations: Report on the Eleventh Session (10–19 April 1985)*. Economic and Social Council, *Official Records*, 1985, Supplement No. 8, UN publication, Sales No. E/1985/28, p. 40.

[112] UNCTC, "Data Services in Latin America and the Caribbean" (New York: UNCTC, 1985), mimeo.

¹¹³ *Commission on Transnational Corporations: Report on the Tenth Session (17–27 April 1984), Economic and Social Council, Official Records, 1984, Supplement No. 8,* UN publication, Sales No. E/1984/18, p. 32. See also "Message Delivered by Mr. Carlos del Campo, Personal Representative of Ambassador Porfirio Muñoz Ledo, President of the Group of 77 in New York", to the Second IBI World Conference on Transborder Data Flow Policies (Rome: IBI, 1984), mimeo., p. 2.

Conclusions

Data industries, and within them especially data services, are the pole around which economic development is being restructured. Internationally, trade in data services (or transborder data flows) is important for three reasons: it is a growing economic activity in its own right; it increasingly furnishes the infrastructure for international trade in goods and services and for the activities of transnational corporations; and it increases the tradeability of many other services. Recognizing the importance of transborder data flows, various fora have begun work on a number of aspects of this phenomenon. One of them, the OECD, has got so far as to adopt, in 1985, a Declaration on Transborder Data Flows—the first international public-policy instrument for trade in data services.

The adoption of this instrument occurred at a time when transborder data flows were already being seen in a broader context, namely that of trade in services in general. Since TDF are a service themselves, this is not surprising. In addition, the role of these data flows in increasing the tradeability of other services means that data services are a core service and that any discussion of them is intertwined inextricably with that of trade in services in general.

Discussions on an international regime for trade in services have begun in GATT. They are fuelled primarily by a desire to reduce barriers to trade in services (or to keep them as low as possible) and to ensure that various mechanisms are established through which this can be done. The US is actively promoting these discussions at the bilateral, regional and international levels and the developed market economies as a group have concluded that such a regime is desirable. These countries are likely to proceed, either by themselves or with the participation of others, with the establishment of an international regime for trade in services. In either case, data services—because of their nature as a core service—are likely to be one of the most important service areas to be covered. And in either case, the resulting international regime is bound to become an important parameter for economic development in general and for international service trade in particular. Furthermore, by regulating international trade in services, this regime is likely to have a considerable influence on the growth of the domestic service sector—which accounts for the largest share of GDP in most countries.

A curious aspect of the current international discussion of services is that it focuses on *trade* in services and not on *FDI* in services. This is curious for a number of reasons:

- As documented earlier, the value of services delivered to foreign markets via foreign affiliates of transnational corporations of major developed countries is double that delivered via trade; in the case of the US, sales of foreign service affiliates are, in fact, five times higher than service exports.

- The barriers facing FDI in services are probably considerably higher and more common than those facing trade in services.
- The 1984 US Trade and Tariff Act provides a comprehensive and integrated framework for vigorous action on both trade *and* FDI in services. In fact, the Act is remarkable for the extent to which it sees trade and FDI as interrelated, an approach that is particularly important for services.
- Negotiations in GATT are already complicated by the introduction of the new issue of trade in services. Since trade in services also involves certain FDI aspects, this further complicates the GATT negotiations. Conversely, a resolution of the FDI issues cannot but facilitate the trade negotiations.
- Finally, the last GATT round has lasted six years, and the new round is not likely to be much shorter, especially in the light of the complicating factors just mentioned. On the other hand, a framework (even if non-binding) for FDI—which would also cover services—is within reach: the United Nations Code of Conduct on Transnational Corporations.

Yet, in spite of all these facts, the clear emphasis of the international discussion on services has been on trade and not on FDI in services. Before elaborating on some of these points, an effort to understand the reasons for the neglect of the FDI dimension is in order.

- One reason could be that trade is a less sensitive matter than FDI and, therefore, lends itself to faster action and results. FDI involves the control of economic activities by foreigners and some key issues surrounding FDI—right of establishment, national treatment, nationalization and compensation, dispute settlement, role of international law—belong to the most intractable international public-policy issues, particularly between developed and developing countries. It should be noted, however, that the validity of this observation is tempered by the fact that an international framework for FDI is within reach.[1]
- Perhaps more importantly, the growing role of trade in data services in its own right and the role of these services in turn as the infrastructure for trade in both goods and services make it urgent to adopt measures that maintain the present largely unrestricted international environment for TDF. And this can perhaps best be achieved in the framework of an agreement on services in general. In particular, to the extent that TDF become the lifeblood of the operations of transnational corporations, the interest of these corporations in a stable and predictable regime for trade in data services increases very significantly.
- The increase of tradeability of certain services because of the advent of TDF opens vistas for trade in these services which are considerably more promising in their potential than FDI in services, especially given the fact that the share of service production entering international trade is markedly lower than that of industry. An international framework that permits the dynamic expansion of trade in these services could, therefore, be very desirable. By the same token, the advent of TDF may make FDI in certain services comparatively less important, in so far as the establishment of foreign affiliates may no longer be a precondition for delivering these services to foreign markets.

- Finally, and perhaps most basically, most participants in the international services debate may simply be unaware that FDI in services is more important than trade in services in delivering services to foreign markets, and thus fail to give sufficient attention to FDI.

Whatever the relative importance of these factors, the basic fact remains that FDI is considerably more important than trade in delivering services to foreign markets and it is likely that this will remain so in the foreseeable future. Sooner or later this economic reality will assert itself in the international discussions on an appropriate framework for international transactions in services. Besides, as discussed earlier, some of the key concepts discussed in the trade context (e.g., right of presence, establishment trade) are very close to FDI concepts, or actually overlap with them because it is usually quite difficult to determine the point at which trade in a service ends and local production of the same service through FDI begins. For a number of services, trade may, therefore, be inextricably linked to FDI, with the implication that a regime for trade in services may only have a full value if certain FDI issues are resolved as well.

Some efforts have, in fact, been made as regards the FDI side of services— but only at the bilateral and regional levels, where services have, at least to a certain extent, been covered by bilateral investment protection treaties and OECD instruments. There are also some signs that a few developed market economies, led by the US, wish to introduce issues relating to FDI in services in the international discussion. For these countries, the preferred forum is GATT. But since GATT clearly has no competence regarding FDI, the subject could be introduced there only under the aspect of trade-related FDI issues. The recent developments in US trade law discussed in chapter III and the emphasis given to such concepts as right of presence as a trade concept suggest that this is, in fact, a possibility. The advantage of this approach is of course that it would permit the simultaneous examination of trade and FDI issues in services and would not require a separation of issues that are so closely linked.

One must, however, examine whether it is feasible to solve the services FDI issues in the context of GATT and, if so, whether it is possible without extended delays. For one, FDI issues in this approach would be dealt with in an indirect way only, namely from the *trade-related* angle. In other words, it would be very difficult to face FDI issues squarely and on the basis of their own merit. Given the importance of FDI in services, this may simply not be good enough. On the other hand, any direct discussion of FDI issues in GATT is bound to be opposed by many countries, and probably not only developing countries, because GATT clearly has no mandate to deal with FDI. The efforts to include trade in services in GATT have already been strongly resisted by a number of countries because GATT is seen as having no competence in this matter. These (and other) countries can be expected to object even more vehemently to the inclusion of FDI aspects in the GATT services discussion, thus adding to the strain on GATT and further delaying any agreement. The last GATT round lasted six years. The introduction of the entirely new issue of services into GATT is not likely to speed up the new round. If FDI issues are added to that, ten years for the next round may not be an inconceivable time-span.

Such delays would certainly increase the likelihood that new barriers to trade in services would be established, especially in the area of data services. For, if data services are in fact as important as they are generally believed to be, it is only a question of time before more and more countries pursue strategies that maximize the location of data services on their territories, using all measures permissible to advance this objective. In a sense, therefore, the establishment of a multilaterally agreed framework for international transactions in services is a race against time. It is a race during which differing national frameworks are likely to be established and restrictive national actions are likely to proliferate, probably leading to costly and disruptive conflicts. Conversely, since international transactions in data services are still largely unrestricted, swift multilateral action could perhaps prevent a Balkanization of public-policy frameworks for data services.

For those interested in creating a stable and predictable framework for international transactions in services, all this suggests that they ought to press ahead in GATT with the establishment of a regime for trade in services while, at the same time, pursuing with even greater interest the establishment of an international FDI framework which also covers services. The adoption of an FDI framework would not only cover the by far more important component of international transactions in services but could also diffuse the thorny FDI aspects in the service-trade debate and thus contribute to their solution. Such an approach calls, of course, for an adjustment of priorities in the international politics of trade and FDI in services, especially on the part of the United States, in that considerably more attention would have to be given to the formulation of an international framework for FDI (without, of course, giving up the efforts in the trade area).

Such an adjustment in priorities not only seems to make economic and political sense but it could also be crowned with success without much delay. The reason is that the adoption of an international framework for FDI, the United Nations Code of Conduct on Transnational Corporations, is within reach.

The recognition of the need for a comprehensive international framework for FDI, supported by all states, predates the services discussion. It is grounded in the fact that although FDI has become the most important international economic activity, no framework comparable to that provided by GATT for trade and the IMF for finance exists for FDI. All countries, including the most important developed countries, concur that such a framework in the form of a Code of Conduct is needed and they are joined in this assessment by the international trade union movement and the international business community. As recently as 1984, for instance, the Global One Hundred, a group of international business executives mostly from transnational corporations, adopted a statement in which this group urged that the international agenda include, among other things, the establishment "of an international organization to create and enforce rules for foreign investment, as GATT does for world trade, with powers to protect the rights and security of investors and of host countries."[2]

Negotiations on a Code of Conduct began in 1977 in the framework of an Intergovernmental Working Group on the Code of Conduct established by the United Nations Commission on Transnational Corporations. In 1983, these negotiations were continued in a special session, open to all states, of the Commission on Transnational Corporations.[3] The United States, the United Kingdom, the Federal Republic of Germany, France, Switzerland, and Sweden are among the leaders in these negotiations on the part of the developed countries; Mexico, Brazil, Egypt, India, Pakistan, and Bangladesh are among the leaders on the part of the developing countries. It is taken for granted that the Code will be adopted by consensus, not only because this is the normal procedure of the Commission but also because a Code which is not supported by the principal home countries would lose much of its effectiveness. Furthermore, on the insistence of the developed countries, the Code is almost certain to be a voluntary instrument. Nevertheless, it could still become the basis on which stronger obligations could be built, if and when this is desired by all countries.

The negotiations on the Code are an effort to define—in a balanced manner and with the participation of all countries—the rights and responsibilities of both transnational corporations and governments, among the latter especially those of host countries. Accordingly, one central part of the Code lays down broad guidelines for the activities of TNCs; almost all the provisions in this part have already been agreed upon. Their main thrust is to encourage transnational corporations to maximize their contribution to the development process while minimizing any negative effects that may be associated with their activities. This part of the Code does not go beyond what had been agreed upon by the developed countries of the OECD in the framework of that Organisation's "Guidelines for Multinational Enterprises."

Another central part of the Code lays down guidelines for the behavior of governments vis-à-vis TNCs; a number of the provisions in this part are also agreed upon and formulations exist for the remaining ones which are close to consensus. Their main thrust is to establish a stable and predictable framework for FDI and the activities of TNCs. When adopted, these provisions would, for the first time, specify in an international agreement what governments can or cannot do in relation to foreign investors. They will cover such issues as the applicability of international law or obligations; nationalization, compensation and dispute settlement; fair and equitable treatment; national treatment; choice of law; and a number of other principles that are considered important by governments and are central to the conduct of international business. In short, the Code will contain all the elements required for an effective framework for FDI.

Together, these two central parts of the Code, which are complemented by provisions dealing with inter-governmental cooperation and implementation machinery, will indeed establish a framework defining the rights and responsibilities of TNCs and governments in the area of FDI. In this manner, the Code will contribute to the stability and predictability needed to develop mutually satisfactory relations between TNCs and countries. At the same time, it would help to reduce tensions and conflicts between corporations and governments, thereby decreasing the risks of costly and disruptive confrontations.

Although the negotiations on the Code predate the services discussions, the Code would fully cover FDI in services and thus establish an international framework for this activity. In fact, the Commission on Transnational Corporations has special competence in services because, since its inception in 1975, it has dealt with a number of service industries (including banking, insurance, advertising, shipping, and tourism) on the basis of studies prepared by the Centre on Transnational Corporations. In addition, the Commission has, as discussed earlier, paid special attention to TDF.

At the beginning of 1986, the negotiations on the Code had reached a stage at which, with a certain amount of political will, they could be concluded in two or three sessions of two to three weeks' duration each.[4] On the substantive side, the single most important obstacle concerns some fine legal differences on how exactly to refer to international law or obligations as far as the application of the Code is concerned. However, an independent group of experts from business, trade unions and academia from developed and developing countries which is advising the Commission agreed within two weeks in June 1985 on a text which settled the principal outstanding issues.[5] On the political side, the single most important obstacle concerns the question of whether less than a handful of key countries really want the Code. The reluctance of a few of them may well reflect general mistrust of the United Nations. More importantly, it may reflect simply a concentration on trade issues combined with a lack of awareness of the importance of the FDI dimension in international service transactions, the advanced stage of the negotiations of the Code, and the implications of an agreement on an FDI framework for the negotiations on trade in services. Be that as it may, the economic and political realities are clear: those who wish to deal with international transactions in services without delay would be well-advised to pay close attention to the Code of Conduct on Transnational Corporations. It is likely that, if the United States strongly favored the adoption of the Code, it could be finalized within a year.

The stakes are high. Obviously, therefore, it is of paramount importance that all countries that have not yet done so identify their interests and examine especially the implications of an international regime for trade and FDI in services for the development of their own service sector and especially its data-service component, with a view to ensuring that any agreement takes their needs into account as far as possible. In this process, special attention has to be given to the rapidly changing underlying technology. More specifically, countries must make sure that they consider trade and FDI in services on the basis of where technological developments are likely to be in the early 1990s, and not where they had been in the early 1980s. If this is not done, a number of the issues they address may well be obsolete by the time an international framework is established, while new ones have not yet been perceived by all parties involved.

It has been observed for the US that "information policy must be given higher-level policy attention. . . . Information wars will be difficult to deter. The United States must begin to assemble an information policy today if it wishes to avoid the high cost of unpreparedness tomorrow."[6] If this is true for the US—which has taken the lead in this field—it is a fortiori true for other countries and especially for most developing ones. If serious policy attention is not paid to trade and FDI in data services, if countries are not prepared for international negotiations, they may well suffer serious disadvantages for the development of their data resources and therefore for their economic development in general.

At the beginning of 1986, most countries were certainly not prepared for negotiations. In fact, the imbalance of awareness and preparedness between developed market economies on the one hand and developing and socialist countries on the other was striking. The OECD has for years put considerable resources into work on international service transactions, conducted a number of sectoral studies, engaged in in-depth examinations of a conceptual framework for international transactions in services, and even adopted several instruments dealing with aspects of the subject. The developing and socialist countries, on the other hand—leaving aside a few country studies and a few discussions in SELA—have done practically no preparatory work. They are where the OECD was at the end of the 1970s (when the services discussion began there), if not at the beginning of the 1960s (when the OECD adopted the first instruments which also cover services).

In this situation it is unavoidable that those who are prepared determine the questions asked, the concepts discussed, the direction taken and the solutions explored—in short, they determine the agenda, if not the outcome of the negotiations.

While this imbalance may have some temporary advantages for those who are prepared, it is decidedly *not* the basis for creating a lasting international framework for service transactions. For one, this situation is bound to slow down negotiations because unprepared countries will have to undergo their learning process during the negotiations. More importantly, however, any framework that is not built on a full appreciation of the interests of all countries involved is not likely to be a stable and durable one. Rather, as soon as it becomes apparent that certain interests have not been considered, the countries affected will seek revisions, thus putting the entire framework into question with—costs and disruptions for everyone.

In the light of this, the US policy of encouraging the examination of international transactions in services in a number of forums is a policy of enlightened self-interest. It is now for the other developed countries and especially the developing and socialist countries to prepare themselves as well and to define their interests. Given the importance of the service sector in general and of data services in particular, the establishment of a framework for international transactions in these fields is inevitable. The only questions are what, when, where and how.

Notes

[1] The argument could be made that the FDI side of service transactions for the developing countries could be dealt with through bilateral investment treaties. As indicated earlier, however, these treaties are regarded with reservations by the developing countries in general, and a number of the most important among them have refused to sign such treaties. In any case, it appears to be opinio juris that the existence of a network of bilateral treaties containing basically (or even verbatim) the same clauses does not in and by itself constitute customary international law. (Bilateral extradition and air-transit treaties, for instance, widely use the same language, but it is not claimed that the network of these treaties constitutes customary international law binding on third parties.) See Oscar Schachter, "Compensation for Expropriation", *American Journal of International Law*, 78 (January 1984), p. 126.

[2] The Global One Hundred, "A Statement of the Global One Hundred" (New York: Business International, 1984), mimeo., p. 2.

[3] For the text of the draft Code see, *The CTC Reporter*, 12 (Summer 1982), pp. 3–4, 23–26.

[4] For a discussion of the "Outstanding Issues" see, *The CTC Reporter*, 18 (Autumn 1984), pp. 8–14. For formulations that can resolve these issues, see "Solutions to Principal Outstanding Issues in the Draft Code of Conduct on Transnational Corporations", E/C.10/1986/S/2 of 11 December 1985.

[5] See "Statement of the Expert Advisers", *The CTC Reporter*, 20 (Autumn 1985), pp. 18–19.

[6] Joan E. Spero, "Information: The Policy Void", *Foreign Policy*, 48 (Fall 1982), p. 156.

Annex I

Recommendation of the OECD Council
Concerning Guidelines Governing the Protection
of Privacy and Transborder Flows of Personal Data

(OECD, *Guidelines on the Protection of Privacy and Transborder Flows of Personal Data* [Paris: OECD, 1981], pp. 7–12)

THE COUNCIL,

Having regard to articles 1(c), 3(a) and 5(b) of the Convention on the Organisation for Economic Co-operation and Development of 14th December, 1960;

RECOGNISING:

that, although national laws and policies may differ, Member countries have a common interest in protecting privacy and individual liberties, and in reconciling fundamental but competing values such as privacy and the free flow of information;

that automatic processing and transborder flows of personal data create new forms of relationships among countries and require the development of compatible rules and practices;

that transborder flows of personal data contribute to economic and social development;

that domestic legislation concerning privacy protection and transborder flows of personal data may hinder such transborder flows;

Determined to advance the free flow of information between Member countries and to avoid the creation of unjustified obstacles to the development of economic and social relations among Member countries;

RECOMMENDS

1. That Member countries take into account in their domestic legislation the principles concerning the protection of privacy and individual liberties set forth in the Guidelines contained in the Annex to this Recommendation which is an integral part thereof;

2. That Member countries endeavour to remove or avoid creating, in the name of privacy protection, unjustified obstacles to transborder flows of personal data;

3. That Member countries co-operate in the implementation of the Guidelines set forth in the Annex;

4. That Member countries agree as soon as possible on specific procedures of consultation and co-operation for the application of these Guidelines.

Annex to the Recommendation of the Council
of 23rd September 1980

GUIDELINES GOVERNING THE PROTECTION OF PRIVACY
AND TRANSBORDER FLOWS OF PERSONAL DATA

PART ONE:
GENERAL

Definitions

1. For the purposes of these Guidelines:
   a) "data controller" means a party who, according to domestic law, is competent to decide about the contents and use of personal data regardless of whether or not such data are collected, stored, processed or disseminated by that party or by an agent on its behalf;
   b) "personal data" means any information relating to an identified or identifiable individual (data subject);
   c) "transborder flows of personal data" means movements of personal data across national borders.

Scope of Guidelines

2. These Guidelines apply to personal data, whether in the public or private sectors, which, because of the manner in which they are processed, or because of their nature or the context in which they are used, pose a danger to privacy and individual liberties.

3. These Guidelines should not be interpreted as preventing:
   a) the application, to different categories of personal data, of different protective measures depending upon their nature and the context in which they are collected, stored, processed or disseminated;
   b) the exclusion from the application of the Guidelines of personal data which obviously do not contain any risk to privacy and individual liberties; or
   c) the application of the Guidelines only to automatic processing of personal data.

4. Exceptions to the Principles contained in Parts Two and Three of these Guidelines, including those relating to national sovereignty, national security and public policy ("ordre public"), should be:

a) as few as possible, and
b) made known to the public.

5. In the particular case of Federal countries the observance of these Guidelines may be affected by the division of powers in the Federation.

6. These Guidelines should be regarded as minimum standards which are capable of being supplemented by additional measures for the protection of privacy and individual liberties.

PART TWO:
BASIC PRINCIPLES OF NATIONAL APPLICATION

Collection Limitation Principle

7. There should be limits to the collection of personal data and any such data should be obtained by lawful and fair means and, where appropriate, with the knowledge or consent of the data subject.

Data Quality Principle

8. Personal data should be relevant to the purposes for which they are to be used, and, to the extent necessary for those purposes, should be accurate, complete and kept up-to-date.

Purpose Specification Principle

9. The purposes for which personal data are collected should be specified not later than at the time of data collection and the subsequent use limited to the fulfilment of those purposes or such others as are not incompatible with those purposes and as are specified on each occasion of change of purpose.

Use Limitation Principle

10. Personal data should not be disclosed, made available or otherwise used for purposes other than those specified in accordance with Paragraph 9 except:
    a) with the consent of the data subject; or
    b) by the authority of law.

Security Safeguards Principle

11. Personal data should be protected by reasonable security safeguards against such risks as loss or unauthorized access, destruction, use, modification or disclosure of data.

Openness Principle

12. There should be a general policy of openness about developments, practices and policies with respect to personal data. Means should be readily available of establishing the existence and nature of personal data, and the main purposes of their use, as well as the identity and usual residence of the data controller.

Individual Participation Principle

13. An individual should have the right:
   a) to obtain from a data controller, or otherwise, confirmation of whether or not the data controller has data relating to him;
   b) to have communicated to him, data relating to him
      i) within a reasonable time;
      ii) at a charge, if any, that is not excessive;
      iii) in a reasonable manner; and
      iv) in a form that is readily intelligible to him;
   c) to be given reasons if a request made under subparagraphs (a) and (b) is denied, and to be able to challenge such denial; and
   d) to challenge data relating to him and, if the challenge is successful, to have the data erased, rectified, completed or amended.

Accountability Principle

14. A data controller should be accountable for complying with measures which give effect to the principle stated above.

PART THREE:
BASIC PRINCIPLES OF INTERNATIONAL APPLICATION:
FREE FLOW AND LEGITIMATE RESTRICTIONS

15. Member countries should take into consideration the implications for other Member countries of domestic processing and re-export of personal data.

16. Member countries should take all reasonable and appropriate steps to ensure that transborder flows of personal data, including transit through a Member country, are uninterrupted and secure.

17. A Member country should refrain from restricting transborder flows of personal data between itself and another Member country except where the latter does not yet substantially observe these Guidelines or where the re-export of such data would circumvent its domestic privacy legislation. A Member country may also impose restrictions in respect of certain categories of personal data for which its domestic privacy legislation includes specific regulations in view of the nature of those data and for which the other Member country provides no equivalent protection.

18. Member countries should avoid developing laws, policies and practices in the name of the protection of privacy and individual liberties, which would create obstacles to transborder flows of personal data that would exceed requirements for such protection.

PART FOUR:
NATIONAL IMPLEMENTATION

19. In implementing domestically the principles set forth in Parts Two and Three, Member countries should establish legal, administrative or other procedures or

institutions for the protection of privacy and individual liberties in respect of personal data. Member countries should in particular endeavour to:
  a) adopt appropriate domestic legislation;
  b) encourage and support self-regulation, whether in the form of codes of conduct or otherwise;
  c) provide for reasonable means for individuals to exercise their rights;
  d) provide for adequate sanctions and remedies in case of failures to comply with measures which implement the principles set forth in Parts Two and Three; and
  e) ensure that there is no unfair discrimination against data subjects.

PART FIVE:
INTERNATIONAL CO-OPERATION

20. Member countries should, where requested, make known to other Member countries details of the observance of the principles set forth in these Guidelines. Member countries should also ensure that procedures for transborder flows of personal data and for the protection of privacy and individual liberties are simple and compatible with those of other Member countries which comply with these Guidelines.

21. Member countries should establish procedures to facilitate:
  i) information exchange related to these Guidelines, and
  ii) mutual assistance in the procedural and investigative matters involved.

22. Member countries should work towards the development of principles, domestic and international, to govern the applicable law in the case of transborder flows of personal data.

Annex II

Convention of the Council of Europe for the Protection of Individuals with Regard to Automatic Processing of Personal Data

(*European Treaty Series*, No. 108 [Strasbourg: Council of Europe, 1981], pp. 2–11)

PREAMBLE

The member States of the Council of Europe, signatory hereto,

Considering that the aim of the Council of Europe is to achieve greater unity between its members, based in particular on respect for the rule of law, as well as human rights and fundamental freedoms;

Considering that it is desirable to extend the safeguards for everyone's rights and fundamental freedoms, and in particular the right to the respect for privacy, taking account of the increasing flow across frontiers of personal data undergoing automatic processing;

Reaffirming at the same time their commitment to freedom of information regardless of frontiers;

Recognising that it is necessary to reconcile the fundamental values of the respect for privacy and the free flow of information between peoples,

Have agreed as follows:

CHAPTER I—GENERAL PROVISIONS

Article 1:
Object and purpose

The purpose of this convention is to secure in the territory of each Party for every individual, whatever his nationality or residence, respect for his rights and fundamental freedoms, and in particular his right to privacy, with regard to automatic processing of personal data relating to him ("data protection").

Article 2:
Definitions

For the purposes of this convention:

a. "personal data" means any information relating to an identified or identifiable individual ("data subject");

b. "automated data file" means any set of data undergoing automatic processing;

c. "automatic processing" includes the following operations if carried out in whole or in part by automated means: storage of data, carrying out of logical and/ or arithmetical operations on those data, their alteration, erasure, retrieval or dissemination;

d. "controller of the file" means the natural or legal person, public authority, agency or any other body who is competent according to the national law to decide what should be the purpose of the automated data file, which categories of personal data should be stored and which operations should be applied to them.

Article 3:
Scope

1. The Parties undertake to apply this convention to automated personal data files and automatic processing of personal data in the public and private sectors.

2. Any State may, at the time of signature or when depositing its instruments of ratification, acceptance, approval or accession, or at any later time, give notice by a declaration addressed to the Secretary General of the Council of Europe:

a. that it will not apply this convention to certain categories of automated personal data files, a list of which will be deposited. In this list it shall not include, however, categories of automated data files subject under its domestic law to data protection provisions. Consequently, it shall amend this list by a new declaration whenever additional categories of automated personal data files are subjected to data protection provisions under its domestic law;

b. that it will also apply this convention to information relating to groups of persons, associations, foundations, companies, corporations and any other bodies consisting directly or indirectly of individuals, whether or not such bodies possess legal personality;

c. that it will also apply this convention to personal data files which are not processed automatically.

3. Any State which has extended the scope of this convention by any of the declarations provided for in sub-paragraph 2.b or c above may give notice in the said declaration that such extensions shall apply only to certain categories of personal data files, a list of which will be deposited.

4. Any Party which has excluded certain categories of automated personal data files by a declaration provided for in sub-paragraph 2.a above may not claim the application of this convention to such categories by a Party which has not excluded them.

5. Likewise, a Party which has not made one or other of the extensions provided for in sub-paragraphs 2.b and c above may not claim the application of this convention on these points with respect to a Party which has made such extensions.

6. The declarations provided for in paragraph 2 above shall take effect from the moment of the entry into force of the convention with regard to the State which has made them if they have been made at the time of signature or deposit of its instrument of ratification, acceptance, approval or accession, or three months after their receipt by the Secretary General of the Council of Europe if they have been made at any later time. These declarations may be withdrawn, in whole or in part, by a notification addressed to the Secretary General of the Council of Europe. Such withdrawals shall take effect three months after the date of receipt of such notification.

CHAPTER II—BASIC PRINCIPLES FOR DATA PROTECTION

Article 4:
Duties of the Parties

1. Each Party shall take the necessary measures in its domestic law to give effect to the basic principles for data protection set out in this chapter.

2. These measures shall be taken at the latest at the time of entry into force of this convention in respect of that Party.

Article 5:
Quality of data

Personal data undergoing automatic processing shall be:

    a. obtained and processed fairly and lawfully;

    b. stored for specified and legitimate purposes and not used in a way incompatible with those purposes;

    c. adequate, relevant and not excessive in relation to the purposes for which they are stored;

    d. accurate and, where necessary, kept up to date;

    e. preserved in a form which permits identification of the data subjects for no longer than is required for the purpose for which those data are stored.

Article 6:
Special categories of data

Personal data revealing racial origin, political opinions or religious or other beliefs, as well as personal data concerning health or sexual life, may not be processed automatically unless domestic law provides appropriate safeguards. The same shall apply to personal data relating to criminal convictions.

Article 7:
Data security

Appropriate security measures shall be taken for the protection of personal data stored in automated data files against accidental or unauthorised destruction or accidental loss as well as against unauthorised access, alteration or dissemination.

Article 8:
Additional safeguards for the data subject

Any person shall be enabled:

a. to establish the existence of an automated personal data file, its main purposes, as well as the identity and habitual residence or principal place of business of the controller of the file;

b. to obtain at reasonable intervals and without excessive delay or expense confirmation of whether personal data relating to him are stored in the automated data file as well as communication to him of such data in an intelligible form;

c. to obtain, as the case may be, rectification or erasure of such data if these have been processed contrary to the provisions of domestic law giving effect to the basic principles set out in Articles 5 and 6 of this convention;

d. to have a remedy if a request for confirmation or, as the case may be, communication, rectification or erasure as referred to in paragraphs b and c of this article is not complied with.

Article 9:
Exceptions and restrictions

1. No exception to the provisions of Articles 5, 6 and 8 of this convention shall be allowed except within the limits defined in this article.

2. Derogation from the provisions of Articles 5, 6 and 8 of this convention shall be allowed when such derogation is provided for by the law of the Party and constitutes a necessary measure in a democratic society in the interests of:

a. protecting State security, public safety, the monetary interests of the State or the suppression of criminal offences;

b. protecting the data subject or the rights and freedoms of others.

3. Restrictions on the exercise of the rights specified in Article 8, paragraphs b, c and d, may be provided by law with respect to automated personal data files used for statistics or for scientific research purposes when there is obviously no risk of an infringement of the privacy of the data subjects.

Article 10:
Sanctions and remedies

Each Party undertakes to establish appropriate sanctions and remedies for violations of provisions of domestic law giving effect to the basic principles for data protection set out in this chapter.

Article 11:
Extended protection

None of the provisions of this chapter shall be interpreted as limiting or otherwise affecting the possibility for a Party to grant data subjects a wider measure of protection than that stipulated in this convention.

CHAPTER III—TRANSBORDER DATA FLOWS

Article 12:
Transborder flows of personal data
and domestic law

1. The following provisions shall apply to the transfer across national borders, by whatever medium, of personal data undergoing automatic processing or collected with a view to their being automatically processed.

2. A Party shall not, for the sole purpose of the protection of privacy, prohibit or subject to special authorisation transborder flows of personal data going to the territory of another Party.

3. Nevertheless, each party shall be entitled to derogate from the provisions of paragraph 2:

a. insofar as its legislation includes specific regulations for certain categories of personal data or of automated personal data files, because of the nature of those data or those files, except where the regulations of the other Party provide an equivalent protection;

b. when the transfer is made from its territory to the territory of a non-Contracting State through the intermediary of the territory of another Party, in order to avoid such transfers resulting in circumvention of the legislation of the Party referred to at the beginning of this paragraph.

CHAPTER IV—MUTUAL ASSISTANCE

Article 13:
Co-operation between Parties

1. The parties agree to render each other mutual assistance in order to implement this convention.

2. For that purpose:

a. each party shall designate one or more authorities, the name and address of each of which it shall communicate to the Secretary General of the Council of Europe;

b. each Party which has designated more than one authority shall specify in its communication referred to in the previous sub-paragraph the competence of each authority.

3. An authority designated by a Party shall at the request of an authority designated by another Party:

a. furnish information on its law and administrative practice in the field of data protection;

b. take, in conformity with its domestic law and for the sole purpose of protection of privacy, all appropriate measures for furnishing factual information relating to specific automatic processing carried out in its territory, with the exception however of the personal data being processed.

Article 14:
Assistance to data subjects
resident abroad

1. Each Party shall assist any person resident abroad to exercise the rights conferred by its domestic law giving effect to the principles set out in Article 8 of this convention.

2. When such a person resides in the territory of another Party he shall be given the option of submitting his request through the intermediary of the authority designated by that Party.

3. The request for assistance shall contain all the necessary particulars, relating inter alia to:

a. the name, address and any other relevant particulars identifying the person making the request;

b. the automated personal data file to which the request pertains, or its controller;

c. the purpose of the request.

Article 15:
Safeguards concerning assistance
rendered by designated authorities

1. An authority designated by a Party which has received information from an authority designated by another Party either accompanying a request for assistance or in reply to its own request for assistance shall not use that information for purposes other than those specified in the request for assistance.

2. Each Party shall see to it that the persons belonging to or acting on behalf of the designated authority shall be bound by appropriate obligations of secrecy or confidentiality with regard to that information.

3. In no case may a designated authority be allowed to make under Article 14, paragraph 2, a request for assistance on behalf of a data subject resident abroad, of its own accord and without the express consent of the person concerned.

Article 16:
Refusal of requests for assistance

A designated authority to which a request for assistance is addressed under Articles 13 or 14 of this convention may not refuse to comply with it unless:

a. the request is not compatible with the powers in the field of data protection of the authorities responsible for replying;

b. the request does not comply with the provisions of this convention;

c. compliance with the request would be incompatible with the sovereignty, security or public policy (ordre public) of the Party by which it was designated, or with the rights and fundamental freedoms of persons under the jurisdiction of that Party.

Article 17:
Costs and procedures of assistance

1. Mutual assistance which the Parties render each other under Article 13 and assistance they render to data subjects abroad under Article 14 shall not give rise to the payment of any costs or fees other than those incurred for experts and interpreters. The latter costs or fees shall be borne by the Party which has designated the authority making the request for assistance.

2. The data subject may not be charged costs or fees in connection with the steps taken on his behalf in the territory of another Party other than those lawfully payable by residents of that Party.

3. Other details concerning the assistance relating in particular to the forms and procedures and the languages to be used, shall be established directly between the Parties concerned.

CHAPTER V—CONSULTATIVE COMMITTEE

Article 18:
Composition of the committee

1. A Consultative Committee shall be set up after the entry into force of this convention.

2. Each Party shall appoint a representative to the committee and a deputy representative. Any member State of the Council of Europe which is not a Party to the convention shall have the right to be represented on the committee by an observer.

3. The Consultative Committee may, by unanimous decision, invite any non-member State of the Council of Europe which is not a Party to the convention to be represented by an observer at a given meeting.

Article 19:
Functions of the committee

The Consultative Committee:

    a. may make proposals with a view to facilitating or improving the application of the convention;

    b. may make proposals for amendment of this convention in accordance with Article 21;

    c. shall formulate its opinion on any proposal for amendment of this convention which is referred to it in accordance with Article 21, paragraph 3;

    d. may, at the request of a Party, express an opinion on any question concerning the application of this convention.

Article 20:
Procedure

1. The Consultative Committee shall be convened by the Secretary General of the Council of Europe. Its first meeting shall be held within twelve months of the entry into force of this convention. It shall subsequently meet at least once every two years and in any case when one-third of the representatives of the Parties request its convocation.

2. A majority of representatives of the Parties shall constitute a quorum for a meeting of the Consultative Committee.

3. After each of its meetings, the Consultative Committee shall submit to the Committee of Ministers of the Council of Europe a report on its work and on the functioning of the convention.

4. Subject to the provisions of this convention, the Consultative Committee shall draw up its own Rules of Procedure.

CHAPTER VI—AMENDMENTS

Article 21:
Amendments

1. Amendments to this convention may be proposed by a Party, the Committee of Ministers of the Council of Europe or the Consultative Committee.

2. Any proposal for amendment shall be communicated by the Secretary General of the Council of Europe to the member States of the Council of Europe and to every non-member State which has acceded to or has been invited to accede to this convention in accordance with the provisions of Article 23.

3. Moreover, any amendment proposed by a Party or the Committee of Ministers shall be communicated to the Consultative Committee, which shall submit to the Committee of Ministers its opinion on that proposed amendment.

4. The Committee of Ministers shall consider the proposed amendment and any opinion submitted by the Consultative Committee and may approve the amendment.

5. The text of any amendment approved by the Committee of Ministers in accordance with paragraph 4 of this article shall be forwarded to the Parties for acceptance.

6. Any amendment approved in accordance with paragraph 4 of this article shall come into force on the thirtieth day after all Parties have informed the Secretary General of their acceptance thereof.

CHAPTER VII—FINAL CLAUSES

Article 22:
Entry into force

1. This convention shall be open for signature by the member States of the Council of Europe. It is subject to ratification, acceptance or approval. Instruments of ratification, acceptance or approval shall be deposited with the Secretary General of the Council of Europe.

2. This convention shall enter into force on the first day of the month following the expiration of a period of three months after the date on which five member States of the Council of Europe have expressed their consent to be bound by the convention in accordance with the provisions of the preceding paragraph.

3. In respect of any member State which subsequently expresses its consent to be bound by it, the convention shall enter into force on the first day of the month following the expiration of a period of three months after the date of the deposit of the instrument of ratification, acceptance or approval.

Article 23:
Accession by non-member States

1. After the entry into force of this convention, the Committee of Ministers of the Council of Europe may invite any State not a member of the Council of Europe to accede to this convention by a decision taken by the majority provided for in Article 20.d of the Statute of the Council of Europe and by the unanimous vote of the representatives of the Contracting States entitled to sit on the committee.

2. In respect of any acceding State, the convention shall enter into force on the first day of the month following the expiration of a period of three months after the date of deposit of the instrument of accession with the Secretary General of the Council of Europe.

Article 24:
Territorial clause

1. Any State may at the time of signature or when depositing its instrument of ratification, acceptance, approval or accession, specify the territory or territories to which this convention shall apply.

2. Any State may at any later date, by a declaration addressed to the Secretary General of the Council of Europe, extend the application of this convention to any other territory specified in the declaration. In respect of such territory the convention shall enter into force on the first day of the month following the expiration of a period of three months after the date of receipt of such declaration by the Secretary General.

3. Any declaration made under the two preceding paragraphs may, in respect of any territory specified in such declaration, be withdrawn by a notification addressed to the Secretary General. The withdrawal shall become effective on the first day of the month following the expiration of a period of six months after the date of receipt of such notification by the Secretary General.

Article 25:
Reservations

No reservations may be made in respect of the provisions of this convention.

Article 26:
Denunciation

1. Any Party may at any time denounce this convention by means of a notification addressed to the Secretary General of the Council of Europe.

2. Such denunciation shall become effective on the first day of the month following the expiration of a period of six months after the date of receipt of the notification by the Secretary General.

Article 27:
Notifications

The Secretary General of the Council of Europe shall notify the member States of the Council and any State which has acceded to this convention of:

a. any signature;

b. the deposit of any instrument of ratification, acceptance, approval or accession;

c. any date of entry into force of this convention in accordance with Articles 22, 23 and 24;

d. any other act, notification or communication relating to this convention.

In witness whereof the undersigned, being duly authorised thereto, have signed this Convention.

Done at Strasbourg, the 28th day of January 1981, in English and in French, both texts being equally authoritative, in a single copy which shall remain deposited in the archives of the Council of Europe. The Secretary General of the Council of Europe shall transmit certified copies to each member State of the Council of Europe and to any State invited to accede to this Convention.

Annex III

U.S. National Study on Trade in Services: Executive Summary

(U.S., Office of the United States Trade Representative, "U.S. National Study on Trade in Services" [Washington: USTR, 1983], pp. 1–9)

This study is a broad examination of services trade issues prepared by the U.S. government under recommendations contained in the GATT Council of Ministers' statement of November 1982. It reflects several years of discussion and analysis within the U.S. government and private sector and is intended to serve as a vehicle for exchanging points of view and information with other governments on issues in the services trade area. The discussion in the U.S. national study is not intended to reach hard and fast conclusions but rather to stimulate a broad international discussion of important trade issues in the world service economy.

A descriptive analysis of services in the world economy is developed in Section 1 of the study. Official statistics show that world trade in services exceeded $350 billion—in all likelihood by a substantial amount; among the top 25 exporters were a number of developing and middle income countries. It is argued that domestic economic developments are increasing the importance of world services trade. For example, the greater sophistication of tradeable goods requires an increase in the trade of support services such as training and maintenance. Also, the information revolution in the world economy has drastically lowered the cost and increased the technical feasibility for many service industries to do business abroad. Changes affecting the transportation, banking and insurance, and communications sectors are discussed as examples of how broad economic change in the world economy is increasing the scope for services trade. Finally it is argued that the potential gains to the world economy from reduced barriers to trade in services parallel gains already achieved from 35 years of liberalization of world merchandise trade.

In Section 2 the focus shifts from the world to the U.S. service economy. Services, including government, now account for two-thirds of U.S. gross national product and 70 percent of U.S. employment. The rapid growth in demand for business services, which now account for an estimated 25 percent of U.S. GNP, together with changing consumer tastes and rising incomes help explain the strong growth of the U.S. services economy. Of the 20 million net new jobs created by the U.S. economy in the 1970s, 90 percent were in services. Much of the new employment is in information services and in jobs in areas with an increasingly technological orientation. Contrary to popular perception, evidence suggests that none of the productivity slowdown experienced in the United States in the 1970s (as in other industrial countries) was caused by the shifting of U.S. employment from goods to service industries.

Traditionally, a substantial number of service activities have been quite heavily regulated in the United States as elsewhere, although U.S. policy has preferred to regulate private firms rather than to own and run government monopolies. Economic regulation has been justified on two principal grounds: (1) the preservation of economic efficiencies associated with natural monopolies in some industries while protecting the public from monopoly abuse; and (2) the elimination of inefficiencies thought to be associated with excessive competition in other industries. As the result of a reappraisal of the economic effects of various regulatory regimes in the 1970s, the U.S. government has acted to reduce regulations and administrative requirements affecting a number of service industries. The current regulatory regimes of 10 service industries are described: accounting, telecommunications, banking, insurance, motion pictures, franchising, aviation, travel agents, legal services and maritime. With the exceptions of domestic air and maritime transport as well as direct broadcast signals, the regulatory review suggests that the U.S. market is generally open to foreign service providers who are, with few exceptions, accorded national treatment.

Trade in many service industries is affected by a number of common, generic problems which raise broad conceptual issues. Analysis and discussion of such issues are likely to be helpful in formulating general principles and potential rules and procedures for trade in services. Section 3 identifies and discusses three major conceptual issues: (1) competition between private firms and government monopolies; (2) distinguishing trade in services from investment in services; and (3) the role of immigration and labor in trade in services.

With respect to the relation between private firms and government monopolies, because of its position at home, a public monopoly may have an unequal advantage vis-à-vis private foreign competitors in transborder services such as aviation or telecommunication. Public monopolies may discriminate between domestic and foreign purchasing firms in supplying services, as in the case of national airline ground servicing monopolies engaging in discriminatory practices against airlines of other nations. When public service monopolies are allowed to compete with private firms in providing services not covered by the monopoly, the inherent power of the domestic monopoly may greatly disadvantage foreign private competition. In each of these three areas the trade issue is whether monopolies should be required to adopt an arm's-length relationship between its domestic monopoly activities and its activities as a competitor internationally or as a competitor domestically in services outside the area of its direct monopoly or as a supplier of services.

The concepts of trade and investment in services are discussed in Section 3 as well. Governments have traditionally separated trade from investment issues and developed separate disciplines for each. If countries are to embark on the formulation of trade rules for services, they must know whether this can be done in a meaningful way without dealing with the more sensitive issue of investment in services. Separating trade from investment issues will require a clear distinction between services (or a component of a service) which are traded (i.e., produced abroad) and services produced locally. Thus, data processing services provided by a foreign computer center through long-distance communications links are clearly trade, while the same services provided locally by a foreign-owned computer processing facility are clearly an investment activity.

Under GATT principles, a product that has overcome legitimate barriers at the border is entitled to full national treatment, that is giving a foreign producer the same access to the domestic distribution system as the domestic producer. This existing GATT approach could be applied to services. Access to a national distribution system would be treated as a trade issue, while ownership of the distribution system would be treated as an investment issue. Access to the distribution system would include the right to negotiate with local businesses to provide distribution and servicing facilities or, where establishment is required to provide a service, the right of the foreign firm to establish itself under the national treatment principle.

While it is important for trade negotiating purposes to make a distinction between trade and investment issues, this does not imply that investment barriers are irrelevant for trade. The ability to invest can often enhance a firm's ability to trade. Parallel efforts to reduce foreign investment barriers are taking place multilaterally under the OECD Code on Investment for developed nations and through Bilateral Investment Treaty negotiations for the United States with its trading partners, particularly developing countries.

A third conceptual issue cutting across all services trade is the role of immigration and labor. The ability of a company to conduct service business internationally depends, in many instances, on the ability of salesmen or professionals with specific skills to move across national borders. Foreign personnel may be needed to set up data processing systems, to audit financial records, to train or supervise workers, to transmit or use other special knowledge, skills, expertise or talent required for commercial activities. Trade in services probably depends more heavily on the movement of people than trade in goods. In spite of this, bilateral agreements such as Friendship, Commerce and Navigation (FCN) treaties, rather than trade rules, cover the international movement of businessmen and technical experts. Recent U.S. experience has been that existing arrangements in this area have been inadequate to meet the needs of service industry trade. It is, however, unlikely that a general approach to visa or professional practice problems will be either feasible or desirable over the foreseeable future. While governments are willing to accommodate individual industry representatives under existing bilateral agreements, no government has been willing to undertake general obligations vis-à-vis the world as a whole. Service trade issues that arise because of restrictions on personnel movements will most likely have to be dealt with in the existing legal framework.

Following the discussion of the three broad conceptual issues, Section 4 of the study reviews existing bilateral and multilateral mechanisms applicable or potentially applicable to services trade. These include FCN treaties, Bilateral Investment Treaties as well as agreements related to aviation, maritime and other sectoral and functional areas.

The Organization for Economic Cooperation and Development (OECD) has attempted to promote liberalization of trade in services and of restrictions on international capital flows through the Code of Liberalization of Current Invisible Transactions and the Code of Liberalization of Capital Movements. The Invisibles Code potentially liberalizes trade in all service sectors, however, its application has been restricted by reservations, derogations and limitations on the scope of liberalization measures set down in the Code. For example, the Code contains no blanket provisions for right of establishment, right to conduct business or national treatment, although the Code does contain the possibility to incorporate such disciplines on an industry-by-industry basis. Right of establishment, right to conduct business and national treatment have all been incorporated into the Invisibles Code with respect to the insurance industry, though numerous reservations and derogations have limited their applicability in fact.

The Invisibles Code has several drawbacks as an instrument for further services liberalization: membership is currently limited to OECD countries; obligations can be circumvented with relative ease; there are no strong enforcement mechanisms; and there is a general, if not complete, absence of the rights of establishment and to conduct business and of national treatment from the listed liberalization measures. In its favor, the Invisibles Code is already in force and, with the requisite political will, could be broadened and strengthened. Operation of the Invisibles Code does play a significant role in the process of conceptualizing standards of conduct for trade in services and may be a tool for increased liberalization as the OECD continues to progress in the management of issues that are of particular importance to specific service sectors.

The Capital Movements Code commits OECD members to progressively abolish restrictions on long-term capital flows among themselves. Its relevance to services trade lies in its application to direct investment and the possibility of extending its scope to include at least some aspects of right of establishment.

Recently, the OECD has focused attention on trade in services. The ministerial statement of 1981 noted that OECD activities on services should move forward expeditiously and that when final results emerge, OECD members should examine the ways and means available to improve cooperation on international trade in services. Work has been initiated on several service industry sectors and conceptual trade issues. Work also has been done in the context of various OECD codes of conduct. These codes and declarations, which rely on voluntary compliance, establish standards to guide members' efforts to liberalize restrictions. Although this voluntarism creates problems of compliance, it is also a strength in permitting less inhibited discussion by governments and greater freedom to concentrate on the more sensitive issues that cannot be addressed contractually.

Contracting parties to the General Agreement on Tariffs and Trade (GATT) are committed to reduce trade barriers and discriminatory practices in international commerce. GATT rules focus on trade in goods and cover services only to the extent that they are incidental to goods trade. Nevertheless, as the Tokyo Round of Multilateral Trade Negotiations (MTN) demonstrated, the GATT can be adapted to changes in the international economy. The MTN addressed for the first time non-tariff measures that had become increasingly distortive to international commerce. Services issues were to be included in the Tokyo Round, but negotiators agreed to postpone attention to this area because of the complexities and degree of effort required to extend GATT rules to non-tariff measures. The GATT continues to be a potentially useful instrument with which to establish trade disciplines for services because it is a contractually binding agreement that applies to a large number of developed and developing countries. Since the GATT is primarily designed to deal with merchandise trade and focuses especially on barriers at the border, such as the tariff, it is clear that a simple, blanket extension of the GATT to services is not possible. Nevertheless, it is equally clear that many of the principles embodied in the articles of the GATT could be relevant to services trade.

The body of the U.S. national study discusses the extension of individual GATT articles to services. Of particular importance to trade in services is the principle of national treatment contained in GATT's Article III. A substantial part of the national treatment discipline exists in respect to internal regulatory practices which are a chief source of restriction on service firms' ability to sell in foreign markets. Most-favored-nation (MFN) treatment is, of course, one of the pillars of the GATT system. In principle it should be applicable to services trade, although the special market structure of certain service industries may require careful consideration of how MFN applies in such cases. Freedom of transit is another GATT undertaking which could have particular significance if fully applied to services, including areas such as communication.

Dumping and subsidies exist in the services as well as the goods area. However, technical problems might make the application of anti-dumping and countervailing duty disciplines to services extremely difficult. The complicated adjustment process involved in comparing home to foreign market prices could raise insurmountable technical difficulties in the absence of specific customs and other documents in many service sectors.

Transparency with respect to rules and regulations affecting trade is equally important for goods and services. The process of making transparent rules and regulations that affect trade in services may be more complicated because of the non-tariff nature of most barriers to services. For this reason, however, application of transparency principles is all the more important for services.

Since governments are prone to supply certain services through state-owned enterprises, GATT principles on state trading enterprises could be particularly significant for services. Although exceptions would have to be accepted to accommodate legitimate national interests, the general strictures against the operation of state enterprises so as to create serious obstacles to trade could be particularly useful if applied to services.

The GATT details the rights and obligations of Contracting Parties when differences arise. It establishes procedures for situations in which one party considers that a benefit that is due under the General Agreement "is being nullified or impaired or that the attainment of any objective of the agreement is being impeded" as a result of specified actions by another party. As indicated earlier, the GATT is the only contractually binding multilateral trade agreement in existence, and consultation/dispute settlement procedures are the operational means by which it is enforced. Any services understanding under GATT auspices should contain similar procedures.

During the MTN, GATT member countries focused considerable attention on non-tariff measures. The core of the Tokyo Round results consists of a series of binding agreements, or codes, aimed at reducing and bringing under more effective international discipline these non-tariff measures. All of the codes provide for consultation and dispute settlement. As presently formulated the codes do not relate to services traded independently of goods. There are three MTN agreements that potentially relate to services or now apply to services in very limited ways when they are traded in conjunction with goods.

The Agreement on Government Procurement is the only MTN code that specifically requires signatories to consider developing rules for trade in services.

Signatories to this agreement are currently obligated not to discriminate against or among the products of other signatories in purchases covered by the agreement. The agreement covers only those government ministries, departments, or entities listed in the agreement. Services are covered by the agreement when they are incidental to the supply of goods purchased by code-covered entities so long as the value of these incidental services does not exceed the value of the procured products. Service contracts per se are not covered. The agreement also provides that signatories shall undertake negotiations by the end of 1983 with a view toward broadening and improving the agreement. As part of this exercise, the agreement explicitly requires that signatories consider the possibility of bringing service contracts under the agreement. These negotiations are now underway.

The Agreement on Technical Barriers to Trade (Standards Code) commits signatories to insure that when governments or other bodies adopt standards and technical regulations, engage in the testing or certification of products (for reasons of safety, health, consumer of environmental protection, or other purposes), these activities shall not create unnecessary obstacles to trade. Significantly, the Standard Code provides that signatories accord national treatment to all other signatories in each part of the agreement where it is relevant. The Code provides for both most-favored-nation and national treatment when testing imported products for conformity with technical regulations or standards. The Code's provisions are not applicable to standards involving services. Consideration could be given to the extension of the Standards Code to the procedures for preparing, adopting and applying standards to trade in services. For example, this might be particularly valuable in the telecommunications sector where specific design, testing, and performance standards sometimes make it impossible for foreign firms to compete with or even interconnect with local systems.

The Customs Valuation Agreement provides detailed rules for the determination of customs value of imported goods for the purpose of assessing duties. The Code rules are designed to set a fair, uniform and neutral system for the valuation of goods for customs purposes and to preclude the use of arbitrary or fictitious customs value. In defining the customs valuation treatment of goods, the Code also covers certain services associated with the goods. For example, post-importation charges for construction, assembly and maintenance are not to be included in customs value. The Code leaves open to national discretion the treatment of insurance, transportation and merchandise handling charges associated with moving goods to the place of importation. While primarily relating to the treatment of merchandise, the Code also prescribes whether or not the value of associated services are to form part of dutiable value. As technological advancement becomes increasingly important in the overall competitiveness of goods, and where the level of technology is principally in the form of a service, foreign customs procedures can undermine the value of new processes that achieve comparative advantage.

Section 5 of the U.S. national study considers various possible approaches for establishing a services trade regime. One approach would be to develop single sector agreements open to all interested parties. Such agreements could be tailored to the economic and regulatory particularities of an individual sector. It would, however, be difficult to maintain a consistent trade liberalizing bias among a number of such independent agreements and some agreements could, in fact, become trade restrictive. Sectoral agreements reached bilaterally might be the easiest of all to negotiate. However, they run the additional danger of establishing restrictions against third countries if market sharing arrangements are included. Given the structure of particular markets and overriding concerns of national security or economic development, somewhat restrictive bilateral agreements may represent the greatest achievable degree of competition. Agreements on civil aviation landing rights are a case in point.

Another alternative would be to negotiate bilateral agreements that cover a large number of service sectors. Such agreements could incorporate an exchange between two governments of concessions or benefits for a variety of service sectors and incorporate a number of general principles such as national treatment and transparency. The concept of most-favored-nation treatment, however, would be abandoned in favor of preferential systems based on reciprocal opportunities. Such bilateral accords might nevertheless operate as models for developing the basic rights and obligations appropriate for a healthy multilateral services trade regime.

Different service sectors have their own unique problems. As noted earlier, many service sectors face common trade problems whose reduction or elimination would facilitate a more efficient trading system. Ideally, all sectors should be moving in the same basic direction, albeit in different ways depending on the sector. In order to accomplish such an objective, services trade could operate under a common framework applicable to all sectors with specific rules set out for individual sectors.

A number of principles and procedural elements should be considered for inclusion in such a framework for services. These principles include national treatment, minimization of distortions to trade, nondiscrimination, the right to sell; procedures include transparency, due process, formal dispute settlement procedures and provisions establishing the relationship of the framework agreement to other existing or future agreements, particularly those applicable to individual sectors.

While a consideration of the possible organization of trade negotiations in services is premature at this stage, discussion can be useful in structuring work programs of a formal or informal nature. At this stage, the U.S. government believes that the most workable approach is along the lines of a framework of principles covering all sectors. However, sector-specific issues must blend into such an approach. These conclusions, however, are tentative, and all countries must maintain a certain flexibility in structuring discussions until such time as national studies are completed and a more meaningful exchange of views has occurred.

There are four appendices to the U.S. national study. The first is a statistical analysis of world trade in services based on data reported by the International Monetary Fund. The second appendix describes U.S. methods of collecting data on U.S. international service transactions as well as efforts to improve U.S. services trade data. The discussion in the second appendix also serves as a basis for explaining the presumption that the value of service industry international transactions are currently underestimated. The third appendix is composed of separate papers analyzing the trade issues in twelve service industries: telecommunications engineering and construction, maritime, banking, insurance, professional services, advertising, motion pictures, travel and tourism, franchising, lodging and aviation. The appendix to be supplied is an inventory of selected trade obstacles faced by U.S. service industry exporters in foreign markets. The listing of the inventory is arranged by service sector.

Annex IV

Statement by the President:
International Investment Policy

("Statement by the President: International Investment Policy", reprinted in US
Department of Commerce, *International Direct Investment*
[Washington: Superintendent of Documents, 1984], pp. 85–88)

I am releasing a major statement on international investment. This statement
was developed by my Senior Interdepartmental Group on International Economic
Policy chaired by Treasury Secretary Regan, and encompasses the views of this
Administration on international investment.

The last time such a policy paper was released was in July of 1977—more
than six years ago. Since then, we have come to view international investment
which responds to market forces as a vital and necessary ingredient in a stable,
growing world economy.

A world with strong foreign investment flows is the opposite of a zero-sum
game. We believe there are only winners, no losers, and all participants gain from
it.

International investment flows significantly affect the United States and world
economies. With the current environment of widespread international debt problems, foreign direct investment flows take on increased importance. As the
preeminent home and host country for foreign direct investment, we have a
substantial interest in the conditions under which those flows occur.

The statement I am releasing enunciates the fundamental premise of our
policy—that foreign investment flows which respond to private market forces will
lead to more efficient international production and thereby benefit both home and
host countries.

It also highlights three other important points. First, our concern with the
increasing use of governmental measures to distort or impede international investment flows. Secondly, our strong support for the concept of national treatment
which extends to foreign direct investors in the United States. And finally, an
enumeration of specific multilateral and bilateral steps the Administration has taken,
and will take, to help liberalize international investment flows.

A free and open international investment climate will play a key role, not
only in sustaining our own economic recovery here at home, but also in resolving
many of the current international debt problems.

Executive Summary

International direct investment plays a vital and expanding role in the world economy. To ensure its maximum contribution to both global and domestic economic well-being, the United States believes that international direct investment flows should be determined by private market forces and should receive non-discriminatory treatment consistent with the national treatment principle.

The United States welcomes foreign direct investment that flows according to market forces. The United States accords foreign investors the same fair, equitable, and non-discriminatory treatment it believes all governments should accord foreign direct investment under international law.

The United States opposes continued and increasing government intervention that impedes or distorts investment flows or attempts to shift artificially the benefits of these flows. These measures include trade-related or other performance requirements, fiscal or financial incentives, and discriminatory treatment of foreign investment.

To counter such measures, the United States will pursue an active international investment policy aimed at reducing foreign government actions that impede or distort investment flows, and at developing an international system, based on national treatment and most-favored-nation principles, that permits investment flows to respond more freely to market forces. The United States will work to protect U.S. investment abroad from treatment which is discriminatory or otherwise inconsistent with international law standards. Under international law, no U.S. investment should be expropriated unless the taking is done for a public purpose, is accomplished under due process of law, is non-discriminatory, does not violate previous contractual arrangements, and is accompanied by prompt, adequate, and effective compensation.

In carrying out its international investment policy, in multilateral institutions, the United States will continue to:

- encourage OECD member governments to adhere to, strengthen and extend OECD investment and capital liberalization instruments;
- explore ways of extending the principles embodied in the OECD instruments to non-OECD countries;
- support efforts to increase awareness of the extent and adverse effects of government intervention in order to build a global political consensus to reduce such intervention;
- work toward increased recognition of intellectual property rights;
- work in the OECD to examine investment problems that affect the service industries, recognizing that for these sectors the opportunity to do business in foreign countries is dependent, in many respects, on the ability to establish foreign operations that are governed by discriminatory investment rules;
- work in the OECD for a "data pledge" which would assure that no new barriers to data flows will be imposed by developed countries; and encourage all countries to join in adopting more open and liberal policies on transborder flows;

- work to ensure that any technology transfers which occur are carried out on a sound commercial basis subject to national security and foreign policy considerations;
- encourage the Multilateral Banks to explore ways to strengthen the private sector role in facilitating financial flows to the developing world;
- support investor access to third-party arbitration to settle investment disputes.

In its relations with individual countries, the United States will:

- provide services and assistance to American investors abroad, and offer the full support necessary to ensure that their investments are treated in accordance with standards of international law;
- seek to ensure that the provisions of U.S. Friendship, Commerce and Navigation treaties and bilateral investment treaties and agreements are fully observed;
- seek to conclude bilateral investment treaties and agreements with interested countries;
- explore other appropriate ways to support private direct investment in developing countries;
- reserve the right to take action against the use of performance requirements and similar policies, consistent with international obligations. The United States will also exercise its rights under existing international agreements.

The United States believes that a combination of multilateral and bilateral efforts will contribute to a more open global climate for investment and thus enhance the prospects for economic growth in the United States and globally.

I. Setting

The United States believes that international direct private investment plays a vital and expanding role in the U.S. and world economies. It can act as a catalyst for growth, introduce new technology and management skills, expand employment and improve productivity. Foreign direct investment can be an important source of capital and can stimulate international trade. Both home and host country economies benefit from an open international investment system.

International direct investment can provide particular benefits to developing countries. Foreign investment capital can help to expand the domestic resource base, augmenting locally-generated investment and foreign concessional flows. Foreign direct investment may be of particular value to developing countries in that it contributes to domestic productive capacity without increasing the debt service burden. Further, developing countries may look to foreign direct investment to create new employment opportunities and to provide needed managerial and technical skills that cannot be gained through foreign trade.

Under present circumstances, however, international direct investment is being prevented from making its full contribution to global economic growth. While the current world trade and monetary systems (as embodied in the GATT and the IMF) developed after World War II remain an important foundation for the long-term growth and prosperity of the world economy, there unfortunately exists no comparable system for international direct investment. There has been inadequate collective restraint on widespread and distortive interventions by both developed and developing governments, attempting to control the flow of foreign direct investment and the benefits associated with it. While the effects of intervention are difficult to quantify, the impact can be negative for home, host, and third countries because intervention distorts international investment and trade flows, thereby preventing the most efficient allocation of resources.

Useful attempts have been made to address this problem, particularly in the OECD, but progress has been slow. The inability to arrive at an international consensus on these issues has created pressures in many countries, including the United States, to abandon more traditional economic policies based on market forces and to move toward still greater government intervention.

In light of these developments, it is important that there be a clear understanding both at home and abroad of U.S. policies with respect to international direct investment issues and how the United States intends to implement these policies.

II. U.S. Policy Precepts

The United States believes that an open international investment system responding to market forces provides the best and most efficient mechanism to promote global economic development. Government intervention in the international allocation of investment resources can retard economic growth.

The United States has consistently welcomed foreign direct investment in this country. Such investment provides substantial benefits to the United States. Therefore, the United States fosters a domestic economic climate which is conducive to investment. We provide foreign investors fair, equitable, and non-discriminatory treatment under our laws and regulations. We maintain exceptions to such treatment only as are necessary to protect our security and related interests and which are consistent with our international legal obligations.

The United States believes that U.S. direct investment abroad should also receive fair, equitable and non-discriminatory treatment, consistent with international law standards. The basic tenet for treatment of investment is the national treatment principle: foreign investors should be treated no less favorably than domestic investors in like situations. Exceptions should be limited to those required to protect national security and related interests. In these cases, foreign direct investment should be accorded treatment consistent with the most-favored-nation principle.

The United States opposes the use of government practices which distort, restrict, or place unreasonable burdens on direct investment. These include such measures as trade-related or other performance requirements (such as local content, minimum export, and local equity requirements), fiscal or financial incentives. Interference with the market mechanism can cause serious distortions in trade and investment flows, encourage the retaliatory use of similar measures by other governments, and precipitate a downward spiral in global investment flows. The United States intends to continue its efforts to reduce or eliminate measures that restrict, distort, or place undue burdens on international direct investment flows. In this regard, the United States will make a particular effort to prevent the introduction by other countries of new measures of this type. Moreover, the United States will continue to attempt to deal with this issue on a multilateral basis, although non-multilateral approaches may be appropriate on a case-by-case basis.

The United States will continue to work for the reduction or elimination of unreasonable and discriminatory barriers to entry of investment. The United States believes that foreign investors should be able to make the same kinds of investment, under the same conditions, as nationals of the host country. Exceptions should be limited to areas of legitimate national security concern or related interests. Because establishment questions are not adequately covered in existing multilateral instruments relating to investment, the United States will encourage broader exploration, identification and discussion of these issues in the OECD and elsewhere.

The United States is particularly concerned with foreign investment rules that prohibit service industries from doing business abroad. Service sectors are among the most dynamic in today's economy, but there exists a number of limitations that inhibit export opportunities. For many service sectors, there is a universal requirement of establishment in host countries, with the competitive success of these industries heavily dependent upon the presence of branches to meet peculiar regulatory requirements. Thus, the investment policies of foreign countries have special importance to the service sectors.

The United States recognizes that international direct investment frequently serves as a vehicle for transfer of technology and can benefit the economic development goals of both home and host countries. Technology transfers should be carried out on a sound commercial basis, subject to national security and foreign policy considerations.

The United States places high priority on the protection of U.S. investment abroad from discriminatory treatment, or treatment which is inconsistent with international law standards. Under international law, no U.S. investment should be expropriated unless the taking (a) is done for a public purpose; (b) is accomplished under due process of law; (c) is non-discriminatory; (d) does not violate any previous contractual arrangements between the national or company concerned and the government making the expropriation; (e) is accompanied by prompt, adequate and effective compensation.

III. General U.S. Objectives

The United States accords foreign investors open access to investment opportunities. What we seek is similar access for United States investors abroad. A major objective of our international investment policy is acceptance of the national treatment principle.

In addition, the United States seeks to:

- strengthen multilateral and bilateral discipline over government actions which affect investment decisions, such as incentives and performance requirements, particularly when such actions distort international trade and investment flows;

- reduce unreasonable and discriminatory barriers to establishment;
- create, through cooperation among developed and developing nations, an international environment in which direct investment can make a greater contribution to the development process;
- foster a domestic economic climate in the United States which is conducive to investment, ensure that foreign investors receive fair and equitable treatment under our statutes and regulations, and maintain only those safeguards on foreign investment which are necessary to protect our security and related interests and which are consistent with our international legal obligations.

IV. Multilateral

The United States will:

- continue to adhere to the OECD Investment Declaration and related Decisions on national treatment, international investment incentives and disincentives, and Guidelines for Multinational Enterprises as adopted in 1976 and reviewed in 1979. We also adhere to the OECD Code of Liberalization of Capital Movements, adopted in 1961, and support its expansion;
- encourage OECD governments to abide by the OECD investment and capital liberalization instruments, and to strengthen and extend these instruments through broader extension of the principle of national treatment and the right of establishment;
- explore ways of extending the principles embodied in the OECD instruments to non-OECD countries. To increase the effectiveness of these instruments on a global basis, the developing countries, and in particular the newly-industrialized countries, need to be brought into any multilateral understanding on investment;
- support efforts to increase awareness of the extent and adverse effects that government intervention, e.g., through performance requirements, can have on the U.S. and world economies. This is essential in order to reduce the predatory use of such measures, and especially to limit the introduction of new measures and the expansion of existing measures. The United States will encourage and actively participate in continued work in multilateral institutions to address these questions;
- encourage adherence by all countries to the Paris Convention for the Protection of Industrial Property, and enactment of effective industrial property laws, guaranteeing recognition of patent, copyright, and other industrial property rights. These are essential for the flow of foreign direct investment into both developed and developing countries. The lack of adequate property rights is a major disincentive to investment in manufacturing facilities and research and development, and to the transfer of technologies. The Paris Convention for Industrial Property Protection is currently undergoing revision under the auspices of the World Intellectual Property Organization. The United States will support continued efforts aimed at improving protection of industrial property rights, fight to maintain

current protection levels where they are adequate and to upgrade protection where it is inadequate, and work to ensure that such principles are upheld in negotiations of codes relating to transfer of technology and transnational corporations which are now underway in the U.N.;

- continue to work in the OECD for a "data pledge" which would assure that no new barriers to data flows will be imposed by developed countries; and encourage all countries to join in adopting more open and liberal policies on transborder data flows;
- encourage adherence to the Code of Capital Movements and support its expansion;
- support the Multilateral Development Banks in their efforts to foster more rapid economic growth in the developing countries. The United States will continue to encourage the Banks to explore ways to develop new programs to strengthen the private sector role in financial flows to the developing world;
- support investor access to third-party arbitration to settle investment disputes, such as the facilities of the World Bank's International Centre for the Settlement of Investment Disputes. The United States believes that governments should effectively support investor access by adherence to the Convention of the Settlement of Investment Disputes between States and Nationals of Other States or the Inter-American Convention on International Commercial Arbitration, and by evidencing their commitment to be bound by third-country arbitral awards by adhering to the Convention of the Recognition and Enforcement of Foreign Arbitral Awards.

V. In its bilateral relations, the United States:

- in cases of expropriation or nationalization of American investment abroad, will provide full support for American investors to ensure that standards of international law are honored by host governments;
- will provide appropriate facilitative services to assist American investors overseas and, in particular, will assist them in obtaining information on the host country investment climate, economic objectives, and investment opportunities;
- will work to ensure that the relevant provisions of our Friendship, Commerce and Navigation treaties are fully observed;
- as a means to facilitate and protect American investment, will seek to conclude bilateral investment treaties and agreements with interested countries. The treaties will contain appropriate provisions on, inter alia, treatment of existing and new investment (including national treatment and most-favored-nation treatment); transfers; dispute settlement; use of performance requirements; and compensation in the event of expropriation;
- will explore, through our bilateral economic assistance programs with developing countries, appropriate ways to increase non-official flows, and will seek to ensure that these programs effectively support private direct investment;
- reserves the right to take unilateral action against the use of performance requirements and similar policies, consistent with our international obli-

gations. The United States is now exercising and will continue to exercise its rights under existing international arrangements, including the GATT and OECD.

The United States believes that a combination of multilateral and bilateral efforts will contribute to the achievement of a more open global climate for investment, and thus enhance the prospects for economic growth in the United States and globally.

Annex V

U.S. Objectives in International Telecommunications and Information Policies

(New York: US Council for International Business, 1984, mimeo)

Clarification of Objectives

It is increasingly evident that efficient and effective telecommunications systems are essential to the growth and development of the economy as a whole. Telecommunications and information products and services, as high-technology, high-growth industries, not only make contributions to healthy innovation and expansion in the economy in their own right, but they also promote increased productivity, greater competitiveness, and higher employment and growth rates throughout the economy. In the developing world, reliable and efficient telecommunications infrastructures can greatly aid local development efforts as well as help attract necessary international commerce and investment. The fundamental principles and policy objectives set forth in this document are designed primarily to promote the growth and efficiency of the telecommunications and information industries. It is important, however, to recognize that achievement of these objectives will also result in direct benefits to the information-and telecommunications-dependent industries in the service, manufacturing, natural resources, and agricultural sectors.

In order to appreciate the full value of an efficient telecommunications and information sector to society, one must look beyond its role in business to the part it plays in technological advancement, education, cultural development, national security, social welfare, and world peace and understanding. The underlying assumption of this paper is that less regulation and a greater scope for private initiative and entrepreneurship will encourage the telecommunications and information industries, thereby bringing widespread benefits to business, consumers, national economies, and world trade.

Principle A: Open International Marketing of Information Processing and Telecommunications Equipment Should be Encouraged On A Fair and Competitive Basis Without Restrictive Trade Barriers

During the 1970s, the demand for terminal equipment increased rapidly, vastly expanding the private market for telecommunications equipment and reducing the share of equipment purchases by the traditional service providers. This trend will continue and, in order to meet the increasingly diversified needs of users, trade in terminal equipment must be facilitated and encouraged. Moreover, greater competition in the terminal equipment market will promote technical advancements, improve the product spectrum for all consumers, and reduce price-cost margins. No harm will be done to the network if equipment attachment is appropriately supervised.

The chief supervisory tool is the national certification (homologation) process which defines the specifications and conditions under which equipment can be connected to the public network. This certification process could, however, be used as an import restriction. Therefore, requirements for attachment of user-provided customer premises equipment should be limited to ensuring protection of the network and network personnel from possible harm caused by such attachment. For a subscriber service specifying standardized protocols, equipment attachment may, in addition, be subject to requirements of compatibility with the service. For instance, in the development of Integrated Services Digital Networks (ISDNs), such requirements should not go beyond physical attachment to the network (beyond Layer One of the Open System Interconnection of the International Standards Organization).

Given that the providers of basic telecommunications services will continue to account for a large share of total equipment purchases, their procurement policies will have a major impact. With due deference to national security considerations, the procurement procedures of the basic service providers should be more open and competitive, allowing all producers to compete on an equal footing.

Recognizing that there are legitimate national security reasons for restricting certain sensitive technologies, national security considerations can be too broadly defined and, many times, the definitions of sensitive technologies are dated. Export restrictions on information processing and telecommunications equipment must be rationalized and clarified. Given the fact that most of this type of equipment can be readily purchased from a number of suppliers in the international marketplace, it makes little sense to restrict exports between friendly nations and detracts from the objective of encouraging free and fair competition in terminal equipment.

Principle B: Users Should Have the Freedom to Choose Among Competitive Suppliers, Including Telecommunications Agencies, for the Supply, Installation, and Maintenance of Their Customer Premises Equipment

In order to meet their varied and distinctive information requirements, users of telecommunications and information products and services must have the freedom to select the most appropriate equipment (compatible with the necessary technical standards for telecommunications), which will be located on their premises and attached to national and international telecommunications networks.

National policies and/or artificial trade barriers that restrict users' freedom of choice without a sound technical justification, and therefore must be revised, include:

- mandatory local sourcing or local content rules;
- overly complex or discriminatory interface standards; and

• rules requiring equipment purchasing and/or leasing to be from one sole entity.

These types of policies not only curtail the efficiency of business and other types of communications, but also tend to restrain the introduction of innovative new technologies (and the concomitant skills) to the local marketplace. In the long run, the economies of countries with restrictive policies will be handicapped in their efforts to compete in the international marketplace.

Principle C: There Should be an Unrestricted and Competitive International Market for Value-Added (Enhanced) Telecommunications and Information Services

A key drawback to encouraging competition is the lack of agreement on what should be competitively offered. Recognizing that the division between "basic transmission" and "enhanced" services is an American definition, an internationally harmonized definition should be agreed upon which provides for division between telecommunications services that have characteristics that justify an exclusive franchise and those telecommunications and information services that are provided in a competitive market environment. By clarifying this division and encouraging competitive forces in as many segments of the industry as possible, innovative new technologies, products, and services will be introduced at the lowest cost to user and consumer. It should be noted that CCITT draft Recommendation I.200, which defines bearer services and tele-services, does not address the need to allow for competitive provision of services that lack justification for an exclusive franchise.

International trade in telecommunications and information services will be encouraged by further work toward bilateral or multilateral trade agreements on services. Such agreements must allow providers of these services entry to or presence in foreign markets and must allow users access to service providers located beyond their borders on an equal basis with local providers or users. Moreover, further work to resolve conflicts of law and the legal questions of national jurisdiction over data wherever they may be collected, processed, used, or stored, would greatly encourage growth and trade in these services.

Principle D: The Encouragement of Innovation In and Development and Application of New Products and Services Should Be Through Competitive Market Forces

The best way to encourage and stimulate technological innovation is to reduce market restrictions, thereby allowing rapid adaptation and application of new technologies. This is particularly true for the telecommunications and information technologies because of the highly dynamic state of the technology and because of the strong demand for these products and services.

Distortions to market indicators, created by such measures as subsidies, cartels, and heavy regulation, serve to weaken the health of these industries, since companies may base strategic decisions on misleading or incorrect market signals.

Products or services, requiring substantial investment, may be developed and brought to market only to find that demand may be far less than projected.

Principle E: Recognizing That There Will Always Be a Requirement for Efficient Public Telecommunications Networks, It is Essential to Continue to Encourage the Development of High Quality Services in Both Developed and Developing Countries

Most developed countries have high quality public telecommunications networks. These networks must be efficiently and effectively maintained and updated in order to ensure that service is universally available to users. In developing countries, however, greater attention and resources should be devoted to installing and developing a sound national telecommunications system. The contribution that telecommunications makes to economic and social growth and development are only recently being documented, and this work should be supported. New and innovative financing tools should be created to support telecommunications infrastructure projects, including private sector financing and development.

Public telecommunications networks in developed and developing countries should be developed in harmony with international standards so as to insure worldwide interconnectability.

Principle F: To Provide Maximum Interconnectability Among National Telecommunications Networks and Services, Reasonable Minimum Standards Should Be Established on an International Basis with User's and Suppliers' Participation

It is vital that the telecommunications networks of countries be able to communicate efficiently with each other. In order to promote interconnectability, a minimum set of international standards should be established by international bodies. These bodies should promote the participation of users and suppliers as well as national telecommunications administrations in their work. It is also important that international standards bodies be used in preference to regional bodies and that close cooperation among the various international standards bodies be encouraged.

To facilitate interconnection of user networks with the public network and with other user networks, internationally-accepted standards for network interfaces should be defined in a way that will promote maximum flexibility. This will be particularly important as Integrated Services Digital Networks (ISDNs) develop. Interface specifications are desirable at each of the possible attachment points to an ISDN (reference points) in order to satisfy demand and to promote technical innovation within the network, in services provided over the network, and in attached customer premises equipment. In addition, ISDN specifications must also provide for numerous gateway interconnections not only between ISDN systems, but also between ISDN and non-ISDN systems, particularly shared industry networks and private networks.

Principle G: Users Should Have the Freedom to Choose From Available Basic Transmission Services; Included Among Such Services Should Be "Transparent" Services, Such As Full-Period Leased Circuits, Which Provide Users with the Greatest Flexibility and Ease of Use

It is to the credit of the national telecommunications administrations that national networks, in general, provide high availability and reliability to all types of users. Users today, however, are concerned not only with reliability, availability, and price/performance, but also with such characteristics as ease of use, expansion capability, security, adaptability to specific requirements, and flexibility to use the same service for more than one purpose. The user's freedom to choose between different telecommunications services and facilities provided the only solid foundation for meeting the varied and specific communications requirements of the user community. Of particular importance to large users is the continued availability of flat-rate international private-leased circuits (IPLCs).

Principle H: Prices Charged for Regulated Telecommunications Services Should Normally Be Based on the Cost of Providing the Services, Including a Fair and Reasonable Rate of Return

Establishment of tariffs for a given regulated telecommunications service is subject to government control either by a regulatory body or by the telecommunications agency. A common objective in the establishment of tariffs is the avoidance of discrimination against any class of user. The best way to avoid the possibility of discrimination in a regulated environment is to relate prices charged for telecommunications services to the costs of providing those services. These costs should be clearly identifiable.

Alternatively, the prices charged for telecommunications and information services provided in a competitive environment will be established by market forces. It is, therefore, important to have a clear and workable boundary between regulated and competitive services.

Principle I: While Attention Should Be Paid to the Protection of Individual Privacy, Proprietary Rights, and National Security, the General and Traditional Free Flow of Information Among Nations Should be Preserved in the Interests of the Advancement of the World Economy

Information flow in its broadest sense is the transfer or exchange of information in any form (graphic, written, spoken, electronic, printed, recorded, or filmed) both within and across national boundaries. The free flow of information has always been vital to society, supporting trade and commerce as well as health, education, the arts, and an open society. Restrictions on the flow of information, particularly on the content or the message, must be kept to a minimum and can be justified only by a genuine need to protect personal privacy, proprietary rights, or national security.

Information is a unique resource. Thus, it is often difficult to establish its exact value and classification and such attempts may discourage information exchange. Its value lies in its use; its utility to successive users can vary between wide extremes and use does not necessarily diminish its value. Information, itself, is also neutral. Its significance depends on the interpretation placed on it and its credibility.

Information is a key resource in national and international investment, trade, commerce, and industry, and an important element in the stimulation of the world economy. Efficient international information flows, together with international trade and investment, promote the optimal utilization of global resources and permit the exchange of data necessary for further innovation. Information can play this role only if it can be accessed and exchanged unimpeded on a worldwide basis.

Annex VI

The Business Roundtable:
International Information Flow

(New York: The Business Roundtable, 1985, pp. 3–8)

A PLAN FOR ACTION:
EXECUTIVE SUMMARY AND RECOMMENDATIONS

A. Importance of International Information Flow (IIF)

. . .

B. Need for Improved International Cooperation in the IIF Area

Currently, there are no internationally accepted principles governing the way in which governments approach the broad economic consequences of IIF-related issues and restrictions. The IIF arena is cluttered with a plethora of national policies, which are at best confusing, and at worst conflicting. Some countries (including the U.S.) have no overall policy in this area, and as a result they often take actions which are themselves conflicting. Companies which attempt to comply with the various, and sometimes conflicting, national policies often find it difficult and costly to do so. Furthermore, since IIF and trade in related information-based services depend heavily upon the use of telecommunications, national telecommunications policies have the effect of inhibiting or encouraging IIF. Thus, IIF policies must be developed in tandem with telecommunications policies.

Within the U.S., no single government agency has the authority for IIF, trade in related information-based services, and the telecommunications policies related to IIF. Companies complain that there is not even a single entity to coordinate IIF policies and to which they can bring IIF-related complaints. In addition, there is no international forum in which countries may bring complaints about the trade-distorting consequences of national IIF and telecommunications policies.

In addition to supporting the activities of other organizations, such as the OECD and the International Telecommunication Union (ITU), the U.S. has urged the initiation under the auspices of the GATT of a process of on-going Multilateral Trade Negotiations which would include as a major component the development of a new set of rules for trade in services and a reduction of existing barriers. IIF and trade in related information-based services would be included as part of these negotiations, and this would also, of necessity, include attempting to reduce the trade-distorting consequences of national telecommunications policies.

In this paper, The Business Roundtable recommends negotiating principles and strategies which it believes the U.S. government should consider in its preparation for any future negotiations. Furthermore, the ambiguity and overlapping concepts and regulatory jurisdictions associated with these issues make the definitional phases of any negotiations on trade in services, which will necessarily encompass IIF issues, critical to ultimate success. The U.S. government should begin an in-depth analysis of the definitional aspects of these negotiations. The analysis should also focus upon the relation of each area to the existing international regulatory structure in that area to determine whether the existing structure is adequate to deal with any problems that may exist.

C. Telecommunications and Information Policy Issues

In the international community, IIF is generally discussed in terms of telecommunications and information policy issues. Following is a list of the more important of these issues, together with a synopsis of the Business Roundtable's views on each.

1. Information Policy Issues
a. Free Flow of Information
- The free flow of information internationally advances the human condition and enhances both national economies and the world economy.
- Governments should seek to facilitate the exchange of information internationally.
- Exceptions to the free flow of information should be as narrow as possible.

b. Privacy and Data Protection
- The Business Roundtable endorses the OECD Privacy Guidelines and urges companies to take reasonable affirmative steps to implement these Guidelines.
- The Business Roundtable supports the social objectives of privacy and data protection, but urges governments to minimize the economic side effects of these laws.
- The scope of these laws should be limited to the protection of the privacy of personal information; they should not be extended to cover legal persons. Issues relating to companies, such as providing adequate protection for corporate proprietary information, are different and should be the subject of a different body of law.

c. Valuation and Taxation of Information
- Information cannot, and should not, be treated like a traditional commodity.
- While there may be limited instances where the taxation of IIF or trade in related information-based services is appropriate (e.g., non-discriminatory sales or value-added taxes or income taxes), such taxation is generally not practical, equitable, or conducive to overall economic growth.

d. Intellectual Property
- The Business Roundtable supports the on-going international efforts to provide adequate protection for corporate proprietary information.

- IIF and trade in related information-based services add few inherently new problems to this area, but they do focus attention upon the need to develop internationally acceptable solutions.

2. Telecommunications Policy Issues

- As the primary distribution channel for IIF and trade in related information-based services, telecommunications is central to the operation of all multinational business activity.
- The Business Roundtable supports the telecommunications policy principles drafted by the ad hoc policy group formed by members of the USA-BIAC Committee on International Information Flows[1] and the National Committee of the U.S. Organization for the International Telegraph and Telephone Consultative Committee (CCITT). These principles stress the need for an unrestricted and competitive international market in the telecommunications sector. They also emphasize the need for companies to have the freedom to choose among competitive suppliers of telecommunications equipment and value-added (enhanced) services.
- As the U.S. begins the process of developing negotiating strategies for IIF and trade in related information-based services, it should take into account the differing national approaches to telecommunications and the activities of the existing international telecommunications organizations. The goal of the U.S. in these negotiations should be to focus attention upon the international trade and investment consequences of national telecommunications policies. In some cases, this may include attempting to persuade other governments that certain of their present or projected policies are or will be barriers to international commerce. The sovereign right of nations to determine their own telecommunications policies is not the issue; rather, it is the international consequences of these national policies that may be subject to legitimate challenge by other countries whose interests are adversely affected.

D. Principles of an International Agreement

Many of the principles which the Business Roundtable has previously endorsed with respect to trade and investment apply to the IIF arena. In addition, there are some new principles which would appear to apply in this area. Some of the more important of these principles, the application of which will have to be thoroughly examined and tested as the development of a model for negotiation proceeds, are:

- *National Treatment*—Foreign suppliers of telecommunications and other information-related products and services should be accorded treatment equal to domestic suppliers.
- *Non-Discrimination*—Foreign companies should receive treament equal to the most favorable treatment accorded companies from a third nation.
- *Market Access*—Foreign companies should be subject to a balanced group of rights which neither impose costly barriers to entry into a national market nor make costly demands for establishment within a market. These rights of establishment and non-establishment must be combined with a

group of balanced rights to send and receive information internationally, as well as to store or process information extraterritorially.

* *Dependence Upon Foreign Sources*—Countries and companies need to have reasonable assurances that the extraterritorial storage and processing of information does not represent an unacceptable risk to their future ability to function. The alternative to some form of assured access to such data is not only restrictive local processing and storage requirements, but also a disinclination to exploit the growing capabilities of international telecommunications and information technologies to the detriment of all international commerce.

* *Transparency*—Governments should make greater efforts to identify laws and regulations that impact IIF and trade in related information-based services. All such laws should be published in a timely and open manner.

* *Government Procurement, Tariffs, and Subsidies*—Current government efforts to use procurement policies, tariffs, and subsidies to support domestic information-related industries threaten to cause severe distortions in international trade. Already, protectionist actions have been met in kind and are on the increase internationally. International negotiations should strive to keep such trade-distorting policies to a minimum and to create adequate international structures to respond to the problems generated by such policies.

E. Strategies for International Negotiations

The Business Roundtable supports the U.S. efforts to pursue issues pertaining to IIF and trade in related information-based services as part of on-going Multilateral Trade Negotiations on trade in services. The Business Roundtable recommends the following strategy for pursuing these negotiations, and is prepared to assist the government in the further investigation and refinement of this approach.

* IIF and trade in related information-based services cannot be counted or measured like traditional commodities. Moreover, any international agreement in this area must not rely upon the kind of government monitoring and regulation of information flows that we are seeking to avoid. Therefore, the best approach in this area appears to be creation of a procedural framework describing under which conditions IIF and trade in related information-based services can and should occur. The principles of such an agreement would be similar to those listed above.

* The U.S. should look to the experiences of previous international negotiations for insights into the present situation. In particular, the U.S. should begin an in-depth analysis of the applicability of the GATT Standards Code model to IIF and trade in related information-based services. The analysis would explore the definitional aspects of the proposed negotiations, the relation to the activities of the existing international telecommunications organizations, and which issues and principles are amenable to a procedural approach similar to that embodied in the Standards Code. Acceptance of the Standards Code model does not automatically imply the use of the Standards Code itself, that the GATT will be the supervising entity for

an ultimate agreement, or that these issues should be treated solely as technical issues.

Notes

[1] USA-BIAC is the U.S. arm of the OECD's Business and Industry Advisory Committee (BIAC).

Annex VII

Information Flows: An International Business Perspective.
Policy Statement Adopted by the Council of the
International Chamber of Commerce

(Paris: ICC, 1983, mimeo)

1. THE BACKGROUND

During the past century there has been a close and synergistic relationship between the development of world trade and communications. As the letter post, telegraph, telephone and telex were successively improved, they stimulated productivity and service levels in existing businesses and enabled new sorts of enterprises to become established. These developments in turn created user demands for quicker, more reliable, more convenient, cheaper and more widespread services and equipment which led to further innovation. Recently the convergence of the rapidly developing technologies of computing and communications has resulted in the introduction of yet another generation of communications media. Starting with data transmission, there has been a continually growing list of new services like facsimile, electronic mail, videotex and video conferencing. The rate of technological innovation is accelerating and the only limits to the services that can be provided seem to be the imagination of the providers and economic constraints. Like their predecessors, these new services are both supplementing and replacing existing media.

This development of information technology has already had effects on the interchange of business information both within and across national boundaries, resulting in economic and social benefits.

In today's increasingly complex business environment, information is a key resource in national and international trade, commerce and industry, essential to the growth and development of individual nations and an important element in the stimulation of the world economy. In an interdependent community of nations, information can play that role only if it flows freely and can be accessed and exchanged on a worldwide basis.

Because of its pervasive nature, information technology has inevitably raised a wide range of new social, economic and juridical issues. Questions have arisen as to how the national interest can be maintained in a world in which information technology is increasingly creating international interdependence—questions relating to the protection of personal privacy, economic sovereignty, the vulnerability of a computerised society, the migration of employment and decision taking. These matters are complex, dynamic and of obvious importance to the international business community. Through its Commission on Computing, Telecommunications and Information Policies, the ICC seeks to contribute to the resolution of these apparent conflicts of interest.

The International Chamber of Commerce, representing the interests of the international business community in some 50 countries, has since its foundation advocated and promoted the free flow of goods and capital, and, more recently, in 1981 in its Document 103/34 Rev. 4, has publicly advocated international work toward a liberalisation of trade in services.

This statement focusses on business views and needs with regard to international information flows, and summarizes the ICC's current thinking on some information policy issues. It is intended that this paper be followed by future statements elaborating ICC positions on the specific issues raised herein.

2. FUNDAMENTAL PRINCIPLES

The ICC position arises from four basic perceptions:

- The intrinsic importance of the efficient exchange of information in the development and growth of modern international trade and commerce.
- The right of a business to communicate freely within and outside its corporate structure.
- The right of business to access and freely utilize national and international communications facilities.
- The necessity of recognizing the worldwide interdependence of modern business communications.

3. NEW LAWS AND REGULATIONS

While the ICC has urged that legislation and regulation be carefully reviewed on the basis of a cost/benefit analysis, it has consistently demonstrated its acceptance of such constraints which are clearly in the public interest, provided they are non-discriminatory, enforceable and do not add to the existing bureaucratic burden. In particular it recognizes the contribution that elements in the regulation of international communications have made to orderly expansion and development.

Within the international business community, however, there are serious fears that the application of new information technologies may be inhibited by the introduction of unwarranted or untimely laws or restrictions. Before any form of additional legislation or regulation is contemplated, the ICC urges that certain criteria should be applied.

- That significant harm be clearly demonstrable, not merely a technical possibility. Regulations should focus on abuse of the information itself and not on the media of transmission.
- That only specific problems be addressed and interference with other parts of the information sector be avoided. An example of the latter has been

the inappropriate inclusion of legal persons in the data protection laws of several European countries.

- The cost/benefit analysis of administration procedures demonstrate that neither unreasonable direct or indirect cost nor delays will be incurred by business.
- That in view of the dynamic state of information technology and the limited legal experience in this field, preference be given to the establishment of national and international codes or other means of ensuring flexibility and avoiding interference with growth and development.
- That regulatory measures be adopted only within an internationally harmonized framework. Due to the transnational character and importance of information flows, it is vital to reach an international consensus on their role.

4. MAINTAINING PERSPECTIVE

The earliest manifestations of the new forms of communications described in section 1 were in transmission of data, which perhaps explains why that has become the focus of attention and debate in national and international fora. This has had the unfortunate consequence of causing data flows, particularly the international exchange of data (sometimes referred to as "Transborder Data Flows"), to be seen outside the broader context described above. The inappropriateness of such a narrow view becomes even more apparent when one considers that current developments in telecommunications will progressively render data transmissions technically indistinguishable from speech, facsimile, telex and the other electronic media already enumerated. Thus, before considering the imposition of laws or regulations specifically aimed at data flows, it is pertinent to question both the wisdom and logic of such discrimination.

5. PROMOTING UNDERSTANDING

Perhaps the greatest dangers for both business and governments lie in lack of knowledge and understanding. Notable research has been undertaken by a number of regional and international bodies, but relatively little factual information is available on the subject. Much empirical work remains to be done to define the issues, comprehend their context and evaluate policy options, while recognising the needs of the business community. In today's economic climate, resources for work of this kind are scarce; the ICC therefore recommends that such activities be carefully coordinated and duplication avoided.

The need for an understanding of the broader issues concerned extends to the general public, since information technology and international communications also have important consequences outside the business field. Health care, education, science, the arts, and national security may all be impacted. The ICC therefore supports the participation of businesses with governments, labour organizations and other interest groups in programs of education in this field.

6. INFORMATION IN BUSINESS

Information is a unique resource. Its value lies in its use, its utility to successive users can vary between wide extremes, and use does not necessarily diminish it. Information is also neutral; its significance depends on the interpretation placed on it and its credibility.

Many companies of all sizes use international data flows to manage their worldwide operations with maximum efficiency. Specific applications include worldwide inventory, sales, production, marketing, planning and financial coordination. This information exchange is thus one of the instruments available for retaining competitive positions in world markets. The primary information sector, comprising the sale of information services to third party buyers, is growing rapidly, which reflects the increased importance attached to information in management decision taking in the manufacturing and the service sectors.

The form of information transmission can be as critical to business as the information itself. Users have a great diversity of needs; their application requirements can vary greatly in terms of expected return, information volume, traffic pattern, etc. They are best served by the availability of a large menu of both enhanced services and communications products.

Attention should be paid to improvement and harmonization of the necessary communications infrastructure, including protocols, standards and other policies. The ICC position with regard to this issue is set out in more detail in its document entitled "The Liberalization of Telecommunications Services—Needs and Limits", which also calls for open and fair competition in the provision of telecommunications.

7. INFORMATION FLOWS AND WORLD DEVELOPMENT

Whilst the greatest impacts of information technology have been felt in the industrialized countries, it is recognized that they will be of growing significance to the developing parts of the world, as the catalytic effect of information becomes understood. International businesses are acting as pioneers in the introduction of these technologies in such countries, stimulating the development of local expertise, the creation of awareness of the benefits and the provision of access to data banks and data processing facilities abroad. The ICC recognizes the need for complementary actions sponsored by governments and international agencies.

8. CONCLUSIONS

The growing integration of the world economy is an acknowledged development in which information technology is a key factor for the growth and development of business. Efficient international information flows together with international trade and investment permit the optimal utilization of global resources and promote the exchange of data necessary for further innovation. In addition, the ICC wishes to point out that the needs of the international business community are not inconsistent with the needs of the community at large—both desire prosperity.

Given this scenario, the ICC urges governments and intergovernmental organizations to consult with business in order to promote policies which encourage the freedom of business communications and to review those that create barriers or hindrances.

The ICC would welcome opportunities for further clarification and detailed discussions in this field.

Annex VIII

Agreement on the Establishment of a Free Trade Area between the Government of the United States of America and the Government of Israel: Declaration on Trade in Services

(United States, Office of the Trade Representative, April 1985, mimeo)

Preamble

The Governments of the United States of America and Israel,

RECOGNIZING the significance of trade in services to their economic and social progress and to the world economy;

NOTING the importance of open international markets for trade in services;

ACKNOWLEDGING that the Treaty of Friendship, Commerce and Navigation between their two nations establishes bilateral rights and obligations which provide for open trade in a broad range of services;

RECOGNIZING that other bilateral and multilateral agreements for certain services sectors are in effect;

Declare that, although the principles set forth below shall not be legally binding, they shall endeavor to the maximum extent possible to conduct their policies affecting trade in services between them in accordance with those principles;

Express their desire to work toward international acceptance of these principles in trade in services.

Principles

1. Definition: Trade in services takes place when a service is exported from the supplier nation and is imported into the other nation. Services encompass, but are not limited to, transportation; travel and tourism services; communications; banking services;[1] insurance; other financial activities; professional services, such

as consulting in construction, engineering, accounting, medicine, education, and law, and the providing of other professional services such as management consulting; computer services; motion pictures; advertising.

2. Each Party will endeavor to achieve open market access for trade in services with the other nation, taking into account the different regulatory regimes for specific service sectors in the two nations.

3. Each Party will endeavor to assure that trade in services with the other nation is governed by the principle of national treatment. Each party will endeavor to provide that a supplier of a service produced within the other nation is able to market or distribute that service under the same conditions as a like service produced within the first nation, including situations where a commercial presence within the nations is necessary to facilitate the export of a service from the other nation or is required by that Party.[2]

4. In situations where services are regulated by political subdivisions, the authorities of each Party responsible for overseeing the operation of this Declaration will consult with such political subdivisions in an effort to assure that such regulations are consistent with the principles of this Declaration.

5. Each Party will endeavor to assure that its regulatory agencies will accord national treatment to suppliers of the service from the other nation, to the extent that such treatment is consistent with those agencies' legal authority, including their exercise of discretion in fulfilling their statutory mandates. The authorities of each Party responsible for implementing this Declaration shall consult with their own regulatory agencies in an effort to achieve consistency with the principles of this Declaration.

6. Each Party recognizes that there may be established public monopolies in the service area with reserved special rights. Nonetheless, each Party will endeavor to provide that, subject to their reserved special rights, such monopolies shall make their purchase and sales of services involving either imports or exports affecting the commerce of the other nation in accordance with the principles of this Declaration.

7. Each Party will make public its domestic laws and regulations affecting trade in services and notify the other Party of laws and regulations which discriminate against a service exported from the other nation. Each Party will provide to the nationals and companies of the other nation reasonable access to established domestic review and judicial proceedings relative to regulations on trade in services.

8. Each Party agrees to consult with the other periodically to discuss specific problems that arise concerning trade in services between the two nations and to review existing regulatory regimes of the two Parties as they affect trade in services.

9. The Parties will review the effectiveness of this Declaration not later than eighteen months from the date that this Declaration is signed. In this review, the Parties will explore further opportunities to strengthen open trade in services between the two nations, including the possibility of transforming the provisions of this Declaration into legally binding rights and obligations.

Notes

[1] For the purposes of this Declaration, commercial banking services are limited to the activities of representative offices.

[2] For example, in the area of commercial banking, the concept of a commercial presence refers to the activities of representative offices, but not to agencies, branches or subsidiaries of commercial banks.

Annex IX

Services in International Trade:
A Summary of Interim Conclusions
by the International Chamber of Commerce

(Adopted by the 146th session of the Council of the International Chamber of Commerce on 17 June 1984 and contained in Document No. 103/70 of 17 June 1984, mimeo)

The ICC has now been working on the subject of international trade in services, and the problems of liberalisation of that trade, for some 4 years. A great deal of ground has been cleared, and much more is now known about the subject.

When the ICC began its work, there was very little general interest in the matter in many of the industries involved, and barely any at all in any of the governments, except in the United States, from which the impetus had come. Now the topic is one of general international and national interest. A great deal of most useful analytical work has been done in the OECD, and some in UNCTAD; and considerable effort is being made by governments and industries in a number of countries to establish the information and the machinery needed for future progress. A beginning—though very modest—has been made towards putting the matter on the agenda of the GATT. Substantive international negotiations are still some way ahead; but we welcome the encouragement given by the 1984 London Summit to press forward with the work on services in the international organisations.

The ICC has now carried its work on the general issues to the point where it has felt able to set out the result in the attached interim summary of its conclusions so far, while continuing its more detailed consideration on a number of aspects.

* * *

1. The service industries, and international trade in services, are now an important element in the economies of most countries, either as exporters or importers or both. This importance now makes it desirable to have an agreed framework of international rules in the services sector.
2. The general principles of international trade, including the benefits from an open trading system, are applicable to trade in services as well as to trade in goods.
3. In general, therefore, the principles on which the GATT is based— multilateralism rather than bilateralism, the removal of impediments,

progress towards liberalisation within an internationally accepted framework—should become the objective of policy.

4. On this basis, the GATT (or some close association with GATT) is the appropriate central forum in which the broad framework should be discussed, and a system of international obligations should be created. But this does not exclude the helpful interest of other international bodies in the necessary background work.

5. Trade in services means both the supply of services across frontiers, where this is possible, and the supply of services which may require some local presence by a non-national or a foreign-owned or controlled supplier. The rules may need to be adapted to accommodate differences of conditions between the one situation and the other.

6. The need for local activity has given rise to considerable discussion about "right of establishment". International discussion about "right of establishment" is immensely complex, and raises issues far wider than the services industries. To enter into that difficult and sensitive area would be counter-productive, and would postpone any outcome on trade in services for very many years. Some more limited objective must therefore be found, by trying to evolve some rules about permitting local presence to the extent necessary to make supply of services possible, and to secure adequate access to the market.

7. Any system must rest on a few basic principles analogous to those of the GATT:

    (i) Non-discrimination (in the GATT usage of that term—i.e. most favoured nation treatment for all countries participating in the system). It would not be viable to have an international framework on a bilateral basis. "Reciprocity" results from mutual acceptance of the obligations by the participants.

    (ii) In the *ideal* system of open trade, there should be complete national treatment—i.e. the market is as open to foreign as to domestic suppliers. But the GATT has a number of limitations on national treatment; most importantly

        (a) those of quite general application, on grounds of national security, public order, etc.

        (b) for balance of payments reasons, in specified circumstances

        (c) for the protection of domestic industry, but then *only* through the use of customs duties; these are the subject of periodic negotiations, and in most countries, and for most products, have been bound against increase.

    There is no reason against (a) and (b) applying to services as to goods. But (c) presents considerable difficulty. Customs duties are not likely to be a generally appropriate method of giving protection to service transactions, and there is no obvious alternative which has the same characteristics of certainty and measurability. The objective should be true national treatment; but it may be necessary to examine the problems of each sector separately, and to arrive at appropriate solutions within the general rules on a sector basis. Whatever is decided for a particular sector should not be supplemented, or undermined, by other covert devices—i.e. once an appropriate method is agreed for a particular sector, there should be national treatment in all other respects. For example, there should not be differential stamp duties or other discriminatory charges. Moreover, any levels of protection so fixed should be the subject of periodic multilateral negotiations, on the same lines as are customs duties.

(iii) The objectives of sub-paragraphs (i) and (ii) above might perhaps be achieved through a broad non-discrimination clause; and the possibility of such a clause should be examined.

8. Full information on all national legislation or administrative measures must be easily available. "Transparency" is an essential element for the conduct of trade.

9. Equality before the law: where regulatory or supervisory systems are in force, for whatever purpose, they should not be applied more vigorously (or at greater cost) to services supplied by non-nationals or by foreign-owned or controlled enterprises than to nationals. This should apply to regulations, e.g. for consumer protection, taxation, raising finance, the possession of qualifications, etc. There is no reason to exempt non-nationals from regulations which apply to nationals. But regulations should not be framed in ways which provide covert methods of protection.

10. The objective, ultimately, should be an Agreement on Services parallel with the GATT, and providing a set of agreed general obligations on the conduct of international trade in services, including the possibility of negotiations about the progressive mutual reduction of any barriers which survive. Within such an Agreement, many of the detailed features of the GATT (both reinforcements of the central obligations, like rules about subsidies, and provisions for special derogations, like emergency safeguards) might also be required. There might also have to be some special arrangements for countries "at an early stage of development of participation in international service trade" (to adapt a phrase from the GATT which is more appropriate than the blanket—and not very meaningful—description "developing countries").

As a first step in this direction, there might be an outline Code, which sets out general principles on the above lines, and which would in the first place apply to a list of sectors established by negotiation, and including defined derogations applying to particular sectors as necessary.

Acronyms

ADAPSO	Association of Data Processing Service Organizations
AFIPS	American Federation of Information Processing Societies
ATM	Automated teller machines
ATT	American Telephone and Telegraph Company
BI	Business International
BIAC	Business and Industry Advisory Committee
BIS	Bank for International Settlements
BP	British Petroleum
CAD	Computer-aided design
CAE	Computer-aided engineering
CALAI	Conferencia de Autoridades Latinoamericanas de Informática
CAM	Computer-aided manufacturing
CAP	Common Agricultural Policy
CBEMA	Computer and Business Equipment Manufacturers Association
CBS	Columbia Broadcasting System
CCITT	International Telegraph and Telephone Consultative Committee of ITU
CCTIP	Commission on Computing, Telecommunications and Information Policies
CEC	Commission of the European Communities
CICCP	Committee for Information, Computer and Communications Policy
COC	Commission of the European Communities
CONIN	National Council for Informatics and Automation
CSI	Coalition of Service Industries
CTD	Centre for Technology in Informatics
DSB	Direct Satellite Broadcasting
EC	European Community
EFT	Electronic funds transfer
ESA	European Space Agency
EUREKA	European Research Co-ordinating Agency
FA	Factory automation
FAST	Forecasting and assessment in the field of science and technology
FDI	Foreign direct investment
FMS	Flexible manufacturing systems
GATT	General Agreement on Tariffs and Trade
GNP	Gross national product
GSP	Generalized system of preferences

IATA	International Air Transport Association
IBI	Intergovernmental Bureau for Informatics
ICA	International Communications Assocation
ICAO	International Civil Aviation Organization
ICC	International Chamber of Commerce
IIAC	International Insurance Advisory Council
IIFC	International Investment and Finance Committee
IMF	International Monetary Fund
IMO	International Maritime Organization
INTUG	International Telecommunications Users Group
ISDN	Integrated systems digital network
ITC	International Trade Committee
ITU	International Telecommunication Union
LOTIS	Liberalisation of Trade in Services Committee
MAP	Manufacturing automation protocol
MTN	Multilateral trade negotiations
NASA	National Aviation and Space Administration
NIIO	New International Information Order
NMP	Net material product
NTBs	Non-tariff barriers
NTIA	National Telecommunications and Information Administration
NTP	Network-termination point
NTT	Nippon Telegraph and Telephone Public Corporation
OECD	Organisation for Economic Co-operation and Development
OSI	Open systems interconnection
POS	Point of sale
PTT	Post, telephone and telegraph administration
RACE	Research and Development in Advanced Communications Technologies for Europe
R&D	Research and development
SBS	Satellite Business Systems
SDI	Strategic defense initiative
SEI	Special Secretariat of Informatics
SELA	Sistema Economico Latino-Americano (Latin-American Economic System)
SITA	Société internationale de télécommunications aéronautiques
SNA	Systems network architecture
SPAC	Services Policy Advisory Committee
SPC*	Stored program control
SWIFT	Society for Worldwide Interbank Financial Telecommunication
TDF	Transborder data flows
TIPS	Technical Information Pilot System
TNC	Transnational corporation
UNCITRAL	United Nations Commission on International Trade Law
UNCTAD	United Nations Conference on Trade and Development
UNCTC	United Nations Centre on Transnational Corporations
UNESCO	United Nations Educational, Scientific and Cultural Organization
USTR	United States Trade Representative
WIPO	World Intellectual Property Organization
WTO	World Tourism Organization

675

3